# Donald and Melinda Maclean

## Idealism and Espionage

Chelmsford Press                    Briarcliff Manor, New York

*When a society is regulated by principles favoring narrow class interests, one may have no recourse but to oppose the prevailing conception and the institutions it justifies in such ways as promise some success.*

John Rawls, *A Theory of Justice*

*"The lines of loyalty in the 1930s ran not between but across countries . . . Never has there been a period when patriotism, in the sense of automatic loyalty to a citizen's national government, counted for less."*

Eric Hobsbawm, *The Age of Extremes*

Chelmsford Press
Briarcliff Manor, New York

ISBN-13: 978-0692204313
ISBN-10: 0692204318

*For Jane*

# Acknowledgments

First, as is proper, the archivists: Liz Baird, Wolfson College; Sue Donnelley, Library, The London School of Economics and Political Science; Mark Dunton, The National Archives; Shelly Glick, Briarcliff Manor Public Library; Amanda Goode, Emmanuel College Archivist; Matthew Herring, York University; Colin Harris, Special Collections, Bodleian Libraries, University of Oxford; Caroline Herbert, Churchill Archives Center, Churchill College; Liz Larby, School Archivist, Gresham's School; Patricia McGuire, King's College, Cambridge; Don Skemer, Curator of Manuscripts, Department of Rare Books and Special Collections, Firestone Library, Princeton University; Tracy Wilkinson, Assistant Archivist, Archive Center, King's College, Cambridge; Robert Winckworth, Archives Assistant, University College, London, Records Office.

The following also have been helpful: Richard Aldrich, Rupert Allason, Geoffrey Andrews, Gill Bennett, Katherine Bucknell, Paul Broda, Adrian Clark, Frank Costigliola, Stella Dracheva, Jill Edwards, Stephen Ellis, Michael Goodman, John Haffenden, Henry Hardy, Peter Hennessy, Heather Kiernan, Simon Kinder, Jane MacKillop, Evangeline Monroe, Gerald Monroe, Antony Percy, Sergei Peregudov, Jill Perlman, Serhii Plokhii, Mark Pottle, Sir Adam Ridley, Senator Charles Schumer, Christopher Sinclair-Stevenson, Richard Smith, Peter Stansky, Peter Steel, Landon Storrs, Paul Trewhela, Tom Wallace, Natasha Walter, Peter Watson, Kathryn Weathersby.

Errors are, of course, my own. I would be grateful to have them brought to my attention so that they might be corrected.

## Table of Contents

# Donald and Melinda Maclean

## Idealism and Espionage

# Introduction

If we seek to understand something more about Hobsbawm's short twentieth century, the lives of Donald and Melinda Marling Maclean are ready at hand for the purpose. As a British diplomat, Donald Maclean was an observer of and participant in many crucial events from the late 1930s to the early 1950s. As a spy he had some influence on those events, possibly more influence than is generally known. Finally, for nearly half his working life, he was a Soviet academic, moving steadily closer to the dissident circles that shortly after his death would give rise to the "new thinking" associated with Mikhail Gorbachev. In all this he worked closely with his American wife, the former Melinda Marling, who, aided by the chauvinism of the time (and this), played her role so well as to be nearly invisible.

As the Cold War has been over for a quarter of a century, perhaps we can begin to consider the middle fifty years of the twentieth-century in the same way we would any other period of history. "Begin," because we can only begin to do so, as although the main actors are long since dead, some of the institutions and individuals implicated in the Cold War remain and remain influential. Indeed, it might be said that some of the voices from Cold War institutions from the winning side are more powerful than ever, having few countervailing institutions to call them to account. We can, nonetheless, "bracket" those voices, as the philosophers put it, in order to write drafts of the history of that time from a different point of view.

At the level of technical historiography, in addition to being an attempt to write about aspects of the history of the period without the usual grand narratives, this study, like my earlier studies of James Jesus Angleton and Guy Burgess, is an attempt to integrate the history of secret intelligence matters with political and intellectual history, something that has often been called for by Christopher Andrew and others. Max Weber, in his essay on "Objectivity" in the Social Sciences, said that "the choice of the object of investigation and the extent or depth to which this investigation attempts to penetrate into the infinite causal web, are determined by the evaluative ideas which dominate the investigator and his age" and that it is a matter of common decency that the investigator declare, to the best of that person's ability, the point of view from which the investigation proceeds.

Concerning the point of view from which this investigation proceeds, a first step is to avoid the rhetoric of both journalistic and seemingly scholarly writing about espionage. Here is a typical characterization of Guy Burgess: "Burgess was known to be a drunk, a homosexual and the seediest kind of intellectual flaneur . . ."[1] That rather neatly sums up the usual rhetorical devices deployed by journalists contemporary with Burgess and Maclean, like Cyril Connolly, Goronwy Rees and Malcolm Muggeridge, and journalists active today. They are useful, those devices, the sneer and the smear, useful for making their object unsympathetic (except, perhaps, to other drunks, homosexuals and intellectual flaneurs), but not useful instruments for the historian. Such characterizations are not meant to lead to understanding; they are meant to prevent it.

A more fruitful approach might be derived from a remark made by Richard Crossman, then a Labour Party MP, during the House of Commons debate on "Former Foreign Office Officials (Disappearance)" on November 7, 1955. He said: "Everyone who faces the world's dilemmas today finds his national loyalties in conflict with others.

> We have talked about Russia, but there might be a conflict between our national loyalty and American interests. The Russians are not the only people who have secret services. I can conceive of a time when an Englishman might think it his duty to pass information on to America, feeling he had a moral duty to do so, and then, later, he might well be proved to be a traitor if the world went the wrong way for him.[2]

Crossman points to the question of treason. Some countries celebrate as heroes people other countries revile as traitors. "For the Soviets Maclean was a hero of the revolution . . . Most [British] people see

14

Maclean as a damaging traitor who caused deep distress in the Anglo-American relationship."[3] One would conclude from such judgments that it is best to avoid talk about treason and traitors when writing about espionage matters.

Underlying all of these difficulties for the historian is what people in the West "know" about the period. This ideological construction has it that the Cold War was a heroic Anglo-American effort to contain an aggressive Soviet Union. George F. Kennan, the American diplomat who coined the word "containment" struggled through the second half of the twentieth-century against this distortion of his analysis. He saw the Soviet Union's actions as essentially defensive, if opportunistic, and those of the United States as aggressive and excessively militarized. This was an analysis shared by the Macleans. If a reader finds this interpretive framework difficult to accept, I can only quote Oliver Cromwell: "I beseech you . . . think it possible you may be mistaken."

That said, the following pages will avoid characterizing the Macleans by epithets masquerading as descriptions (or diagnoses) and try, instead, to describe who they were, what they did and the effects of their actions on their chosen world: the political.

**Introduction: Notes**

---

[1] Crossman, Richard.
http://contentdm.warwick.ac.uk/cdm/compoundobject/collection/rcc/id/1277/rec/1

[2] Hansard, Commons, November 7, 1955, 1538

[3] Kerr, Sheila. "Investigating Soviet Espionage and Subversion: The Case of Donald Maclean," in Hoare, Oliver (ed.) British Intelligence in the Twentieth Century, London: Routledge, 2003, p. 104. Kerr's deeply researched work is essential to any consideration of Maclean's career(s). In addition to her published articles, now see her LSE dissertation, supervised by Robert Cecil, which I have had digitized and made available on-line from LSE.

# Donald and Melinda Maclean

## Idealism and Espionage

## Chapter One

*Paris Before the War*

One evening in December 1939, Donald Maclean walked into the Café de Flore and saw Melinda Marling and her sister Harriet.[1] Melinda Marling was a 23-year-old American from a family background that Maclean would have assumed was something familiarly Mayfair. She had been born in Chicago, where her father, Francis Marling, was advertising manager for the Pure Oil Company. Her mother, also Melinda, the men of whose family had been for generations lawyers, military or navy officers, left Francis Marling in 1928 and took her three daughters to Switzerland. The girls were put into a school near Lausanne (in Vevey, a setting for *Daisy Miller*, on the one hand, and, on the other, the headquarters of Nestlé). After a decent interval Mrs. Marling went to New York, the Marling girls remaining in Europe for their lessons and their holidays, the latter of which they spent at Juan-les-Pins in France. While the girls perfected their French, Mrs. Marling obtained a divorce and soon married Charles Dunbar, a vice president of Whitaker Paper, a newsprint firm. In July, 1931, her daughters joined the Dunbars in New York, Melinda Marling being enrolled in the Spence School. Between 1934 and 1938 Melinda Marling lived in the Dunbar apartment on Park Avenue and enjoyed Manhattan. Perhaps she went to dances and nightclubs. Perhaps she spent time in the summers at her step-father's farm, "Merriebrook" in the Berkshires, or in the houses of friends on the North Shore of Long Island. Perhaps she went to Communist rallies and meetings. Unlike her sister, she did not go to college.

In the summer of 1938 Melinda Marling returned to Europe to attend lectures in art appreciation and French literature at the Sorbonne.[2] She stayed at first with a bourgeois French family, as a young woman of her class would, then, breaking that pattern, took a room in the then decidedly unbourgeois Hotel Montana next door to the Café de Flore. Concerning the Flore,

> In 1939 . . . the big stove, in the middle of the Café, was [an invitation for lingering] and the writers didn't deprive themselves of benefiting from it. Simone De Beauvoir was actually one of the first to adopt it. Jean-Paul Sartre wrote: "We installed ourselves completely: from 9 to 12 am, we worked, then we had lunch, and at 2 pm we came back and spoke with friends we had met, until 8 pm. After having dinner, we received people with whom we had fixed an appointment. This could seem strange to you, but at this Café, we were at home" . . . At that time, the Café looked more like an English club than a café: those lifelong friends or even those who met the day before gathered around tables and were from 10 to 12 people. Anyone could be one of them on condition that he knew how to make himself modestly or brilliantly accepted.[3]

Sartre had just written *Nausea* and *The Wall*. He and de Beauvoir, in the midst of the early iterations of their complicated love lives, were inventing Existentialism. Sartre and de Beauvoir and one or another young girl at one table, Giacometti and Tristan Tzara at a second, Dora Maar, waiting for Picasso, at another. Sartre and de Beauvoir, although of the Left, of course, were more interested in the geometry of passion than in events of the outside world, such as the Munich crisis. At least so one gathers from their letters. Melinda Marling and her sister were to be found nearby, as Melinda, at least, was "one of the most popular denizens of Saint-Germain-des-Prés, known and liked by most of the habitués of the Flore, the Deux Magots, and the Brasserie Lipp—where she frequently ate her meals."[4] This from Geoffrey Hoare's book, *The Missing Macleans*, which appears to have benefitted from the cooperation of Mrs. Dunbar and her daughters. It was their story and Hoare passed it on.

Melinda Marling had been in Paris for a year before her sister Harriet—beginning her Smith College junior year abroad—joined her. Does a year at the Café de Flore equal a degree from Smith

College? Melinda Marling may have gone to nightclubs and dances, lectures, museums in Paris, as she may have done in New York. She might have gone to Communist rallies and meetings. She may have had love affairs. It was Paris, after all, and she was a young woman living in a hotel on her own.

Donald Maclean, with his Cambridge First French, tall, blond, the perfect model of the young British diplomat, would have had the opportunity to participate in those conversations in the Café de Flore. (His friend Robert Cecil noted Maclean's comfort with bohemian life.) But, unlike Sartre's friend Nizan, or his own friend Philip Toynbee, Maclean had not abandoned the Party after the Molotov-Ribbentrop Pact. Nor ever would. After all, he had provided the information about Chamberlain's intentions in the weeks before the Pact that had contributed to Stalin's decision to agree to an alliance with Germany.

Maclean described Melinda Marling to his NKVD[5] liaison (and mistress) Kitty Harris in this fashion: "She's a liberal, she's in favour of the Popular Front and doesn't mind mixing with Communists . . . There was a White Russian girl, one of her friends, who attacked the Soviet Union and Melinda went for her." According to Harris, Maclean later told Melinda Marling that he was a Communist and a spy in order to make himself seem more interesting to her. "She's actually promised to help me to the extent she can . . ."[6] This was probably not good news for Harris on either the personal or political levels. Maclean's views and after-hours activities were supposed to be deep secrets, not bait for a seduction. There was other bait. Melinda Marling, who all her life wrote frequently to her mother, had at first told Mrs. Dunbar that she was not "in the least bit interested in him." Six months later, when she very much was, she sent her mother this description: "He is six foot tall [a considerable under-estimate], blonde with beautiful blue eyes, altogether a beautiful man.

He has all the qualities for a husband (at least, I think). He is the soul of honour, responsible, a sense of humour, intelligent, imagination, culture, broadminded (and sweet), etc. Of course he

21

has faults but somehow they don't clash with mine – except that he is stubborn and strong willed. I needed that as I was drifting along getting nowhere.[7]

Despite his beautiful blue eyes, she seems never to have any illusions about him. A couple of months after they met, she sent him a note with advice that she would often have occasion to repeat: "If you do feel an urge to have a drinking orgy, why don't you have it at home – so at least you will be able to get safely to bed? Anyway, do try to keep young P. from completely demolishing your apartment."

Evidently "P.," Philip Toynbee, and Maclean had at least once gotten very drunk and Toynbee had wrecked Maclean's apartment.[8] It was, of the pair, Toynbee who was then the more outrageous drunk. As Toynbee was a recurring presence in the lives of the Macleans, it might be best to introduce him now. He was the son of the historian, Arnold Toynbee and Rosalind Murray, who was the daughter of Gilbert Murray and Lady Mary Howard. He had been famous at Oxford as a Communist and famous in the Castle Howard circle (which centered on the Bonham Carters) as a charming alcoholic. While still at school he had become a disciple of Esmond Romilly, Clementine Churchill's nephew, who eloped with and then married Jessica Mitford. (Churchill had sent a warship to Spain to fetch them in a failed attempt to keep them from marrying.) Mitford said that their parties in London often ended with Toynbee going from one to another of those women remaining, asking each in turn to sleep with him, until, surprisingly often, one or another did. Toynbee, his drinking, and helpfulness in the wrecking of apartments, would be crucial at a later stage of Maclean's career.

Toynbee, also a novelist and poet, was a journalist for most of his adult life. In the autumn of 1938, Frank Pakenham (who seems to have been rather close to those on the border between the public and secret Left) had purchased the Labour newspaper the *Birmingham Town Crier* and appointed Toynbee editor. Toynbee in turn hired Auden to review books, Richard Crossman to write on foreign affairs.[9] Crossman would lead the post-war left opposition to Ernest Bevin's foreign policy. Auden had just written *Spain:* "To-day the

22

deliberate increase in the chances of death,/The conscious acceptance of guilt in the necessary murder . . . History to the defeated/May say Alas but cannot help or pardon." Toynbee said that during the late 1930s he had become close to Donald Maclean, whom he had known earlier, of course, given their families. (Violet Bonham Carter, daughter of Prime Minister Asquith, was a friend of Maclean's parents, as Sir Donald Maclean had been Asquith's lieutenant in the Liberal Party, etc., etc.) In the late-1930s, Toynbee thought Maclean unchanged, but quieter.

When on May 16th, 1940, as the German army approached Paris, the British Embassy sent home all wives and female staff and the American Embassy urged all other Americans to leave. At which point Donald Maclean proposed to Melinda Marling. She asked for time to think it over, perhaps in America, but Maclean was persistent and she was pregnant. (She seems later to have easily become pregnant, but, on the one hand, she had not—that we know of—become pregnant earlier, and, on the other, it *was* Paris and if they had wished, the pregnancy could have been terminated relatively safely.) In any case, they became engaged on June 8th, Melinda Marling writing to her mother the next day:

> Please don't feel hurt that I haven't let you know before about my decision to marry Donald. But honestly I didn't know whether to or not. We decided very suddenly because it seemed to be the only chance as the Embassy is liable to leave Paris for some Godforsaken little place in the country . . . I am sorry I haven't given you more details about Donald and I know you must be very worried and also probably disappointed at my marrying an Englishman.[10]

(The last phrase may only mean that such a marriage would imply residence far from Park Avenue.) After some difficulty in finding an official to perform the ceremony, they were married, on June 10, 1940, in the Mairie of the Palais Bourbon district.[11] (Mrs. Dunbar placed a marriage announcement in *The New York Times,* as was to be expected.)

Donald Maclean would travel his road to Moscow hand in hand with his wife. (Literally so: they often were seen holding hands at diplomatic receptions, something sufficiently unusual to draw comment.) Even Upper East Side Spence girls in twinsets and pearls can have political opinions and act on them. As she would. As for him, he had decided long before which path to take.

The French government deserted Paris amid chaotic scenes reminiscent of those seventy years earlier during the Franco-Prussian War. The Macleans "with the friend in whose car they were travelling, got only as far as Chartres, and they spent their first married night in the car, parked in a field . . .

> After reporting to Bordeaux, where the British Embassy had established itself, they [spent] two days in a village not far from Biarritz . . . on June 23, they went on board a British destroyer that sailed in the late afternoon. Three hours later . . . they were transferred to a British tramp steamer returning from delivering coal to South America, and in it they made a fantastic ten-day journey to England. There was little food and practically no fresh water on board the ship, which was now crowded with refugees. Melinda shared the cook's cabin with three other women, and Donald and the men slept in the passage outside.[12]

In retrospect it may have seemed a romantic beginning to married life.

## Chapter One: Notes

---

[1] He was either with Robert McAlmon, the American publisher of the Lost Generation, if Geoffrey Hoare (that is, Melinda Maclean) is to be believed, or Mark Culme-Seymour, if the *Sunday Times* journalists are to be believed—most likely the latter. See: Page, Bruce, Leitch, David and Phillip Knightley. Philby: The Spy Who Betrayed a Generation. London: Andre Deutsch, 1968, p. 85. Culme-Seymour was making a living in Paris as a journalist while pursuing Princess Hélène Marie de la Trémoïlle. On the other hand, it *could* have been McAlmon. McAlmon's book, Being Geniuses Together came out in the late summer of 1938. After that McAlmon moved to Dampierre, a small village on the outskirts of Paris, where he remained until the summer of 1940. He spent March and April 1939 in Rochefort and Maintenon, in July in Chatelaillon, returning to Paris in early August. See: Smoller, Sanford J. Adrift Among Geniuses: Robert McAlmon, Writer and Publisher of the Twenties. University Park and London: The Pennsylvania State University Press, 1975, p. 275. I have not been able to locate the relevant volume of Philip Toynbee's diary, which might throw some light on this.

[2] Hoare, Geoffrey. The Missing Macleans. New York: The Viking Press, 1955, pp. 43-46.

[3] http://www.cafedeflore.fr/accueil-english/history/1939-45/ accessed May 16, 2013.

[4] Hoare, pp. 51-2.

[5] This organization had many names during the history of the Soviet Union: the Cheka (1917-22), the GPU (1922-3), the OGPU (1923-34), the NKVD(1934-41), the NKGB (1941-6), the MGB (1946-53), then the KGB. It will be referred to here as "NKVD" until the change to KGB.

[6] Damaskin, Igor with Geoffrey Elliott. Kitty Harris: The Spy with Seventeen Names. London: St Ermin's Press, 2001, pp. 192-3. See also "Sketches," p. 48.

---

[7] Cecil, Robert. A Divided Life: A Biography of Donald Maclean. London: The Bodley Head, 1988, p. 60, citing Hoare.

[8] Cecil, p. 60, citing Hoare. This is a tangled tale, difficult to interpret, given the fact that Toynbee's papers are not currently well-ordered. It seems that at the date indicated Toynbee was in the British Army and had been since the beginning of the war.

[9] Toynbee, Philip. Friends Apart: A Memoir of Esmond Romilly & Jasper Ridley in the Thirties. London: MacGibbon & Kee, 1954, p. 139.

[10] Hoare, p. 48.

[11] Hoare, p. 65. They had known each other for nine months.

[12] Hoare, p. 68.

# Chapter Two

## *Socialists, Communists, Tories, Empire and the Dole*

We are in the habit of thinking about spies as living in a nearly sealed compartment of history: Smiley's people, alone with their tobacco pipes, mackintoshes, faithless wives and fog. That is, perhaps, more or less true in some cases. But other spies—Donald Maclean and Guy Burgess are as good examples of this as any— lived *in* the general history and society of their day. They were revolutionaries who might have chosen different forms of action— parliamentary, as did Stafford Cripps—or as overt members of the Communist Party—as did John Cornford and Eric Hobsbawm. The goals of Cripps and, for that matter, the goals of his vastly underestimated senior colleague, Clement Attlee, were not far distant from those of the Macleans, Burgess, Cornford and James Klugmann. Cripps, for example, spent much of the 1930s trying to forge an alliance between the Communist and Labour parties and in the 1940s and as ambassador and Chancellor, supported an alliance between Great Britain and the Soviet Union (as did Attlee for a few years). At about the time that Donald Maclean chose the road that ultimately led to Moscow, Attlee was contemplating a Labour Party in power ruling by decree and martial law. The extreme measures that seemed necessary to these people—from, say, Orwell on the right to Nye Bevan and Cripps on the left—in order to change the political and economic system of the day were a reflection of the extreme nature of that system.

The British Left between the wars was opposed by the representatives of those who benefitted from that system. The loyalties of those on the Right, as with those on the Left, ran across national boundaries. Many of the British aristocracy sent their daughters to Nazi Germany to be "finished" by, or with, handsome young SS officers (Unity Mitford being only the most notorious).[1] A much-lauded figure like Ernest Bevin began his career dedicated to building a better life for "his people"—British trades unionists—and eventually became what must be called an "agent of influence," if that term has any meaning at all, for the American government. Or perhaps, to use a particularly vile phrase shared between particularly unsavory commentators in the United States and the Soviet Union of the day, a "useful idiot": useful to the military high commands of the United States and the British Empire and useful as well to those American political and corporate interests intent on dismantling and absorbing the economic foundations of the British Empire.[2] Bevin, loyal to the membership of the Labour Party but also, wittingly or unwittingly, to General Montgomery and General Motors, was a tragic figure. Chamberlain and his Cabinet colleagues were not. They followed the traditions of the Conservative Party from its decades-long efforts to reduce the standard of living of the vast majority of the British people in order to increase corporate profits, to their natural consequences on the international stage: alliances, or would-be alliances, with Fascist Italy and Nazi Germany, the casual bartering away of the freedom and lives of people in countries far away of whom they knew, and wished to know, nothing.

The sentimental historicism of what may be called elite popular culture of our time conceals the day to day reality of life for most people in England, Britain, the British Empire, of the first half of the twentieth century behind a screen of high literature and high tea, Mrs. Dalloway's morning shopping expeditions and the exquisite reproductions of the mise-en-scène of country house life. Those were not the experiences that formed the political consciousness of people like Donald Maclean, awakened from similar dreams by the rise of fascism and the collapse of the world economic system. The system has been—somewhat patchily—repaired, the dreams dusted off and returned to their duty, screening good citizens from too much reality. It, once again, seems incredible that tall, blond, privileged Donald Maclean threw in his lot with the bloodstained dictator of Soviet Russia. One answer is that Stalin was far away. Neville Chamberlain and Philip Snowden, the owners of coal mines and the managers of the Dole, near at hand.

Donald Maclean came to political consciousness in the early 1930s, when the British ruling class was, as it had been for a century or more—the most powerful group of men in the world. They controlled the industries, mines, agriculture, fleets, banks and trading companies of the United Kingdom as well as the agriculture, industries, mines and trade of the largest and most populous empire ever known. They were incomparably richer than the workers of their own country and inconceivably wealthier than those living in the lands they controlled beyond the seas. The salary of the Prime Minister toward the end of the period – £10,000, fifty times that in today's currency – may be taken as typical for the men of the ruling class (although traditionally it was *unearned* income in that amount that was required for admission to the inner circle). A British coalminer, dockworker, worker in a shipyard, may have received £100 a year, for which, say, the miners of the Tredegar Valley dragged with chains between their lacerated bare legs carts filled with coal through tunnels the height of a four year old.[3] The enormous number of women "in service" often had very little monetary income, working all their waking hours for nothing more than food, shelter and uniform clothing. The situation in regard to wealth, property, was more extreme than that of income. Many, perhaps most, British families owned only household goods, while a few others owned city houses and country houses and much of the countryside itself. In 1905 half the British national income went to 12% of the population.[4] The share of the top 10% was over 90%, that of the top 1% was 70%.[5] The United Kingdom was not, to say the least, a just society.[6] This income and wealth inequity, as, if not more, severe than that today, was considered by those who benefitted from it the natural order of things.

As Maclean and his classmates at Gresham's School and Cambridge knew, the average worker in the Empire, say in Bengal, lived on less—much less—than his or her counterpart in the United Kingdom. Peasant families in Bengal survived on a diet below the minimum provided to prisoners in the local prison, at an effective level below which they would not, in fact, have survived. It was a nice calculation. It should go without saying that the difference between what they were paid and the value of what they produced

29

financed the Empire. That is why there was an Empire. In the first instance they paid for the colonial governments themselves, in the form of taxes, both direct and indirect, such as the notorious salt tax. But more importantly, from the point of view of those living on unearned incomes in England, they generated extraordinary dividends. "By the eve of World War I, Britain . . . owned foreign assets equivalent to nearly two years of national income . . . Capital invested abroad was yielding around 5 percent a year in dividends, interest, and rent . . ." [7] Investments in India as often as not paid dividends of 10%; in South Africa double that. As a consequence, during the entire nineteenth century, the economic growth rate of the Indian Empire was zero, profits that might have financed investment in Bengal were transferred to the Home Counties.[8] The whole glittering pageant of Mayfair parties and country house weekends, Parliament and the Monarchy, was supported by an immense inverted pyramid resting on the coolie's bowl of rice, the miner's bread and drippings. The bowl of porridge snatched from the widow's grasp became, by the magic of finance, the canapés in the ballroom, the roasted partridge on the groaning sideboard, the undergraduate's witticism, the debutante's smile, the MP's cigar.

The division between those who labored and those for whom they labored was obvious to all, was *made* obvious to all: declared by education, clothing, speech, stature and health. The percentage of young adults who went to Oxbridge in those days was little more than a rounding error, one, perhaps two percent of their generation. The white dinner jacket that Philip Toynbee hid at the bottom of his suitcase, under the bed he shared with an old miner when out recruiting for the Communist Party, was the essential uniform of his class, a uniform as foreign to his bed-mate as that of a Sikh dragoon. The accent Toynbee shared with his Bonham Carter cousins, that Donald Maclean shared with the foreign office and secret intelligence service grandee Gladwyn Jebb, was acquired (or reinforced) at the institutions that also, as it happened, taught the classical and modern languages, mathematics and some science, but most importantly taught how to give orders and expect obedience.[*] Their ultimate flowers included eloquent Home Secretaries balancing their ciceronian periods in the Palace of Westminster as they condemned to starvation whole communities indiscriminately in Tyneside or Bengal.

As we shall see, Donald Maclean, like his school friend James Klugmann, gradually became aware that the Liberalism of their parents's generation was an inadequate response to the growing world crisis. While the Ministers and their servants in Whitehall had an entire world empire over which to worry and to rule, for most residents of pre-World War II Great Britain, the range of concerns was much narrower: food, housing, family, friends and the labor that sustained them. They had little time left for Imperial anxieties.[9] For most people the dominant fact of the inter-war period was the precariousness of employment. Unemployment had reached crisis proportions soon after the end of the First World War. In formerly industrial areas, such as Tyneside, there were towns where the men thrown out of work at the end of the war never again found employment.[10] The unpublished memoirs of a Northumberland local Labour Party activist, Dorothy Robson give a vivid picture of life as lived by most British subjects before the Attlee Government. She remembered that her "Uncle Sam Grice was a 'puddler' a skilled job, well paid, but dangerous.

> Shortage of orders had caused the firm he worked for to close, temporarily. This was very serious, for there was not unemployment benefit in those days. It's true, one could apply for 'poor relief,' but one must be really destitute which meant having sold all your worldly goods except your bed, but you must also have led a blameless life, if it could be proved that you or your wife had an 'affair' or been drunk recently then you were not respectable, outdoor relief would be refused and the family would be offered the workhouse . . . Often the Relieving officer

---

[*] Donald Maclean and his brother Ian were both enrolled in the ROTC at Gresham's.

would investigate and woe betide he who dared to cling to some cherished article or be caught out in a lie: the penalty was prison. This Act was administered by a committee of men and women of the affluent class, many of them sanctimonious, self-righteous, unsympathetic humbugs, who although known as 'Guardians of the Poor' were in fact 'Guardians of the Rates.'[11]

The "Guardians of the Poor" were a part of what seems in retrospect to have been a quite extraordinary system in which the few affluent, by virtue of their incomes, were given administrative and juridical authority over the great majority of the inhabitants of Great Britain, as justices of the peace, school governors, and the like. The rule of the "haves" over the "have-nots" was blatant, juridical, and taken—by the former—as a law of nature. James Klugmann, would later express this in the form of dogma to which Donald Maclean subscribed: "The existing British state was not, as reformism claimed, a neutral body. It was a *capitalist* state. Despite all the liberties and rights won in hard struggle by the working people, it remained, in essence, an expression of the power and authority of the capitalists. It was the *dictatorship* of the capitalists."[12] Of course not all the "haves" were capitalists. Some were members of the professional classes, some harvesters of rents. But Britain was the birthplace of industrial capitalism and that set the tune. According to Ernest Bevin's biographer, Alan Bullock, "What gave intensity to every [industrial] dispute was the underlying moral conflict between two opposed attitudes.

Employers and management still largely held to the view summed up in that phrase of the early industrial revolution "masters and hands". They were the masters, the men who took the decisions, who hired or fired the hands as they thought fit, without any need to give a reason or to consider how their decisions might affect the men they employed. In their eyes, their employees were "hands" to whom they repudiated either obligation or relationship other than to pay a wage, and that at the lowest rate possible. For a hundred and fifty years working-men had hated and repudiated such a view. They too, they

claimed, were human beings, not to be treated as if they were
creatures of a lower order, without rights or status. From this
sense of outrage, from rebellion against their inferior social and
moral status, quite as much as from indignation at the actual
poverty in which so many working-class families lived, sprang
the bitterness of the class war.[13]

Among the great symbolic events of the interwar period, two were
particularly searing for the generation to which Donald Maclean
belonged. One, of course, was Spain. The other, earlier, was the
General Strike. Both were associated with a sense of shame and the
taint of betrayal. Maclean was a young boy during the General
Strike. But as he grew older its effects were visible all around him, in
the starving mining villages and the willingness of successive Tory
Governments to starve other members of the working class: the
willingness of Labour ministers like the Chancellor, Philip (later
Lord) Snowden, to do so as well.

The men in the bars and smoking rooms of Parliament were fully
aware of the vital connection between the miseries of the peasants of
the Raj, those of the British working class (i.e., most people living in
the United Kingdom) and their own comfort. They knew it so well
that the course of honors, as it were, for the "Guardians," began in
the opium or judicial service of Bengal, say, or in the tax collection
offices in Shanghai, before they returned home, now future members
of the great and the good, to the quiet dignity of Whitehall. James
Klugmann, in his history of the British Communist Party, would
give some examples of this career pattern from the point of view of a
Party stalwart:

> The normal training for Police Commissioners and high Home
> Office officers is a period in the Empire, so that after the
> experience of "putting down the natives abroad" the official is
> apt at 'putting down the natives' at home. Sir John [Anderson]
> was joint undersecretary to the Lord Lieutenant of Ireland in
> 1920. After the Home Office (1922-1932) he was to enrich his
> "putting down" experience as Governor of Bengal, 1932-1937,

33

returning, still more experienced, as Home Secretary, 1939-1940.[14]

The Imperial Guardians, consuls and proconsuls, are gone now, leaving their descendents in decent county obscurity: some more or less rich people calling one another by titles as odd and obsolete as those of the Masons; a happy few securing their incomes by authenticating the details in movie scripts or acting in the films made from them; stockbrokers with double-barreled names. Once, not so long ago, their kind ruled the quarter part of the world.

## Chapter Two: Notes

---

[1] http://media.nationalarchives.gov.uk/index.php/suddenly-all-roads-led-to-munich-1936-why-i-wrote-winter-games/

[2] Smith, Raymond. Ernest Bevin, British Officials and British Soviet Policy, 1945-47 in Deighton, Ann (editor) Britain and the First Cold War. New York: St. Martin's Press, 1990, pp. 32 ff.

[3] James Klugmann noted that "The founders of the British Communist Party understood that the British capitalists were not merely the exploiters of the 45,000,000 in Britain, but of the 450 millions, one-quarter of the world's population, who inhabited the British Empire. They deduced from this that victory over British capitalism could only be achieved as the victory of *all* exploited subjects of British capitalism through the *alliance* of the British working class and its allies at home with the colonial peoples struggling for independence against British imperialism." Klugmann, James. History of the Communist Party of Great Britain. Volume One: Formation and Early Years, 1919-1924. London: Lawrence & Wishart Ltd., 1968, p. 158.

[4] Bullock, Alan. The Life and Times of Ernest Bevin. Volume One: Trade Union Leader, 1881-1940. London: Heinemann, 1960, p. 13.

[5] Piketty, Thomas, Capital in the Twenty-First Century. Translated by Arthur Goldhammer. Cambridge, Massachusetts: The Belknap Press of Harvard University Press, 2014, p. 344.

[6] See Rawls, John. A Theory of Justice. Cambridge, Massachusetts: The Belknap Press of Harvard University Press, 1971, p. 7: "The justice of a social scheme depends essentially on how fundamental rights and duties are assigned and on the economic opportunities and social conditions in the various sectors of society."

[7] Piketty, p. 121.

[8] Sen, Amaryta. "The rate of economic growth was close to zero percent a year for about 200 years when India was part of the British Empire." Amartya Sen Interview: India Must Fulfill Tagore's

Vision, Not Gandhi's." O'Malley, J. P. The Spectator, August 20, 2013,
http://blogs.spectator.co.uk/books/2013/08/amartya-sen-interview-india-must-fulfil-tagores-vision-not-gandhis/ accessed November 13, 2013.

[9] For example, the word "India" does not even appear in the hundreds of pages of the memoirs of Dorothy Robson.

[10] A situation reprised in the nearby mining districts during the Thatcher regime fifty years later and yet again in more widely dispersed areas in the second decade of the twenty-first century.

[11] Robson, Dorothy, Memoirs, p. 109.

[12] Klugmann, p. 40.

[13] Bullock, p. 253.

[14] Klugmann, James. History of the Communist Party of Great Britain. Volume 2: The General Strike: 1925-1926. London: Lawrence & Wishart Ltd., 1969, p. 40, note 3.

# Chapter Three

## *From Tiree to Cambridge*

Donald Maclean's father, Sir Donald Maclean, was the pro forma leader of the Parliamentary Liberal Party from the 1918 election to that of 1922, a period when the leader of his Party, H. H. Asquith was not in Parliament. Sir Donald was a Scotsman whose family moved from Tiree, in the Inner Hebrides, to Wales, toward the end of the period of the clearings of the Argyll estates. His father, John Maclean, was a shoemaker. His mother, Agnes Macmellin, was "a Scottish matriarch who lived to the respectable age of ninety-one and who spoke Gaelic to her family to the end of her days . . . [she] was the dominant, driving force of the family. It was at her insistence that the Macleans had migrated to Wales."[1] Born in 1864, Sir Donald, following the path of social and economic ascent deeply embedded in folklore about the Scots, used the grammar school education he received in Southwest Wales to qualify as a solicitor in a Cardiff law firm and on his second try was elected to Parliament for Bath on the Liberal ticket in 1906. The next year he married Gwendolen Devitt, an Englishwoman sixteen years younger than he, from Oxted, Surrey.* She was the daughter of a magistrate who became chairman of a brokerage (Lewis and Peat) specializing in rubber from Ceylon, neatly illustrating the connections between county gentry and colonial enterprise. Maclean later became a partner in a second law firm, this in London: Church Rackham & Co.[2] In 1910, after switching to the Scottish constituency of Peebles and Selkirk, Maclean became Parliamentary Private Secretary to the Liberal Chief Whip and in 1911 Deputy Chairman of Ways and Means. By 1916 he was a Privy Councillor and Chairman of the Treasury Committee on Enemy Debts. He was knighted in 1917 and became Chairman of the Reconstruction Committee on the Poor Law.[3] His brother, Sir Ewen Maclean, had a career as dazzling. He

---

* Donald and Melinda Maclean's last English home was in Tatsfield, for which Oxted was the nearest railroad station.

was a surgeon, obstetrician and gynecologist, President of the British Medical Association in 1928-9.[4] It was a long way from Tiree.

Sir Donald was the godfather of Mark Bonham Carter, son of Violet Bonham Carter and Asquith's grandson. We catch a glimpse of Maclean in the letters of Violet Bonham Carter, campaigning for Asquith in the Paisley by-election in 1920, Maclean chatting to Asquith "about the fate of Constantinople" and later, simply as "Donald" during his effort to return to Parliament.[5] From late 1922 to mid-1929 Sir Donald practiced law and Liberal politics outside of Parliament until he was again returned in the 1929 election, the first in which the electorate included all adults. An indication of Sir Donald's frank speaking style can be gleaned from an observation about then Prime Minister David Lloyd George. On March 27, 1922, Sir Donald remarked in the House of Commons:

> We know what will happen next Monday. The Prime Minister will come down here with all his unequalled gifts of raising issues which are not absolutely relevant to the question which is before the House, and, before the Debate has gone far, the personality of the Prime Minister will be the supreme issue of the day.[6]

Sir Donald and Lady Gwendolen Maclean had four sons and a daughter. Ian, the eldest son, was sent to Gresham's school in Norfolk, studied law at Emmanuel College, Cambridge, was awarded an Ordinary degree, practiced law with no great interest through the 1930s, and died in World War II, a navigator on an Special Operations Executive (SOE) flight over Denmark. Their second son, Andrew, who had health problems, also was sent to Gresham's, but did not finish school and immigrated to New Zealand, where he lived apparently happily enough. Donald Duart Maclean, their third son, was born on May 25th, 1913 in London, in due course following his brothers to Gresham's and then, like his eldest brother, on to Cambridge. The fourth son, Alan, also went to Cambridge and the Foreign Office. He finished his career as a publisher. Their sister, Nancy, was also employed by the Foreign Office, marrying an American diplomat named Robert Oetking.

Donald Maclean, then, was a child of a section of the British ruling class, not of the aristocracy (as his Soviet friends would believe), but of that group to which his older contemporaries, Attlee and Cripps belonged—call it the clerisy—united, in this case, with his mother's family of colonial merchants. His father was a representative of "the good" part of "the great and the good" who considered themselves the natural governors of Great Britain and the eventually-to-be-gradually-emancipated nations of the Empire. In August, 1922, during a debate on the Indian Civil Service, Sir Donald enunciated the Liberal position on India:

> You cannot stop the progress of India; it is impossible. It is a world movement to a different, and, I hope, a better, state of things, and if we are sympathetic, if we are full of understanding, and if we are wise, judicious and restrained in our language, I am quite certain the day will come—it may be distant, but that day may yet come in our time—when in this vast Dominion, with all our faults—and they are very great—with which we have discharged a duty to the admiration of impartial onlookers, that great country, with all its diversities of race, creed and tongue, will perform an even better and nobler part in the great circle of self-governing Dominions within the great Commonwealth which we call the British Empire.[7]

That was the great Liberal hope; perhaps misguided, but not entirely without merit.

Gresham's, where Sir Donald sent his sons, is an independent school near Norwich, founded in 1555, strongly linked to the professional classes of the City of London (originally it was especially associated with the Worshipful Company of Fishmongers). Until then a country grammar school, Gresham's was reinvigorated, circa 1900, by new money from the City, with what was considered a progressive curriculum, emphasizing the sciences and modern languages as part of the preparation of its students for Oxbridge or careers in the City. We have a description of Gresham's from W. H. Auden, who was at the school in the early 1920s: "The first condition for a successful school is a beautiful situation and in that respect we were . . . very fortunate . . .

> Watching a snow storm come up from sea over the marshes at Salthouse, and walking in a June dawn . . . by Hempstead Mill are only the two most vivid of a hundred such experiences . . . If the buildings were not lovely . . . they were better than many, and comfortable. Class-rooms were warm and well-lit. In my own house we had dormitories with cubicles . . . and studies, shared with two or three others for the first two years, and single afterwards . . . Fagging, during one's first year or so, was extremely light, hot water was plentiful, and the cooking, if undistinguished . . . was quite adequate . . .

> We had a magnificent library . . . the labs were excellently equipped, all the staff were conscientious and some efficient . . . Athletics were treated as they ought to be treated, as something to be enjoyed and not made a fetish of . . . I can't say that we were given any real sense of the problems of the world, or of how to attack them, other than in vague ideals of service . . .

Auden's primary criticism of the school in his time was its honor system, requiring boys to report on one another if rules were broken, turning each student into a spy on all the others, a situation Auden compared to Fascism.[8] Auden disliked the system; Benjamin Britten, a slightly younger contemporary of Donald Maclean, loathed it and suffered under it. Maclean's feelings in this regard are unrecorded. Perhaps he found the training useful.

From a political point of view, Auden is associated with Spain, that graveyard of young British Communists and poets. But before Spain there was the British General Strike, which demonstrated to those who particpated in it, and to their younger siblings, such as Donald Maclean, the limits of working class direct action and governmental justice. It seemed to close off the trades union route to a just society and to demonstrate the identity of purpose of, say, the mine owners and the Conservative Party.

The General Strike began in the coal fields. Coal was the largest British industry, employing more than a million workers. Large swathes of the country were devoted to it, especially in Wales and the North. The company towns of South Wales were evolving into union towns as "The Fed," the South Wales Miners' Federation, gradually built in that isolated countryside something like a socialist community, with its own schools, clinics, libraries and social organizations. Unsurprisingly, relations between the miners and the owners were never good, the former holding the latter in often-justified contempt, as exploitative drones, the latter seeing each request for a wage increase or safety demand as a form of theft. The owners, supported by the Government, thought to increase profits by depressing wages. (The Washington Consensus *avant la lettre.*) The crisis that led up to the General Strike began in the spring of 1925, when "the mine owners again presented their programme of lower wages and longer hours.

> The Miners' Executive . . . responded with the slogan, *Not a penny* [less], *not a minute* [more]; and called on the other Unions for help. On May Day—Labour Day—there was called a special meeting at the Memorial Hall in Farringdon Street, at which representative after representative went up to the table to hand over his Union's promise to come out with the miners. Over three and a half million workers were put at the disposal of the T.U.C. [Trades Union Congress] General Council; but it was still not certain that they would be called out. The leaders were deeply concerned to prevent the strike; they "grovelled," as J. H. Thomas said, in the attempt to get any concession at all which they could take to the miners. They got none . . . [9]

The crisis was compounded in April when Churchill, then Chancellor, decided to return to the gold standard at the pre-war relationship of the pound to the dollar.[10] This over-valued the pound and put British trade at a disadvantage. In his pamphlet *The Economic Consequences of Mr. Churchill,* [John Maynard] "Keynes fastened on the effects of a restoration of the gold standard on British industry . . . By returning to the gold standard at the pre-war parity of the pound with the dollar, Keynes argued, the pound was over-valued by as much as ten per cent . . . In order to avoid pricing

41

themselves out of overseas markets, the export industries . . . would have to drive their costs down by an equivalent amount . . . by reducing wages."[11] A Government minister, knowing little of these things, makes a disastrous decision on the basis of advice from the very serious officials around him, all of whom agreed, and as a consequence, families in Wales, already surviving at the subsistence level, are told they must live on lower incomes, have less food, succumb more readily to disease, so that the owners may have higher profits.

Arthur (A. J.) Cook, Secretary of the Miners' Federation from 1924, "Twice imprisoned for his strike activities and now a member of the Communist Party and the Minority Movement . . . was the advocate of uncompromising class-war and a policy of direct industrial action."[12] On July 29th, Prime Minister Baldwin told the miners' leaders "All the workers of this country have got to take reductions in wages to help put industry on its feet." Not seeing why increased investments in industry need come from workers' wages rather than from owners' profits, on the 30th the T.U.C. voted to strike at midnight on the 31st. On the 31st the Government intervened, freezing wages (e.g., preventing reductions) until May 1, 1926.[13]

The report of the Royal Commission on the Coal Industry, "The Samuels Report," was published on March 10, 1926. It called for reorganization of the industry (fewer mines and miners), but not nationalization; wage reductions, but not longer hours. It was not accepted by the mine owners, the miners or the Government. The owners issued an ultimatum, abrogating existing agreements as of April 30th.[14] On May 1st the miners agreed to place the conduct of the dispute in the hands of the General Council of the T.U.C.[15] Members of the General Council met with members of the Cabinet all through May 2, to no avail. It is difficult to conclude that the Cabinet was negotiating in good faith. Having had a year to prepare for a national strike, they were ready to implement their plans. Having had a year to prepare for a national strike, the unions had no plans at all. The Cabinet broke off negotiations over the seemingly minor matter of a work action at the *Daily Mail.* "As the evening shifts ceased work on the night of 3$^{rd}$ May [1926], the whole transport system of the United Kingdom came to a standstill."[16] The Conservative Government implemented what amounted to a plan for war. Churchill "denounced British workingmen as 'the enemy'."[17] "Volunteer drivers for trains and lorries and special constables were recruited from ex-officers and from the universities. This was class war, in polite form."[18] Looking back, forty years later, James Klugmann wrote:

> The Tory Government might have set out to prove the truth of Lenin's writings on the State . . . Baldwin, Churchill and the Government took it for granted that the State was *their* State, the State of British capitalism, and proceeded to mobilize and use it for *their* aims . . . Troops were concentrated in the main industrial areas, armed convoys defended Government supplies and strike breakers. Cruisers [warships] were dispatched to the north-east . . ."[19]

The Government, with its control of communications and its demonstrations of military force, won a conflict that the T.U.C. did not wish to wage. On May 12$^{th}$ . . . at a meeting with Baldwin and members of the Cabinet, "The T.U.C. offered unconditional surrender."[20] The news of the General Council's decision to end the strike was greeted, not with relief, but with disbelief and anger."[21] When the General Strike "was called off by the General Council on May 12 [1926], the number of strikers was at its highest peak, the enthusiasm of the strikers greater and their organisation stronger than at any moment of the Nine Days."[22] The General Strike was a disaster for the trades union movement. Both membership and militancy declined.[23] The miners, abandoned, continued their strike for months until starvation forced them back down the pits on the owners' terms. The General Strike, and its failure, was at once an expression of social, political and economic relations of the time and a formative influence on the way that people of Maclean's generation thought about their society. For some, the failure illustrated the strength of the state and the governing class. Others wondered what would be necessary to bring about a more just society in a country where the Government was willing to declare

43

war on miners who objected to a reduction in their wages. For people like future Labour Party Ministers Stafford Cripps and Ellen Wilkinson, the failure of the General Strike closed off trades unionism as a road to a just society.[24] For men like Bevin, the union movement became a way, instead, to gradually improve conditions for "his people" within the constraints of an unjust society.

For at least some of the younger members of the ruling classes, the General Strike was like some inexplicable natural disturbance—a storm or an earthquake. The editors of *The Gresham*, the student paper, commented in a surprisingly even-handed way in June of 1926: "In the first few weeks of this summer the country has passed through a period of storm and stress unequalled since 1918.

A lightning General Strike has disorganized transport, trade and industry and has inflicted suffering upon thousands throughout the length and breadth of the land. Like the War, it produced a great outburst of loyalty on both sides, great efforts and great achievements. Unlike the War, it has passed off rapidly; but in this it bears out the resemblance, that it has left behind it an aftermath of suffering far smaller, indeed, but yet something which will not easily be wiped away . . . But, in spite of all that has happened, the original problem . . . still remains to be solved.

However, later in the same issue of *The Gresham,* in the report of the doings of the school's old boys at Cambridge, we find accounts of decidedly more partisan actions, if equally charitable sentiments: "It is all over; very suddenly it seemed; and life is very full trying to recover from a week's manual labour, to pick up the broken threads of work and face a Tripos due in three weeks.

It would fill too much space to recount all the doings of C.O.G.'s [Cambridge Old Gresham's] but a few examples will show that we were well represented in the two thousand Cambridge volunteers.

Bagnall-Oakeley performed varied feats of motor cycling for the Secret Service, clearing roads and convoying food. Bourne could be seen at Cambridge station, with a dirty face and a barrow, acting as a very professional porter. Others, such as

Wansbrough-Jones, Rosenthal, Craig and Keysell acted as special constables under Scotland Yard. Corry distributed newspapers to Suffolk. Stamp and Robinson obtained private work in Poplar, carting flour in lorries. (Stamp's definition of a dead weight is now a "sack of flour".) They only escaped mishap by keeping up a speed of 25 m.p.h., which discouraged attack. The Secretary was general railway man at Bletchley, sleeping on a railway carriage. While patrolling the line on the last day with two friends he had to meet an organized attack of several score of strikers, but the "sports" at Gresham's stood him in good stead and at the end of a mile and a half the hounds gave up the chase.

For all of us it has been an experience we shall not soon forget. The general atmosphere is well illustrated by the story of the undergraduate 'bus conductor. The 'bus had a stone thrown at it and the conductor with the powers of a "special" got off and arrested the thrower. A little later the driver stopped to know what the commotion was about. "He won't pay his fare to the police station," said his partner," and I tell him if he doesn't I will knock his head off"; and the poor fellow did pay. But it had its other side. Bitterness is not a pleasant thing to experience, especially when the feeling is not reciprocated. Probably it has made us more determined than ever to break down the system of the "Two Nations" which still exists, though it is so long since Disraeli inveighed against it.

Ian and Andrew Maclean, both then at Gresham's School, "took minor strike-breaking jobs, one as railway porter, the other as delivery boy," following the lead of their father, who was following his leader, Asquith, in opposing the strike.[25]

Donald Maclean arrived at Gresham's late in the summer of the General Strike, too late to participate with his brothers in "minor strike-breaking jobs," soon enough to hear their stories. He studied French, Mathematics and Science; Latin, German and Physics; doing well, often trading places in the prize listings in German and French with James Klugmann, his friend from a middle class London Jewish family. Klugmann and Maclean became close, studying together,

45

discussing books and current affairs. Klugmann spent some school holidays with Maclean's family. Donald Maclean was not always found studying with Klugmann. Like his older brother, Ian, he was active in the school sports, playing cricket for his house in 1927, 1928 and 1931, rugby in 1928 and 1930 and hockey in 1930 and 1931. He was a school Prefect in 1931.

The political atmosphere of the school can be traced in the pages of *The Gresham,* particularly in the accounts of the activities in the Debating Society. During Maclean's first and second year, that political atmosphere was conservative. His brother, Ian, who was then Captain of the Headmaster's House, on October 16, 1926, fresh from strike-breaking, moved that "In the opinion of this House the tyranny of Fascismo (sic) is preferable to that of Trade Unions."

> The Hon. Mover urged the House to lay aside its patriotism in considering the motion before it. He compared the tyrannies by motives and the accomplishments of the tyrants; Mussolini, he said, had higher motives and greater accomplishments to his credit than had Mr. [A. J.] Cook. In conclusion, he subjected the miners' leader to a scathing and bitter attack.

The Headmaster, taking part in the general discussion, "Thought that the Trade Unions did not inflict a real tyranny. He pointed out what power of good they had in the past, and, although he deplored many of their actions, he considered that they were indispensable to the industrial welfare of the country." After much discussion, some serious, for and against, the motion lost by four votes out of 48. In the Spring, at the meeting of the Debating Society on Saturday, March 5th, 1927, A. L. Hutchinson, President of the Cambridge Union and a Gresham's old boy (O.G.), moved that "This House would welcome an over-whelming Labour victory at the next general election." The motion lost by 75 out of 115 votes. Late in the year, on November 5, the Debating Society considered a motion that "In the opinion of this House a Conservative Administration is best suited to the British temperament." The motion was carried by 115 out of 173 votes.

Away from the Debating Society, in July 1930, a German prize had gone to Klugmann, a French prize to Maclean. The following October Klugmann won a French prize, Maclean a prize in History and in July, 1931, a German prize. Turn and turn about, Maclean and Klugmann honed their languages, studied their history.

The general election in May, 1929, had again brought Labour to power. This time it was the largest party in the Parliament, but once more without an absolute majority. Sir Donald Maclean, one of the relatively small group of Liberal M.P.s to survive the election, joined the Government. Good to its word, the Labour Government resumed diplomatic relations with the Soviet Union in October. But it was still the Government of the Empire for all that. In December Gandhi began a new campaign of civil disobedience, aiming at independence for India. After marching to the sea and gathering salt, in defiance of the Imperial salt tax, he and 50,000 others were imprisoned. There were probably fewer political prisoners in the Soviet Union that year. Foreign (as opposed to colonial) affairs were handled quietly and smoothly by Arthur Henderson, the Foreign Secretary; in Britain itself relations between owners and workers settled down to a series of collaborative negotiations. Union leaders, led by Ernest Bevin, sought to transform the unions into partners with business. As with the first Labour Government, the Labour ministers worked with civil servants who maintained continuity with the Conservative Party's policies. Ellen Wilkinson commented: "During the brief tenure of the Labour Government, it was amusing to notice how the higher Civil Service so obviously regarded itself as the caretaker for the real owners during the temporary occupation of the poor relations. Any Minister foolish enough to quarrel with his own entourage, therefore, could soon be brought to heel . . ."[26] A murmur of "Yes, Minister," could be heard.

In late October, 1929, the American stock market crashed. Within a few months trade between Great Britain and the United States was at a standstill and the world's financial markets began to freeze. British unemployment went from one million to two to two and a half million by December 1930. This was nearly 20% of the insured labor force.[27] Snowden, writing the Chancellor's playbook to be followed by some of his distant successors, dealt with a crisis in demand by cutting government expenditure, particularly on items affecting the poor and unemployed, and attempting to balance the budget—for "moral," rather than economic reasons—on their backs, thus reducing demand. In August, 1930, there was a speculative, perhaps political, run on the pound. The bankers insisted on more punitive reductions in the budget. In an action without precedent (or successor) in Great Britain, Prime Minister Ramsey MacDonald went to the King and proposed a "National Government," including both the Conservatives and the Liberals, with MacDonald himself remaining as Prime Minister. The National Government was formed on August 24, 1930, with a cabinet of four Conservatives, four Labour Party members and two Liberals. On August 31st the Labour Party in MacDonald's home district expelled him and the executive of the National Union of Railroaders accepted the resignation of his colleague J. H. Thomas (Minister of Employment and then Secretary of State for the Dominions) and denied him a pension.

On September 8, Snowden, still Chancellor, presented his budget, again slashing government expenditures. The salaries of teachers, for example, were cut by 15%. The budget passed without significant support from those members of the Parliamentary Labour Party not in the Government. They went into opposition against its own former leaders. Forty years later, Ralph Miliband observed: "Given the fact that Britain was in 1931 one of the richest countries in the world, and blessed with one of the richest ruling classes in the world, it is surely amazing that there were actually found rational men to argue that the saving of a few million pounds a year on the miserable pittance allowed to unemployed men and women and their children was the essential condition of British solvency . . ."[28] On September 15 the sailors of the Atlantic Fleet at Invergordon, whose loyalty, it was thought, had been tampered with by Communists in 1923, decided that their loyalty had been tampered with by the actions of the National Government itself. They mutinied when their pay was cut more than that of other state employees.[29] The

Government could cope with unhappy teachers. Mutinying sailors were another matter. Cuts were equalized to 10%, benefitting the teachers as well as the sailors.[30] A few days later the gold standard was abandoned (the Labour Government had been told that this was impossible), the pound fell against the dollar, imports became more expensive, exports cheaper, the British economy congealed into the form it took for the remainder of the decade: massive unemployment in Wales and the North; mild prosperity in the Southeast; good profits for the owners and bankers.

The consequences of Snowden's budget were not felt in the City. They were felt in the country.

> Industrial Britain in the Depression: the empty dockside streets with the little knots of men drifting away from the calling-on stands; the silent pits, with the miners squatting on their heels against the walls of the labour exchange; the shabby industrial towns of the North and Midlands, the dirty, crowded tenements of working-class London, with the ragged, sallow-faced children playing in the courts.[31]

On November 2, 1930, Sir Donald Maclean, now a member of the National Government, had addressed the League of Nations Union branch at Grisham's under the title "What the League has done and what it is doing." A few months later, on March 1, 1931, at another meeting of the League of Nations Union of the school, his son Donald read a paper in defense of a theoretical belief in the League of Nations, much in the spirit of the elder Maclean's speech four months earlier: "That in the light of individual experience, the animal in man could be overcome, and that that was the fundamental belief of the League.

> He attacked those who took it for granted that there would never be another war; it was they who were living in a Fool's Paradise, and not believers in the League of Nations, who saw the danger, and were doing their best to avert it.

He was seventeen years old and, as his younger brother Alan would comment some time later, already a political animal.

On February 28, 1931, the motion before the Debating Society was "This House condemns Socialism both in theory and in practice."

> D. D. Maclean, speaking fourth, deplored the distinction between private and public morality. Socialism would carry into a wider sphere the domestic virtues of service, liberty and justice. It was absurd to say that it was incompatible with human nature, for it already existed in municipal tramways, health service, and education. The practical aims of Socialism were Nationalisation, a legal minimum wage, and an extension of co-operative concerns.[32]

The motion condemning Socialism lost by 48 votes to 51. Maclean, and the school, or, at least, the Debating Society, were moving "forward from Liberalism" toward Socialism. In addition to Socialism, or perhaps as part of it, the atmosphere of the school was taking on a certain hostility to the United States, or to the British image of the United States. *The Gresham's* leader, December 12th, 1931 asserted that "One of the most prevalent tendencies of the modern world is that of placing one's trust in novelties, simply because they are new, and, as may be realised, this is not only an erroneous but even a dangerous idea.

> This tendency has reached its height in the United States of America, where it is imagined that wireless, motorcars, airships, television, and the like are all steps along the road to a perfect civilisation. But surely civilisation must rest on some more stable foundation than material comforts, and one is tempted to ask whether a country which makes no provision for its ten million unemployed, and which has so little culture of any kind, is really civilized.

It has been an oddity of political commentary, especially during the Cold War, that criticism of the United States, even of this cultural type, has often been taken to be evidence of a lack of loyalty, especially by American commentators seemingly unaware of that the United Kingdom was not a somewhat backward section of the United States.

Harold Macmillan, that complex figure, recalled that "after 1931, many of us felt that the disease was more deep-rooted.

> It had become evident that the structure of capitalist society in its old form had broken down, not only in Britain but all over Europe and even in the United States. The whole system had to be reassessed. Perhaps it could not survive at all; it certainly could not survive without radical change . . . Something like a revolutionary situation had developed, not only at home but over-seas."[33]

According to the nearly entirely unreliable memoir of Alan Maclean, Klugmann and Maclean had read Marx at Gresham's, and become Communists. "Although they took it very seriously nobody else did and I believe that Mr Eccles, the Headmaster, and my father were rather pleased that these two clever boys were already responsible enough to take their own political line. They would grow out of it and no doubt be a credit to all concerned. They didn't."[34] In the fall of 1931 Maclean—and Klugmann—had left Norfolk for Cambridge. Klugmann was at Trinity, Maclean a couple of minutes away at Trinity Hall. The December *Cambridge O. G. Letter* noted that "Maclean and Klugmann may be seen striding down King's Parade during the intervals between lectures engaged in earnest discussion . . ."

\*    \*    \*

> Stendhal's "pistol shot in the theatre", the thrust of political exaction & ideology into personal circumstance, as the author writes, have always been at and for me . . . I was of the generation hit by the pistol shot in the thirties.
>
> *Guy Burgess to Harold Nicolson, 1962.*

Until he went to Cambridge, Donald Maclean's world had oscillated between his school, isolated in its corner of Norfolk, and his home in London, open to the great world of Imperial politics and the political party and quasi-familial connections of Asquithian Liberalism. He was a contemporary of the younger generation of the Asquith/Bonham Carter family, who spent classic Brideshead weekends at Castle Howard, where took place competitions between such as Jasper Ridley and Philip Toynbee for the attention of the Bonham Carter daughters. Toynbee recalled those nearly pre-1914-war-golden-summers of the last generation of gilded English youth. "In the summer of 1933, when I was seventeen, I had fallen in love with a girl two years younger than myself.

> We had been staying together [at Castle Howard] which still, at that late hour, was providing the robust pleasures of a long Whig tradition. At this time it was a house of children, for my five cousins were growing up in it, and there were young parties there all through the summer holidays.[35]

No one ever thought Toynbee beautiful, but some so thought the young Donald Maclean.

Maclean took his school prize French and German, improved by summer holidays on the Continent, and settled into Trinity Hall for further language study and "during the intervals between lectures engaged in earnest discussion" with James Klugmann and, no doubt, John Cornford: the Lenin of the Fens.[*] Maclean had not had Guy Burgess's shining career in school; he would not send off sparks at Cambridge. He simply did, as expected, very well. Cambridge, for all its physical isolation, was in its own way an Imperial center, its high tables hosting the Empire's rulers, its students' and dons' rooms sheltering those who in due time would take their place, or replace them. It was also a microcosm of British society: from the employees of the college, such as the waiters organized by Guy Burgess, called and treated as servants; to the workers in the town; on through the shopkeepers, like F. R. Leavis's father, and up to the students, dons

---

[*] Perhaps it was during one of those holiday visits to Germany that he became friendly with Unity Mitford. See: Mosley, Charlotte, ed. *Love from Nancy. The Letters of Nancy Mitford.* Boston and New York: Houghton Mifflin Company, 1993, p. 327.

and officials of the colleges. In the same way, politics was represented by the Pitt Club Tories, baying on the playing fields and the courtyards like their own fox hounds, through the great and good of the slowly disintegrating Liberal Party, of whom Keynes was the exemplar, attempting to save and temper capitalism by sheer force of will, and then on to the many shades of the Left, from the Socialists (Labour, Independent and Guild) to the card-carrying Communists of the CPGB, to the Trotskyites, to the non-Party communists, eventually to others, less visible.

Sir Donald Maclean died of heart failure on June 15, 1932, at the end of Donald Maclean's first year at Cambridge, leaving his widow well-off, if not wealthy by the standards of her class. It is probably too much to say that his son's liberalism died with him. There was not much left of it by then. Donald Maclean had, perhaps, one term, perhaps a bit more, of ordinary undergraduate life—lectures and Hall, tutorials and sports, weekend parties in London or in the country—before he, with much of the rest of Cambridge, was called to attention by Stendhal's pistol shot in the theater. The classic, inevitable, text is from *The Communist Manifesto:*

> Finally, in times when the class struggle nears the decisive hour, the progress of dissolution going on within the ruling class, in fact within the whole range of old society, assumes such a violent, glaring character, that a small section of the ruling class cuts itself adrift, and joins the revolutionary class, the class that holds the future in its hands. Just as, therefore, at an earlier period, a section of the nobility went over to the bourgeoisie, so now a portion of the bourgeoisie goes over to the proletariat, and in particular, a portion of the bourgeois ideologists, who have raised themselves to the level of comprehending theoretically the historical movement as a whole.

Maurice Dobb, an economist (easily cast in the role of one of the bourgeois ideologists in question), and J. D. Bernal, a scientist, were the elders of Communist Cambridge. Dobb had been one of the first university intellectuals to join the Communist Party of Great Britain (the CPGB), doing so at a time when the Party hardly knew what to do with intellectuals. Bernal, a brilliant, charismatic and extraordinarily promiscuous crystallographer, visited Soviet Russia early on, bringing Soviet scientists into communication with their British peers. He was loyal to the CPGB and other Communist organizations all his life. Loyal, in his way, also to his lover, Margot Heinemann, Cornford's "heart of the heartless world," herself a historian of the CPGB.

Dobb and Bernal worked together to acquaint promising undergraduates with the Party and visa versa. It is said that Guy Burgess met Dobb as early as November 1931, when Dobb gave a presentation on Communism to the Cambridge Historical Society.[36] In the usual accounts of these matters the first Cambridge undergraduate Communist is said to have been David Haden Guest, a mathematician, who became familiar with the Nazi ways of doing things when they threw him into prison while he was on sabbatical studying at Gottingen. Haden Guest responded to this experience in good dialectical fashion by establishing a Communist group at Cambridge in April, 1932. Its membership included Maurice Cornforth,[*] first a philosopher, studying with Wittgenstein, then a Marxist philosopher and popularizer, and two or three others, one of whom may have been Burgess. The treasurer was H. A. R. "Kim" Philby, the son of St. John Philby, a sort of obese Lawrence of Arabia. James Klugmann joined at the group's formation or shortly thereafter. Donald Maclean became the Secretary of the Cambridge Communist cell.[37] This small group of Communists soon decided to move from their limited proselytizing activities with workers in the town to "a more concentrated effort in the University itself."[38] Within a short time the group had twenty-five members and had openly affiliated with the Communist Party of Great Britain. These undergraduate efforts probably do not lend themselves to the fine distinctions of organizational designations and timing that some observers would like to draw. Be that as it may, in 1932 and 1933

---

[*] Cornforth married James Klugmann's sister Kitty.

there were at least two or three dozen Cambridge undergraduates, Maclean among them, who had begun to see themselves as, and to be seen as, Communists.

Depression-era unemployment in Britain peaked at the beginning of 1933, reaching an unprecedented level. The transformation of the Cambridge Socialist Society, which had been a Labour Party organization, in style if not in name, was part of a broader movement propelled by the National Government's coup d'état and the world crisis. The left wing intelligentsia of the Labour Party rallied— without leaving the Labour Party—to the newly formed Socialist League, an overtly Marxist "ginger" (that is, pressure) organization first led by G. D. H. Cole (a Guild Socialist) and Ernest Bevin, then, after Bevin's departure, by Sir (Richard) Stafford Cripps, an immensely successful intellectual property lawyer, nephew of Sidney and Beatrice Webb, son of a Labour Party Minister.[39] The Socialist League was financed and dominated by Cripps, who never quite became Britain's first communist Prime Minister (but was, with Dalton, its most radical Chancellor), and included on its Executive Committee Clement Attlee, Sir Charles Trevelyan (like Maclean's father and Lord Halifax, a sometime President of the Board of Education), Aneurin (Nye) Bevan, Ellen Wilkinson, Cole and Harold Laski (an LSE academic)—a Cabinet, or perhaps a Presidium, in waiting.[40]

On August 28, 1933, *The Times* published an account of a presentation by Cripps, "Problems of the Socialist Government." Cripps declared "that the first task of the Socialist Government would be to pass an Emergency Powers Bill empowering the Cabinet to establish socialism without consulting Parliament." According to *The Times,*

> Sir Stafford Cripps foresees that the measure would not pass the House of Lords and the Crown. If it was decided to continue in power unconstitutionally the upshot would be a conflict with the Crown and the House of Lords and the Judiciary, throwing the country into confusion. This would lead to a capitalist uprising, which would have to be quelled by force . . . The Socialist

55

> League also is committed to the passing of an Emergency
> Powers Act. Mr. G. D. H. Cole . . . the chief exponent of the
> league's policy, declares: "We cannot set limits to the degree of
> dictatorial power which, under the stress of an emergency, the
> Socialist Government would have to assume."

The Socialist League's answer the classic test for loyalty—do you advocate the overthrow of the government by sedition or violence?—was unhesitating: violence. Such was the atmosphere of the times.

By the beginning of his second undergraduate year, the year of the formation of the Socialist League, Donald Maclean was becoming well-known around the university. *The Granta*, then a Cambridge student magazine, ran a series of interviews of representative students in 1933-34 called "The Undergraduate in the Box."[41] The fourth, published on November 8, 1933, was of Donald Maclean, differing from the others as apparently having been written by Maclean himself. It begins with the question of personality. "But which one?" "Maclean" asks. He claims to have three: "The first is 'Cecil', who is the caricature of an aesthete, 'slipping into my velvet trousers', talking about Picasso and F. R. Leavis.

> The second is 'Jack' who, when asked how he spends his time,
> replies (in the jargon of the period) . . . "Oh I just crack around,
> you know. Buy a few club-ties here and smash up a flick there.
> Bloody marvelous.' . . . When 'Jack' is dismissed, by being told
> 'you'd better go and oil your rugger boots,' one recalls that all
> through the winter of 1932-3 [Maclean] had, in fact, played
> rugger for his college. Finally, 'Fred', the hard-working one, is
> paraded and boasts that he belongs to eleven societies and has
> read one of them 'a paper on Lessing's *Laokoon* (in German, of
> course)'. 'Fred' concludes that he hopes to get a first-class
> degree . . . Asked which of these personalities he prefers,
> [Maclean] replies: 'I like them all equally.'[42]

Amusing, in a way one might expect of a serious undergraduate.

A few days after Donald Maclean's auto-interview there occurred an event, famous in Cambridge at the time, that might be taken as marking the public emergence of the Thirties Generation:

"The Armistice Day Riots." The details of the event are complicated, if not unusual; there have been many similar occasions over the past three-quarters of a century. November 11, Armistice Day, was—and is—an occasion for remembering the war dead, which is for some reason often associated with support for the military. The Cambridge movie house, the Tivoli, had put on *Our Fighting Navy* (not an anti-war film), the showings of which were disrupted by anti-war demonstrators, who made it known that they planned to march to the War Memorial on Armistice Day. Such as Maclean's alter-ego "Jack" and his friends decided to disrupt the march, which turned into a running fight between the student groups. Julian Bell and Guy Burgess made a rather spectacular intervention in Bell's car, "armored" with mattresses, which they ran at the "Jacks." Maclean, in "Fred" mode, was conspicuous among the marchers. After this no more velvet trousers; no more rugger.

The following term Maclean published in the Trinity Hall student magazine, of which he was editor, some "Dare Doggerel. Nov. 11" claiming that "Rugger toughs and boat club guys . . . know they've chosen the losing side," and an article asserting that "England is in the throes of a capitalist crisis . . ." A satire in the same issue referred to "The tomb of Donald Maclenin in red Bakelite in Market Square." Maclean's political beliefs could not have been more public. Robert Cecil recalled that "in his final year Maclean had become a campus figure and most of us knew that he was a communist.

> My own enlightenment occurred one morning, when I dropped into his "digs" in Bridge Street. He had a commodious room on the first floor, furnished with at least one good leather armchair. He proffered me one of his expensive Balkan cigarettes, adding that I must not stay long, as his whole morning had already been wasted by an argumentative Buchmanite, trying to convert him to Moral Rearmament. "Why so much effort?" I wanted to know. "I'd be a feather in their cap," he replied, "because I'm a communist." [43]

Which left no doubt at all.

Although the Depression battered Britain unevenly—the Southeast was only mildly affected—as we have seen, the North and Wales were devastated. At the beginning of 1934 "In London 8.6% of the population was unemployed, in Oxford and Coventry, 5%, even in Birmingham no more than 6.4%. In Abertillery the figure was 50% and in Merthyr Tydfil 61.9%, although many of the men had already left to seek work elsewhere."[44] Beginning in 1932 Communist Party activists had decided to bring the economic crisis now endemic in "the special areas" —Wales and especially the Northeast—to the attention of the more comfortable residents of London with a series of "hunger marches" by the unemployed. The first of these, that fall, was met by police violence when the marchers attempted to present a petition to Parliament. The marches continued through the early 1930s, the most famous, the Jarrow Hunger March, led by Ellen Wilkinson, others were led by various combinations of Communists and independent organizations on the left. In February, 1934, again according to Robert Cecil, "the Cambridge University Solidarity Committee, of which [Maurice] Cornforth was secretary . . . linked with similar committees along the route to be taken by hunger marchers . . . who were coming south to attend a Congress of Action at Bermondsey Town Hall . . .

> We duly joined the march and . . . I looked ahead and saw the tall figure of Donald, striding purposefully along, arm in arm with some genuine proletarian. His face wore a look of dedication that I could not hope to emulate.[45]

At the rally in Hyde Park at the culmination of another march Maclean was briefly detained by the police, released when his social status was ascertained.

Maclean's undergraduate career ended when he received, as expected, a first class degree. Now what? What was a Communist recent graduate to do? For Maclean and his friends, it was clear that marches, no matter how dramatic, were not enough.

## Chapter Three: Notes

[1] Hoare, p. 57.

[2] Cecil, p. 10.

[3] Douglas, Roy. Biography of Sir Donald Maclean. http://www.liberalhistory.org.uk/item_single.php?item_id=51&item =biography, accessed May 1, 2013.

[4] Obituary, Glasgow Harold, October 14, 1953, page 3.

[5] Pottle, Mark (ed.). Champion Redoubtable: The Diaries and Letters of Violet Bonham Carter: 1914-1945. London: Weidenfeld & Nicholson, 1998, p. 114; p. 165.

[6] http://hansard.millbanksystems.com/commons/1922/mar/27/foreign-affairs#S5CV0152P0_19220327_HOC_311

[7] http://hansard.millbanksystems.com/commons/1922/aug/02/civil-service-india#S5CV0157P0_19220802_HOC_334

[8] Auden, W. H. "Honour," in Greene, Graham. The Old School. London: Jonathan Cape, 1934, pp. 1-12.

[9] Cole, Margaret. Growing Up Into Revolution. London: Longmans, Green and Co., 1949, p. 120.

[10] Bullock, Alan. The Life and Times of Ernest Bevin. Volume One, p. 265.

[11] Bullock, Volume One, pp. 265-6.

[12] Bullock, Volume One, p. 264.

[13] Bullock, Volume One, pp. 277-8.

[14] Bullock, Volume One, p. 292.

[15] Bullock, Volume One, p. 304; 307.

[16] Bullock, Volume One, p. 315.

[17] Bullock, Volume One, p. 246.

[18] Bullock, Volume One, p. 245.

[19] Klugmann, James. History of the Communist Party of Great Britain. Volume 2: The General Strike: 1925-1926. London: Lawrence & Wishart Ltd., 1969, p. 172.

[20] Bullock, Volume One, p. 335.

[21] Bullock, Volume One, p. 317.

[22] Klugmann, Volume 2, p. 119.

[23] Bullock, Volume One, p. 353.

[24] However, Wilkinson moved slowly to the right during her political career. Of course, she had plenty of territory to cover: "If Ellen [Wilkinson] was not a prime mover in the formation of the Communist Party of Great Britain, she was certainly active during its creation. As a representative of the National Guilds League she attended the preliminary 'unity' conferences and doubtless was present at the actual inception of the Party in London in July 1920. Thereafter she became a keen advocate for the Red International of Labour Unions (RILU), formed 'to win unions from the policy of class collaboration to that of class struggle.' The RILU was formally established during the summer of 1921 at a conference in Moscow, which Ellen [Wilkinson] attended with Robin Page Arnot, Tom Mann and Harry Pollitt." Vernon, Betty D. Ellen Wilkinson 1891 – 1947. London: Croom Helm, 1982, p. 63.

[25] Cecil, p. 18.

[26] Vernon, p. 103. This also seems to have been the case during the first Labour Government: "Labour Ministers were appointed, but instead of proceeding to cleanse their Ministries of the most reactionary of their permanent officials and advisers, they not only maintained them, but lauded them to the skies, listened to them, obeyed them. In their turn, the permanent civil servants quickly lost their first fears of their Labour Ministers, took them over, tamed them, and lauded them in their turn." Klugmann, James. History of the Communist Party of Great Britain. Volume One: Formation and Early Years, 1919-1924. London: Lawrence & Wishart Ltd., 1968, p. 273. Matters were more complex, if not wholly different, during the Attlee government.

[27] "In June 1929, when it took office, the number of unemployed registered at the Labour Exchanges was 1,163,000, just under ten per cent of the insured population; in October 1930, after fifteen months

of a Labour Government, it stood at 2,319,000; by December at 2,500,000, just under 20 per cent." Bullock, Volume One, p. 449.

[28] Miliband, Ralph. Parliamentary Socialism: A Study in the Politics of Labour. London: Merlin Press, Second Edition, 1972, p. 185.

[29] "The Fleet arrived at Invergordon on Friday, the 13th, and shore leave was given that night. There was some disturbance in the Canteen and several men addressed the other men present on the subject of the reductions in Naval Pay. On Monday, the 14th., the WARSPITE and the MALAYA proceeded to sea to carry out Exercises. On Monday night further meetings and disturbances took place in the Canteen and the men present agreed that the Fleet should not be allowed to go to sea the next day. On Tuesday morning [in some ships] the men fell in when ordered and carried out the normal work of the day and prepared for sea, but in other ships the men refused to fall in.

"When the signal to weigh was made on Tuesday morning, a large number of the men in each ship mustered on the Forecastles and refused to allow the anchors to be weighed." National Archives, U.K., Letter to Sir Clive Wigram, Private Secretary to the King from Sir George Chetwode, the Naval Secretary, 16th September 1931 (ADM 178/129).

[30] Taylor, A. J. P. English History: 1914—1945. New York and Oxford: Oxford University Press, 1965, pp. 295-6.

[31] Bullock, Volume One, p. 518.

[32] Maclean, despite his Socialism and Pacifism, was active in the school's Officer Training Corps, attaining the rank of Sergeant.

[33] Macmillan, Harold. Winds of Change: 1914-1966. London: Macmillan, 1966, p. 283.

[34] Maclean, Alan. No, I Tell a Lie, It was the Tuesday: A Trudge Round the Life and Times of Alan Maclean. London: Kyle Cathie Limited, 1997, pp. 4-5.

[35] Toynbee, Philip. Friends Apart: A Memoir of Esmond Romilly & Jasper Ridley in the Thirties. London: MacGibbon & Kee, 1954, p. 37.

[36] Costello, John. Mask of Treachery. New York, William Morrow and Company, 1988, p. 203. There is no reason to suspect that Costello invented this detail.

[37] Sketches of History, the Russian Foreign Intelligence Service. Moscow: International Relations, 1997, p. 41.

[38] Stansky and Abrahams, p. 104.

[39] Clarke, Peter. The Cripps Version: The Life of Sir Stafford Cripps. London: Allen Lane, The Penguin Press, 2002, pp. 26-55.

[40] Miliband, Ralph. Parliamentary Socialism: A Study in the Politics of Labour. London: Merlin Press, Second Edition, 1972, pp. 196-7.

[41] In October, 1951, an M.I.5 officer read *Granta* and *The Cambridge Review* for 1929 to 1934 and noted that "Undergraduate in the Box" also featured Margot Heinemann (PF.53,236). TNA KV 2/3822 (Michael Redgrave PF.56,268).

[42] Cecil, Robert. A Divided Life: A Biography of Donald Maclean. London: The Bodley Head, 1988, pp. 27-8.

[43] Cecil, pp. 29-30.

[44] Bullock, Volume One, pp. 539-40.

[45] Cecil, p. 31.

# Chapter Four

## *The Man on the Park Bench*

Communism's birthplace was Germany, for decades its international language was German, and while Stalin was building his Socialism in One Country, the internationalist flame was tended in Mitteleuropa by a generation of German-speaking revolutionists.

In the years around 1934 the young men and women of Maclean's generation, class and political views, were at a decision point of which, perhaps, they were not fully aware. The Labour Party was largely discounted—they were too young, and too middle class, to view it with the ardent faith of someone like Nye Bevan. And although they might agree with the analysis of the Socialist League, there was no obvious place within it for them. That left varieties of affiliation with the Communist Party and other degrees of fellow-traveling. But the forces that would place Donald Maclean on the path to Moscow were not those of the Communist Party of Great Britain. Coincident with the push to the left from the Socialist League and local Cambridge Communists, there was the pull of international Communism, manifesting through the front organizations of Willi Münzenberg and through the Communist International, the Comintern, itself. Within the Comintern, it was, perhaps oddly enough, the Austrian Communist Party that was to exert the strongest influence on Maclean and his fellow student would-be revolutionaries. The Austrian Communist Party had an importance far beyond what might have been expected from a Party in one of the smaller successor states of central Europe. Vienna had been a center of Marxist theorizing before the First World War and after the war there was Red Vienna, a virtual city-state governed by the Social Democratic Party. The Guernica of Red Vienna was the Austrian army's shelling of the model workers' housing project, Karl Marx-Hof, by the Dollfuss dictatorship during February 12-15, 1934. The leaders of the rebellion, the February Uprising, Socialist and Communist alike, were hunted down by the police and right wing militias, murdered, forced into exile or underground.

A year before the February Uprising, having finished his degree, Kim Philby, Treasurer of the Cambridge Communist group, had decided that he wished both to improve his German and work for the Communist Party by spending some time in Vienna. Stephen Spender and John Lehmann and other young British leftists, not all of whom were members of the Party, were also attracted to Vienna during this period. Towards the end of his life, Philby said: "Once you have a decision, you must act," which sounds as if it may have been his motto.[1] Therefore Philby, having decided, *acted*. He went to see Maurice Dobb, asking for an introduction to the leadership of the Austrian Communist Party. Dobb seems to have taken this as a matter of course (no doubt it happened every morning and twice at tea time), but, given the Austrian Party's then-underground status, he could not, or said he could not, put Philby in touch with them directly. Instead, Dobb gave Philby an introduction to the head of the International Organization for Aid to Revolutionaries (IOAR) in Paris, which, Dobb told Philby, was a Communist front organization. The IOAR, also known as International Red Aid, had been established soon after the Russian Revolution by the Comintern. Its mission was to pay for the legal defense of Communist Party activists.[2] As such, its relationship to the Communist Party was not hidden and therefore it was not literally a front organization, but the IOAR did bear a family resemblance to components of Willi Münzenberg's Congress-of-Cultural-Freedom-like empire of support organizations, magazines, newspapers, film companies, conferences and such. As it happened, Dobb was Münzenberg's main contact in Cambridge.[3]

Philby put Dobb's letter in his pocket and set out on a very long journey. "I went to the man," Philby told Russian journalist Genrikh Borovik sixty years later. "Unfortunately, I do not remember his name or address. I do remember that he had a small office in a large establishment that looked like a newspaper office. Lots of telephones, typewriters, and people talking, typing, calling—they were all busy." That office in Paris was, as likely as not, part of Münzenberg's decentralized publishing house. Philby told Borovik that he quickly found the person he was looking for and handed him the letter from Dobb. The man, whose name Philby "could not remember," did not hesitate: "'Let's do this,' he said. 'I will give you a letter of recommendation to the head of the Austrian Committee for Relief from German Fascism, and you can develop your own contacts there.'" Philby, in the fairy tale way that he told these stories, said that he then immediately went to Vienna with the second letter. He had £100 with him, enough to live on for a year in Depression-era Vienna. Philby's Paris letter, as promised, brought him into contact with the Viennese branch of IOAR. He was sent on to the section in Alsegrund, the ninth district, of the city, which was run by a young Communist, Litzi Friedmann.* (This is a university neighborhood, the part of the city in which Freud and his family were then—still—living. Freud's home was a walk of about twenty minutes from Friedmann's apartment.) Philby became the treasurer of the district IOAR (perhaps based on his Cambridge experience, perhaps more because of the money he was carrying, much of which went to the cause). He also became Friedmann's lover. He was initiated into the work of the Communist underground, drafting and printing leaflets, raising and distributing money, acting as a courier between Vienna, Prague and Budapest. When the February Uprising took place, Philby and Friedmann did what they were asked to do, which did not, quite, include fighting. (Philby cinematically describes walking arm and arm with Friedmann through the barricaded streets, holding his British passport high above his head, like an icon in a procession.) It was at this time that Friedmann's friend Edith Suschitsky identified Philby as a promising recruit for the NKVD. When the uprising was crushed, Philby and Friedmann married, perhaps so that Friedmann could emigrate to Britain, and in April, 1934, they left Vienna for London.

It was while Philby was in Vienna that Willi Münzenberg founded the World Committee for the Relief of the Victims of

---

* Friedmann's circle included Edith Suschitzky (Tudor-Hart), a photographer, and Engelbert Broda, a scientist, of whom more later.

German Fascism and organized the publication in August 1933 of the *Brown Book on the Hitler Terror and the Burning of the Reichstag*. Most of the writing of *The Brown Book* was done by Münzenberg's chief assistant, that much traveled figure, Otto Katz, who was, perhaps, a model for *Casablanca's* Victor Laszlo.[4] Amongst the varieties of those associated with the Communist Party, the various Communist parties, at this time, Katz's evangelical role on the international scene was similar to that in Britain of John Strachey, whose *The Coming Struggle for Power* and *Why You Should Be a Socialist* converted many. The publication of Katz's *The Brown Book* was followed by a well-publicized "London Legal Commission on the Reichstag Fire." Comintern agents like Katz were of great interest to the British secret police, their activities in Britain carefully documented. They knew all about Otto Katz. His frequent travels to and from London while helping to organize the Legal Commission were watched, as were his meetings and companions.[5] For example, on August 30th, 1933, Special Branch intercepted a telegram stating that it was "imperative" for Katz to travel to England for a meeting with Cripps in connection with the Legal Commission. On September 28, 1933, it was noted that Katz "spent some time at the house of Mrs. Haden Guest [P.F. 40391] on the evening of Wednesday, Sept. 27th . . . There is no doubt that he is doing a great deal of work in helping to bring various German refugees into this country."[6] The "P.F." reference is to Mrs. Haden Guest's *personal file* in the archives of the British secret police.[7] Katz's meetings and correspondence were used to diagram the relationships between Cripps, then a Member of Parliament, and members of the British and foreign Communist parties. For example, among much else on Katz, the British secret police files contain the following: On "the 15th December 1933 Sir Ernest Holderness [of the Home Office] informed us that he had received letters from Ellen Wilkinson and Mr. D. N. Pritt urging that Otto KATZ should be allowed here for a further session of the Legal Commission on the Reichstag Fire. Sir Ernest was anxious to know whether we were prepared to waive our objections.

Captain Liddell saw Sir Ernest Holderness and Mr. Maxwell and informed them that from M.I.5's point of view if exception was to be taken at all to visits to this country by foreign Communists, Otto KATZ was about as bad a case as could be found. He was closely associated with Willi MUNZENBERG and in fact was being used as a cover for MUNZENBERG's correspondence, sent by Lord MARLEY and others from this country.

We have evidence to show that KATZ, on his previous visits to this country, had always got in touch with members of the Communist Party, and in view of the presence here of the International Secretariat of the League Against Imperialism which had been transferred from Germany, and of KATZ's previous associations with this body, we thought that it was highly probable that he would be bringing instructions of one kind or another. We therefore regarded his visits here as extremely undesirable.

Mr. Maxwell thought that agitation here against the Reichstag Trial had probably done the German Communists more harm than good. On the other hand he thought that as the Legal Commission had been previously allowed to hold its sessions here, it would be difficult to exclude important witnesses from its final session. He and Sir Ernest also thought that questions would be asked in the House and that representations might be received from [Labour Party leaders] Mr. Lansbury and Mr. Arthur Henderson. Captain Liddell said that as far as M.I.5 were concerned, there was no objection to the Secretary of State telling the House exactly who KATZ was and giving the names of the organisations which he represented. These had been banned by the Labour Party at their Conference at Hastings, and branded in the "Communist Solar System". Mr. Maxwell did not think these arguments would be very effective with the Labour Party. They would merely say that they knew all about these organisations etc. etc., but that they were sufficiently broad-minded to allow free access to this country for their enemies.

It was agreed that Sir Ernest Holderness should put up a minute to the Under Secretary of State, but the result was a foregone conclusion.

Mr. Grant telephoned the following day to say that KATZ was to be allowed to land.

The file also contains an intercepted letter from Christopher Isherwood, in London, to Gerald Hamilton, in Paris dated a few days later: "Katz is here, as you know. I am too busy to see much of him, but his impressions of London don't seem favourable. . . ." Katz, then, was in contact with the Cambridge group of Communists around the Haden Guests; with Labour Party leaders Ellen Wilkinson, Lansbury and Henderson; with D. N. Pritt, a Labour Party lawyer who would be elected to Parliament in 1935 and in 1952 defended Kenyan rebels against the Empire, and with Isherwood's set, including Auden and Gerald Hamilton: "Mr. Norris" himself. The distinctions that appear clear, retrospectively, among the various shades of the Left, were much less clear at the time, least of all to M.I.5, which thought, for example, that Hamilton was running guns to V. J. Patel in India. (This last is an interesting idea for a play, "Mr. Norris in Bombay.")

Back in London from Vienna, newly married and without financial resources or local Party contacts (as he thought), Philby looked for work, unsuccessfully, and attempted to join the Communist Party of Great Britain by the straight-forward expedient of knocking on the door of its King Street headquarters and asking to be signed up. He was told to wait for six weeks while they checked up on him. "Name two or three people who can vouch for you." Perhaps he named James Klugmann. Perhaps he named Maurice Dobb. In any case, while the CPGB said that they were investigating him, Philby's wife arranged for him to meet "a serious person." They took a taxi, switched to a second going in the opposite direction, got on and off cars in the Underground. After three or four hours of this they reached Regent's Park, which was near where they had started.

Friedmann handed Philby off to a man sitting on a park bench: "Otto," an NKVD "illegal."[8] Miranda Carter, in her exemplary biography of Anthony Blunt, explained that term as follows: "The illegals, who operated on their own and were not attached to any Soviet delegations, came into their own in the late 1920s . . .

> Political idealists and internationalists, moved by their own experiences and the suffering they had seen to try to change the world, they had been recruited by the NKVD because they were intelligent and deeply committed. They had gone underground because they had been persuaded that it was necessary for the survival of Communism and the USSR.[9]

"Otto" was a pseudonym of Arnold Deutsch, a paladin of the Comintern. He was born on May 21, 1904, in Vienna, into a middle class family. According to the Russian Federation's Foreign Intelligence Service, which has a highly complimentary profile of Deutsch on its website, his father, a former agriculture teacher from Slovakia, was at the time of Deutsch's birth a businessman. Deutsch, who was eventually fluent in German, English, French, Italian, Dutch and Russian, became a member of the Austrian Socialist Union of students in 1920 and in 1924 joined the Communist Party of Austria, receiving a doctorate from the University of Vienna in 1928. He worked in the underground section of the Comintern from 1928, traveling as a messenger and courier to Romania, Greece, Syria, and Palestine. In January, 1932, Deutsch went to Moscow, transferring from the Austrian Communist Party to the Soviet Communist Party, and a few months later, on the recommendation of the Comintern, started working in the Foreign Department of the NKVD. After a short period of training, Deutsch left to work abroad as an "illegal," continuing to act as a courier, contacting those who might be useful in case of war (say, as radio operators), repeatedly traveling between Paris and Vienna.

The NKVD's work in Britain had been complicated by the break in diplomatic relations between the British Empire and the Soviet Union in 1927. The staff of the remaining Soviet institutions in London were under intensive Secret Branch surveillance. In such circumstances, espionage by those under legal cover was difficult and dangerous, as any slip could be used to compromise other employees of Soviet institutions and serve as an occasion for another political scandal. For this reason Moscow Center had decided to focus its efforts on the deployment of an illegal network of agents. Some of those in France and Austria, who had been convinced by Deutsch to cooperate with Soviet intelligence, were sent to Britain. At the end of 1933, Deutsch himself was sent to Britain, where he enrolled in the Psychology course at the University of London. In the 1933-34 academic session he lodged at the White Hall Hotel, Kensington Gardens Square, while taking courses in Phonetics and Spoken English (for foreign students). In the 1935-36 academic year he took twenty Lectures on the Nervous System (part of a Neurology course); Higher Mental Process (under Sir Cyril Burt[*]); Psychology of the Learning Process and a seminar on the "recent results and views in contemporary Psychology." In November, 1935 he moved into Flat 1, Lawn Road Flats, Lawn Road, N.W.3, a famous modernist project in Hampstead, which had been completed a year earlier. In April, 1936, he moved to a larger flat, number 7, when his wife joined him.[10] Other well-known people who lived there include Agatha Christie and, a bit later, Walter Gropius, Marcel Breuer, and Lázló Maholy-Nagy, the latter three forming something of a Bauhaus colony. It was a fashionable address for a certain, rather restricted, intellectual circle, who happened to be immune to the English taste for semi-detached villas in yellowish-brown brick.[11]

The Russian Foreign Intelligence Service profile of Arnold Deutsch is particularly careful to record Deutsch's scientific expertise, stating that while studying at the University of London Deutsch had been granted six patents. In addition to his work as a recruiter and then as the supervisor, "the control," of a number of agents, Deutsch used his scientific knowledge to develop new technical tools that, it was said, significantly improved the efficiency

---

[*] At first well-known for his studies on the heritability of intelligence, then, after his death, for questions about those studies.

of the NKVD. He developed several types of high grade codes and proposed the use of infrared rays in night vision devices and in photography at night and on cloudy days, etc. At a time when the NKVD almost never used radio, Deutsch's recommendations led to the development of new radio equipment. He also designed simulators for pilots, tank crews, sailors and artillerymen. He was the very model of the New Soviet Man, although Austrian.

Three of the agents Deutsch took with him from Vienna helped him and other NKVD agents with the processing and photography of intelligence materials. One was Edith Suschitzky, the daughter of Socialist bookstore owners in Vienna. She had trained as a Montessori teacher there, before studying photography at the Bauhaus. Suschitzky, like her friend Litzi Friedmann, had married a British subject as a way to escape Vienna. In her case the husband was Alex Tudor-Hart, a doctor, and through him she received British citizenship as Edith Tudor-Hart. According to the British secret police files: "In August, 1933 Dr. A. E. Tudor-Hart went to Vienna and married Edith SUSCHITZKY [sic] with whom he returned to this country a few weeks later.

By April 1935 they were no longer living together, although they remained in touch, and in April 1940 they were said to have been recently divorced . . . In April 1935 Edith Tudor-Hart is known to have been running a photography business at 158, Havistock Hill, N.W. and to be in contact with a number of alien and British Communists. Her photographic business, which transferred later to 68, Acre lane, S. W. and afterwards to 17 Duke Street, Oxford Street, W., did well. In February 1938 invoices for a Leika camera and other photographic material used by Percy GLADING [the head of a group of British Communists recruited for espionage on behalf of the Soviet Union] showed that these goods had been supplied by the Westminster Photographic Exchange Ltd., and the General Electric Co., to Edith TUDOR Hart at 68 Acre Lane . . . The police reported on 23.7.38 that a group of the Austrian Communist Party had been functioning in London for several months under the leadership of Engelbert BRODA (q.v.), and that Edith TUDOR HART had been delegated by the central Committee of the C.P.G.B. to act as liaison with the Austrians. In March 1941 she was reported [          ] as a member of the Central Committee, and accountant of the Austrian Communist Party here.[12]

Tudor-Hart, like Friedmann, had been a courier for the Austrian Communist Party in Vienna, then after moving to London, for the Comintern. As a photographer, she had a connection with Ramsey and Muspratt, the Cambridge photographers famous for their portraits of John Cornford, Guy Burgess, Donald Maclean and (the) others. Engelbert Broda, mentioned in the secret police report just quoted, was an Austrian scientist who during the Second World War worked on the Tube Alloys atomic energy project at the Cavendish Laboratory, Cambridge. Broda himself returned to Austria after the war and had a distinguished career at the university there.[13] It is likely that his work and political views in Cambridge brought him into contact with J. D. Bernal. Special Branch files include a "Report re Engelbert Broda and the Austrian Communist Party Group in London. Secret.

A group of the Austrian Communist Party composed principally of refugees who have come to England has been functioning in London for several months and meeting at regular intervals. Mrs Edith Tudor-Hart has now been delegated by the Central Committee of the Communist Party of Great Britain to act as a liaison between the Central Committee and this group and to assist in its control. The leader of the group is Engelbert Broda, an Austrian, whose address is kept secret from all, even Mrs. Tudor-Hart, who only knows his telephone number and communicates with him by that medium . . . Broda is being used by the Left Book Club to give lectures to groups on political conditions in Germany and Austria.[14]

According to M.I.5, Edith Tudor-Hart and Broda were "intimate" from 1942 to 1947.[15] Tudor-Hart was a link, possibly a linking agent, between the underground Austrian Communist agents, the British agents known as the Cambridge Five (through Deutsch and Philby) and the overtly Communist scientists around Bernal.

The Russian Foreign Intelligence Service's biography of Deutsch comments that with Deutsch's arrival in London "Work at the illegal residency significantly quickened." Crucially, it was Deutsch's idea to recruit students from Oxbridge who would likely be in a position later in life to influence the foreign policy of Britain. (Norman Holmes Pearson had a similar idea, and function, at Yale after the Second World War, recruiting students from "Third World" countries for the C.I.A.[16]) In a relatively short period of time Deutsch had identified a group of sympathizers who could in turn identify likely undergraduates in the educational institutions that trained personnel for the highest echelons of the British administration. (Dobb, presumably, was one such talent agent.) Deutsch focused his efforts on the Cambridge, Oxford and University of London training schools of the elite and on the technical personnel of the Ministry of Foreign Affairs. According to the Russian Foreign Intelligence Service, Deutsch recruited more than twenty people in England, not just the famous five.[17]

Litzi Friedmann had told Deutsch that Philby had attempted to join the Communist Party of Great Britain. Deutsch, on that day in Regent's Park, said to Philby: "The Party doesn't play a big part in British life. If you were to sell the *Daily Worker* in working-class neighbourhoods of London that would be a fine thing, of course. But you can help Communism in a much more real and palpable way. You can undertake a real and important job . . . [as] an infiltrator for the Communist anti-fascist movement."[18] Philby, perhaps flattered, perhaps from a certain idealism, perhaps for other reasons, agreed to undertake this work. Deutsch then asked him to break off all public connections with known Communists. He also asked for a list of possible recruits to join him in underground work with the Comintern, against Fascism, for peace, as Philby understood it. Philby accordingly visited Cambridge in September 1934 to advertise his abandonment of the Communist Party and to look for recruits. He gave Deutsch a list of seven men. The list was topped by

Maclean, who had just received his first class degree in modern languages.

On instructions from Deutsch, during Christmas vacation 1934, Philby invited Maclean to his flat in London. Philby gave Borovik this account of their conversation: "A modest table was set.* After preliminary chitchat they moved to business.

[Philby] began by assuring his friend that he did not doubt Maclean's intentions to follow the convictions that they had both reached at Cambridge. Nor did he doubt that a brilliant career at the Foreign Office awaited his friend . . . But how did Maclean plan to combine his convictions with work in the Foreign Office?

Philby needed hardly to wait for Maclean to reply, supplying the answer himself: "He could serve the Communist movement without leaving the Foreign Office, moving swiftly up the ladder, having a brilliant career and not despising himself for it . . ." Philby, telling the story more than half a century after the event, said that he remembered that Maclean only asked one question: "Do you mean Soviet intelligence or the Comintern?" Philby told Borovik that he responded that "To tell the truth, I don't know. But the people I could introduce you to are very serious, they work in a very serious international anti-fascist organisation, which may be tied to Moscow." Maclean said that he wished to discuss Philby's suggestion with James Klugmann, as, apparently, Klugmann had been talking about Maclean working with him in the CPGB.† Philby (no doubt on instructions from Deutsch), said that it was impossible for Maclean to mention the matter to Klugmann, but that Maclean could have a few days to think it over himself.

---

* This sounds like a reflexive Russianism—referring to zakuski, and not necessarily a literal account of the occasion, which more likely had only a bottle of whiskey on the table.
† The British secret police had opened a file on "Klugman, N. J." on October 12, 1934, finding that he was corresponding with Jan Gillett at the Federation of Student Societies concerning a speaker on Spain. They noted his attendance at the World Congress of Students Against War & Fascism in Brussels at the end of December. (TNA KV/2/788).

Two days later Maclean, perhaps after having in any case discussed the matter with Klugmann, agreed to join Philby in the Communist underground. Maclean's meeting with Deutsch was in a café, rather than in a park, it being London in December. "After the meeting at the café, Deutsch told Kim that his friend was already officially 'one of us' . . . And so Donald Maclean . . . became an agent in December 1934."[19]

Others on Philby's list followed, first of all Guy Burgess. After Burgess guessed that Maclean's apparent loss of interest in Communism was a screen for a secret, Maclean, despairing of his ability to deceive Burgess, arranged for Burgess to meet Deutsch.[20] It is not recorded whether the meeting was in a park or a café. Perhaps it was in a pub. Anthony Blunt soon followed. He later recalled that he, at least, thought that they were working for the Comintern.[21] In any case, they did not think of themselves as working for Russia. They told one another, they told themselves, that they were working for peace, that the international Communist movement was a bigger thing than the Soviet Union. Just as the class-based Government of Britain had affinities with and supported similar governments elsewhere, while being at the same time the center (or with that of the United States, one of the two centers) of capitalism, so the Communist government of the Soviet Union, although central to the world Communist movement, did not sum it up. Many, even those not working with the charismatic Arnold Deutsch, thought the same during those years.

Philby seems in his account of Maclean's recruitment to go out of his way to avoid involving Klugmann in the story. Klugmann himself was to be recruited by Deutsch in 1936. However, "Klugmann's role differed from those of his contemporaries; he was seen more as a talent-spotter in identifying likely recruits—not dissimilar to his work amongst communist students at Cambridge . . ." For example, the next year "He had . . . grown friendly with John

Cairncross,[*] a retiring, working-class Scot sympathetic to communism, with whom he shared an interest in German and French literature.

> Cairncross had been a postgraduate student at Trinity and by 1937 was now working at the Foreign Office. After unsuccessful attempts were made by Burgess and Blunt to recruit Cairncross, Klugmann was approached and reluctantly agreed, on the approval of Harry Pollitt, the CPGB's general secretary . . . On a May evening in 1937, Klugmann, who had returned briefly from Paris, introduced the unsuspecting Cairncross to "Otto" in Regent's Park . . .[22]

Deutsch was apparently fond of Regent's Park in the Spring. Klugmann's role may not have been as different as all that from the roles of Maclean and Burgess. He was very close to Edith Tudor-Hart and Litzi Friedmann. According to his M.I.5 file, at the end of the Second World War he met with them, Margot Heinemann, and others in that circle within hours of his return from Yugoslavia, where he was credited, or blamed, with securing British support for Tito—blamed, then credited, then blamed. Klugmann had delivered an entire nation to the Soviet sphere of influence. For a time. This was surely at least in the same league as the work done by his Cambridge friends.[23]

"Once you have a decision, you must act." Philby, Maclean and Burgess could have followed Philip Toynbee, John Cornford, Dobb, Bernal, Spender, John Strachey and Hobsbawm, into open work for the Party: writing, teaching, organizing. (Toynbee's Oxford summer vacation in 1936 was spent in "communist activity, 'in and out of meetings' from Vienna to Geneva and Paris . . ."[24]) They chose instead that most seductive of alternatives: secret action. Thus Dr. Arnold Deutsch, who at their age had been already a veteran militant of the Austrian Communist Party, reached into the heart of the British Empire and persuaded a group of young men, "of good

---

[*] Klugmann (as well as Blunt) had lived on the same staircase as Cairncross at Trinity College in 1934.

family," who were on the verge of publicly joining the British Communist Party in order to help create a Communist Great Britain, to work instead, underground, for the Comintern, or Soviet intelligence, which eventually turned out to be the same thing.

They were not far outside the mainstream of the British Left at that point. As we have seen, Stafford Cripps—ex- and future- Labour Minister, soon to be on the Labour Party's National Executive Committee—was talking and writing about the necessity for violence and unconstitutional rule if Socialism was to succeed. The laconic Clement Attlee agreed. At this point Cripps, according to his biographer Peter Clarke, "Staked everything on working-class solidarity and the benign influence of the world's only non-capitalist power, the Soviet Union."[25] How was one to act on that strategy? If one were a member of Parliament and wealthy, like Cripps, one could create an organization to educate and agitate—the Socialist League. If one were a recent graduate one could choose the path pointed out by Deutsch: silence, cunning, and exile, to wrench an apposite phrase from a different context.

Maclean, like Philby, like Burgess, declared to Cambridge that he had abandoned Communism.* Burgess and Philby set upon creating Fascist bona fides—Philby dutifully, Burgess with some glee. Maclean had considered traveling to Russia to teach English or staying in Cambridge and applying for a Fellowship to write a thesis on Calvin and the rise of the bourgeoisie. Instead, encouraged by Deutsch, he began to study at one of the London establishments which specialized in such things, cramming for the Foreign Office examinations to be given in August 1935.[26] He lived with his mother in her flat in Kensington. During holidays they were joined by his younger brother Alan and sister Nancy, who were both otherwise at boarding school.[27] Alan Maclean warmly remembered his relationship with his brother—eleven years older—at this time: "He was the best sort of big brother to me.

---

* Klugmann told the British secret police in 1944 that he had left the Communist Party in 1935 (KV 2/788).

77

Gentle, funny, tolerant and understanding, he always had or
made time for me . . . I had the run of his large bed-sitting room
on the top floor and at weekends when he wasn't working we
would often amuse ourselves by singing duets from a songbook
of sea shanties and "traditional" English songs . . . Sometimes
we sang together and sometimes he got out a recorder which he
was learning to play and picked out the tune to accompany my
wavering treble . . . Donald was always ready to take me with
him if he was going to a movie . . . The fact that he'd given up
being a Communist didn't seem to surprise anyone. Our mother,
who was ambitious for all of us, told me many years later that
she hadn't minded him being a Communist at the time but that it
hadn't seemed to her to be very "useful".[28]

Maclean crammed at "Scoones" "located on the upper floors of an
old house near the British Museum, which was the domain of
Monsieur Turquet . . . The chief subjects taught, in addition to
French and German, were Modern History and Economics."[29] The
French and German would have been easy enough. Maclean had
been studying them all through his time at Gresham's and Trinity
Hall.

His interview for admission to the Foreign Service was of the
type familiar within what was later called the Establishment. It was
practically a family gathering. The chairman of the interviewing
board was Sir Horace Rumbold, the father of Maclean's friend and
fellow cramming student (Sir) Anthony Rumbold, whose career in
the Foreign Service would parallel Maclean's. The only female
board-member was Lady Violet Bonham Carter. As we have seen,
she was a good friend of the Maclean family: "her sons and
daughters had virtually grown up with Maclean." At some point
Maclean was asked about his political opinions. They had heard
about his undergraduate Communism. "Yes, he conceded, he had
strong political sympathies, adding, "And I haven't entirely shaken
them off." The interviewing board was charmed.[30]

That fall Maclean, having passed the examination, was
welcomed into the Foreign Office and joined the Travellers' Club, as

was to be expected. He also "adopted what his friend Philip Toynbee called his 'society Bolshy role'.

Attired in white-tie and tails and sometimes flaunting a cloak, Maclean was a very acceptable escort in the London season for "the Liberal girls"; daughters of leading Liberals, such as the Bonham Carters and Sir Archibald Sinclair. They danced to "Body and Soul" and "Smoke Gets in Your Eyes", and there was not much political talk. If there was, Maclean baffled his questioners with a mixture of flippancy and illusory frankness, as when he observed "my future lies with the oppressors rather than the oppressed."[31]

Toynbee was an open Communist, like Klugmann and Cornford: a recruiter. He was well-known as having been the first Communist President of the Oxford Union: "I had joined the [Oxford] University Communist Party at the end of my first term, and month by month from December 1935 onwards I retired further and further into this busy and secretive hive.

There was a song which we would ruefully sing at our evening socials:

> Dan, Dan, Dan!
> The Communist Party man,
> Working underground all day.
> In and out of meetings,
> Bringing fraternal greetings,
> Never seen in the light of day.

I was not a clandestine member of the party, but sat on the little iceberg peak above the submarine majority, revealing, as we used to say, "the Face of the Party" . . . I was sent to international conferences in Paris and Brussels, in Geneva and Valencia; I was sent to live with unemployed communist [sic] miners in the Rhondda Valley . . . The girls whom I hastily and clumsily loved were all communists, and my most intimate friends were fellow members of the Party.[32]

Maclean had "first met Toynbee at a ball in the summer of 1936 . . .

Afterwards they went to a 'Negro night-club, ending up with a dip in the Serpentine "as the sun rose over the park". Toynbee wrote many years later: "When he heard that I was a communist . . . he told me that he used to be one as well, that he was still a Marxist, but that his interests now lay with the ruling classes. I was shocked and fascinated by this ingenious monster, but charmed, above all, by his lazy wit and sophisticated good humour."[33]

Toynbee went to Spain as a "student delegate" of the Communist Party over Christmas that year and a couple of months later nearly brought A. J. "Freddie" Ayer (with whom he shared a staircase at Oxford) and Ayer's wife, Renée, into the Party.[34]

At the end of May and in mid-November of 1936, as if to illustrate how, in Hobsbawm's formulation, the lines of loyalty during this period ran across national boundaries both for those on the Right as well as for those on the Left, the former Secretary of State for Air, Lord Londonderry, played host to the German Ambassador, Joachim von Ribbentrop at Londonderry's homes in Northern Ireland. Londonderry in turn visited Germany six times between the beginning of January and the time of the Munich agreement. And then, of course, there were (most of) the Mitfords. Such friendly gestures were taken by those in the highest Nazi Party circles as evidence of sympathy to their cause by a segment of the British aristocracy, not least of all Edward the VIII. It was these gestures and beliefs that underlay Hitler's "peace offers" early in the Second World War and Hess's mission. It is said that they had a mistaken idea about the governance structure of the British Empire, believing that if they could, in various ways, seduce the aristocracy, they could influence the foreign policy of the Empire. Perhaps they were so mistaken; perhaps not.

## Chapter Four: Notes

[1] Borovik, Genrikh. (Ed. & Introduction by Phillip Knightley). The Philby Files. London: Little, Brown and Company, 1994, p. 12.

[2] McMeekin, Sean. The Red Millionaire: A Political Biography of Willi Münzenberg, Moscow's Secret Propaganda Tsar in the West. New Haven: Yale University Press, 2003, pp. 165ff.

[3] Andrew, Christopher and Gordievsky, Oleg. KGB: The Inside Story. London: Hodder & Stoughton, 1990, p. 151.

[4] "Katz was a Czech Jew and, like Münzenberg, an unconventional, cosmopolitan Central European of great personal charm who seemed far removed from the doctrinaire Stalinism expected of Communist Party apparatchiks. During the 1920s Katz had built up a remarkable range of contacts in publishing, journalism, the theatre and the film agency. 'In Hollywood,' wrote Babette Gross, Münzenberg's 'life partner', 'he charmed German émigré actors, directors and writers. Katz had an extraordinary fascination for women, a quality which greatly helped him in organizing committees and campaigns.'" Andrew and Gordievsky, pp. 147-8.

[5] TNA, KV2/1382ff. One of the watchers insinuated that Katz and Wilkinson had on at least one occasion shared a hotel room for a night.

[6] He was referred to here as "Rudolf" Katz. Rudolf Katz was a member of Guy Burgess's set. See my *Guy Burgess: Revolutionary in an Old School Tie.* M.I.5 knew the difference, but occasionally became confused. The "P.F." reference indicates that Special Branch maintained a file on Mrs. Haden Guest.

[7] For the David Haden Guest/Engelbert Broda reference, see: Broda, Paul: Scientist Spies: A Memoir of My Three Parents and the Atom Bomb. Leicester, U.K.: Matador, 2011, p. 38.

[8] Borovik, p. 26.

[9] Carter, Miranda. Anthony Blunt: His Lives. London: Macmillan, 2001, pp. 154-5.

[10] Personal communication from Robert Winckworth, Archives Assistant, University College London Records Office and Perlman, Jill. The Spies Who Came into the Modernist Fold: The Covert Life in Hamstead's Lawn Road Flats. Journal of the Society of Architectural Historians. Vol. 72, No. 3 (September 2013), p. 362.

[11] Burke, David. The Lawn Road Flats: Spies, Writers and Artists. Woodbridge, Suffolk: The Boydell Press, 2014.

[12] TNA. KV 2/1013.

[13] http://www.telegraph.co.uk/news/worldnews/europe/russia/5300954/New-spy-book-names-Engelbert-Broda-as-KGB-atomic-spy-in-Britain.html

[14] Borda, p. 65-6.

[15] Broda, p. 97.

[16] See my "Ideological Origins of American Studies at Yale," American Studies, Vol. 40, No. 2: Summer 1999.

[17] Russian Foreign Intelligence Service, http://svr.gov.ru/history/dejch.htm accessed May 3, 2013.

[18] Borovik, Genrikh. The Philby Files: The Secret Life of the Master Spy – KGB Archives Revealed. Edited and with an Introduction by Phillip Knightley. London: Little, Brown and Company, 1994, p. 28.

[19] Borovik, p. 45-7. Sketches of history, the Russian Foreign Intelligence Service. Moscow: International Relations: 1997 places this a month earlier. His codename apparently was "Weise".

[20] Borovik, p. 48-9.

[21] Cecil, p. 33.

[22] Andrews, Geoff. James Klugmann, a complex communist 27 February 2012 accessed on May 12, 2013 at http://www.opendemocracy.net/geoff-andrews/james-klugmann-complex-communist

[23] Klugmann's file includes an amusing series of communications between M.I.5 and S.O.E, with the former chasing Klugmann about the Mediterranean theater, endeavoring to prevent the latter from employing him, to no avail, as he was promoted from private to

major, using his Serbo-Croatian in Yugoslavia and his Arabic in Palestine. At one point S.O.E. replied to M.I.5's information that Klugmann was a Communist by asking how that could matter when Britain was allied to the Soviet Union, where everyone was a Communist.

[24] Toynbee, Philip. Friends Apart: A Memoir of Esmond Romilly & Jasper Ridley in the Thirties. London: MacGibbon & Kee, 1954, p. 71.

[25] Clarke, p. 62.

[26] Cecil, p. 36.

[27] Maclean, Alan. p. 18.

[28] Maclean, Alan, pp. 18-19.

[29] Cecil, p. 39.

[30] Cecil, p. 40. Sketches of History, the Russian Foreign Intelligence Service has a story about a letter of recommendation from Baldwin, p. 43.

[31] Cecil, pp. 41-2.

[32] Toynbee, Philip. Friends Apart, p. 37; pp. 60-2.

[33] Cecil, p. 42.

[34] Rogers, Ben. A. J. Ayer: A Life. New York: Grove Press, 1999, p. 136.The love life, so-called, of this group was incredibly complicated. It is better to assume that Ayer had sex with any woman named than not, while Renée did her best to match his record. In the autumn of 1936 Ayer had an affair with Inez Pearn, then a Communist, later the first wife of Stephen Spender, and a couple of years later with Marion Cummings, wife of the poet e.e., and Renée, the following year, began an affair with Stuart Hampshire, philosopher and spy. And so forth. The Cummings were great friends of James and Cicely Angleton during the Cold War. Angleton once said, perhaps of people like these: "Once an agent, always an agent—for someone."

# Chapter Five

*Foreign Office: London and Paris*

As the first step in his career, or, perhaps, one should say as a first step in his "careers," Maclean was assigned to the League of Nations and Western Department of the Foreign Office in October, 1935. The Department was responsible for the Netherlands, Spain, Portugal and Switzerland as well as the League, but it was the League that mattered. On October 3, by way of a welcome to the new Foreign Service officer, Italy attacked Abyssinia. The League applied economic sanctions: credits and some exports to and imports from Italy were forbidden.[1] The crucial issue was oil: without it, Italy could not fight a war; with it, the war could not be stopped. A meeting of the Cabinet on December $2^{nd}$ decided to add oil to the sanctions regime against Italy.[2] But over the next few days the Cabinet back-tracked, fearing that if oil was embargoed Mussolini would declare war on the British Empire, a thought that apparently inspired apprehension in Prime Minister Baldwin, Foreign Secretary Hoare and the Chancellor, Neville Chamberlain. In any case, the international oil trade in those days was dominated by U.S. companies and, as Standard Oil did not wish to lose a market, there would be no embargo of oil, whatever the Cabinet decided.

Hoare went to Paris and reached an agreement with Pierre Laval, the French Foreign Minister, on an offer of a partition of Abyssinia to be presented to Mussolini and Haile Selassie.[3] The second half of the 1930s would be a period in which the British and French became habituated to offering bits of other countries to the dictators. However, in this case, after the Hoare-Laval Plan leaked to the French press, there was outrage in Britain and Hoare was forced to resign in favor of Anthony Eden. In the next few months the Italian armies remained on the offensive, employing poison gas and other modern weapons, defeating the less well-equipped armies of Haile Selassie, who went into exile on May 1, 1936.[*] Neville Chamberlain

---

[*] The head of the Egyptian Red Crescent organization during the Abyssinian war was Ismail Daoud, of whom more later.

called for the end of sanctions on June 10, 1936. They were withdrawn on the 18th. Why enforce sanctions after a war, when they had not been enforced during it?

Taking note of these events, Hitler ordered his army to reoccupy the Rhineland on March 7, 1936. He was prepared to withdraw at any sign of resistance (and the army chiefs were prepared to overthrow him if he did not). There was no resistance. A meeting of the Council of the League of Nations was held in London, where only Maxim Litvinov, representing the Soviet Union, proposed sanctions against Germany. The proposal was rejected. Hitler countered with an offer of a twenty-five year non-aggression pact, saying "he had no territorial claims in Europe." Asked for clarification, he did not reply.[4]

The reaction to the Abyssinian and Rhineland affairs contributed to a novelty in British society: the rise of a mass socialist culture not restricted to the trades union movement, on the one hand, or the Oxbridge and elite socio-parliamentary groups related to the Webbs, on the other. The Left Book Club was an early indication, and a propellant, of this change. It was organized by the publisher Victor Gollancz in association with Stafford Cripps and the communist publicist John Strachey. The Club was in a sense the propaganda and education arm of the Socialist League, but it was much more than that, helping to form the distinctive leftist culture that was to remain for the rest of the century characteristic of large swathes of British society. Ronald Blythe, in *The Age of Illusion,* judged that "The Left Book Club was launched at just the right moment and had an immediate and sparkling success.

It set out to educate and then to organize ordinary men and women into building a United Front against fascism. The books came out monthly and cost two and sixpence each. They were accompanied by a magazine called *Left Book Club News,* which was soon simply *Left News* and from the very start there was a sense of belonging and, at long last, *doing* which had an extraordinarily heartening effect. It attracted members from all classes and all political parties, and from the more progressive

85

element in the Church . . . Members formed regional groups, discussion centres, and attended meetings . . . Nearly half the books commissioned by the Club each year were written by Communists . . . The success of the Club depended greatly upon keen local support and proselytizing in a given area . . . In the Depressed Areas unemployed men worked out a scheme of group membership, with three or four people contributing to the monthly 2s. 6d. and sharing the same book.[5]

Dorothy Robson remembered that she had "helped form the Left Book Club" in her Depressed Area mining town of Morpeth, Northumberland, where she was later the first Labour Party and first woman Councillor. "There were about 30 of us, all professional types and we met monthly in Dixon's Café. We were also members of the League of Mothers Union and some attended the same W[orkers] E[ducation] A[ssociation] class as I . . . [When] the Townswomen's Guild was introduced into the town. I was not invited to join because they said I was not a lady."[6] Which places the membership of the Left Book Club among the fine class distinctions of provincial British society.

The Club published its cheap volumes on a wide range of subjects. Contributors included Clement Attlee, G. D. H. Cole, George Orwell and Ellen Wilkinson. One of those orange-jacketed books was *Forward From Liberalism* by Stephen Spender. Forward to where? Spender names his destination in the first line of the book: "I have been asked to write a book on my approach to communism . . ." Spender's idea of communism, in 1937, was utopian: "By a free people, I understand 'from each according to his ability; to each according to his needs.' By 'his needs,' I do not understand wealth only, but the whole inheritance of knowledge and culture possessed by our civilization, and the creative effort of the future life . . . I am a communist because I am a liberal . . . in the modern world communism—the classless, internationalist society—is the final goal of liberalism."[7] News, perhaps, at Castle Howard.

Maclean was the most junior officer in the League of Nations and Western Department and not anywhere near the decision-making levels of the Foreign Office and Government. Nonetheless, many, if not most, of the cables and memoranda dealing with the Abyssinian and Rhineland affairs crossed his desk along with those pertaining to more routine matters. By early 1936 he was delivering large quantities of secret documents to his NKVD contacts, who were surprised and pleased.[8] He met regularly with Deutsch or Deutsch's supervisor, another Comintern illegal, Theodore Maly, handing them the most important documents that passed through his department at the Foreign Office. The documents were photographed on a "flat carrier" at the NKVD residency and given back to him so that the next day he could return them to their proper places in the Foreign Office files. For use in cases when he could only hold very valuable documents for a few hours, Maly gave him a camera so that Maclean could photograph them himself. In addition to the documents Maclean provided to Maly and Deutsch, he helped the cause by telling them, inter alia, that "the British read all the telegrams of the Communist International and American and German coded telegrams and attempted the Soviet ciphers."[9] The Soviets deduced from his reports that there were British agents within the Soviet Ministry of Foreign Affairs and in the Münzenberg organization. The consequences for those suspected of being the persons in question can be imagined.

This brings us to some basic questions about Donald Maclean's espionage career to which we will return again and again: What did he know? What did he provide to Soviet secret intelligence? What use was made of it? Concerning the first question, he knew about information in two categories of materials. One category consists of documents to which as far as possible he is known to have had access: documents with a positive connection to Maclean, for example, reports that he drafted or documents about which he commented and documents that in the course of his routine duties it is improbable that he did not see, such as those falling within his area of responsibility. The second category consists of documents that he may have seen. These include materials generally circulated to those at his level in the Foreign Office and materials to which he may have gained access without arousing suspicion, including those that may have been referred to in conversations, official or casual.

Concerning the second question, Sheila Kerr, who wrote a London School of Economic dissertation on Maclean, assumes that everything that we know that Maclean had access to and everything to which he may have had access, was given by him to Soviet foreign intelligence. This is a reasonable, Angletonian, assumption. A counterintelligence official, like the Cold War chief of the C.I.A.'s counterintelligence staff, James Angleton, would have a professional obligation to act on such an assumption. That does not mean that it is literally true. Maclean may not have seen some otherwise available materials because he happened to be ill or on leave on a particular day. He may have judged some materials trivial or irrelevant. The assumption that everything he could have sent to Moscow he did send to Moscow is not a sufficient basis for determining what Moscow knew. On the other hand, if Maclean could have seen some specific document or heard of some matter, it cannot be assumed that he did not or did not then send it along. That said, we might prudently proceed with the understanding that material to which he had access was more likely than not sent to NKVD headquarters.

And then what? It seems that at the peak of Maclean's career the material he sent (and that sent by Burgess, among others) went to Beria, the Soviet secret police chief, and that relevant materials went on to Molotov at the Soviet Foreign Ministry and some made it all the way to Stalin. How were these materials used? This is a much more difficult question than the difficult questions we have already examined. If Kim Philby knew that so-and-so was an M.I.6 agent and soon thereafter so-and-so was murdered, we have a fairly good causality chain. But if Maclean saw an appraisal of a political situation and even if the Soviet leadership subsequently acted in such a way as to give the impression that they had knowledge of that appraisal, the chain of causality is much less certain. They might have known about that appraisal from other sources; they might have guessed; they might have acted in that way coincidentally. On the other hand, it would also be a mistake to be too cautious. It is unlikely that nothing Maclean was uniquely positioned to know and send to Moscow had political effects. It is likely that much that Maclean was uniquely positioned to know and send to Moscow had political effects, on certain occasions changing the course of history.

\* \* \*

The Spanish Civil War began in mid-July of 1936 when a group of generals revolted against the Spanish Republic. It was at first thought that they would succeed in a few days, but the rebels failed to take Madrid and what had begun as a coup became a war of attrition, with Italy and Germany openly supporting the rebels from the beginning. Soon the Soviet Union announced it would support the government as long as Italy and Germany supported the rebels.[10] Spain became a cause, *the* cause, of the Thirties for those on the left, for none more so than Maclean's friends from Gresham's and Cambridge. Julian Bell drove an ambulance for the Republic's forces, as W. H. Auden had said he wished to. John Cornford fought and died there, as did David Haden Guest. Philby wrote news stories from the Nationalist side, strengthening his Fascist bona fides. On the other hand, from the point of view of the Government in London, the Spanish Civil War was a distraction, complicating efforts to reach an understanding with Mussolini and to find a way to "appease" what it considered the well-justified grievances of Germany in regard to the Treaty of Versailles.

An international "Non-Intervention Committee" was set up with headquarters in London under the chairmanship of Ivor Windsor-Clive, the Earl of Plymouth, Parliamentary Under-Secretary of the Foreign Office. In November, 1936, Maclean was given the task "of compiling a summary of Soviet infringements of the Non-Intervention agreement."[11] There is just a possibility that this was done with malice aforethought, as a prophylactic for the immature opinions of a promising junior official. In any case, according to the record of a Cabinet meeting that month, "The Secretary of State for Foreign Affairs reported that the International Non-intervention

89

Committee was continuing its work of examining alleged breaches of
the Non-Intervention Agreement.

> In view of the many breaches, however, it was impossible to
> maintain the present position . . . The Cabinet were reminded
> that telegrams were pouring in every day revealing a steady
> importation of arms into Barcelona from Russia, and to some
> extent to other ports from other countries. The Non-Intervention
> Agreement was being continuously broken, and it was suggested
> that to maintain the International Committee was a sheer farce.

> While this was not contested, it was pointed out that it was the
> existence of the Committee that enabled the French Government
> to maintain a neutral position. If it disappeared they would
> hardly be able to escape from allowing the exportation of arms to
> the Spanish Government. The object of the Agreement had been
> to prevent the Spanish Civil War from, spreading into the rest of
> Europe, and for this purpose it was still effective.[12]

One might infer that in the view of the British Cabinet, the purpose
of the Non-Intervention Committee was not to prevent the spread of
the Spanish Civil War, which even at the time must have seemed
unlikely, but, in the first place, to limit the Soviet Union's efforts to
provide resources to the Spanish Government, and, in the second
place, to keep the French, Popular Front, government from doing the
same. The Committee, and parallel British efforts, were ultimately
successful in the latter instance, but not in the former. Maclean's
information about the attitudes and decisions of the British
Government, if transmitted to Moscow, might have been useful there
for planning activities in Spain, particularly those that the Soviet
leadership wished to keep secret.

Meanwhile, Maclean had other bits of information to send to
Moscow. We now know from Russian sources that in early October,
1936, Maclean reported to Maly and Deutsch that he had met a
certain David Footman of the Foreign Office and surmised that he
was connected with the British intelligence services. They decided to
have Burgess make contact with Footman in order to attempt a
penetration of British secret intelligence.[13] This was to be a slowly

maturing project. It was not until May 25th of the next year that Burgess wrote to Footman that he thought that he "might not be just the person to give some travel talks of a rather personal nature."[14] Footman submitted a script, "Albania, Fish and a Motor Car," which was broadcast on August 2nd. He submitted other scripts, one of which was accepted and was sufficiently successful to be broadcast first in November and then again in January, 1938. As Maclean had surmised, Footman's civil service responsibilities had to do with secret intelligence. He had served as the Belgrade resident of M.I.6, then as head of the political section in London.[15] In December, 1938, perhaps at Footman's suggestion, Burgess resigned from the B.B.C. and joined Section D of M.I.6, where, in due course, Philby joined him.[16] In this way Maclean, working with Burgess, facilitated the penetration of British foreign intelligence by agents of the Soviet foreign intelligence service.

There is a depiction of Maclean at this stage of his career in John Cairncross's autobiography. Cairncross writes that early in February, 1937, he was transferred to the Western Department, responsible for, among other matters, the Foreign Offices interests in Spain. "It was in the Spanish Section that I first made the acquaintance of my new colleague and immediate superior, who was much the same age as I, and who had entered the Diplomatic Service a year earlier.

Donald Maclean . . . was a tall, mild-mannered figure. He was clearly an up-and-coming official, highly intelligent, most competent in his work and always friendly, though he never expressed strong views either in conversation or on paper. He rarely discussed foreign politics and the only opinion I heard him express was the need for Britain to rearm . . . We never developed a close relationship. He enjoyed dining out in the small cosy restaurants in Soho and seeing the latest plays . . . Towards the end of my stint with the Department Maclean confided to me that I did not make the right impression because I was too spontaneous and oblivious of conventional behaviour: it was not so much a question of having the wrong view, though this was also noted, as not coming from the right background.[17]

Cairncross was taken to his Regent's Park meeting with Arnold Deutsch by James Klugmann a few months later, in May, 1937.

Donald Maclean was careful to keep his distance from the rising tide of left-wing activism, frequenting, instead, the festivities of the aristocracy. In June he served as his friend Anthony Rumbold's best man at the latter's wedding to Felicity Ann Bailey, granddaughter of the Earl of Inchcape, Chairman of the P and O steamship company. Mark Culme-Seymour, who was a friend of Maclean's during this time, later said that he "used to spend two or three evenings a week with Maclean.

> They would have a few bitters at the Commercial—Maclean was not yet a heavy drinker—and afterwards favoured a game of billiards at the nearby Temperance Hall. Maclean was always inquiring whether there were any parties in the hope that he might meet a girl . . . "He never talked to me about anything except people in general and girls in particular," Culme-Seymour recalls. "I didn't think of him as a political person, rather the reverse."[18]

Culme-Seymour was a much-married man (as seems to have been habitual in the Culme-Seymour family). He was married to Babette Patric-Jones from 1935 to 1938; to Princess Hélène Marie de la Trémoïlle from 1941 to 1949; to Patricia June Reid-Graham from 1956 to 1966 and to Mary Darrall Riely in 1973, each marriage lasting longer than the one before until he ran out of time.[19] It was perhaps the end of his marriage to Babette Patric-Jones and his courtship of Princess Hélène Marie de la Trémoïlle that in 1938 brought him to Paris, where he became acquainted with the American heiress Melinda Marling.

Be that as it may, when not at the Foreign Office, having a few bitters at the Commercial, attending at the weddings of the aristocracy or socializing with Toynbee and the Liberal Girls, Maclean was with Deutsch or Deutsch's fellow illegal, Theodore Maly, who met their agents, including Philby and Burgess as well as Maclean, in a safe-house, which was run by a woman called Kitty Harris. She opened the door for them, brought them coffee and biscuits, occasionally cooked supper.[20] Late in 1937 Maclean found that when he went to the agreed and back-up places and times for meetings with his Soviet contacts there was no one there to meet him. The London residency of the NKVD had closed. Deutsch had had to leave the U.K. in mid-1937, not at the behest of Moscow, but because his student visa had expired. Maly, on the other hand, had been recalled to Moscow and executed. It was not a good year to be an employee of the NKVD. Survival rates were not high. (Deutsch, most unusually, survived the purges, only to die during the war when the ship he was traveling on to America was attacked and sunk by German aircraft.[21]) At first, after the NKVD's London residency closed down, Edith Tudor-Hart acted as the conduit between operatives and a "cut-out," the Communist activist Bob Stewart, who reported to the Soviet embassy.[22] This was not good tradecraft. Stewart was watched by Special Branch, which, however, seems not to have watched closely enough. Deutsch was eventually replaced as the primary London contact of Soviet foreign intelligence by Anatoli Gorsky, who had arrived in 1936 under legal cover as an official of the Soviet Embassy.* In any case, one day, early in 1938, when Maclean once more went to the assigned meeting place at the assigned time, there was Kitty Harris, who swiftly gave him the recognition phrase. "'You hadn't expected to see a lady, had you?'" she said, most likely in an accent with a foundation of cockney overlaid with Canadian and American vowels. "'No, but it's a pleasant surprise,' he replied quickly." She was probably not like any other "lady" Maclean had met, with that accent, among other unusual qualities.

Harris was thirteen years older than Maclean, a highly experienced underground worker for the NKVD. She had been born in London, the daughter of a Jewish shoemaker from Bialystok. (It is probably of no significance that Maclean's grandfather had also been

---

* Gorsky was at first the assistant Resident, then rose as his superiors were recalled to Moscow. Gorsky himself went to Moscow (but not to the Gulag) in March, 1940 and was subsequently sent back to London.

a shoemaker, as had Stalin's father, for that matter.) The family moved to Winnipeg, Canada, when she was nine and by the time that she was thirteen years old she had finished with all the conventional schooling she would have and was working in a cigar factory. (Perhaps one of the reasons that the NKVD called her "Gypsy.") She then worked as a seamstress, joined the Industrial Workers of the World, moved with her family, once again, this time to Chicago when she was about twenty, became the secretary of the local of the Amalgamated Clothing Workers and joined the Communist Party, USA, in January, 1923. Two years later, in fact or in effect, she married Earl Browder. (Browder was to become perhaps the most prominent American member of the Comintern and later the head of the Communist Party in the United States.) Harris transferred from the American to the Soviet Communist Party in 1927 and in the following year she and Browder went to Shanghai, where Browder became secretary of the Pan-Pacific Trade Union and Harris became a Communist Party courier. In 1929 Browder and Harris went to Moscow and then Harris went on to the United States where she worked in the American Negro Labor Congress. She was recruited by the Foreign Intelligence section of the OGPU (one of the manifestations of the Soviet secret intelligence service) in 1931 and in 1932, having separated from Browder, she was sent to Berlin (her time there perhaps overlapping with that of Deutsch), and then in October, 1935, as Maclean was joining the Foreign Office, returned to Moscow, where she was trained in radio operation, photography and cryptography. In April, 1936, she was sent to Paris as the radio operator for the NKVD station there, was back in Moscow in January 1937 for further training and in May was sent to London to work for Gregory Grafpen, an NKVD official under official cover.[23] Harris may have had only three or four years of formal education, but she was obviously an intelligent, highly trained, multilingual, agent of Soviet foreign intelligence with a most interesting passport (or passports).

At their first meeting under the new arrangement, Maclean "advised [Harris] to rent a flat in a 'nice' part of town, which might be more expensive but would be better from a security point of view" because it would be difficult to explain it away if one of his friends saw him in "some God-forsaken part of London." Accordingly, with her £50 a month allowance from the Comintern (probably at least as much as Maclean's Foreign Office salary at the time), she took a flat in Bayswater, which was nice enough, it seems.[24] Twice a week Maclean filled his briefcase with the Foreign Office papers he had collected, like any dutiful member of the staff intent on working at home after hours. He "would first head off to Oakley Street," where he was living at the time, "and then leave his flat a little while later and take a taxi to some randomly selected street corner, where he would pay it off, walk on a little way and then hail another. Sometimes, if he though there was the slightest risk, he would repeat the manoeuvre, get out on a street near Kitty's and complete his journey on foot . . ." As if he were paying a call on one of the Liberal Girls, Maclean included flowers and chocolates with his gifts of Foreign Office papers. Maclean would present Harris with the flowers and chocolates and empty his briefcase. Harris, with her professional training, would photograph the papers.[25]

During this early part of his career in espionage, Maclean was able to furnish information to the Soviet Union in regard to three crucial events: Munich, the Molotov-Ribbentrop Pact and the Russo-Finnish War.

### Munich

Soviet Foreign Minister Maxim Litvinov had completed a Franco-Soviet Mutual-Assistance Pact on May 2, 1935, and two weeks later a Czechoslovak-Soviet Pact. The issue, as it would be three years later, had been how these pacts were to be effective in case of a German attack on Czechoslovakia. The Soviet answer was to attempt to reach transit right agreements with at least one of the two states—Poland and Romania—separating the Soviet Union from

Czechoslovakia. The Soviet Union picked the Romanian route between its frontier and that of Czechoslovakia: "Immediately after the signing of the pact with Czechoslovakia, Soviet Commissar of Defense Kliment Voroshilov assured Czechoslovak President Edvard Bênes that the Red Army would come to the assistance of Czechoslovakia in the event of war *with* or *without* the consent of Romania" to transit of the Red Army.[26] The Romanian government and army at first agreed that the Red Army could move through Romania to support Czechoslovakia, but then equivocated. On the other hand, the Romanian transportation system was so inadequate for this purpose that the question was more or less academic. Polish transit rights for the Red Army were vital to Czechoslovak defense.

Germany had occupied the Rhineland, in violation of the Treaty of Versailles, in March, 1936. Two years later, on March 12, 1938, it had annexed Austria. The German-speaking population of the western provinces of Czechoslovakia, the Sudetenland, afforded the pretext for Hitler's next move. The American Ambassador in Germany reported to the Secretary of State on May 6, 1938, a conversation with the Soviet Chargé d'Affaires in Berlin in which the latter "stated that Russia would under no circumstances move to the military assistance of Czechoslovakia unless France moved.

> He added that French action in turn certainly depended on British action. He said furthermore that Russian military support of Czechoslovakia was complicated by the attitude of Poland and Rumania, especially the former, which was that the passage of troops over her territory would be regarded as a cause for war [with the Soviet Union]. He trusted, however, that the attitudes of these two states could be overcome provided general common actions were joined against Germany.[27]

Therefore, in order for German plans against Czechoslovakia to be stopped by, say, Soviet intervention, Poland (or, alternatively, Romania) would have to agree to the passage of the Red Army along its transportation system, Britain would have to support French intervention and, perhaps, intervene in some way itself. The key was the attitude of the British Government.

Czechoslovakia was a pawn from every point of view except its own. From the point of view of the German government it was the final piece in the pattern of more or less non-military initiatives setting up the board for war. From the point of view of the French and British governments it was a link in the system of French alliances meant to restrain Germany, or, alternately, the Soviet Union. From the point of view of the Soviet Union it was a buffer between Germany and the Soviet Union and a token of the Soviet Union's status in the ensemble of European powers. Given the ambivalence of British and French attitudes, the Soviet leadership calculated that Soviet support for Czechoslovakia had to be linked to that of France, otherwise that support might well be used as an excuse for the cancellation of the British and French commitments to Czechoslovakia and de facto support for German moves east. Running that logic in reverse, failure of Britain and France to fulfill their commitments to Czechoslovakia would read in Moscow as de facto British and French support for German aggression against the Soviet Union. On May 16th, 1938, William C. Bullitt, the American Ambassador in France, reported that he had spoken with the French minister, Bonnet, who told Bullitt that he had asked Litvinov "what the Soviet Union would do if Germany harmed Czechoslovakia. Litvinov had replied that the Soviet Union would wait to see what France would do . . ." Bonnet also told Bullitt that the Polish Government had "stated categorically that if a Russian Army should attempt to cross Poland to attack Germany or to defend Czechoslovakia, Poland would at once declare war on the Soviet Union and that the Rumanian Foreign Minister had said the same.[28]

These were the understandings that were in place when on May 19, 1938, there were reports of major German troop movements in the vicinity of the Czech border. Czechoslovakia called up reserves and manned the border fortifications. There was the possibility of Soviet intervention on the side of Czechoslovakia, but Romania now had settled into a policy of studied ambiguity, complicating matters already sufficiently complex.[29] On May 21st, the Foreign Secretary, Viscount Halifax telegraphed instructions to Sir Nevile Henderson, the British Ambassador in Berlin, concerning the message the latter should convey to the German Government: "His Majesty's Government, as the German Government well know, are doing their utmost to promote a peaceful solution of [the Sudeten] question.

They have been using all their influence with members of the Czechoslovak Government including the President himself in the direction of a just settlement . . . You should add that if, in spite of His Majesty's Government's efforts, a conflict arises, the German Government must be well aware of the dangers which such a development would involve. France has obligations to Czechoslovakia and will be compelled to intervene in virtue of her obligations if there is a German aggression on Czechoslovakia . . . In such circumstances His Majesty's Government could not guarantee that they would not be forced by circumstances to become involved also.[30]

Halifax did not eschew double negatives. Perhaps he found their obscurity useful. The next day Halifax cabled the Ambassador in Paris, as follows: "It is of utmost importance that French Government should not be under any illusion as to attitude of His Majesty's Government . . . in the event of failure to bring about peaceful settlement in Czechoslovak question.

His Majesty's Government have given the most serious warnings to Berlin . . . But it might be highly dangerous if the French Government were to read more into those warnings than is justified by their terms . . . His Majesty's Government would of course always honour their pledge to come to the assistance of France if she were the victim of unprovoked aggression by Germany. In that event they would be bound to employ all the forces at their command . . . If, however, the French Government were to assume that His Majesty's Government would at once take joint military action with them to preserve Czechoslovakia against German aggression, it is only fair to warn them that our statements do not warrant any such assumption . . .[31]

Such communications (a classic diplomatic sequence) showed that the British Government's support of the French commitment to

Czechoslovakia was not as solid as it appeared. This would, no doubt, have been of interest in Moscow.

In an attempt to clarify matters, at least from the point of view of Whitehall, on the 25th Foreign Secretary Halifax informed the British Cabinet that "he was sending Mr Strang, of the Foreign Office, to Prague that very day to obtain some idea of the atmosphere in that city.

> Mr Strang was to go on to Berlin, where he would spend the second day, returning to London on Friday. In the meantime the Foreign Office would be examining the ideas of a plebiscite and a system of neutrality. He asked for no decision, but he had wished the Cabinet to know the lines on which he was working .
> . . In the course of a short discussion the plan of Czechoslovak neutrality, accompanied perhaps by a Cantonal system as in Switzerland, was commended. A plebiscite was felt to offer greater difficulties.[32]

Not that the Czechoslovak government was consulted on this perhaps commendable plan.

Maclean had been sent to Prague on May 23rd, in advance of Strang. According to Igor Damaskin's reading of the Soviet archives, in Prague "Maclean and his colleagues were housed in the [British] embassy . . .

> Maclean's responsibility was the handling of the DEDIP traffic, messages that were regarded as too sensitive to be handled by the cipher clerks and had to be deciphered by an official, and he was thus well-placed to obtain and pass on copies of cables on everything that the Foreign Office was doing in Berlin, Prague, Paris and other European capitals over this critical period. He also passed on information on the organisation of the British intelligence effort in Prague, and one particularly important message was a report on what a cryptographer named Stevens had told him about British successes in breaking all the Soviet codes.[33]

Damaskin slides from Maclean was "well-placed to obtain and pass on cables" to "He also passed on information on the organisation of the British intelligence effort in Prague." Apparently the archives explicitly mention the latter and Damaskin infers the former. It is a reasonable inference. Aside from the code issue (which, like the poor, is always with us), the importance to the Soviet Union of Maclean's access to "everything that the Foreign Office was doing in Berlin, Prague, Paris and other European capitals over this critical period" was to help inform Soviet decision-making in the light of German aggression and British intentions. Presumably, Maclean's reports could have allowed the Soviet leadership to follow the Foreign Office's thinking virtually from day to day. Where was the British Empire going to draw the line? Or, and this was the Kremlin's greatest fear, was the British Empire not going to draw a line limiting German ambitions, but instead planning an alliance— overt or tacit—with Germany against the Soviet Union? The Soviet leaders had vivid memories of British support for the Whites in the Russian Civil War and knew that many, if not most, of the British Government and armed forces leaders would rejoice in the disappearance of Communist Russia. At what point then, or in what direction, lay safety? The immediate issue, from the point of view of the Soviet Union, was whether the situation would develop in such a way as to oblige it to send forces into Czechoslovakia just at the moment when Stalin was quite busy decimating the senior officer corps of the Red Army.

The issue, from the British Foreign Office point of view, was that as Britain was bound by treaty with France to support that country if it was a victim of aggression, and France had similar treaties with Czechoslovakia and the Soviet Union, if Germany invaded Czechoslovakia, both France and the Soviet Union would, in principle, be bound to go to war with Germany and then the British Empire, in principle, would be bound to do so as well. The Imperial General Staff said that they were not ready for war with Germany. Chamberlain and his "friends in the House" did not want to fight Germany, particularly, or especially, in alliance, however indirect, with the Soviet Union. The supposed critical point was the German demand that the inhabitants of the Sudeten region should be allowed to vote on the issue of autonomy. However, all involved knew that this was merely the first step toward the dismembering of the Czechoslovakian state. On Strang's return to London on May 31st, he met with Halifax, Alexander Cadogan (Permanent Undersecretary of the Foreign Office) and senior Foreign Office official Orme Sargent, reporting that he had been "told by [B. C.] Newton [British Minister at Prague] that the root problem was not the presence of the Sudeten Germans but the fact of a Slav state thrust into the heart of Germany and having treaties of mutual assistance with France and Russia."[34] Cadogan had noted in his diary for May 24th that Halifax "wants to sever French-Czech and Czech-Soviet connections."[35] If Halifax had said this to Cadogan, it is possible that others in the Foreign Office realized that this was the direction of his thinking and had discussed it within Maclean's hearing. It would have been apparent in Moscow that severing those connections would mean the end of Czechoslovakia and one more step on Hitler's road to Moscow, or, at least, to Kiev and the western Ukraine wheat-basket.

On August 2nd, Lord Runciman was sent to Czechoslovakia as a mediator between the Sudeten Germans and the Czechoslovak government, at the initiative of the British Government.* The American Chargé in London reported on August 16th that Czechoslovak Foreign Minister Masaryk had told him that the Soviet Ambassador in Prague had assured *him* that Stalin had decided that if Czechoslovakian were attacked Russia would come to its assistance "the minute that France moves."[36] The next day he reported a talk with the Soviet Ambassador in London, Ivan Maisky, who said he was not at all sure that France would fight if Czechoslovakia were invaded, which added nuance to Stalin's assurances.

One day that summer, "Maclean turned up at [Harris's] flat carrying a huge bunch of roses, a bottle of wine and a box holding a

---

* A parallel would have been for the British Government of the day to have sent a mediator to the United States after the election of Lincoln, without consulting Lincoln. In either case it would have been clear to all concerned that the British Empire was "tilting" in favor of the rebellious parties.

locket on a thin gold chain. "He had ordered dinner from a local restaurant, and they sat eating it and listening to Glenn Miller on the radio.

> That was the first night they made love, and true to her training she reported the event to her controller, Grigoriy Grafpen, next day . . . Harris went on being entirely open in her reports, even telling her controllers that she and Maclean began and ended every meeting with sex. Sometimes this had adverse effects on their work. Telegrams from Moscow complained: "The material in the last two pouches turned out to contain only half of each image. What was the problem? Moreover in the last batch, many of the pages were almost out of focus . . ."[37]

Harris wore the gold chain and locket for the rest of her life.

When not thus otherwise occupied, "Over the period they worked together in the safe-house, Maclean handed Kitty [Harris] a vast quantity of documents, which, as the files show, the senior levels of Soviet intelligence and the country's leaders (for the most part, in this period, Stalin, Molotov and Beria) evaluated as 'important' and often 'very important'.

> Even if he had accomplished nothing else, Maclean made an invaluable contribution by passing over the plain texts of enciphered cables [vital for code-breaking efforts] . . . [S]ome papers whose sensitivity made them absolutely impossible to remove from the Foreign Office . . . Maclean memorized . . . and he relayed to Kitty his conversations with colleagues, statements at official meetings and verbal directives given by senior officials . . . Maclean also provided some SIS material to which he had access . . . [including] intercepted Comintern traffic.[38]

Maclean's contributions to that point therefore included materials to help Soviet code-breakers in their attempts to read British secret communications and materials that pinpointed for them which Soviet codes were insecure, in addition to the diplomatic materials vital to Molotov and Stalin as they attempted to guide the Soviet Union through the developing crisis. Here, if Damaskin's account is accurate, we have at least one confirmation that, even at this early date, Maclean's work was reaching the Soviet Union's leaders and was taken seriously.

And so passed the summer of 1938. Maclean and Toynbee were much together that year. Maclean's affair with Harris, his "older woman," paralleled, but lasted longer than, that of Philip Toynbee with Julia Strachey, which almost precisely occupied the second quarter of 1938. Toynbee enjoyed the sexual attention and the devotion of Strachey; she enjoyed the sexual attention and was made unhappy by his lack of devotion. It was—and is—a familiar pattern.[39] There is no reason to believe that Harris had similar cause for unhappiness that year. After all, in addition to personal satisfactions, she and Maclean had their work together, which must have been satisfying for her in itself. It was, indeed, the peak of her career.

In September, 1938, the situation in Czechoslovakia reached the critical point Hitler had carefully planned, but not quite in the way in which he had planned it. The Czechoslovakian President, Bênes, and Chamberlain, worked in parallel to give him what he asked for, the Sudeten region, but not what he had wanted: the occasion for military action. The pretext for war was to be disorder in the Sudeten region. The puppet Nazi leadership there dutifully demanded autonomy. The belief was that it would not be granted and that it would then serve as an excuse for a German invasion of Czechoslovakia. On September 2nd, Soviet Foreign Minister Litvinov suggested to his French and British colleagues that they respond together to German aggression against Czechoslovakia and begin staff talks with one another. (He also sent Maisky, the Soviet ambassador in London, on the same day, to see Churchill, implicitly asking the latter to communicate to Halifax Soviet willingness to send forces to Czechoslovakia if the League of Nations recognized German aggression against Czechoslovakia.[40]) Litvinov's proposals were not answered until the 11th, when they were rejected by the British and French governments—part of what would be a pattern of lagging Western responses to Soviet communications in this period. In the meantime, on September 4th, Bênes had agreed to the Sudeten demands. On September 8th Daladier told Bullitt that the Soviet Union was concentrating large force on the borders of Romania.[41] On September 13th, deprived of a pretext, the puppet leaders of the Sudeten area attempted to revolt anyway. The attempt failed. (Czechoslovakia had a large, modern, army, perhaps superior to that of Germany at that time.) Daladier telephoned Chamberlain and suggested that the British and French governments should invite the Germans to a conference on the Sudeten dispute. Chamberlain's French was not good. He had difficulty in understanding Daladier and the message was finally transmitted through the British Ambassador in Paris.[42] On September 15th, the Romanian Foreign Minister, moving back to an earlier position, "told the British delegate at the [League of Nations] meeting, Count de la Warr, that in the event of war, 'supplies [from the Soviet Union] would probably pass . . . through Romania to Czechoslovakia and he thought there would be no difficulty in such a case in allowing transit, especially for aeroplanes.'"[43] Chamberlain might not have thought this was good news. From that point on the Czechoslovakian crisis followed two tracks: the well-known British efforts to dismember the country in order to "appease" Hitler and the less well-known Soviet efforts to find an opportunity to defend Czechoslovakia, primarily with air power, in order to keep Hitler far from the Soviet frontier.

Chamberlain, in his own version of air power, flew to Munich on September 15th to meet Hitler at his vacation home in Berchtesgaden. "Hitler later told Polish Ambassador Jozef Lipski that he was "taken aback to a certain extent by Chamberlain's proposition to come to Berchtesgaden . . . He thought Chamberlain was coming to make a solemn declaration that Great Britain was ready to march."[44] Chamberlain instead at once offered the separation of the Sudeten Germans from the rest of Czechoslovakia, a gift, reminiscent of his earlier offer of parts of Ethiopia to Mussolini. The French premier and foreign minister, Daladier and Bonnet, went to London on September 18th, where Daladier argued that Hitler did not want some Czechoslovak provinces, but the domination of Europe.[45] He was right, of course, but Chamberlain could not be persuaded to alter his policy. On September 18, the Czechoslovak Foreign Minister, Krofta, repeated to the American Minister in Prague the message he had given to Count de la Warr three days earlier, that "all was prepared for the passage of Soviet troops over Romania"[46] The British and French governments demanded of President Bênes on the 19th that he agree to a German occupation of the Sudeten provinces, including his country's frontier defenses, and abandon the Soviet (and other eastern European) alliance(s). If he did not agree the two great powers would cease to support him, as they claimed to be doing, against the Germans. This became an ultimatum on the 21st, to which Bênes somewhat inexplicably agreed. The next day Chamberlain again flew to Germany, where this time he met Hitler at Godesberg. Hitler tried to salvage the situation, from his point of view, by demanding immediate occupation of the disputed provinces. He was finding it frustratingly difficult to get a war started.

On September 22, as Poland moved military forces to the Czechoslovak border in support of Germany, the Czechoslovak Foreign Minister asked the Soviet Union to warn Poland that an attack on Czechoslovakia would void the Polish-Soviet Non-Aggression Treaty of 1932. The Soviet Union complied on the 23rd. Also on the 23rd, in spite of the theoretical abrogation of the Czechoslovak-Soviet treaty implied by the Czechoslovak acceptance of the Anglo-French ultimatum, the Soviet Union announced that it would stand by the treaty.[47] Red Army infantry, tank and air units had been mobilized at Kiev on the 21st. On the 23rd similar forces in Belarus were mobilized, including armored trains, and moved to the frontier. Light and heavy bombers were put on alert. On the 23rd antiaircraft units were mobilized around Leningrad, Kalinin, Belarus, Kiev, Kharkov and Moscow, while reserves were called up. In all, "sixty infantry divisions, sixteen cavalry divisions, three tank corps, and twenty-two tank and seventeen air brigades" were mobilized.[48] There were still ambiguities about the routing of Soviet forces to Czechoslovakia. Because of the inadequate Romanian rail network, "[o]f the five Soviet army groups mobilized and posted to the frontier in September 1938, four were stationed on the Polish border, one on the Romanian border."[49] The Soviet Union was reported to have sent perhaps 60 SB-2 fast bombers to Czechoslovakia, via Romania, for use by the Czechoslovakian air force.[50] However, Soviet diplomats in Prague and Moscow once again emphasized that the Soviet Union would not "lend military assistance to Czechoslovakia except in common action with France."[51] Such was the situation in the East.

Sir Eric Phipps, the British Ambassador in Paris, was convinced that the French would not put up any resistance to German ambitions. On September 24th Phipps sent his notorious cable to London, stating that "All that is best in France is against war, *almost* at any price . . ."[52] The "almost" was an unnecessary modifier. The motto of "all that is best in France" (presumably the wealthy families who dominated the economy) was "Better Hitler than Blum," the Jewish leader of the Popular Front. Maclean later wrote that "From the early summer of 1940 until the end of the war, all but a small fraction of the French big bourgeoisie went over from alliance with Britain to alliance with Germany."[53] The pro-German sentiments of the French military high command were, if anything, stronger, and they were in a position to act on them, as they most likely did in 1940.[54]

A dramatic series of Cabinet meetings took place in London, during which Halifax, at the urging of his assistant, Sir Alexander Cadogan, switched sides, opposing Chamberlain's wish to accede to Hitler's demands. It was then widely expected that war would break out at any moment. On the 26th the Foreign Office issued the following communiqué:

> The German claim to the transfer of the Sudeten areas has already been conceded by the French, British and Czechoslovak Governments, but if in spite of all the efforts made by the British Prime Minister a German attack is made upon Czechoslovakia the immediate result must be that France will be bound to come

to her assistance, and Great Britain *and Russia* will certainly stand by France.[55] (Emphasis added.)

The following day Chamberlain ordered the First Lord of the Admiralty, Duff Cooper, to mobilize the fleet (or allowed Cooper to do so). The next day after that Hitler agreed to the conference at Munich, from which Chamberlain returned with a piece of paper promising eternal peace between Germany and the British Empire. In return Hitler promised not to act against Czechoslovakia before 1 October, taking the Sudeten area in an orderly way between then and the 10th, thereby providing a fig-leaf of legality to Chamberlain's surrender of the sovereignty of Czechoslovakia.[56] The Soviet forces stood down. As a quid pro quo for Mussolini's chairman's role at Munich, on October 4th France recognized the Italian conquest of Ethiopia.

Maclean had watched the unfolding Munich Crisis from a privileged position within the Foreign Office, at one point, during his assignment in Prague, privy to the most secret British communications. What conclusions would he have drawn? The American journalist Walter Lippmann wrote: "In sacrificing Czechoslovakia to Hitler, Britain and France were really sacrificing their alliance with Russia. They sought security by abandoning the Russian connection at Munich, in a last vain hope that Germany and Russia would fight and exhaust one another."[57]

Maclean, and Stalin, no doubt shared this opinion.

*      *      *

At the end of September, 1938, while Chamberlain commuted to the Rhineland and Bavaria, the Foreign Office transferred Maclean to the Paris embassy. The NKVD sent Harris along with him.[58] Paris for a British diplomat in 1938 was a plum assignment: the center of Western culture, a city of museums and art galleries, cafes and bookstores, night clubs and specialized hotels. Janet Flanner had described it for *The New Yorker's* readers ten years before: "Paris was still a beautiful, alluring, satisfying city.

107

It was a city of charm and enticement, to foreigners and even to the French themselves. Its charm lay in its being in no way international—not as yet. There were no skyscrapers. The charm still came from the *démodé* eighteenth- and nineteenth-century architecture that marked the facades of the private dwellings and the old-fashioned apartment houses . . . On warm summer days the *bateaux mouches,* the Seine's small excursion boats, took one out as far as Saint-Cloud and brought one back to the Louvre. Seated on their hard, uncomfortable outdoor benches, one felt that one was traveling on a nineteenth-century picnic. On hot afternoons the French women on the café terraces quietly drank lemonades and the French men consumed their inferior French beers. In winter the big terraces like that of the Deux Magots were heated by large *bracieri,* filled with coals.[59]

Maclean moved into a large apartment in the rue de Bellechasse, near the Invalides, on the Left Bank. "It was sparsely furnished and guests sat around . . . on collapsing sofas or orange-crates . . . A book-shelf held a few of his Marxist texts, some Tauchnitz paperbacks and the orange jackets of editions from Victor Gollancz's Left Book Club."[60] Special training in espionage would not have been necessary to ascertain Maclean's political views. A glance at his bookshelf would have shown that he had indeed moved forward from his family's Liberalism.

The *Sunday Times* team of journalists who wrote about Maclean after he went to Moscow believed that soon after his arrival in Paris Maclean "became a habitué of the Deux Magots and Café de Flore in St Germain where he met the sculptor Giacometti and Tristan Tzara, the surrealist poet who had founded the Dada movement."[61] Perhaps the *Sunday Times* journalists were romanticizing. It is at least as likely—rather more likely—that he looked up his old friend James Klugmann. Maclean's apartment in the Rue de Bellechasse is a twenty minute walk to 71 Rue du Cherche-Midi in the area of the Odeon Theatre, where James Klugmann lived from 1935 to 1940. Geoff Andrews has found that Klugmann, "on the recommendation of the CPGB leadership . . . [had] moved to Paris in 1935, ostensibly

108

to carry out postgraduate research, but in reality to work for the World Student Assembly for Peace, Freedom and Culture (RME), a Comintern-controlled organisation with a membership of some 1,500,000 members in forty-six countries . . . In Paris, he divided his time between the *Bibliotheque Nationale* and the RME offices, where as the organisation's political secretary he organised student campaigns and raised 'Aid for Spain.'"[62] Also, as the British secret police noted on May 2, 1936, campaigns for "Chinese students in their struggle for independence."[63]

Eric Hobsbawm recalled that RME "operated out of one of those small dusty Balzacian backstairs offices so characteristic of unofficial pre-war politics, in the ill-named Cité Paradis, a gloomy dead-end in the 10th *arrondissement,* and later in a more ambitious locale [97 Boulevard Arago, after February, 1938] on the Left Bank.

> Its most obvious public activities were to organize periodic world congresses, which Cambridge and other student volunteers helped to prepare . . . I spent all the summer of 1939 working on the technical preparations for what would be the largest of these congresses, which ended a few days before Hitler invaded Poland . . .[64]

Klugmann, accompanied by his friend, Gresham's classmate, and Oxford Communist, Bernard Floud, visited India, Sri Lanka, Singapore, China, and the United States that year, "a remarkable tour during which he met Jawaharlal Nehru and Mao Zedong, and addressed large student gatherings on questions such as Indian independence and opposition to the 'colour bar' in the United States . . ."[65] Which indicates, among other things, the unsurprising facts that there was communication between the Cambridge and Oxford Communist student groups, both open and clandestine, and that Maclean would have found Paris filled with old friends from Oxbridge. Toynbee (of course) was there, perhaps more drunken than usual, until at the end of November he married Anne Powell, the nineteen year old daughter of a Colonel who insisted he was not a Blimp, thereby proving it, and a Mayfair woman, whose money supported the family.

109

Floud and Klugmann had co-operated with Otto Katz in founding the World Student Committee Against War and Fascism, a predecessor, or earlier version, of RME. In 1938 Münzenberg and Katz established a magazine, *Die Zukunft* (The Future), in Paris, for which E. M. Forster, Harold Nicolson and other liberals wrote. In Robert Cecil's opinion "its editorial office would have been for Maclean both a congenial and a convenient meeting place, as he began, with increasing self-confidence, to revert to his favoured "Bohemia'."[66] Given Cecil's use of the subjunctive to indicate matters which he wished to assert without quite saying so, this places Maclean in the company of the Comintern's best-known organizers of front organizations: Münzenberg, Katz and Klugmann. Perhaps such company seemed merely bohemian at the time. After all, Nicolson, for one, was then of unimpeachable respectability, his private life still private. The offices of *Die Zukunft* would have been a convenient place for Harris, or even Maclean himself, to drop off the films of the documents he thought might be of interest in Moscow. Another person who was living in Paris at this time, who was close to people then close to Maclean, was Litzi Philby, who was acting as the linking agent for Kim Philby as he reported to *The Times* and Soviet Intelligence on the Spanish Civil War from the Fascist side. She met Philby at various sites in the south of France, exchanging messages to and from her Soviet control officer in Paris. Litzi Philby had a luxurious apartment in Paris and a place in the country, gave lavish parties all paid for by Philby's allowance from *The Times.* Looking back from the security of a certain eminence in the German Democratic Republic, she saw this period as the most pleasurable of her life.[67]

\* \* \*

For at least the first year of Maclean's time in Paris he continued his affair with Kitty Harris and she for that time and perhaps longer continued to photograph the bulging briefcases full of papers he brought her. She would then take the film to a "drop" of some kind, perhaps the offices of *Die Zukunft,* where it would be collected by someone from the Soviet embassy, or by yet another cut-out, and then sent by the diplomatic bag to Moscow, or, if it contained urgent documents, developed and enciphered in the embassy and transmitted to Moscow by radio. There Maclean's contributions joined the flow of documents from Burgess, Blunt, Cairncross and others, as well as the more routine communications from embassy officials. The documents were deciphered, if necessary, graded for importance, translated into Russian and sent up to Stalin, Molotov or Beria, as appropriate.[68]

What would Maclean have been able to see at the Paris Embassy that would have been of interest to Stalin? Paris was, still, the most important British embassy: "During the first forty years of this century, if Britain can be said to have had a special relationship with any great power, it was with France and not the United States . . . In the inter-war period . . . British diplomacy was far more concerned with concerting its policy with the French than with the American Government . . . 'the traffic of information and consultation' between London and Paris was then consistently heavier than between London and Washington."[69] According to Robert Cecil, who was there, "The Embassy was a small, closely-knit body and the two Third Secretaries saw virtually everything–not only the telegrams and formal despatches, but even the Ambassador's personal letters to Sir Alexander Cadogan."[70] In other words, Maclean could have seen, if he wished, anything in European affairs involving the Foreign Office and a selection of Foreign Office correspondence concerning all other parts of the world, not only current, but also the materials that resided in the files, such as the Ambassador's appraisals of French attitudes before Munich. And he certainly would have wished to do so.

From this body of documents he would make his own selection concerning matters he thought might have been of interest in Moscow, such as Halifax's letter to Phipps of November 1st, conceding German dominance of Central Europe, or the record of the conversations Halifax and Chamberlain had with the French ministers on November 24th. On that occasion Chamberlain asked Bonnet, the French foreign minister, whether they had thought would happen if Germany attempted to detach the Ukraine from the Soviet Union by subversion, rather than invasion and the Soviets called upon the French to help suppress the revolt. Bonnet replied that the Franco-Soviet treaty only obligated France to come to the assistance of the Soviet Union in case of invasion by a foreign power. The tone of Halifax's memorandum, and of the conversations it recorded, were such as to minimize French commitments to its alliance with the Soviet Union.[71] If it had been obtained by Maclean, or through other means, it would no doubt have contributed to the evolving calculations taking place in Moscow concerning the correlation of forces as Europe prepared for war.

Maclean had arrived in Paris during the Munich conference, "at which Chamberlain and Daladier demonstrated that they were prepared to entrust Czechoslovakia to Hitler's mercy rather than form a common front against him with Stalin.

> So much the Soviet dictator could observe for himself; but it was certainly of great advantage to him, as he conducted his "agonizing reappraisal" of Soviet foreign relations, to have a source in the Paris Embassy well placed to report that in France the will to fight was conspicuously lacking.[72]

We can go further than that in our interpretation of the events known as Munich. The conventional view is that Chamberlain, taking the foreign policy of the British Empire into his own hands, attempted to "appease" the "understandable" ambitions of the German government to correct what were seen as the injustices of the Versailles settlement. That this entailed as its price the destruction of the Czechoslovakian democracy mattered little to Chamberlain. He was the head of the Government of the world's greatest empire, after all. There were reasons of state to consider, reasons of state taking precedence over sentiments about democracy and the rhetoric of politicians from places of little more consequence than, say, Wales. This was not how the matter was viewed from Moscow. The Soviet treaty with Czechoslovakia, and that with France, were part of a strategy to reduce the isolation of the Soviet Union and to protect it against the obvious plans of German aggression. Chamberlain's maneuvers, illuminated by the information sent to Moscow by Maclean, increased the diplomatic and military isolation of the Soviet Union, leaving it without allies against German expansionism in the East. Indeed, as seen from Moscow, Chamberlain's goal in the Munich negotiations would seem to have been exactly that. There was no question of Hitler's plans for the Soviet Union. He had laid them out clearly enough, and often. They were plans that by means of the Munich negotiatons Chamberlain sought to help implement.

In this way the information Maclean provided to the Soviet secret intelligence services contributed to the process in which Stalin decided to find a substitute for his "Western" strategy: the alliance with Nazi Germany.

Following on the Munich conference and the subsequent loss of Czechoslovakia as a barrier to German eastward expansion, a possible stage in those preparations, from the point of view of Stalin and his colleagues, was another visit to a dictator by Chamberlain, this to Mussolini. Chamberlain and Halifax and their retinue traveled to Rome in early January, 1939, by train, not airplane, arriving on the morning of the 11th and remaining until the 14th. Their extensive talks with Mussolini, who was viewed as occupying the territory between a possible ally and an unfriendly neutral, were aimed chiefly at an attempt to convince him to intervene with Hitler to tone down the aggressive gestures of the latter and to settle outstanding issues with the French government. It was a friendly set of meetings, with cultural tours laid on and long talks in chilly, palatial, reception rooms. If nothing else, it sent a clear message that the British Government was, literally, willing to go far toward friendship, or, at least, negotiations, with the dictators.

In spite of the Roman atmospherics, early in February, as the Spanish Republic collapsed, the British Government thought it necessary, in effect, to issue a guarantee to France in case the Italian forces in Spain continued on north over the Pyrenees. (All pretence of the exclusively Spanish nature of Franco's forces having been

113

dropped long before.) At the end of February Chamberlain announced that Britain would recognize the Franco regime. Janet Flanner, no friend of the Spanish Republic, described what followed in her March 1$^{st}$ letter to *The New Yorker:*

There has never been anything in modern history like the recent flight of the Catalonian army and civilian population into France. Since the exodus was without precedent, nobody was prepared to take care of it. When the French frontier roads were finally opened, about three hundred thousand Spaniards—soldiers, civilians, women, and children, all hungry, exhausted, and in a panic—swept down on the two hundred thousand French inhabitants of the Pyrénées-Orientales . . .[73]

Two weeks later (March 15) the German army occupied Prague.

### The Molotov-Ribbentrop Pact

In mid-February, 1939, Chamberlain told Joseph Kennedy, the American Ambassador in London, that he did "not take the possibility of a Russian-German alliance seriously. He says they are both so distrustful of each other that it would never work out . . ."[74] A potential Anglo-German alliance was another matter. During March there was a trade agreement between the Federation of British Industries and the corresponding German organization, including possible credits from Britain to Germany to facilitate trade between the two nations on a cartel basis. In a "vulgar" Marxist interpretation, such an agreement was tantamount to an alliance between the two countries. This Anglo-German agreement was followed by the German occupation of the remainder of the Czech lands.

Tacking the other way, at the end of the month the British Government sent "a proposal to Poland, France, the Soviet Union, Rumania, Turkey, Greece and Yugoslavia asking them if they were prepared to take concerted action with Great Britain in case of further German aggression against any one of them."[75] France and the Soviet Union said that they were. Chamberlain, under pressure from the public and Parliament, out of concern about either an Italian offensive against France or a German offensive against either Holland or Poland, and, perhaps, out of personal pique, on April 3rd issued a "guarantee" to Poland. It was the end of—overt—appeasement. In Cripps's opinion, "The policy of appeasement had been adopted not through love (or even fear) of Hitler, but because the Government misguidedly saw Hitler as a bulwark against Bolshevism."[76] It still did in the Spring of 1939, and would so see Germany for decades to come. Chamberlain, confident in his own wisdom, told Ambassador Kennedy that he felt that "he can make a deal with Russia any time now."[77] From the middle of April to the middle of May, 1939, the British Government "sought openly for a one-sided Soviet pledge of assistance 'if desired',"[78] that is, the Soviet Union was to promise to come to the aid of the British Empire and its allies, but they would not need to come to the aid of the Soviet Union. On the 17th the British proposed to the Soviet Union that it too guarantee Poland and Rumania against a German attack. The next day the Soviet Union sent a telegram to the Foreign Office countering by suggesting a British, French and Soviet agreement for mutual assistance and protection of all states bordering on the Soviet Union in the west. A week later the British Government turned down the Soviet proposal.[79] Phipps told Daladier, on April 27th, that he thought that Poland should negotiate with Germany over Danzig.[80] By the first of May the three-way negotiations between the British, French and Soviet governments had reached an impasse: the British insisting on a unilateral Soviet guarantee of Poland and Rumania, while the Soviets and the French wished to have tri-lateral mutual aid guarantees. (Apparently Phipps, opposed to a Soviet alliance, did not convey the French proposal to the Foreign Office.[81]) Stalin, looking over the diplomatic chessboard, dismissed the western-oriented Maxim Litvinov as Soviet Foreign Minister, replacing him with Vyacheslav Molotov.[*] The American Ambassador in Paris, Bullitt,

---

[*] The dismissal of Litvinov, which was not fatal for him, removed a barrier to Soviet negotiations with Nazi Germany, as Litvinov, who was the

115

met with the anti-German British Foreign Office official Sir Robert Vansittart and asked "if he felt that Stalin's dismissal of Litvinov had been occasioned by the dilatory and almost insulting policy which the British Government had pursued vis-à-vis the Soviet Union since Hitler's invasion of Czechoslovakia."[82] The question was obviously a statement of opinion.

On May 8th, Phipps informed Bonnet (and, perhaps, through Maclean, Stalin) "that the British Government was still opposed to accepting the French proposal to the Soviet Union since the British Government was loath to give any guarantee whatsoever to the Soviet Union."[83] Concerned that Phipps was still not conveying the French view to the British Government, Daladier began to conduct Anglo-French discussions through the French Ambassador in London. On May 19th Chamberlain gave a statement in the House of Commons concerning the negotiations with the Soviet Union. Leo Amery, a Conservative Member of Parliament, commented in his diary: "The trouble with Neville is that he is being pushed all the time into a policy which he does not like, and hates abandoning the last bridges which might still enable him to renew his former policy. So he vainly tries to avoid a war alliance with Russia."[84] A few days later, in Paris, Halifax told Daladier that he expected that the negotiations with the Soviet Union would be concluded in July, if necessary on the basis of the Soviet proposals for reciprocity previously rejected by the British Government.

At this point there were beginning to be rumors in Paris "with regard to offers that the German Government was making to the Soviet Government."[85] On May 24th the British Government sent a draft proposal of a reciprocal agreement on the Soviet terms to the French Government for its approval. The proposal was given to

---

designer of the multi-national treaty regime the Soviet Union had sought and Germany opposed, was Jewish, which made matters difficult in negotiating with the anti-Semites in Berlin. Stalin made a further gesture to the latter by ordering the removal of many other Jewish senior Foreign Ministry officials .

Molotov in Moscow on the 27th, who "read it giving every sign that he was familiar in advance with its contents."[86] On June 3 Halifax rejected an offer from Cripps to go to Moscow to negotiate an agreement, perhaps fearing he might succeed.[87] From the end of May to the last week of July, "the British tried to devise a formula which would look like a straight alliance and which would yet would bar a Soviet initiative . . . the British would cooperate with Soviet Russia only if Poland were attacked *and agreed to accept Soviet assistance . . .*"[88] [Emphasis added.] In other words, any Anglo-Soviet joint military assistance to Poland depended on Polish agreement, and Beck, the Polish Foreign Minister, could be relied on never to agree. Indeed, he had threatened war with the Soviet Union the previous year if the Red Army had tried to cross Polish territory to assist Czechoslovakia.

Hugh Ragsdale, an authority on the Soviet Union's policy during the Munich Crisis, observed: "If the British and the French were suspicious of Moscow, Moscow had reason enough to be suspicious of them in turn. The publicly announced policy of appeasement in Britain had since the Rhineland crisis of 1936 facilitated Hitler's movement in one distinct direction, after all, the direction toward the border of the USSR."[89] In December, 1937, Litvinov had told a correspondent for *Le Temps*, as relayed by the French Ambassador in Moscow, "if they are abandoned by us, the Soviets would consent to serious sacrifices in order to obtain from Germany at least a truce that would assure them the several years of respite that they need."[90] It had been a clear warning. "Even after Munich, even after the Anglo-French issuance of the guarantee to Poland, [Soviet Ambassador [Maisky in London] suspected the continuation of efforts in the British cabinet to make a deal with Berlin . . ."[91] On the first of July, 1939, the British Ambassador in Paris told the American Ambassador that if Germany attempted "to take Danzig, and Poland should resist, Great Britain would declare war on Germany at once."[92] But Maisky had good reason to be suspicious. In July, Sir Horace Wilson had held conversations with Helmuth Wohlthat, commissioner of the German Four-Year Plan and in the first few days of August with German Ambassador Dirksen, concerning an Anglo-German non-aggression pact and trade agreement, including colonial concessions by the British to the Germans.[93] However, by the end of June the British Government had decided to accept the Soviet terms for what would be, in effect, an Anglo-French-Soviet alliance, committing each to the defense of the others and all to the defense of Poland and the small nations of Europe. British and French negotiations with the Soviet Union continued through July, at the end of which it was agreed to begin military staff talks toward the end of the first week of August. It was about this time that the German Ambassador in Moscow began increasingly friendly conversations with Molotov, while trade negotiations between the two countries also were making progress.[94]

Then, in what has become a legendary sequence of events, the British and French military missions were sent to Leningrad by sea, which took about four days, as if there were no urgency to the matter.[95] When they finally reached Moscow, there was an unexpectedly dramatic scene: "The Anglo-French negotiations of a military alliance with Moscow were opened on 12 August . . .

> As a matter of convention, the Soviet negotiator, Marshal Kliment Voroshilov, exhibited his own diplomatic powers, which authorized him, quite simply, both to negotiate and to sign a military convention with the visitors. He then asked for an exhibit of the presumably similar powers of the Anglo-French delegation . . . [The French had similar powers.] British Admiral Reginald Drax, on the other hand, demurred, saying that he had no written powers, that he had been authorize to negotiate but had no powers to sign . . . Marshal Voroshilov then asked for a presentation of the military plans that the visiting delegations had in mind. Admiral Drax said that he had no precise plan.[96]

And so it went, with Voroshilov presenting detailed plans, the French following and the British demurring. On August 14, Marshal Voroshilov asked the British negotiators "the decisive question . . . 'Can the Red Army move across North Poland . . . and across Galicia in order to make contact with the enemy?' The British and now even the French could not answer. The talks ran to a standstill. The Poles refused to admit the Red Army."[97] Colonel Beck said that this would be tantamount to a new partition of Poland. After the non-response to Voroshilov's question Stalin's chessboard showed only one remaining move.[98] A week later the talks ended. Hitler had proposed to Stalin on the 15th that serious German-Soviet talks should begin, and that the German Government would send a high-ranking official to Moscow. A German-Soviet commercial agreement was signed on the 19th. On the 22nd came the announcement that Ribbentrop was on his way to Moscow to sign a Russo-German non-aggression pact. Beck had been quite correct, in a Delphian sense, in his prediction of a new partition of Poland.

Maclean saw the cable traffic moving between the British and French representatives in Moscow and their respective foreign offices in London and Paris and at each stage would have been able to send those messages to Moscow and to advise Stalin of the British response to Soviet proposals.[99] Those cables and the records of Cabinet discussions in London make it clear that the British Government, and the Imperial General Staff, could not bring themselves to embark on a political and military alliance with the Soviets. The politicians distrusted the Soviet Government; the military had a low opinion of the Red Army. And, in any case, the whole foundation of Chamberlain's policy was the belief—hope— that just one more concession, or, failing that, just one more threat, would put an end to Hitler's adventurism. Or better yet, turn him to the east. Why then entangle the British Empire with Russia, its historic enemy with which it might soon be at war? On the other hand, the leader of the extreme Left in Parliament, Stafford Cripps, commented: "The principle for which we Socialists believe it is worth fighting is working-class freedom and no one will convince me that I can forward that aim by fighting against the Soviet Union."[100] Maclean, of course, went further, fighting, in his way, for "working-class freedom," which he at this point identified with the survival of the Soviet Union.

## Donald and Melinda Maclean

Donald Maclean was probably one of the few people on the Left who was neither surprised nor dismayed by the Molotov-Ribbentrop Pact. He knew that the Soviet Union had offered to intervene on behalf of Czechoslovakia before Munich. He knew that offer was rejected by Chamberlain. He knew with what lack of seriousness the British Government had negotiated with the Soviet Union that summer. He could see the cards held by each of the players. Now he could just wait to see how well Stalin would play his, knowing what Stalin knew, thanks in part to Maclean, about the cards held by Chamberlain. The Molotov-Ribbentrop Pact was signed on August 23, 1939. That day Chamberlain sent a message to Hitler offering, once more, his good offices for negotiation in regard to Poland, what Bullitt, who was shown it by the British Charge d'Affairs, called "a new Munich."[101] Chamberlain repeated to Hitler his suggestion of negotiations on August 28th. Hitler accepted the offer on the 29th, demanding that a Polish negotiator reach Berlin the next day. Discussions and diplomatic activity continued until, having securing its eastern flank, Germany invaded Poland on September 1.

Philip Toynbee began his "war diary" on September 7th, 1939, with a retrospective account from the previous Thursday, August 31.

There was the usual sitting in the Flore, buying every edition of the Paris-Soir. It seemed very likely that a new Munich was brewing, and we were all feeling sick and depressed. The war of nerves had produced in me only the most profound irritation . . . I got steadily drunker. At the Select were a lot of Americans who couldn't get home—slow, rather tedious cynicism.

Toynbee continued to get drunker, eventually all his money was stolen by prostitutes and he was picked up by the police and thrown out of their car far from where he was staying.

I woke on Friday [September 1] with a furious hang-over, mental, moral and physical. All my resolutions had been broken: I was ill and depressed. There would be no war and I should drift on into increasing squalor and decay . . . At Dupond's I read the Journal and found that Hitler had at last made his conditions known. It appeared that he'd have no less than Danzig and the corridor. "And he'll get them." I thought, when suddenly there was a stir and movement in the café, everybody craning to read the headline of a first copy of Paris-Midi . . . I craned too, and read. "Hitler attagne la Pologne." Later I read the paper through. German armies had invaded Poland from Prussia, East Prussia, Silesia and Slovakia . . . I walked to the Flore . . .

Toynbee reflected, as he walked from one café to another that the war would solve his personal problems, subsuming them in the greater issues. Arriving at the Flore he found that "Balthus and his Swiss wife were there, and the little bearded painter . . . Everyone was gay and excited, except handsome Balthus. He was to be called up on the fourth day of general mobilization."

The British declaration of war in 1939 was a declaration of war by the British Empire, most importantly, in addition to Great Britain itself, India, which furnished millions of soldiers and laborers to the Empire's war effort as well as something like a billion pounds sterling in finance. The Dominions—first Australia and New Zealand then South Africa and Canada—followed over the next two weeks, involving every continent except Antarctica. For many months after the declarations of war on Germany and its allies the British Minister for War's reports to the Cabinet were limited to the phrase: "No activity on the Western Front." On the other hand, there was considerable activity on the Eastern Front. The Soviet Union, according to the arrangements made during August, invaded Poland on September 17th and Poland, as well as the intervening Baltic states, quickly ceased to have an independent existence. The surviving units of the Polish armed forces made their way through the Balkans to Romania (where Beck himself was interned and later died), and on to the west. The Soviet Union sovietised its sector of Poland and the Baltic countries, dispossessing the feudal landlords and, for the moment, giving land to the quasi-serfs (beneficiaries of the demesne-robot [sic] system) on the large estates. The following month Soviet Ambassador Maisky, in London, hedging the bets then on the table, suggested talks on Anglo-Soviet trade. Cripps began conversations with Halifax as to whether he should be part of a trade delegation to be sent to Moscow.[102]

On October 26th Cripps made his "test question" speech concerning the future of India. "Britain's commitment to democracy, he maintained, could only be validated by a firm commitment to Indian self-government, to be fully implemented after the war, but with an interim instalment at once . . . [The Viceroy] Linlithgow had candidly told Gandhi, by contrast . . . that 'it was not a question of fighting for democracy', to which he did not believe the Government committed 'in the slightest degree'."[103] Churchill, soon to become Prime Minister, agreed with Linlithgow and would fight the war on that basis: for Empire, not for democracy. It was clear to those on the left in Britain, and later, in the United States, who they were fighting against—Nazi Germany, Fascist Italy and Imperial Japan—it was less clear, particularly in Britain, which governmental and socio-economic system they were fighting for. Could Britain practice social democracy at home and colonialism over the seas?

The governments of the British Empire and the French Republic had declared war on Germany to protect Poland. At least that was they said to the newspapers. Logically, as the Soviet Union had also invaded Poland, they should have declared war on it as well. This would have been safe enough: the Red Army was even farther out of reach than the German. However, at a meeting of the War Cabinet on November 1, 1939, Halifax said that the British Empire "'would not be justified in adding to our present burden by declaring war on Russia unless and until the United States of America had definitely ranged themselves on our side' . . . The War Cabinet agreed . . . that 'Great Britain and France are at present in no position to undertake additional burdens and that we cannot, therefore, from a military point of view, recommend that we should declare war on Russia.'"[104] In any case, all through November the Cabinet was considering a trade agreement with the USSR. That proposed with Germany had been abandoned some months earlier.

## *The Russo-Finnish War*

As Germany converted its sector of Poland into a charnel house, life in Britain and France continued, by and large, as before. Workers mined coal from the pits and manufactured goods in factories; bankers did whatever it is that bankers do; the ten percent of the population considered middle class lived well enough, their betters did . . . better, while the unemployed scavenged and went hungry. The war was three or four months old by the time Maclean met Melinda Marling at the Café de Flore, and although Poland had become merely a geographical expression, neither the British nor the French armed forces had been engaged in anything more than maneuvers. Sartre, for example, having been called up, was moving about Alsace with a small meteorological group, writing daily letters to de Beauvoir and other women (or girls, as the case may be), working on his diary and beginning to think about *Being and Nothingness.* Balthus had been called up, as anticipated, but was demobilized after a month and went to Switzerland to paint cats (or girls, as the case may be). In Britain, during these months of "Phony War," unemployment remained high; Ministers, seeing no reason to mobilize for war, were aghast when it was suggested that the RAF might attack private property in Germany; habitués of the Gargoyle Club in Longon formed specialized anti-aircraft units characterized by Bloomsbury attitudes and brightly colored silk pajamas.

At the end of November, 1939, Halifax informed the War Cabinet that the Soviets had announced that there had been an incident on their border with Finland and that they had demanded that the Finns withdraw their forces twenty or so kilometers from the point on the border closest to Leningrad. Halifax said that he would raise the matter with the Soviet Ambassador. The War Cabinet took note of the Foreign Secretary's statement.[105] Two days later the War Cabinet learned from the Secretary of State for War, Hore-Belisha, that there were three-quarters of a million soldiers concentrated on the border between Finland and the USSR, with roughly equal numbers on each side. The Finns had suggested that each withdraw

25 kilometers. The Soviets said that this would place their army inside the Leningrad suburbs (where, ironically, it would be soon enough), and abrogated the Finnish-Soviet non-aggression pact, claiming hostile acts by the Finns. The War Cabinet of the British Empire made note of these statements.[106] By December 1st Soviet troops had crossed the Finnish frontier in several places and were rumored to have captured the nickel mines at Petsamo, in the far north. This was of great concern to the British and French governments, as the nickel and iron ore mines in the area of the northern borders of Norway, Sweden and Finland were the chief sources of those vital materials for the German war machine. The War Cabinet believed at this point that the Red Army would make short work of the Finnish army and having obtained their objectives in the north, the Soviet Union would turn its attention to the Balkans (always considered by the Government of the British Empire to be the chief object of Russian ambitions).[107] This would have opened the possibility for a British-Italian alliance to thwart a Russian move through the Balkans to the Straits. It would be 1914 all over again.

A week later, the British Empire and Dominions began shipping aircraft and other means of war to Finland and considering facilitating the recruiting and transportation of volunteers.[108] The Finns were successfully defending themselves against the Soviets on the ground (the reports about Petsamo apparently incorrect), while suffering from aerial bombardments of military installations and civilian population centers. In addition to receiving supplies from the British and the French, they were receiving supplies, including aircraft, from Italy (which was playing a quite ambiguous role) and possibly from, or at least through, Germany as well. The British Government was keeping the American government informed about these complex matters, in hope of involving the United States in an ill-defined enterprise, which might have appeared, in Moscow, to be an incipient alliance between the British Empire, France and Italy, with American support, against the Soviet Union.[109] At least some War Cabinet discussions were communicated to the Paris embassy and most probably thence, via the Embassy's Third Secretary, to

Moscow. The Soviet leaders would have found Maclean's communications of increasing, and finally, perhaps, of crucial, interest for their conduct of the war with Finland.

The French proposed toward the end of December that they and the British encourage Norway and Sweden to take active measures in support of Finland.[110] Just before the end of the year, Churchill, then First Lord of the Admiralty, raised the issue of direct British (and French) intervention in the war between Finland and the Soviet Union in order to block iron ore supplies to Germany, speculating about the type of event that might serve as a pretext.[111] This became less of a speculation after mid-January, 1940, when in response to a request from Finland for some tens of thousands of "volunteers" for the early summer, the War Cabinet began to consider the technical arrangements this would entail.[112] Two weeks later, the French government proposed sending an expeditionary force composed of Polish units to intervene. The War Cabinet thought this unwise, or impractical, but nevertheless thought it appropriate to begin to consider alternatives.[113] Soon enough these included plans for sending regular British and French forces to Finland in the late spring or early summer.[114] During a War Cabinet Meeting on January 29, 1940, "the Prime Minister [Chamberlain] observed that events seemed to be leading the Allies to open hostilities with Russia."[115] Stafford Cripps, stopping in Chungking in January during a private round the world trip, to his surprise was asked by the Soviet ambassador "whether there was any likelihood of Britain and Germany combining against Russia."[116] He thought it an odd question. Of course, Cripps was not privy to the War Cabinet discussions. The British Ambassador in Paris may have been better informed. If he was, so was Stalin.

At a meeting of the War Cabinet on February 2, 1940 the Chief of the Naval Staff introduced a "Report on Intervention in Scandinavia." He said that although the report had not been discussed in detail during the recent visit of the Chiefs of Staff to Paris, there had been a discussion of the French project for a landing at Petsamo. He said that "the vital importance" of obtaining control of the northern Swedish ore fields was recognized by the French. General Ironside, Chief of the Imperial General Staff, then said that the head of the French army, General Gamelin, had offered no objection to the diversion of troops from England and a British division from France to carry out "the big project" of stopping Germany's iron ore supplies. He added that General Gamelin thought that the Germans were unlikely to attack in the west in 1940 and that if the Germans were forced to engage in a conflict in Sweden it would entirely preclude an attack in the west.[*] The French plan for an attack on Petsamo included a landing of British and French forces in cooperation with the Finns and the dispatch of 30-40,000 "volunteers" to central Finland, to replace Finnish forces needed for the attack on Petsamo. After the landing at Petsamo, the plan was to cut the railway to Murmansk. Halifax intervened, saying he had just received a telegram from the Paris embassy, recounting a conversation between Phipps and Alexis Leger (the administrative head of the French Foreign Office, who was also the poet Saint-John Perse, as it happened.) Leger explained that the French plan was to create a diversion at Petsamo, to force the Germans to attack Southern Sweden, which would result in a Swedish appeal to the British and French, who would then seize the Norwegian port of Narvik.

After some discussion the War Cabinet decided that the French plan was "not well thought out" and had little chance of achieving the objectives of preventing a Soviet occupation of Finland, bringing

---

[*] There is a curious story in Malcolm Muggeridge's memoir, *The Infernal Grove,* about the replacement of General Ironside by General Brook as Commander-in-Chief, Home Forces. According to Muggeridge it was—or may have been—occasioned by Ironside's "frequenting" of a house in Holland Park associated with fascists, possible former members of the Anglo-German Fellowship. In other words, the Commander-in-Chief was suspected of sympathy with the enemy. Which might explain his eagerness concerning the prospects of the Scandinavian War, loyalties—left and right—in those days running across national boundaries.

Sweden and Norway into the war on the side of Britain and France, and cutting off the German ore supplies. The War Cabinet instead favored simply informing the Finnish government that the British and French were willing to send forces to their assistance, but that this depended on the agreement of the Norwegians and the Swedes. If they declined, then the onus for the defeat of Finland would lay with them. If they accepted, British and French forces could be landed at Narvik and sent across northern Scandinavia to seize the Gallivare iron-ore fields. The British forces would be regular Army units but, as with the French plan, described as "volunteers." The War Cabinet agreed to this, particularly to the suggestion "that any forces sent to Finland . . . would have to be units of the armed forces of the Crown who would volunteer for this Service, on the model of Italian "non-intervention" in Spain,"[117] which was interesting in the light of Chamberlain's policy during the Spanish Civil War. The differences between the French and British plans was that the former envisioned Petsamo as the initial target, bringing Sweden and Norway into the conflict by means of the German reaction, while the latter focused on Narvik and bringing Sweden and Norway in by diplomatic means. Both governments were in agreement that an expedition would soon take place and that it would have three aims: stopping the Soviet conquest of Finland, seizing the iron ore and nickel mines in the far north of Scandinavia, and bringing Sweden and Norway into the Western Alliance.

In addition to the planning for an offensive in the far north, the Paris staff talks included plans to attack Baku, the Soviet Union's oil center in the south, in order to cut off oil supplies from the German and Russian armies.[118] Therefore, in March, the British positioned light bombers at Middle Eastern and Indian air bases in preparation for attacking the Baku oil fields. At a meeting of the Cabinet as late as April 21st, Halifax relayed a telephone message from Phipps stating that the French had suggested discussions concerning "operations in the Caucasus."[119] There were also plans to lay mines at the mouth of the Volga and to send submarines into the Black Sea to stop the oil tankers that were delivering Soviet oil to the Germans.

Churchill had first thought of attacking the oil fields twenty years earlier, at that time with the rationale of helping the Monarchists defeat the Soviet government in the Russian Civil War. It was an idea to which he clung through shifting versions of the rationale for the action.

It is highly unlikely—nearly impossible—that Maclean was unaware of the Anglo-French planning that winter, positioned as he was in the Paris Embassy, where, as Robert Cecil assures us, he saw everything he wished to see. If Maclean knew about the Anglo-French planning, within a day or two of the meetings described above, Stalin would have also known about it. Before the bombing of Baku or the invasion by the 30-40,000 "volunteers" could take place, Stalin, perhaps acting on Maclean's information, suddenly ended the war with Finland.[120]

Even after the Finnish Field Marshal, Mannerheim, accepted Russian armistice terms, on March 12th, the Royal Air Force "continued to make detailed plans for raids on the Soviet oil center at Baku . . . ."[121] There was also continued British planning, perhaps not as good as it should have been, for seizing Narvik. British planning for the proverbial "next day" after the occupation of the ore fields is difficult to ascertain. Perhaps there was none. Or perhaps it was assumed that the Soviet Union would simply collapse under the impact of the assumed capture of Leningrad by the Finns and that the Germans, annexing the Ukraine, would make peace and everyone would live happily ever after. A. J. P. Taylor, taking a view that is perhaps too Olympian, judged the planning of the British Government in regard to Finland as simply inept or a matter of fantasy. It may have been fantastic and inept, but not the less serious for all that.

\* \* \*

There was a noticeable presence of Comintern Englishmen in Paris during those spring months of 1940. There was Klugmann, running his student organization; Kim Philby, who was working for

*The Times* as a correspondent at the headquarters of the British Expeditionary Force in France, and Guy Burgess, then in addition to his responsibilities to a number of British secret intelligence organizations, producing propaganda radio programs. Burgess had taken the novelist Rosamond Lehmann to Paris in order for her to do one of the broadcasts. But then ignoring Lehmann, Burgess had used the trip to Paris to look up "some of his old contacts."[122] These could have included all of the above as well as Maclean, Litzi Philby, Edith Tudor-Hart and perhaps Harris.[123] (Harris remained in Paris until the German Army arrived.[124]) Not to mention the denizens of his favorite Parisian nightclubs.

On April 9th, 1940, Germany perhaps realizing that British interest in Narvik threatened their ore supply, which traveled by ship down from the arctic through Norwegian territorial waters, invaded Norway (and Denmark, in passing, as it were). In June the Norwegian government would be replaced, eponymously, by one led by Quisling. On May 10th Germany again attacked in the west, occupying the Netherlands on the 14th, Belgium—perhaps not without royal assistance—on the 28th. General Gamelin's sources of information about German plans seem to have been unreliable. Amid dramatic scenes in Parliament Churchill, in spite of his role in the Norwegian debacle, became Prime Minister on May 10th, on the understanding that, as opposed to Chamberlain or Halifax, he would not make peace with Germany. The Labour Party leaders, having refused to serve under Chamberlain, came into the new coalition Government under Churchill. "Speak for England," Leo Amery had shouted to the Labour Party deputy leader, Greenwood, not realizing that Labour would, indeed, speak for England for the next quarter of a century and more. Attlee was soon Deputy Prime Minister and most of the Labour Party leadership were in ministerial or sub-ministerial roles. (Bevin as Minister of Labor and National Service was charged with keeping the factories going without strikes. He was made MP for Wandsworth, site of the notorious prison, so that he could serve in the Government.)

At this point we can calculate a subtotal of Donald Maclean's efforts on behalf of the Comintern. According to Igor Damaskin, "The material supplied by Maclean to Soviet intelligence from the day he joined the Foreign Office to the moment he left France in June 1940 fills forty-five boxes in the archives, each containing more than three hundred pages."[125] Say, 14,000 pages: about fifty pages a week, which would have kept Kitty Harris busy with her camera at their weekly meetings, but is by no means an impossible workload. Nor would it necessarily be noticed at the Foreign Office or the Paris Embassy that Maclean took home ten or twenty pages of materials every day or two. If asked, he could say he was studying them, which he was. On the other hand, that quantity of documents would have given the responsible Soviet officials quite a clear idea of British attitudes and decisions concerning matters of interest in Moscow. After Maclean moved to Paris, the flow of documents provided a good view of French attitudes and decisions, in addition to the condition of Anglo-French relations and French relations with other countries of interest, such as Czechoslovakia, Italy and Poland, as well as Germany. Litvinov and Stalin knew, for example, about British attitudes toward possible Soviet support for Czechoslovakia during the Munich Crisis.[126] Later, during the winter 1939-40, Molotov and Stalin would have been able to keep abreast of Anglo-French support for Finland as it changed in character from supplies of material to planning for armed intervention. Was it a coincidence that just as Anglo-French planning for an expeditionary force in northern Scandinavia reached fruition, Stalin suddenly brought the conflict to an end?[127] Doing so saved the Soviet Union from a war with the British Empire and France, and possibly with Germany as well. Or, looked at from Whitehall, Stalin's sudden decision derailed, for the time, British plans for a conflict with the Soviet Union, perhaps in alliance with Germany, while giving Germany, let us say, the Ukraine as a quid pro quo for peace with the British Empire.

We will see that these sudden decisions by Stalin, otherwise puzzling, become more easily explained knowing that he had a

confederate (often more than one) reading the cards, as it were, of
the other players.

## Chapter Five: Notes

---

[1] See, inter alia,
http://filestore.nationalarchives.gov.uk/pdfs/small/cab-24-257-cp-35-186.pdf

[2] http://filestore.nationalarchives.gov.uk/pdfs/small/cab-23-82-cc-50-35-18.pdf

[3] Taylor, A. J. P. English History: 1914—1945. New York and Oxford: Oxford University Press, 1965, pp. 384-5.

[4] Taylor, A. J. P., pp. 385-6.

[5] Blythe, Ronald. The Age of Illusion: England in the Twenties and Thirties, 1919-1940. London: Phoenix Press, 2001, pp. 112-5.

[6] Robson, Dorothy. Memoirs. Unpublished. In the possession of the author.

[7] Spender, Stephen. Forward From Liberalism. London: Victor Gollancz Ltd, 1937, p. 137; pp. 20-3.

[8] Sketches of History, the Russian Foreign Intelligence Service. Moscow: International Relations, 1997), p. 44.

[9] Sketches of History, p. 45, more or less direct quotation.

[10] Taylor, A. J. P., p. 394.

[11] Cecil, p. 46.

[12] Meeting of the Cabinet Wednesday, 18th November, 1936, at 11.0 a.m. TNA CAB/23/86

[13] Sketches of History, p. 46.

[14] Contributors, Footman, David, Talks file 1, 1937-1962, PP/GB 27th May, 1937, B.B.C. Written Archives Center, Caversham.

[15] Jeffery, Keith. The Secret History of MI6. New York: The Penguin Press, 2010, pp. 285-6.

[16] ". . . in the course of his regular visits to Broadcasting House, Footman seems to have decided that Burgess was worth introducing to M.I.6." West, W. J. Truth Betrayed. London: Duckworth, 1987, p. 63.

[17] Cairncross, John. The Enigma Spy: The Story of the Man Who Changed the Course of World War Two. London: Century, Random

House, 1997, pp. 56-7. There is some confusion here about which Foreign Office department is meant.

[18] Page, Bruce; Leitch, David and Phillip Knightley. Philby: The Spy who Betrayed a Generation. London: Andre Deutsch, 1968, p. 82.

[19] Mosley, Charles. editor, Burke's Peerage, Baronetage & Knightage, 107th edition, 3 volumes (Wilmington, Delaware, U.S.A.: Burke's Peerage (Genealogical Books) Ltd, 2003), volume 1, page 992. Hereinafter cited as Burke's Peerage and Baronetage, 107th edition.

[20] Damaskin, Igor with Geoffrey Elliott. Kitty Harris: The Spy with Seventeen Names. London: St Ermin's Press, 2001, p. 149.

[21] According to the Russian Foreign Intelligence Service, Deutsch's passport expired in November 1937. It had been assumed that he would leave for New England on a business visa, but British counterintelligence had become interested in Deutsch and to protect him Deutsch was recalled to Moscow. After returning to the Soviet Union, the Deutsches received Soviet citizenship and passports in the names of Stephen Lang and Josephine Pavlovna. Deutsch became a senior researcher at the Institute of World Economy of the Academy of Sciences, where he worked until 1941. Reactivated by the NKVD, he was at first assigned to the East, but, the routes being closed by the war, was reassigned for work in Latin America. At the end of October 1942 Deutsch and his assistant sailed from Arkhangelsk for the United States via Iceland on the transport "Donbass," which was sunk by German aircraft. Deutsch was not among the survivors. See article on Deutsch in Sketches of History. The Deutsches had a daughter who attended an event in connection with Edith Tudor-Hart's photography in Vienna (personal communication from Dr. Paul Broda) in 2013.

[22] Forbes, Duncan. "Politics, Photography and Exile in the Life of Edith Tudor-Hart," in Behr, Shulamith and Marian Malet. Arts in Exile in Britain 1933-1945: Politics and Cultural Identity. Amsterdam and London: The Yearbook of the Research Centre for

German and Austrian Exile Studies, 6, Institute of Germanic Studies and Romance Studies, University of London, p. 73.

[23] This account is from Svetlana Chervonnaya's website "Documents Talk.com," which refers to the article "Svjaznaja Dzhipsi – 'Tsyganochka'," in *Ocherki po istorii rossiiskoi vneshnei razvedki*, Moskva: "Mezhdunarodnye otnoshenija", 2003, tom 4, 1941-1945, s. 259 ("The Courier 'Gypsy'," *Essays on the History of Russian Foreign Intelligence*, Moscow: "International Relations," 2003, vol. 4, 1941-1945, p. 259. Damaskin's book is apparently from the same source.

[24] Damaskin, p. 163-4. According to the "Sketches," Harris was Maclean's fifth contact (p. 46).

[25] Damaskin, p. 171.

[26] Ragsdale, Hugh. The Soviets, the Munich Crisis, and the Coming of World War II. Cambridge: The Cambridge University Press, 2004, 54; 58.

[27] FRUS, 1938, Volume I, p. 492.

[28] FRUS, 1938, Volume I, p. 502.

[29] Ragsdale, p.77.

[30] Viscount Halifax to Sir N. Henderson (Berlin) No. 169 Telegraphic, FOREIGN OFFICE, May 21, 1938, 3.45 p.m. Repeated to Prague (No. 94), Paris, Rome, Budapest and Warsaw.
[Source: *Documents on British Foreign Policy,* (London, 1949), Third Series, vol. I, no. 250, pp. 331-2.]

[31] Viscount Halifax to Sir E. Phipps (Paris). No. 141 Telegraphic. Foreign Office, May 22, 1938, 4.30 p.m. [Source: *Documents on British Foreign Policy,* (London, 1949), Third Series, vol. I, no. 271, pp. 346-7.]

[32] TNA CAB/23/93; Cabinet 26(38). Conclusions of a Meeting of the Cabinet held at 10 Downing Street, S.W.1., on Wednesday, The 25th May, 1938, at 11.0 a.m.

[33] Damaskin, p. 175; 176.

[34] Dilks, David. (ed.) The Diaries of Sir Alexander Cadogan, O.M.: 1938-1945. New York: G. P. Putnam's Sons, 1972, p. 83. Actually, a

glance at a map would show that it was not the heart of Germany into which Czechoslovakia was metaphorically thrust.

[35] Dilks, p. 80.

[36] FRUS, 1938, Volume I, p. 546.

[37] Walter, Natasha, Spies and Lovers. The Guardian, May 10, 2003.

[38] Damaskin, pp. 167-8.

[39] Strachey, Julia and Partridge, Frances. Julia: A Portrait of Julia Strachey by Herself and Frances Partridge. Boston: Little Brown and Company, 1983, pp. 154-8.

[40] Ragsdale, pp. 88-9.

[41] FRUS, 1938, Volume I, p. 583.

[42] FRUS, 1938, Volume I, p. 594.

[43] Ragsdale, p. 91.

[44] Ragsdale, p. 94.

[45] Around the time of Daladier's visit to London, Maclean joined the former Secretary of State for the Colonies, Baron Harlech, William Ormsby-Gore, on a fishing trip to Scotland. Given its reverence for the British aristocracy, Moscow Center most probably could scarcely believe its luck in having acquired an agent with the entrée at that level.

[46] Ragsdale, p. 82.

[47] Ragsdale, p. 112.

[48] Ragsdale, pp. 113-4. Ragsdale citing the memoirs of Marshal M. V. Zakharov. Other Soviet sources differed only in details.

[49] Ragsdale, p.167.

[50] Ragsdale, p. 83.

[51] FRUS, 1938, Volume I, p. 634.

[52] Dilks, p. 104.

[53] Maclean, Donald. British Foreign Policy Since Suez. London: Hodder and Stoughton, 1970, p. 76.

[54] See: May, Ernest R. Strange Victory: Hitler's Conquest of France. New York: Hill and Wang, 2000.

[55] Dilks, p. 106.

[56] Taylor, A. J. P, pp. 425-7.

[57] Steel, Ronald. Walter Lippmann and the American Century. Boston: Little, Brown and Company. An Atlantic Monthly Press Book, 1980, p. 372.

[58] Damaskin, Igor with Geoffrey Elliott. Kitty Harris: The Spy with Seventeen Names. London: St Ermin's Press, 2001, p. 182.

[59] Flanner, Janet. Paris was Yesterday: 1925-1939. San Diego: Harcourt Brace Jovanovich, Publishers, 1988, p. xxi-xxii.

[60] Cecil, p. 53.

[61] Page, Bruce, Leitch, David and Phillip Knightley. Philby: The Spy Who Betrayed a Generation. London: Andre Deutsch, 1968, p. 83.

[62] Andrews, Geoff. James Klugmann, a complex communist 27 February 2012 accessed on May 12, 2013 at http://www.opendemocracy.net/geoff-andrews/james-klugmann-complex-communist

[63] TNA KV/2/788.

[64] Hobsbawm, Eric. Interesting Times: A Twentieth-Century Life. London: Penguin, 2002, pp. 122-3.

[65] Andrews, Geoff. James Klugmann, a complex communist 27 February 2012 accessed on May 12, 2013 at http://www.opendemocracy.net/geoff-andrews/james-klugmann-complex-communist

[66] Cecil, p. 56.

[67] Honigmann, Barbara. A Chapter from My Life. An extract translated by John S. Barrett from Ein Kapitel aus meinem Leben. Munich: Carl Hanser Verlag, 2004, pp. 75-93. http://www.litrix.de/mmo/priv/15847-WEB.pdf

[68] Modin, Yuri. My Five Cambridge Friends: Burgess, Maclean, Philby, Blunt and Cairncross. New York: Farrar Strauss Giroux, 1994, pp. 43-5.

[69] Maclean, Donald. British Foreign Policy Since Suez. London: Hodder and Stoughton, 1970, pp. 38-9.

[70] Cecil, p. 57.

[71] TNA CAB 24/280

[72] Cecil, p. 52.

[73] Flanner, p. 201.

[74] FRUS, 1939, Volume I, p. 17.

[75] FRUS, 1939, Volume I, p. 84.

[76] Clarke, 158.

[77] FRUS, 1939, Volume I, p. 140.

[78] Taylor, A. J. P. English History: 1914—1945. New York and Oxford: Oxford University Press, 1965, pp. 446-7.

[79] Dilks, David. (ed.) The Diaries of Sir Alexander Cadogan, O.M.: 1938-1945. New York: G. P. Putnam's Sons, 1972, p. 175ff.

[80] FRUS, 1939, Volume I, p. 177.

[81] FRUS, 1939, Volume I, p. 248.

[82] FRUS, 1939, Volume I, p. 248.

[83] FRUS, 1939, Volume I, p. 251.

[84] Barnes, John and David Nicholson (eds.). The Empire at Bay: The Leo Amery Diaries, 1929-1945. London: Hutchinson, 1988, p. 553.

[85] FRUS, 1939, Volume I, p. 256.

[86] FRUS, 1939, Volume I, p. 264.

[87] Clarke, Peter. The Cripps Version: The Life of Sir Stafford Cripps, 1889-1952. London: Allen Lane, The Penguin Press, 2002, p. 101.

[88] Taylor, A. J. P., pp. 446-7.

[89] Ragsdale, Hugh. The Soviets, the Munich Crisis, and the Coming of World War II. Cambridge: Cambridge University Press, 2004, p. 173.

[90] Ragsdale, p. 31.

[91] Ragsdale, pp. 183-4.

[92] FRUS, 1939, Volume 1, p. 196.

[93] Ragsdale, pp. 174-5.

[94] FRUS, 1939, Volume I, p. 332.

[95] Taylor, A. J. P., pp. 446-7.

[96] Ragsdale, p. 177 ff., from Falin, V., ed. Soviet Peace Efforts on the Eve of World War II (September 1938-August 1939). 2 vols. (Moscow: Novosti, 1973, 2: 144-7 (No. 379).

[97] Taylor, A. J. P., p. 447.

[98] But see Gorodetsky, Gabriel. "The Dramatis Personae behind the Ribbentrop-Molotov Pact." February 26, 2013. http://www.youtube.com/watch?v=ZVOh1yS-Qag

[99] Cecil, p. 54.

[100] *Tribune*, September 22, 1939, quoted in Clarke.

[101] FRUS, 1939, Volume I, p. 354.

[102] Clarke, p. 111.

[103] Clarke, p. 116.

[104] TNF CAB/65/2/1.

[105] TNF:CAB/65/2/30. War Cabinet Meeting, November 27, 1939

[106] TNF CAB/65/2/32, War Cabinet Conclusions, November 29, 1939.

[107] TNF: CAB/65/2/35, War Cabinet Meeting of December 2, 1939.

[108] TNF: CAB/65/2/45, War Cabinet Meeting of December 11, 1939

[109] TNF: CAB/65/2/46, War Cabinet Meeting of December 12, 1939.

[110] TNF: CAB/65/4/20, War Cabinet Meeting of December 21, 1939

[111] TNF: CAB/65/4/30, War Cabinet Conclusions of December 27, 1939

[112] TNF: CAB/65/5/16, War Cabinet Meeting of January 17, 1940.

[113] TNF: CAB/65/5/16, Report by Chiefs of Staff Committee January 28, 1940.

[114] TNF: CAB/65/57, War Cabinet Meeting of January 31, 1940

[115] TNF: CAB/65/5/26.

[116] Clarke, 157.

[117] TNF: CAB/65/11/23, War Cabinet Meeting of February 2, 1940

[118] Cecil, p. 57.

[119] TNA, CAB/65/6/44

[120] This story can be followed in the diplomatic traffic preserved in the Foreign Relations of the United States (FRUS) for 1940.

[121] Smith, Bradley F. Sharing Secrets with Stalin: How the Allies Traded Intelligence, 1941-1945. Lawrence, Kansas: University of Kansas Press, 1996: pp. 9-10.

[122] Driberg, p. 56.

[123] Newsletter, Foreign Intelligence Service, Russian Federation, January 25, 2004, http://svr.gov.ru/smi/2004/bratishka20040125.htm. See also National Archives (UK), KV2/1014 for Tudor-Hart's role as a courier during this period.

[124] "Returning to the Cambridge Five: Triumph or Failure?" Newsletter, Foreign Intelligence Service, Russian Federation, April 3, 2008, http://svr.gov.ru/smi/2004/bratishka20040125.htm

[125] Damaskin, p. 197.

[126] Sudoplatov, Pavel and Anatoli Sudoplatov. Special Tasks: The Memoirs of an Unwanted Witness—A Soviet Spymaster. Boston: Little, Brown and Company, 1994, p. 95.

[127] Of course matters were not quite that simple: they hardly ever are. There were other factors, such as the reluctance of Norway and Sweden to allow passage of an Anglo-French military force, under the threat of German intervention, and the conviction of the Finnish military that the Red Army would launch an overwhelming offensive as soon as the Spring thaw arrived. But whatever counterfactuals are put into play, Stalin's access to Anglo-British planning was undoubtedly a significant factor in his decision-making process.

# Chapter Six

## London in the Blitz

*September 7<sup>th</sup>, 1940: "The next raid started at 8:10 p.m. In the second wave, the Germans sent 318 bombers as well as accompanying fighter planes. They dropped 300 tons of high explosive bombs and thousands of smaller incendiary ones. Throughout the second raid, the burning docks brilliantly illuminated London for the next wave of bombers. Now areas outside of the East End as well as the East End itself were relentlessly attacked. The fires at the docks could be seen for 30 miles. This raid lasted from 8:10 p.m. in the evening until 4:30 the next morning.*[1] Peter Stansky, The First Day of the Blitz, p. 48.

*16 September 1940: It has come to a state where none of us can be sure that we shall meet each other the next day and we begin to look for a gap in the party. Bombs have been raining around here, Berkeley Square, Park Lane, and Regent Street.* Charles Ritchie, The Siren Years, p. 67.

The personnel department of the Foreign Office was confused by the irregular arrival in London of the staffs of the Western European embassies in June, 1940. Tours of duty were not over; assignments had not been decided; there were many delicate decisions to be made and no time at all in which to make them. They eventually settled Donald Maclean, prematurely transferred from Paris, into the General Department, which included liaison responsibilities with the Ministries of Shipping, Supply and Economic Warfare, accomplishing this by October, toward the end of the Battle of Britain. The department head was Nigel Ronald, replaced in 1942 by John H. Le Rougetel. Maclean, as a matter of routine, promoted to the rank of Second Secretary, may have felt that he had been given a second rate assignment, away from the mainstream of the political departments of the Foreign Office. Nonetheless, as Sheila Kerr has observed, it was a good assignment from the point of view of his other career: "As a second secretary, Maclean would have seen almost everything of any importance, and what he did not see he would be able to learn at work or socially."[2] Information is the life-blood of intelligence and the General Department of the Foreign Office was the central exchange for information from British embassies, military and naval forces and secret intelligence organizations all around the world. As he had in Paris and as he would in Washington and Cairo, Maclean read the "departmental float" of telegrams, letters and memoranda received and sent, the Foreign Office Print and relevant cabinet conclusions. He read the OPTELS telegrams concerning the war, INTELS, concerning political, diplomatic and economic developments and the Weekly Political Intelligence Summary, giving the view of the day as seen from Whitehall.[3] He would have found enough of interest to at least fill his fifty pages a week ration for the NKVD.

With Harris in Moscow and other parts, Anatoly Gorsky, after a spell in Moscow, took up his cover assignment at the Soviet Embassy in London in November of 1940. Gorsky had been handling eighteen (not five) agents in Britain when he had been recalled to Moscow. On his return, first as an attaché, then as Second Secretary of the Embassy of the Soviet Union, he re-established contact with his network of agents and restored the flow of documents on British war, foreign and domestic matters from London to Moscow.[4] One of those agents, John Cairncross, remembered that "I would turn up on the first Saturday of each month at 5 o'clock at Piccadilly Circus: he would ask me the way to the Strand Hotel.

> After a few moments, I was then to catch up with him by Underground a considerable way out to the suburbs and double back in order to make sure I was not being followed. I had no difficulty in recognising him when he finally re-appeared: his impeccable clothes, the unfailing formal hat (Otto had always gone unhatted), and the round, moonlike bespectacled face allowed no mistake . . . he reminded me of the need to observe

all the outward proprieties in his role as "the perfect foreign gentleman". His instructions were always that, if I was spotted in his company, I was to say that he was a Czech engineer.[5]

Cairncross's description of Gorsky's clothing and demeanor is in marked contrast to the usual image of Soviet foreign intelligence personnel in the espionage literature. Perhaps that image, with its emphasis on ill-cut suits and such, is metaphorical. In any case, it is likely that Donald Maclean followed a routine with his Soviet contacts similar to that followed by Cairncross.[6]

The numerology of the Cambridge Five tends to obscure the actual extent of NKVD success in Britain from the arrival of Deutsch in 1934 to the departure of Burgess and Maclean in 1951. John Cairncross, denying that he was one of the Five, claiming to be a singleton with a particular loathing for Anthony Blunt, named Leo Long and Goronwy Rees, among others, as sometime agents, along with Klugmann. Michael Straight, the Whitney heir, was for a time conspicuous in the Cambridge group. There was also a still-obscure Oxford group of Soviet agents and a group associated with refugee members of the German Communist Party, such as the economist Jurgen Kuczynski and his sister Sonja, who was Klaus Fuchs' contact.[7] We might add, in London, at least Litzi Friedmann Philby and Edith Tudor-Hart, associated with the Austrian Center, both recruiters for and supporters of the network. Tudor-Hart was close to Engelbert Broda, the Austrian refugee scientist who was an early participant in the Tube Alloys project at the Cavendish Laboratory in Cambridge, as well as being a central figure among the exiled Austrian Communists in Britain. The British secret police were not unaware of this activity. For example, the watchers, who were deeply suspicious of the Austrian Center, had an informer close to Edith Tudor-Hart, as well as spending much effort following her around London. On May 6, 1942, they watched her send a small parcel to "Dr. E. Broda" c/o. Cavendish Laboratories, Cambridge.[*][8]

---

[*] The next day she visited Martha and Anna Freud at their home. Anna Freud was treating Tudor-Hart's son for a serious mental illness.

(Apparently obtaining the addressee from the postal clerk after Tudor-Hart entrusted him with the package.) The British secret police saw of many of the dots, but failed to connect them.

Economic warfare meant obtaining needed supplies for the British war effort and attempting to deny them to the Germans. The Minister of Economic Warfare was Hugh Dalton of the Labour Party, who was as well the minister in charge of the Special Operations Executive, busy, if only in tired cliché, setting Europe ablaze. Maclean's colleagues were Patrick Reilly[*] at the Ministry of Economic Warfare, where Frederick Leith-Ross was the Minister, and Victor Rothschild, then an M.I.5 counter-sabotage official, particularly expert at defusing bombs.[†] The activities of the General Department of the Foreign Office were closely integrated with economic warfare and with those of the wider Intelligence community. Maclean was soon considered the Foreign Office's expert in the field of counter-sabotage, particularly as it touched on the activities of Communists in the factories and in the political arena. As such, he had access to the information available on these matters, the actions contemplated and taken concerning them by the Home Security Executive and M.I.5.

In A. J. P. Taylor's "just so" story of the first year of the war, the Ministry of Economic Warfare was Chamberlain's favored means for winning, or at least not losing, the war with Germany. It would remain so for Churchill and, therefore, Maclean had not in fact been

---

[*] Patrick Reilly, who had been at All Souls after taking a first at New College, Oxford, was a diplomat with extensive connections in the intelligence community. He would be an Assistant Under-Secretary in the Foreign Office during Maclean's final tour there.

[†] Rothschild was one of Guy Burgess's friends. He rented Burgess and Anthony Blunt a house, where Teresa Mayor, who would marry Rothschild, also lived. That house, like the house of the Penroses and that of the Empsons, figure in many of the more riotous stories about life in the Blitz. There are other stories told about Victor Rothschild, Teresa Mayor and their friends. Rothschilds attract purveyors of stories.

shuttled off to a siding, as it might have appeared. However, according to Robert Cecil, "This was not a field in which diplomats of those days claimed much expertise . . . I recall overhearing two of my seniors complaining about a three-hour meeting that had been discussing how to deny wolfram to the Germans.[9] 'What,' said one testily, '*is* wolfram anyway?'" Wolfram is also known as tungsten. During World War II wolfram was essential for making the special steel used the armor of tanks. Nearly all of Europe's production of wolfram is from Spanish and Portuguese mines.[10] Both during and after the war it was a crucial bargaining chip in Franco's negotiations with the Allies in regard to, among other things, oil. It was, perhaps, Maclean's access to information about minerals, their sources and control, that was his introduction to the world that was coming into existence under the name Tube Alloys, and which, as the Manhattan Project, was vitally important when he was assigned to the Washington embassy.

The British Empire had declared war on Germany as if war were a matter of exchanges of those pieces of paper so highly valued by Neville Chamberlain. It was not that the Empire had not been preparing for war; to Chamberlain's credit, rearmament had been underway at a rapid pace. But the future participants—Germany no less than the Soviet Union, France and the British Empire—had all been preparing for a war a bit later, circa 1942. At first it seemed as if they would all hold to that timetable, despite the exchange of pieces of paper to the contrary. As we have seen, as late as March, 1940, the configuration of forces was still in flux. It was quite possible, as the Soviets no doubt believed, that there would have been a reversal of alliances at that point, with the British Empire and France in at least a de facto alliance with Germany and Italy against the Soviet Union, beginning with an expedition to Finland, but including activities in the south, in the Baku oil fields and possibly the Ukraine as well. Stalin's precipitous conclusion of the war with Finland complicated matters, which were only clarified for a time when Germany seized Norway to secure the supplies of iron ore thought threatened by Churchill's naval maneuvers.

Records of discussions in the British Cabinet show little anxiety about the war—certainly not as an existential issue—until shortly before Dunkirk. And then, in a matter of weeks, crucial members of the French army's leadership in effect defected to the Germans; much of the French air force flew out of the war to North Africa; the plans of the French navy were doubtful at best and the British army, with all its equipment, was trapped on a beach at the Channel. Peace negotiations were considered, then, seemingly by a hair, not undertaken and the decision was made to continue the war, to "plod on," as Churchill put it, hoping that something would turn up— "something" always being the United States of America, or, more specifically, President Roosevelt. During the early summer of 1940 there was some anxiety in Washington that if Britain were occupied by Germany, as seemed likely enough, the British Fleet might fall into the hands of the latter and become a threat to the United States. On August 8, 1940, Lord Lothian, the British Ambassador in Washington, offered reassurance in the form of a quotation from a declaration made by Churchill on June 4th: "We shall never surrender and even if . . . this island or a large part of it were subjugated and starving, then our empire beyond the seas, armed and guarded by the British Fleet, will carry on the struggle . . ." At which point, something did turn up. Reassured that Churchill's intention was that the war would be carried on by His Majesty's Government in Canada, as it were, armed with the British Fleet and Churchill's oratory, President Roosevelt proposed exchanging ships (destroyers and others) and military equipment for bases on British possessions in the West Indies and North and South America.

The United States had expressed interest in leasing basing facilities on British possessions in the West Indies sometime earlier. In the summer of 1940 this idea became linked with that of the provision of military equipment and ships to the British Empire to replace and greatly add to the equipment lost at Dunkirk and the mounting losses at sea. While the earlier expression of interest had been for the use of parts of British facilities, now the discussions concerned 99-year leases of land on which *American* bases could be

145

built.[11] Three of the "drivers" of American foreign policy were involved. Two were governmental. From the point of view of Congress and the American military, the leases were an early step toward what would become a world-wide screen of bases meant to keep any future hostilities from American shores. At the same time, there was an increasing interest in American business circles in post-war civil aviation, for which an international network of airfields was essential. From the British point of view, although old and many not in good repair, the ships exchanged for the leases were desperately needed for anti-submarine warfare and, perhaps more importantly, with them Roosevelt and Churchill established a precedent for American material support for the British war effort. Maclean, in the Foreign Office's General Department, had some junior responsibility at the London end of the base discussions, familiarizing him with those specifically and the evolving practice of Anglo-American negotiations in general. It was at this time that in Maclean's Foreign Office role, "He learned to juggle two contradictory British interests, the protection of British economic interests from aggressive American competition and the establishment of Anglo-American accord as the cornerstone of British wartime strategy and postwar security."[12]

On November 23, 1940, British Ambassador to the United States Lord Lothian told American reporters: "Well boys, Britain's broke; it's your money we want." Lend-Lease, which followed, was characterized as "An Act to Further Promote the Defense of the United States." It came into effect in March, 1941 and was eventually extended not only to the British Empire but to other Allied nations, including the Soviet Union. Lend-Lease, unlike the bases-for-destroyers agreement, had a large positive effect on the financial situation of the British Empire, providing enormous quantities of supplies—not by any means all weapons of war—which otherwise would have had to be purchased, and by that point there was nothing left to Britain with which to purchase those supplies.

For those who had been troubled by the German-Soviet alliance, political matters became less troubling when, on June 22, 1941,

Germany invaded the Soviet Union. All Spring the intelligence summaries that Maclean routinely read, and probably as routinely passed on to his NKVD contacts, alternated between predicting a German peace bid and a German invasion of the Soviet Union. For weeks previously messages had reached Stalin from his agents in Germany, Switzerland and Japan, as well as from British governmental sources, that an invasion was imminent.* It was, perhaps, exactly because the British Government was sending both conflicting and confirming messages that Stalin disbelieved the flood of information from other sources. If the British Government—which just a year earlier had come within days of entering the war between Finland and the Soviet Union, against the latter—warned of a German attack on the Soviet Union, it was not unreasonable to believe that this was (another) attempt to break the alliance between Germany and the Soviet Union and that the agents were conveying disinformation. Ruling circles in Moscow were so convinced that there was about to be a reversal of alliances that, "When war broke out, 'all believed', later recalled [former Foreign Minister] Litvinov, 'that the British fleet was steaming up the North Sea for a joint attack with Hitler on Leningrad and Kronstadt'."[13] After all, just a month earlier, Cripps, in an ill-conceived attempt to unfreeze his negotiations with them, had warned the Soviets that the British government might seek a separate peace with Germany.[14] The leaders of the Soviet Union continued to fear, or anticipate, a reversal of alliances until, finally, it actually occurred in the immediate post-war period.

It was generally assumed that the Soviet Union would be overwhelmed by the German forces as quickly as had Poland and France. This seemed a reasonable assumption, especially after the immense Soviet losses of men and territory in the summer and fall of 1941. Although the German Army (assisted by that of Finland) did

---

* The messages went directly to Stalin, as Moscow Center had been virtually emptied by Stalin's purge of the Soviet foreign intelligence apparatus.

147

not quite break through to Leningrad in September and was thrown back at the Battle of Moscow on December 6, it seemed unstoppable in the south, occupying the Ukraine region and the Crimea and hoisting the Swastika on the peaks of the Caucasus in the fall of 1942. Reasonable observers might well have thought that by the end of 1942 the Soviet Union, if it existed at all, would be an impoverished, purely Asian state with its western border on the Urals, its industrial plant and best agricultural land, as well as all its great cities, in the hands of Germany, at which point Germany would be able to concentrate again in the West. But then, as if choreographed by the puppet master in the White House, on December 7th, 1941, the Japanese Empire implemented its Southern Strategy, attacking the bases of British, French, Dutch and American power from Java to Hawaii. Germany and its European allies immediately did Roosevelt and Churchill the favor of declaring war on the United States. The United States, which in any case had for some months been allied with the British Empire in every way except militarily, became a belligerent. The home countries of the Macleans, and the nation the system with which they most sympathized, were now all allied. Paul Trewhela has observed that this "was prime time for the Communist Parties.

> Up to a point, they became adjuncts of the war-time governments of the Allied powers . . . Political distinctions became very blurred . . . Once the awkward period of the Pact was out of the way, it was business as usual, only better than ever, since every assistance to the Soviet Union—no matter how extreme—could be justified in terms of the struggle against Nazism.[15]

The new alliance between the British Empire and the Soviet Union extended to their respective secret intelligence services. Each set up an overt office in the capital of the other and developed extensive liaison relationships. For example, Ivan Adreyevich Chichayev, an NKVD officer, served as the Soviet link with S.O.E. and M.I.5 and then with their American opposite number, O.S.S.[16] Given Maclean's contacts with S.O.E., Chichayev was a likely "customer," direct or indirect, for some of his information.

Instead of the expected German final victory, the last few months of 1942 made Germany's eventual defeat simply a matter of time. A dramatic passage in the Memoirs of Ivan Maisky, Soviet ambassador in London, marks the moment: "On the morning of 20 November I received from Moscow an urgent message from Stalin Addressed to Churchill. It stated:

> We have begun offensive operations in the Stalingrad area, in its southern and north-western sectors. The objective of the first stage is to seize the Stalingrad-Likhaya railway and disrupt the communications of the Stalingrad group of the German troops. In the north-western sector the German front has been pierced along a 22-kilometre line and along a 12-kilometre line in the southern sector. The operation is proceeding satisfactorily.[17]

Within a few weeks the Red Army had destroyed the German and Romanian forces at Stalingrad and lifted the siege of Leningrad. Forces of the British Empire defeated those of Germany and Italy at El Alamein in Egypt. American and British Imperial forces captured Algeria and Morocco from Vichy.

Perhaps exhilarated by this turn of events, during his "end of the beginning" speech at the Lord Mayor's luncheon on November 10, 1942, Churchill declared "I have not become the King's First Minister in order to preside over the liquidation of the British Empire." The centerpiece of the Empire, India, was vital to the British war effort. The British Empire drew on Viceregal India for two and a half million men for the army of British India, nearly equaling the United Kingdom's contribution, which peaked at 2.9 million. Those listening to Churchill's declaration would have been aware that Churchill was not just making rhetorical points. Gandhi, in a speech on August 8, 1942, had initiated the "Quit India Movement," with a call for passive resistance to British rule. Churchill had Attlee order the arrest of the entire Indian National Congress leadership, from Gandhi and Nehru to local activists. President Roosevelt urged Churchill to release the prisoners and give

India independence, to no avail. More than 60,000 people were imprisoned and most remained in prison until the end of the war. Six months after the mass imprisonment of Indian political activists, and a month or two after Churchill's Lord Mayor's Luncheon speech, a famine began in Bengal that lingered through the remainder of 1943. Numbers are disputed, as they are with most great famines, but it is perhaps sufficiently indicative to say that "millions" died. As with the Ukrainian famine a dozen years earlier—and others since—it was not so much an absolute lack of food as the diversion of supplies from an area not favored by a government to another that was favored that caused the famine. In this case Churchill prevented the Secretary of State for India, Amery, from sending food supplies to the stricken areas and the Viceroy exercised restraint in taking local palliative measures.[18] "Churchill's only response to a telegram from the government in Delhi about people perishing in the famine was to ask why Gandhi hadn't died yet."[19] The mass arrests of the leadership of the Indian Congress Party and even the Empire's "passivity" in regard to the Bengal Famine were consistent with, if not integral to, Churchill's personal postwar planning, his intention to preserve, and if possible, to expand the British Empire. India was to remain the keystone of the Empire supporting, and supported by, a great arc of client kingdoms extending along both shores of the Mediterranean.[20] This vision was not one that President Roosevelt, and much less people like the Macleans, found attractive.

As Britain's involvement in the war went into its third year, relations between the British Empire and the United States began to deteriorate. During Maclean's time in the General Department of the Foreign Office, "the three most contentious issues in Anglo-American relations were civil aviation, oil and the future of shared bases.

In February, 1943, Maclean warned his Foreign Office superiors that if American ambitions to dominate the world's air services were not controlled, British civil aviation would be "left to the wolves". Government policy aimed for the "internationalisation of civil aviation", to guarantee a share for Britain without antagonising America. Relations deteriorated and by the summer civil aviation had created a crisis in Anglo-American relations.[21] Civil aviation might seem a dull subject, but during the 1940s it was central to British Imperial prospects, both in itself, and symbolically. It might be said, with all due rhetorical exaggeration, that the British Empire itself was essentially a world-wide transportation and communications system, based for centuries on its great merchant fleet—under the protection of the Royal Navy—and increasingly in the twentieth century on civil aviation. Imperial Airways, founded in 1924, gradually surveyed and then implemented routes through the Middle East first to India, of course, and then on to China and Cape Town. By the late 1930s there was regular service on flying boats throughout the Empire. At the beginning of the war, the British Government formed British Overseas Airways Company (B.O.A.C.) as a state airline. It, and its airfields, were considered an asset of Imperial significance. The United States, on the other hand, had a number of large private airlines which saw B.O.A.C. simply as a competitor.

And then there was oil. Although the United States was the dominant supplier of oil to oil-importing nations (a factor in the attempted sanctions regime against Italy during the Abyssinian affair), Britain controlled oil production and refineries in the Persian Gulf area, primarily in order to secure fuel supplies for its navy. Excluded from the Near Eastern fields by the San Remo agreement, American oil companies had begun to take an interest in the Arabian peninsula states in 1932 and would form the Arabian American Oil Company (ARAMCO) in 1944.

(We should here take note of an issue, little mentioned in the grand narratives of the Cold War, that would become of crucial importance. In the later summer of 1943, the British government's Post-Hostilities Planning Committee issued a report on the Middle East, finding, in part, that "the oil pipelines and lines of communication with oil-producing states passing through Palestine were of major concern to the United Kingdom. The peace and security of the country would, therefore, be of the 'utmost

151

importance', and its continued occupation by British forces after the war would be essential."[22] This policy appraisal would be unchanged during the early post-war period and would be important for Donald Maclean's work in Cairo. What the 1943 report pointed to, and arguably what would control Imperial policy in Palestine for the next decade or more, was not the fate of Jews or Arabs in Palestine, but the lines of communications, the oil pipelines passing through that area, and its airfields and naval installations as well.)

The third issue was that of shared military bases. As American involvement in the war grew, there grew also a sentiment in certain American governmental circles that all, or most, of the world-wide system of military and naval bases of the British Empire "should" come under American control, although that logic was not recognized in Whitehall.

Maclean himself, from his Marxist perspective, saw the central problem in Anglo-American relations as "Anglo-American economic warfare in the field of foreign exports and investments." By January, 1944, Foreign Office officials were increasingly uncomfortable with the fact that Britain had become dependant on America for military and economic aid. Maclean and his colleagues "feared and resented American economic competition."[23] In an usual coincidence of attitudes, conservative, that is, imperialist, Britons more and more saw the United States as a threat to the Empire, while those on the left saw it as a threat to the socialist future toward which they were working. Without American financial help and military manpower, the British Empire could not survive against, much less defeat, Germany and Japan. But it increasingly appeared that the price of that assistance would be the Empire itself and the alternative social democratic future of Britain.

\*   \*   \*

*Buildings black with soot cried out for a lick of paint. Boarded-up windows presented a blank face to the world. Mean terraces, with now and then a gap, fizzled out in piles of rubble. Acres of bomb sites and bricks, bricks meticulously counted and piled up: so many bricks in a devastated landscape. After five years of war, the people looked tired and worn. There they were in their shabby clothes, queuing for buses, or walking purposefully along, not bothering to give the bomb sites a glance. Women holding string bags stood patiently in long lines outside shops, resignation on their faces . . . the all-pervasive smell . . . of coal smoke in the dam chill, but something else too. Dust! Dust so acrid you could taste it in the mouth.* Maureen Waller, London 1945, p. 1[24]

The Macleans had stayed with Donald Maclean's mother for the first two weeks after they arrived in London from Paris in 1940, and then moved to a hotel, the Mount Royal, near Marble Arch, where they lived until the late summer and the beginnings of the Blitz. Bombed out of the hotel, they rented a furnished flat in Mecklenburgh Square, near King's Cross railway terminus. This was their home until they moved to Washington in 1944. The Square was bracketed by bombs during the Blitz, but not itself hit. Donald Maclean with his friend Robert Cecil served his turn in the Home Guard during the nightly air raids, "pushing incendiaries off the roofs of government buildings," as did many others.[25] Melinda Maclean sailed to New York in a convoy at the end of November, 1940, for the birth of the child conceived in Paris the previous Spring. A boy was delivered on December 22, but did not live. Melinda Maclean spent the next few months recovering in New York, leaving for London on the Dixie Clipper on April 30, probably via Lisbon.[26] In London, Melinda Maclean became absorbed in the Liberal Establishment of her husband's family—such as the Bonham Carters and their friends in Gloucester Square—and the Fitzrovian Bohemia where both she and her husband were as comfortable. She packed parcels—war work which she shared with novelist, memoir writer and demimondaine Barbara Skelton's sister Brenda,[27] and when "women were conscripted, Melinda worked in the Times Book Shop, where," according to Hoare, "she was very successful–she was interested and efficient and, like all her family, had charming manners."[28]

Barbara Skelton recalled that "One evening in the Café Royal, I ran into the diplomat, Donald Maclean. He suggested I offer my services as a cipher clerk to the Foreign Office and said he would be my sponsor." Skelton dutifully went to Cairo, as she told the story, where her services to the Empire included cipher matters, no doubt, as well as entertainment during the long voyage out for the crew and other men and, once there, for King Farouk (or visa versa), involving belts and such.[29] It is not recorded whether Maclean was questioned about his sponsorship of Skelton. But, of course, no one ever complained about her performance as a cipher clerk. A bit later Skelton was the mistress, then, rather inexplicably, the wife, of Cyril Connolly (who pimped her, in the most literal sense of the term, to the by then-exiled King Farouk), and deeply embedded in the London publishing and arts worlds centered on Connolly's magazine *Horizon* (for which Philip Toynbee also wrote). Skelton's story places Maclean in 1942 as a frequenter of the café society that reacted so violently against him ten years later. Connolly would be one of the leaders in the publicity campaign against Maclean and Burgess. M.I.5 would think that he rather over-did it.

The Macleans spent some of their wartime evenings wandering through the dark streets of London from pub to pub, avoiding the bomb sites and the crowded air-raid shelters. Some evenings they might have been found at the Gargoyle Club, half an hour's walk from Mecklenburgh Square, less from the Foreign Office or the Times Book Club. For a young couple who had met at the Café de Flore, the Gargoyle Club was, at least socially, war-time London's closest approximation to such familiar scenes. In other ways it could not have been more different. It had a ballroom with mirrored mosaic walls; a "Tudor" dining room and a rooftop dining area and garden. These were connected by a very small elevator, which occasionally stopped between floors, providing opportunities for semi-public sex for those so inclined.[30] The Gargoyle was a place for cheap lunches and drinks for writers, artists and those comfortable with their company and late evenings for everyone from Harold Nicolson to Cyril Connolly and Francis Bacon. Caroline Blackwood was later a member, as were Mamaine Paget (who married Arthur Koestler) and Barbara Skelton, Antonia Fraser, Douglas Cooper, Lucian Freud, Constant Lambert, David Sylvester, Michael Redgrave, Frederick Ashton, Kenneth Tynan, Richard and Anne Wollheim, various Tennants, Angela and Mark Culme-Seymour, John Maynard Keynes, Bertrand Russell, Clive and Vanessa Bell and Duncan Grant, a Mitford or two, Augustus John, Philip Toynbee (of course), Victor Rothschild, Roland Penrose and Lee Miller, Anthony and Violet Powell, a few Stracheys, Brian Howard, A. J. Ayer, Nancy Cunard, Guy Burgess . . . Well, everybody, really. It was "the one place where the Home Office, the Foreign Office, Bohemia, the sodden aristocracy, the odd Russian, the odd Hungarian could *all* go without it looking odd at all . . ."[31] Many Gargoyle stories feature a drunken Philip Toynbee rolling on the floor with one person or another with whom he had had a quarrel; others feature Guy Burgess, his pals, and his interesting offers of presumed pleasure to strangers. It was a place the Macleans could meet Toynbee and Burgess and such without arousing comment. There would be nothing similar in the next city to which Maclean was assigned.

Maclean "worked exceptionally hard during the war often appearing tired and worn." He had become the Foreign Office's expert in economic warfare, civil air matters and military bases, not to mention wolfram. Anthony Eden himself praised Maclean's "admirably clear assessments." It was decided that his next posting would be to the all-important British Embassy in Washington. As Kerr noted: "Given Maclean's sparkling performance in the General Department and his familiarity with Anglo-American issues, his transfer to Washington was logical." His Soviet interlocutors were no doubt pleased. "In Washington he would have access to the most highly classified information at the crossroads of Anglo-American diplomacy, just when the balance of world power was to be renegotiated."[32]

155

## Chapter Six:  Notes

[1] Stansky, Peter. The First Day of the Blitz. New Haven: Yale University Press, 2007, p. 48.

[2] Kerr, Sheila. An Assessment of a Soviet Agent: Donald Maclean, 1940-1951. Unpublished thesis, Department of International History, London School of Economics and Political Science, January 1996, p. 64, citing personal information from Robert Cecil.

[3] These matters of Maclean's office routine are from Kerr, who apparently was told about them by Robert Cecil, Maclean's sometime deputy and friend.

[4] Svr.gov/ru/gishtory/gors.htm accessed November 25, 2013.

[5] Cairncross, John. The Enigma Spy. The Story of the Man Who Changed the Course of World War II. London: Century, Random House, 1997, pp. 80-1.

[6] Sudoplatov states that Gorsky "assigned Vladimir Borisovich Barkovsky as the case officer for Maclean because as an engineer, Barkovsky was capable of dealing with the technical details." Sudoplatov, Pavel and Anatoli Sudoplatov. Special Tasks: The Memoirs of an Unwanted Witness—A Soviet Spymaster. Boston: Little, Brown and Company, 1994, p. 173, n. 1. There is some confusion about the route by which information about the British decision to attempt to develop an atomic bomb reached Moscow. Some say that it was Cairncross, who denied it. The Foreign Intelligence Service of the Russian Federation's account of Donald Maclean's career implies that it was Maclean.  Perhaps, as usual, there were many routes.

[7] TNA KV 2/1871-80

[8] TNA KV 2/1013.

[9] There was much activity about wolfram. George F. Kennan, counselor of the U.S. legation in Lisbon in the fall of 1942, was assigned to "help block the Portuguese from supplying wolfram to Germany." Kennan, George F. The Kennan Diaries. Costigliola, Frank (ed.). New York:  W. W. Norton, 2014, p. 152.

[10] Acheson, Dean. Present at the Creation: My Years in the State Department. New York: W.W. Norton & Company, Inc., p. 53.

[11] FRUS, 1940, The British Commonwealth, the Soviet Union, the Near East and Africa, pp. 60 ff., esp. 65.

[12] Kerr, p. 66.

[13] Gorodetsky, p. 114.

[14] Gorodetsky, p. 12.

[15] Personal communication, citing Simons, H. J. and R. E. Class and Colour in South Africa 1850-1950. London: Penguin, 1969, p. 540.

[16] TNA KV 2/3227.

[17] Maisky, Ivan. Memoirs of A Soviet Ambassador: The War: 1939-43. Trans. Andrew Rothstein. New York: Charles Scribner's Sons, 1967, p. 333.

[18] There are many sources on this subject. A contemporary account of the view from Whitehall can be found on pages 909 and following of The Empire at Bay: The Leo Amery Diaries, 1929-1945, edited by John Barnes and David Nicholson, London: Hutchinson, 1988.

[19] "The Ugly Briton," by Shashi Tharoor, Time Magazine, November 29, 2010, citing Mukerjee, Madhusree, Churchill's Secret War.

[20] Treasury hopes for the cancellation of the debt to India continued until the end. See, for example, the letter from Sir W. Eady to Mr. R. H. Brand at the Washington embassy of 22 December 1945. Bullen, Roger and Pelly, M.E. Documents on British Policy Overseas, Series I, Volume IV. London: Her Majesty's Stationery Office, 1987, p.15.

[21] Kerr, p. 90 citing 73. TNA FO 371 364611 W2415, Minute by Maclean, 11 February, 1943. TNA FO 371 364341 W5584, Minute by Maclean, 11 April 1943. TNA FO 371 364381 W1068, Minute by Le Rougetel, 9 July 1943.

[22] Lewis, Julian. Changing Direction: British Military Planning for Post-war Strategic Defence, 1942-1947, Second edition. London: Frank Cass, 2003, p. 61.

[23] Kerr, p. 89, citing TNA FO 371 42552/ W367, Memo by Maclean, 10 January 1944.

---

24 Waller, Maureen. London 1945: Life in the Debris of War. London: John Murray, 2004, p. 1.

25 Cecil, p. 63.

26 FBI records. Cecil has her staying in New York until the fall, returning in a convoy. See also Hoare, Geoffrey. The Missing Macleans. New York: The Viking Press, 1955, pp. 69-70. The Dixie Clipper, a Boeing 314 operated by Pan Am, was later used to take President Roosevelt to the Casablanca Conference. The Wikipedia article on the Boeing 314 provides some detail:

> Pan Am's "Clippers" were built for "one-class" luxury air travel, a necessity given the long duration of transoceanic flights. The seats could be converted into 36 bunks for overnight accommodation; with a cruising speed of only 188 miles per hour . . . The 314s had a lounge and dining area, and the galleys were crewed by chefs from four-star hotels. Men and women were provided with separate dressing rooms, and white-coated stewards served five and six-course meals with gleaming silver service. The standard of luxury on Pan American's Boeing 314s has rarely been matched on heavier-than-air transport since then; they were a form of travel for the super-rich, at $675 return from New York to Southampton, comparable to a round trip aboard Concorde in 2006.

27 Skelton, Barbara. Tears Before Bedtime. London: Hamish Hamilton, 1987, p. 27.

28 Hoare, pp. 69-70. Adult women in Britain 60 years and younger were registered and required to choose a job from an approved list by Spring, 1941. Conscription for women began with young adult single women in December, 1941, extending to nearly all adult women by mid-1943. www.bbc.co.uk/history/british/britain_wwtwo/women_at_war_01.shtml accessed May, 25, 2013.

29 Skelton, p. 52.

30 Luke, Michael. David Tennant and the Gargoyle Years. Weidenfeld and Nicolson. London, 1991, p. 32.

---

[31] Luke, p. 194.
[32] Kerr, 94-5.

# Chapter Seven

*Washington*

*Learning from Venona*

*Maclean, guided by purely ideological motives, entered into collaboration with Soviet intelligence. While holding high posts in the British diplomatic service, he rendered enormous services to* [the Soviet Union], *especially at the end of the war and during the first postwar years.* Steve Hirsch[1]

Donald Maclean was sent to Washington in the late Spring of 1944, just before D-Day. This was, perhaps, the high point of Roosevelt's grand alliance. (However, in a sign of things to come, President Roosevelt "in a semi-jocular manner" said during a Cabinet meeting on March 16, 1945, that "the British were perfectly willing for the United States to have a war with Russia at any time."[2]) Even as much as six months later, just before Roosevelt's death, General MacArthur, of all people, told Secretary of the Navy James Forrestal that he hoped that the Soviet Union would send at least sixty divisions into Manchuria to draw off the main force of the Japanese Army during the projected American invasion of the Japanese home islands.[3]

During the course of the war Washington had replaced Paris as the most important of British embassies. Maclean's colleague, Philip Mason, noted in mid-May of 1944 that the Anglo-American partnership "implie[d] full consultation on all major and many minor issues."[4] The consultations and discussions between all levels of the Foreign Office and the State Department that took place during the war usually went through the British Embassy in Washington, where the former Foreign Secretary, Lord Halifax, was Ambassador. Andrew Roberts, Lord Halifax's biographer, observed of the British

Washington embassy that: "So paramount was American goodwill that the diplomatic service ear-marked its brightest talents for service there.

> These men were of such high caliber that they were to provide many of the Foreign Office's top Ambassadors and Deputy Under-Secretaries for the next two decades. Sir George Middleton (who with Redvers Opie and Donald Maclean used to make up a tennis four with Halifax[5]) considers the wartime Washington Embassy to have been "probably the apogee of British Diplomacy."[6]

The scope of Maclean's relatively narrow initial responsibilities in Washington were laid out in a letter of March 27, 1944, in which his future colleague Michael Wright informed him that "our provisional idea is that you should take on all Near Eastern questions including India, all shipping questions, telecommunications and the supervision of the activities of Underwood who deals with travel arrangements, trans-Atlantic passages, etc. We think you may also have to take on Spain and Portugal."[7] His responsibilities were soon drastically expanded beyond those listed by Wright. Maclean would be working at the center of what would become the Atlantic Alliance, eventually privy to virtually all communications between Foggy Bottom, the White House and Whitehall, in a position of trust inferior to no other British official of his seniority.

Donald Maclean, it must be emphasized, was an outstanding, a model, British diplomat, in much the same way that Kim Philby was a model counterintelligence officer. He was admired, deferred to, trusted. And from a certain point of view he was what he appeared to be. There was never a question that he did his best at the tasks entrusted to him. Those tasks were of the highest importance to the British Empire. At the same time he performed other tasks, those also of the highest importance, to advance the cause he had pledged ten years earlier on a bench in Regent's Park. In regard to his performance of *those* tasks, Kerr observed "It is only possible to speculate that his reports showed the same qualities as those he showed in his official work and later in his book on British foreign

161

policy: that he was rational, politically astute, scholarly, and not prone to any severe ideological distortions."[8] (Kerr was wrong, as we shall see. We can do more than speculate about his reports to Moscow.) When Maclean's dual role became public the entire intertwined social, professional and political worlds of some of the most powerful people in the British Empire, shattered.

Melinda Maclean, who had lived abroad for six years, was now, for the only extended period of her married life, home in America. On their arrival in New York City on May 6, 1944, again pregnant, she at first lived with her mother and step-father in their apartment on Park Avenue, but for most part spent that summer at her step-father's farmhouse in the Berkshires in South Egremont, Massachusetts, while Donald Maclean stayed with Embassy friends in Washington.[9] It was not easy finding housing in wartime Washington. In a communication from Lord Halifax to the Foreign Office of May 31, 1944, the Ambassador noted that "Maclean and Middleton [who with his wife had travelled on the same ship as the Macleans] are having great difficulty in finding suitable accommodation within approved rent limits.

> Fact is that in spite of restrictions, rents at any rate of furnished accommodation, have risen in past year and continue to rise. Would you be prepared to approve $200 unfurnished* rent for Maclean and $250 furnished for Middleton? They will of course do their best to get accommodation at lower rates but must know upper limit you would be prepared to sanction as options cannot be obtained and any offer has to be taken up at once.[10]

During this period Donald Maclean visited his wife at the Dunbar's Berkshire farm about once a month, taking the train from Washington to Pennsylvania Station in New York City, then a taxi to Grand Central Terminal, by train from there to Hillsdale, New York, and then again by taxi to the farm.[11]

---

* The Maclean household effects were to come through on September 14, 1944.

An FBI interviewee in 1951, almost certainly Mr. Dunbar, "stated during all his contacts with Maclean he never suspected that Maclean was in any way 'more liberal than Roosevelt,'" perhaps a deliberately ambiguous statement. Dunbar then "volunteered the observation that Melinda would have been much more the type to furnish Russia with info than Maclean was.

> When asked to explain this he said that he did not want it understood that he thought Melinda was in any way a radical or Communist, but said that she was a "social misfit" and seemed to look down upon American social life. He said that on many occasions at the farm in Massachusetts, Melinda left a party or social gathering and retired to her room stating in effect that she was bored. [12]

Evidently Dunbar, the paper company executive, did not get along with his step-daughter. On the other hand, Melinda Maclean apparently remained in touch with, and on friendly terms with, her natural father. Francis Marling was interviewed in Chicago by the FBI in June, 1951. He said that he had visited his daughter and son-in-law "on several occasions during MACLEAN'S* residence in Washington, D.C., from 1944 to 1948" and had "irregular correspondence with [them] . . . since that time . . . [he] described MACLEAN as level-headed and personable who, to his knowledge, entertained no Communist philosophies.

> MACLEAN, while in Washington, D.C., worked exceedingly hard at his job and appeared to be continually under pressure and great strain, which [Marling] believed to be caused by the demands of his work for the British Embassy and not because of any intrigue or dissatisfaction with the English or American governments. [13]

Donald Maclean, using his new housing allowance of $200 per month, eventually found a house at 2710 35th Place, just around Observatory Circle from the British Embassy. [14] He gave as a

---

* The FBI and its British and Soviet counterparts often capitalized names in cables.

reference his colleague P. H. Gore-Booth, later head of the British Diplomatic Service (and before that one of the final four suspects as the Soviet agent code-named "Homer"). Melinda Maclean gave birth to a boy, by Caesarean, in New York City on September 23, 1944.[15] The, now three, Macleans (and a nurse for the baby) were firmly installed in the Washington house by Christmas.[*] All through their time in Washington the Macleans vacationed at Cape Cod, Florida or Quoque (in the Hamptons), Long Island, where Melinda and her sister Harriet rented a house and they all went sailing, played golf and tennis during the summer months and Donald Maclean went horseback riding with Harriet Marling.[16] For the first year in Washington they had two Jamaican maids, who, proving unsatisfactory, had to be fired by Mrs. Dunbar, who took care of such things for her daughter and son-in-law. They were replaced by a French woman who had been Donald Maclean's maid in Paris.[17] As soon as the Macleans were settled in Washington, Lady Maclean traveled from London to see the newest member of the clan. She met then for the first time Mrs. Dunbar and Melinda Maclean's sisters, Catherine and Harriet, who were regular visitors to 35th Place. According to Robert Cecil, one of the Embassy second secretaries fell in love with Harriet Marling, was turned down, threatened suicide and had to be sent back to London.[18] This is the only reference in the literature to Harriet Marling as a femme fatale. Melinda Marling Maclean, as she matured, was another matter.

Diplomats at a foreign post, as Washington was for Donald Maclean, have as a matter of routine intensive social duties in which their wives were expected to participate, almost as if they, too, were part of the diplomatic service. The Macleans had parties, both grand and informal, to attend and gave their own cocktail parties, including

---

[*] Donald Maclean applied for insurance for a 1937 2-door Plymouth Sedan on July 11, 1945, describing himself as "First Secretary at H. M. Embassy" (FBI, Philby, Burgess and Maclean, Part 1). Around Christmas, 1947, the Macleans moved to 3326 P Street, a four bedroom house in Georgetown built in 1776. It was recently (2013) sold for $2.5 million.

a final, "farewell" party at their house in the summer of 1948, which was attended by forty or fifty people.[19] On the informal side, early in his tour of duty in Washington Maclean stopped by Isaiah Berlin's desk at the Embassy. Berlin, the philosopher and raconteur, was at the Embassy writing weekly accounts of American politics for bemused Foreign Office officials. Maclean said: "My name is Donald Maclean, we know a lot of the same people, we know the Bonham Carters, you know Sinclair,[*] you know Cressida Ridley, we ought to have met before, we have a lot of good friends in common. I think we ought to be friends."[20] Apparently Berlin agreed. When interviewed by Michael Ignatieff for this biography of Berlin, Berlin recalled Maclean making another declaration: "I work with Pentagon and State Department people. They're all so pompous. I hear you know some New Dealers. Could you invite some?"[21] As Berlin remembered it, he then asked Katharine Graham to arrange a dinner for young officials who might interest Maclean.

Katharine Graham remembered the occasion for the dinner slightly differently. Graham was accustomed to the formal dinners given by her immensely wealthy family, but "I myself had never given 'a dinner' . . .

> My first attempt at entertaining has stayed indelibly with me for half a century. Jonathan and June Bingham, young friends who had moved back to New York when the war broke out, were visiting for the weekend and I decided to have a few friends over, including Prich[†] and Isaiah Berlin, a relatively new but close friend who was in Washington at this time as an information officer in the British Embassy. The other couple I invited was Donald and Melinda Maclean. Donald was something like a third secretary at the British Embassy and through Isaiah the Macleans became [had become?] friends of

---

[*] Perhaps Kenneth Sinclair-Loutit.

[†] Edward Prichard, was a protégée of Felix Frankfurter, as was Graham's husband Philip, who took over as publisher of the *Washington Post* from his father-in-law in 1946.

mine. The two of them seemed like attractive, intelligent, liberal young people—in short, much like our own circle of friends.

The night of my dinner, conversation went well enough during the meal, which was perfectly peaceful . . . After dinner we moved out of the dining room into our front room, a small area with only space for a sofa, four chairs, and a bench in front of the fireplace. No sooner had we settled don there than . . . Prich and Donald began to tease Isaiah about his social life, which they portrayed as being too conciliatory of right-wing or isolationist people . . . Out of the blue, Donald said to Isaiah, "The trouble with you is you hunt with the hounds and run with the hares. You know people like Alice Longworth; that's disgusting. One shouldn't know people like that. If I thought you knew her out of curiosity, I wouldn't mind so much, But I'm told you actually like her company. That is dreadful . . . she's fascist and right-wing . . . Life is a battle. We must know which side we're on. We must stick to our side through thick and thin. I know at the last moment, the twelfth hour, you'll be on our side. But until then, you'll go about with these dreadful people."[22]

Berlin recalled that "The rest of the room, Kay Graham included, noisily concurred."[23] Berlin told Graham the next day that he would never speak to Maclean again. However, a few weeks after the dinner, in a condolence letter of February 14, 1945, to Cressida Ridley (née Bonham Carter), whose husband, Jasper Ridley, Philip Toynbee's great friend and rival in romance, had died in the fighting in Italy, Isaiah Berlin said that "Donald Maclean is very very nice. I've had a row with him, funnily enough, & then we made it up—I was the aggrieved party as always alas, & although I cannot really forgive him I like him v. much." Later in the letter Berlin suggests (perhaps facetiously) that Ridley take his place at the Washington Embassy: "You might live with the Macleans . . ."[24]

Graham's account of the dinner (which she implies was only the first of many times she socialized with the Macleans) places the Macleans in a specific Washington set, then just forming, later including in addition to the Grahams, the Benjamin Bradlees, Cord

Meyers and James Angletons: the newspaper/C.I.A. axis. They were liberals, in the American sense of the term in those days, politically somewhere between the New Deal and the Wall Street wing of the Republican Party. At home many of the men were hard drinkers with young families and frustrated wives. Shortly after the Macleans left Washington for Cairo, they were replaced in the group by the Kim Philbys, who harbored in their basement Guy Burgess (recalling, in their fashion, the relationship between Rochester and Bertha Mason). The American couples in the group were to become close to John F. Kennedy, husbands and wives close to the President in different ways.

During Donald Maclean's time in Washington he traveled back and forth to London on a regular basis for consultations at the Foreign Office.[25] Yuri Modin, the Soviet memorialist of the Cambridge Five, stated that on those visits Maclean would meet with Guy Burgess and Maclean "apprised him of the information he had collected."[26] The meaning of this is not very clear. Burgess and Maclean had independent means of communication with the Center. Perhaps Modin simply means that they shared information so as to better understand what would be of importance in Moscow. Or, perhaps, they just went pub crawling after dinner at the Gargoyle, grateful for the chance to relax without worrying about—verbal—indiscretions.

When not in London, on Long Island or Cape Cod or at parties in Washington, Maclean was at the Embassy. "In World War Two the Washington Embassy was . . . a mini-Whitehall responsible for co-ordinating British Missions in Washington which conducted the business of war.

> For example, there were British Missions for weapons, food, oil, raw materials, scientific information and propaganda to name but a few . . . There were liaison officers from MI5 and M16 in Washington, and British Security Coordination based in New York. British and American military machines were coordinated through the Combined Chiefs of Staff (CCS). The British Joint Staff Mission, (BJSM) handled a wide variety of military

information, including the exchange of research and development of weapons. It . . . also transmitted classified information on the atomic bomb between London and Washington.

As a matter of routine, the Embassy received telegrams, Cabinet Papers, the Foreign Office Print, the Weekly Political Intelligence Summaries, and copies of any important cables from other Embassies from London. It also routinely collected and analyzed information for policy makers in London. The Embassy's weekly dispatches on political events and opinion in America were essential reading in Whitehall. The Embassy also produced a weekly dispatch on economic matters.[27]

Anatoly Gorsky, Donald Maclean's NKVD contact, followed the Macleans to America, representing Soviet Foreign Intelligence in Washington, first under cover as Secretary in the Embassy, then as Counsellor, moving up the career ladder at a rate of one tour of duty ahead of Donald Maclean himself.[28] Before Maclean's links to Gorsky and his Washington associates had solidified, Maclean communicated with the NKVD through its New York City offices. This became the key, as it were, to an enormous piece of luck for American counterintelligence. Diplomatic and secret intelligence organizations' communications were, as a matter of routine, sent using international cable services. In order to preserve security, the messages were encoded, typically as groups of seemingly random numbers. The American "VENONA" project,* deciphered some

---

* "The U.S. Army's Signal Intelligence Service, the precursor to the National Security Agency, began a secret program in February 1943 later codenamed VENONA. The mission of this small program was to examine and exploit Soviet diplomatic communications but after the program began, the message traffic included espionage efforts as well." National Security Agency, www.nsa.gov/public_info/declass/venona, accessed 12/23/13. The code names here and in the following NKVD messages have been changed to those supplied by the translators. A marginal notation, for example, equates "GOMER" with Maclean, and will be read as "Maclean." There is

intercepted Soviet secret intelligence cables sent during the mid-1940s. The espionage literature has focused on the issue of the identification of the person referred to in the cables as "GOMER," transliterated as "HOMER." There seems no compelling reason to question the identification of Homer as Maclean, especially given a fortuitously deciphered phrase about "GOMER's" wife's confinement. Given that assumption, the cables are useful in establishing Maclean's knowledge of Anglo-American diplomatic affairs and what type of information and appraisals Maclean provided to the NKVD in America and that it then sent on to Moscow.

On June 28th, 1944, six weeks after the arrival of the Macleans in America, a message was sent from the New York office of the NKVD to the chief of NKVD foreign intelligence, Lt. General P. M. Fitin. The translation of the deciphered June 28th cable begins: "V. S. Pravdin's[29] meeting with Maclean took place on 25 June.

> Maclean did not hand anything over. The next meeting will take place on 30 July in New York. It has been made possible for Maclean to summon Pravdin in case of need. London's original instructions having been altered . . . travel to New York where his wife is living with her mother while awaiting confinement . . . on the question of the post-war [relations] of Britain with the United States, France and Spain . . . on the Britain and material . . . on several questions touching British interests . . .[30]

This first cable is about "housekeeping." The message assured Moscow Center that after his travel from London to Washington, Maclean's connection with the NKVD has been re-established, in the first instance with the chief of the New York station, Pravdin, operating under legal cover in New York as an employee of TASS, the Soviet news agency. It is notable that Maclean was of sufficient significance to the NKVD that a meeting as routine as this was with

---

considerable controversy about the VENONA materials, but none about those involving Maclean.

Pravdin, and was reported directly to Fitin. Maclean was provided with means to contact Pravdin when he wished and a second meeting was arranged for the end of the following month, giving Maclean time to settle in at the Washington British Embassy. However, that second meeting was also to take place in New York as Melinda Maclean was then at a critical point in her pregnancy. (It will be recalled that her first child had been still-born.) On this first occasion, although Maclean did not give Pravdin any documents, he did discuss material, perhaps from U.S. Secretary of State Stettinius's April meetings in London, concerning post-war planning in regard to France and Spain. The remainder of the cable could not be deciphered by the code breakers. We are left with fragments, as if from the sands of Egypt.

Post-war planning about Spain was a highly sensitive indicator of internal British and American politics and the relations between them. And, of course, Spain and its future were highly emotional issues for the Soviet Union's people, its leadership and the Spanish Republican exiles in Moscow, of whom the Secretary General of the Spanish Communist Party, Dolores Ibárruri, *La Pasionaria,* was a leading figure. The issue for the British and American governments in 1944 was whether to recognize the government of the Spanish Republic in exile as the government of Spain (as was being done with many European countries), counting the Franco government as a member of the Axis and therefore a belligerent, or to consider Spain as a special case, in the category of neighboring Portugal (both, it will be recalled, producers of worlfram). The French government in exile, many figures in which had ties to the Spanish Republic, was preoccupied with other matters in those weeks immediately following D-Day. The American government was of half a dozen minds on the issue, some of those minds diplomatic, some military, some financial. Churchill appeared to favor leaving Franco in place, having spoken what he referred to as "kindly words" about Spain on May 24, 1944, in the House of Commons. "Surely anyone could tell the difference 'between the man who knocks you down and the one who leaves you alone.'" According to Jill

170

Edwards, "Churchill's speech . . . [had] intensified fears in the Soviet Union of the formation of a Western bloc . . ."[31] consisting of Britain, France and now perhaps Spain, implicitly anti-Soviet. Fitin and his superiors would have valued any material and appraisals of that material about these issues that Maclean provided.

Later that summer, on the night of 2/3 August 1944, the New York station sent a cable to Moscow under the title "Intelligence from Source "H," that is, we will assume, Maclean. The cable was divided into six parts. Part I is labeled as unrecoverable in the VENONA material. Part II was partially recovered. It begins with an apparent reference to some of Maclean's assignments at the Washington Embassy.

> . . . The Committee is . . . on [political] and economic questions for drawing up instructions to EISENHOWER and WILSON* . . . treaties on civilian questions of the type already signed with Holland and Belgium and the treaty with . . . the European Advisory Commission in London will . . . In Washington is/are taking part in the work of the Committee. Almost all the work is done by Maclean who is present at all the sessions. In connection with this work Maclean obtains secret documents . . . work including the personal telegraphic correspondence of Churchill with Roosevelt . . .

More of Parts III and IV were deciphered:

> 2. The U. S, Government will decide to force the British to alter the allocation of occupation zones in Germany in accordance with the existing plan of the European Advisory Commission. 6 weeks ago Roosevelt informed Churchill that the U.S.A. wishes to detach minimal occupation forces . . . involved in the complex political problems of European countries. Churchill replied that the British vital interests lie in the North Sea, Belgium and Holland and therefore he was not in agreement

---

* General Henry Maitland Wilson, at that moment Supreme Allied Commander in the Mediterranean and soon to be Chief of the British Joint Staff Mission in Washington, where he was assisted by Maclean.

with the stationing of occupation forces a long way from these areas. Roosevelt did not agree with this argument. At this stage the British continue to insist on their plan.

This section refers to the debates about the allocation of the zones of the future occupation of Germany, which eventually were decided in favor of placing the British zone in the northwest.

3. In April Richard LAW [Foreign Office Minister of State] passed to the British Government a memorandum written by the War Office and the Foreign Office setting out the British policy with respect to the use of the Army in south-west Europe. The document divides the aims to be pursued into "inescapable" and "desirable". The inescapable [aims] include occupation by the British of the Dodecanese to prevent a struggle for the possession of these islands among Turkey, Greece and Italy. The use in Greece of a large enough force of troops to organize relief, the dispatch to Greece of military units to support the Greek Government, the basing in TRIESTE of adequate troops to control the Italo-Yugoslav frontier and maintain order there . . . Bulgaria, the despatch of adequate troops to Hungary to take part in the occupation, the dispatch of troops to Albania to restore its independence with the British guaranteed . . . weeks ago Maclean was entrusted with the decypherment of a confidential telegram from Churchill to Roosevelt which said that WILSON and the other generals of Britain were insisting strongly on a change in the plan to invade the South of France, suggesting instead an invasion through the Adriatic Sea, TRIESTE and then north-eastwards. Churchill supported this plan. From the contents of the telegram it is clear that Churchill did not succeed in over-coming the strong objection of Roosevelt and the U.S.A.'s generals . . . Yesterday Maclean learnt of a change in the plans . . . and ANVIL will be put into effect possibly in the middle of August. Commenting on this argument . . . the aims that are being pursued by each: Britain – strengthening of her influence in the Balkans; the U.S. A. – the desire for the minimum involvement in European politics . . .

The remainder of the cable as presented in VENONA dribbles off into missing and unintelligible code groups.[32]

*"Maclean was entrusted with the decypherment of a confidential telegram from Churchill to Roosevelt."* Maclean was providing his NKVD contacts with a window into Anglo-American decision-making at the highest level. This is the Holy Grail of espionage, almost never found before twenty-first century hacking of prime ministerial cellphones. Zubok and Pleshakov have observed that "Early in his political career Stalin had learned the art of looking at his enemies' cards . . .

> A KGB veteran recalls that Stalin and Molotov often received information about British-American talks in the 1940s sooner than it could reach the U.S. State Department or the British Foreign Office . . . "Stalin . . . badly needed to know exactly what transpired between Churchill and Roosevelt when they met, so our agents abroad were directed to find out at all costs."[33]

Although nearly all of the cables exchanged by Churchill and Roosevelt were transmitted "via Army" or "via Navy," among those from Maclean's time in Washington, that of June 28, 1944 ("[a few] weeks ago") from Churchill to Roosevelt appears uniquely to have been sent through the British Embassy in Washington.[34]

That cable from Churchill to Roosevelt is a lengthy exposition of the British position in a disagreement between the two governments concerning support for OVERLORD, the invasion of Normandy. It includes detailed figures for the British and American orders of battle in Italy and France. The American position was that Allied forces in the Mediterranean should be concentrated on an attack through the south of France, Operation ANVIL. ANVIL, agreed to at the Teheran Conference by Roosevelt, Churchill and Stalin, was an invasion up the Rhone Valley from Marseille and Toulon. Churchill argued in a cover note that this would involve "the complete ruin of all our great affairs in the Mediterranean" and that therefore he wished to cancel ANVIL. (Those "great affairs in the Mediterranean" being the creation of a ring of allied monarchies from Spain via Greece to Iraq and back via Egypt to Libya.)

Churchill's memorandum argued for a change of plan, for a concentration on the Italian front and, ultimately, a breakthrough into the Balkans. This gambit by the British was blocked by Roosevelt and his generals. Gerhard Weinberg, the historian of the Second World War, observed, in regard to Churchill's alternative to ANVIL: "Whether driving the Germans out of central Italy was worth the cost is at least open to argument; that the alternative to "Anvil," a push into northern Italy and into the Alps toward Austria would have gotten anywhere, is beyond belief. As Stalin had tried to point out to Churchill at Teheran, there were some very high mountains barring that route into Central Europe."[35]

Law's memorandum supplemented and confirmed the material in Churchill's cable and Maclean's interpretation of it ("the aims that are being pursued by each: Britain – strengthening of her influence in the Balkans; the U.S.A. – the desire for the minimum involvement in European politics"). Possessing this cable, Stalin and Molotov were able to compare Churchill's statements to Roosevelt with what he communicated to them, in this instance, and building on that knowledge, more accurately interpret his communications in other situations. Using the June 28 cable and Maclean's comments about the aims pursued by each, they would also be able to analyze the differences in tactics, strategies and goals between Churchill and Roosevelt. This would have reinforced Stalin's faith in Roosevelt as an ally and reinforced, if reinforcement was needed, his distrust of Churchill. We can take it that Maclean's reporting to Moscow was generally at this level of specificity and importance, certainly justifying its expedited routing to the senior decision-making levels in Moscow.

*The Committee . . . treaties on civilian questions of the type already signed with Holland and Belgium and the treaty with . . .* Soon after his arrival in America, Maclean was assigned to an Anglo-American committee to draft a peace treaty with Italy. This was a sore point with Stalin, as the Soviet Union was excluded from negotiations on Italian matters by his western allies. Despite that exclusion, he would have been able to observe Anglo-American negotiations about the future of Italy by way of Maclean's reports. Maclean was also involved with the preparatory discussions for the second Quebec Conference between Churchill and Roosevelt, which took place in September, 1944. On September 5, 1944, the NKVD station in New York City cabled General Fitin that they had been informed by Maclean that Roosevelt and Churchill would "meet about 9th September in Quebec to discuss matters connected with the impending occupation of Germany."* A detailed report from Maclean was transmitted in a cable of September 7, 1944 from New York. The Prime Minister and President discussed occupation zones in Germany, the Morgenthau Plan, Lend-Lease and the war in the Pacific.[36] Stalin, who had decided not to participate in the Conference, was able to audit the Conference nonetheless, as well as the planning for it, through Maclean's efforts. Much of the September 7th NKVD cable consists of an account of the debates around the "Morgenthau Plan" for the deindustrialization of Germany. It begins, however, with a brief summary of the British economic situation: "Maclean's report of 2nd September (the verbatim quotations from the report are in inverted commas):

In connection with the Anglo-American economic talks Maclean points out that "in the opinion of the majority of the members of the British Government the fate of ENGLAND depends almost entirely on AMERICA. They consider that ENGLAND can remain a strong and prosperous power if she maintains the volume of her imports which she can do in two ways:

1. By getting supplies from AMERICA gratis by DECREE or otherwise.
2. By restoring her exports to the required volume.
The immediate aim of the British Government consists in . . . [securing that termination of Lend-Lease?] will be delayed until the end of the war with JAPAN and also

---

* Melinda Maclean, in New York (or the Berkshires), was nearing the end of her pregnancy, which seems sufficiently to account for Donald Maclean's presence New York.

> receiving [a loan or grant?] . . . In negotiation with the U.S. Government the British will advance the following arguments . . .

Maclean's report then returned to the question of the occupation zones in Germany and the discussions concerning the Morgenthau Plan. The Morgenthau Plan, named for the Secretary of the Treasury, was largely created by Morgenthau's assistant, Harry Dexter White, following a suggestion by President Roosevelt. It envisioned the post-war reconstruction of the German economy along the lines of those of Denmark or the Netherlands, essentially agricultural, as a way of precluding a revival of German war-making capacity. Roosevelt and Churchill initially approved of the plan, including the assumption of Britain taking over Germany's role in industrial production and trade, thus stabilizing the postwar British economy.[37] (Roosevelt thought it sufficient that the German population live "at the lowest level of the people they had conquered."[38]) The Plan became moot when much of the agricultural area of Germany was given to Poland at the end of the war, therefore making it impossible for Germany to be agriculturally self-sufficient.

The NKVD cable cites Maclean as referring to an early indication of the currency reform that would be instituted in the Western zones of Germany in 1948: "Morgenthau obtained Roosevelt's consent to the use of yellow-seal dollars* by American troops instead of military marks as had been previously agreed with the British and the Russians. The purpose of this is to turn the American occupation forces into the economic masters of Germany." Then there is the situation in Greece: "Under the influence of Churchill and [British Ambassador Reginald] Leeper, the British intend to set up and keep in power in Greece a government well-disposed towards England and willing to help her and hostile to communism and Russian influence.

Their tactics consist in supporting the King as much as possible but also in leaning on the so-called liberal elements which might

---

* Dollars on which the Great Seal was printed in yellow.

take the King's place if the opposition to him were to become too strong. For military reasons the British were forced to support EAM and ELAS to a certain extent . . . In order to achieve their political ends the British intend to land a British division from Italy in Greece to keep Papandreou in power. As you know, this plan will be realized very soon. The U.S. Government regards the British intrigues in Greece with some suspicion and Maclean hopes that we will take advantage of these circumstances to disrupt the plans of the British and all the more so since the O.S.S. still supports EAM and ELAS.[*]

The Soviet government would have been particularly interested that the British and American governments were discussing plans in regard to the occupation of Germany between themselves and in secret, when this was nominally a matter for consideration by the three allies together. In regard to Greece, despite Maclean's hopes, Stalin had given Churchill a free hand in that country and had no illusions about what that meant to the Greek people.[39]

After a few more fragments the VENONA version of the September 7th cable ends with the signature of Stepan Zakharovich Apresyan, Soviet Vice Consul in New York.[40] It would appear from the use of direct quotation and the first person that this cable was, at least in part, dictated by Maclean. Maclean not only handed documents to his NKVD contacts, but gave them, probably verbally, expert appraisals of matters coming to his attention and in some cases (e.g., Greece) advice. These VENONA materials can serve as a guide to the espionage aspects of Maclean's career. They confirm the degree of access Maclean had from the first weeks of his time in the United States and how he used that access to provide the NKVD with comprehensive information and interpretation of Anglo-American policies and programs across the full range of consultations, negotiations and discussions in Washington.

---

[*] The Greek National Liberation Front (EAM) and Greek People's Liberation Army (ELAS).

The VENONA materials include cables having to do with Maclean from NKVD Washington to Moscow on March 29th and 30th, 1945 and a Russian translation of a telegram sent on the 7th March 1945 from Lord Halifax to the Foreign Office, concerning the negotiations over the future of Poland.[41] And, finally, some fragments of a cable sent by NKVD Washington to Moscow on March 31st which included portions of secret Foreign Office telegram No. 2536 of 16 March 1945 discussing strategy on the Polish question. This set of NKVD cables are signed by Anatoly B. Gromov [Gorsky], at that time first secretary in the Soviet embassy and the NKVD's Washington station chief,[42] which gives us the date by which Maclean's contact point had switched from New York to Washington.

Maclean, then, met his high-level Soviet contacts, who were operating under legal cover, both in New York City and Washington. He sometimes gave them documents (or photographic copies of documents, as he had with Kitty Harris in London and Paris) and sometimes he gave them verbal summaries and commentaries, which apparently were recorded by machine or stenographically. Even the relatively small amount of documents and appraisals to be found in the VENONA materials associated with Maclean nevertheless indicate the nature and overall volume of documents and appraisals Maclean supplied to the NKVD during his time in the Foreign Office. It is reasonable to assume that *everything* Maclean saw and thought relevant and every conversation in which he participated would have been sent on to Moscow. This should be kept in mind when reviewing Maclean's activities as recorded in the Foreign Relations of the United States, summarized below. Concerning the schedule of meetings with the NKVD, there was not one, but two, Macleans to consider. As we will see, it is said that a few years later, in Cairo, Melinda Maclean volunteered to be a courier. Why should that have been the first time? And what better cover for a courier than to be alternately pregnant and a new mother? There was a nurse at home to watch the Maclean children for an hour or so while their mother went shopping or whatever. Between Donald and Melinda

Maclean they could easily pass to his NKVD contacts what Donald Maclean took from the office to work on at home. Something on the order of fifty pages a night again would not seem out of line: three hundred pages a six-day week. Twelve hundred pages a month for the four years they were in Washington.

## Learning from Venona: Notes

---

[1] Hirsch, Steve (ed). MEMO 3: In Search of Answers in the Post-Soviet Era. Washington, D.C.: The Bureau of National Affairs, 1992, p. 195.

[2] Forrestal, p. 36.

[3] Forrestal, p. 31.

[4] FO 371/38508, AN 1886/6/45 quoted in Reynolds, David. From World War to Cold War: Churchill, Roosevelt and the International History of the 1940s. Oxford: Oxford University Press, 2006, p. 320.

[5] ". . . the Lipmanns came up to tea . . . Mrs. Lippman having a rheumatic arm, Walter Lippman and I made up a four with Jack Lockhart and Donald Maclean. We had rather good sets and got very hot." Halifax Diary, Sunday, July 8, 1945; "I had a game of tennis with Harold Butler, Donald Maclean and Jack Lockhart, which was rather fun;" Tuesday, September 11, 1945.

[6] Roberts, Andrew. "The Holy Fox" The Life of Lord Halifax. London: George Weidenfield and Nicolson, Ltd., 1991, page 288. Opie was with the Treasury. Maclean's Foreign Office career would be interwoven with that of Middleton until its end.

[7] FO 115/3610.

[8] Kerr, Sheila. Secret Hotline to Moscow in Deighton, Anne (ed.) Britain and the First Cold War. New York, St. Martin's Press, 1990, pp. 72-3.

[9] The Park Avenue apartment, according to Verne Newton, was at 277 Park Avenue. This was a McKim, Mead & White building occupying the block between 47th and 48th street, with a circular driveway and giant interior court. It has since been replaced by an office building. The Dunbars were not doing well, as a couple, and would soon divorce.

[10] FO 115/3610.

[11] FBI, "Cambridge Five Spy Ring," part 1. Interviewee redacted, probably Dunbar.

[12] FBI, "Cambridge Five Spy Ring," part 1. Interviewee redacted, probably Dunbar.

[13] FBI, "Cambridge Five Spy Ring," part 1. Chicago office. Interviewee redacted, probably Marling.

[14] Rent was actually $175, not including charges for water, heat, electric light, etc. as enumerated in a letter of December 18, 1944, from Halifax to Eden. FO 115/3610.

[15] FO 115/3610, letter from Washington Consulate to British Consulate General, New York of October 18, 1944.

[16] For the travel dates see FBI Cambridge Spy Ring, Part 3. For Quoque, see FBI Cambridge Five Spy Ring Part 34 of 42 and Newton, Verne W. The Cambridge Spies: The Untold Story of Maclean, Philby, and Burgess in America. Lanham, New York: Madison Books, 1991, p. 210. There is a Quoque Horse and Pony Farm at 48 Lewis Road, East Quoque.

[17] FBI Cambridge Five Spy Ring Part 5 of 42.

[18] Cecil, pp. 73-4. There is a reference to a "grim" letter in the FBI files that may relate to this story.

[19] FBI, "Cambridge Five Spy Ring," part 3.

[20] From a tape recording of an interview of Berlin by Michael Ignatieff, courtesy of Henry Hardy.

[21] Ignatieff, Michael. Isaiah Berlin: A Life. London: Chatto & Windus, 1998, p. 128. This does not quite make sense as written. Maclean seems to have asked Berlin to host a dinner party, or to invite others to a party at the Maclean's, but Berlin instead arranged for the Macleans to meet the Grahams. Perhaps there was a dinner at the Maclean's house or Berlin's, then the Graham dinner.

[22] Graham, Katherine. Personal History. New York: Vintage, 1998, p. 155. The Bingham reference is a bit confusing. According to his obituary in the New York Times (July 4, 1986) Jonathan Bingham was a son of Hiram Bingham, sometime Senator and Governor for Connecticut. He was in the Army from 1942 to 1945, then in the State Department from 1945 to 1946, practicing law in New York from 1946 to 1951. He was later a Congressman and diplomat.

[23] Ignatieff, Michael. Isaiah Berlin: A Life. London: Chatto & Windus, 1998, pp. 128-9. The idiom, of course, is "run with the hare

and hunt with the hounds." It is unclear whether it was Berlin or Ignatieff who thought that Maclean would have said that Berlin hunted with the hare.

[24] Isaiah Berlin, Letters 1928--1946, ed. Henry Hardy (New York, 2004: Cambridge University Press), pp. 531-2.

[25] According to FBI records, Maclean returned to the U.S. from the last of these voyages between America and London on April 6, 1947.

[26] Modin, pp. 117-8.

[27] Kerr, pp. 105-6.

[28] Gorsky was to be promoted to the rank of Colonel in 1945 and awarded the Order of the Patriotic War. In 1946 he returned to Moscow and was made Chief of Department 1 of the Foreign Intelligence Service in recognition of his service in the United States, particularly in regard to atomic weapons matters. http://svr.gov.ru/history/gors.htm accessed November 26, 2013.

[29] TASS and NKVD representative in New York.

[30] http://www.nsa.gov/public_info/_files/venona/1944/28jun_kgb_mtg_donald_maclean.pdf consulted August 27, 2013.

[31] Edwards, Jill. Anglo-American Relations and the Franco Question, 1945-1955. Oxford: Clarendon Press, 1999, p. 11; 15.

[32] www.nsa.gov/public_info/_files/venona/1944/2aug_occupation_plans_germany. pdf accessed August 26, 2013.

[33] Zubok, Vladislav and Pleshakov, Constantine. Inside the Kremlin's Cold War: From Stalin to Khrushchev. Cambridge, Massachusetts: Harvard University Press, 1966, p. 23-4, citing Serge Beria and Yuri Modin.

[34] Kimball, Warren F. Churchill and Roosevelt, The Complete Correspondence, Volume III, Princeton: Princeton University Press, 1984, c-718, pp. 214ff.

[35] Weinberg, Gerhard L. A World at Arms: A Global History of World War II, Cambridge University Press, 1994, p. 677.

[36] FRUS, 1944, Conference at Quebec, pp. 253-4.

[37] Skidelsky, v. 3, p. 363.

[38] Forrestal, James. The Forrestal Diaries, ed. Walter Millis. New York: The Viking Press, 1951, p. 10.
[39] See, inter alia: Sfikas, Thanasis D. "Attlee, Bevin and 'A Very Lame Horse': The Dispute Over Greece and the Middle East, December 1946-January 1947." Journal of the Hellenic Diaspora, 18 (2) (1992), 69-96 and Gerolymatos, Andre. Red Acropolis, Black Terror: The Greek Civil War and the Origins of the Soviet-American Rivalry, 1943-1949. New York: Basic Books, 2004.
[40] See this interesting account of Apresyan:
http://www.documentstalk.com/wp/apresyan-stepan-zakharovich accessed August 27, 2013.
[41]

hwww.nsa.gov/public_info/_files/venona/1945/30mar_translations.pdf
[42] www.nsa.gov/public_info/_files/venona/1945/30mar_maclean_message.pdf

*Civil Aviation and Island Bases*

The first two years that the Macleans were in the American capital were a period of transition for both the United States and the British Empire. President Roosevelt died in April, 1945, and with him died both the New Deal and his vision of alliances through which the "three (or four) policeman" of the great powers would work together to keep the peace.[1] President Truman suspended Lend-Lease aid to the Soviet Union on May 11, 1945, restored it, then in August terminated Lend-Lease to both the Soviet Union and Britain. On May 20, 1945, presidential advisor Harry Hopkins, on his way to Moscow on behalf of the new President, commented to a group including Averell Harriman, Charles Bohlen and James Forrestal that "he was skeptical about Churchill, at least in the particular of Anglo-American-Russian relationship; that he thought it was of vital importance that we not be maneuvered into a position where Great Britain had us lined up with them as a bloc against Russia to implement England's European policy."[2]

By the end of the year Truman had other advisors, less willing than Hopkins to maintain Rooseveltian internationalism, and the congressional Republican Party, with their Democratic Party allies from the South, had begun a great purge from public life of those who had constructed the New Deal agencies and programs.

After the 1945 British election and its long delay in the counting of the votes of the uniformed services, Churchill was thrown out of office, cutting short his effort to construct a revived British Empire supported by a system of satellite monarchies. Five years of effective Labour Party domestic administration had accustomed British voters to everyday socialism. Many felt that Churchill "was enjoying the war, running about the world, showing off and accepting homage whilst the quiet Attlee did the real job."[3] It was thought at the time—and later illustrated in a famous cartoon by Low—that although the memory of Churchill as war-leader was revered, the image of Churchill as leader of the Tories was not. He was associated—he had associated himself—with the men, if not the doctrines, of Munich;

with the Dole; with the unemployment of the working class; with the arrogance of the rich and the oppression of the Empire.

Britain suddenly had in Clement Attlee a Prime Minister who was neither an aristocrat nor a member of a family of rich manufacturers, but a lawyer whose formative years had been devoted to social work. He was for democracy in Great Britain and against imperialism abroad. It was quite extraordinary. Labour came to power, impatient to realize their dream of social democracy, having decided years before to do so by decree if necessary. Their crushing majority in Parliament made the dictatorship Attlee and Cripps had contemplated unnecessary. In foreign affairs, at first, Labour, especially Attlee, did not look for a renewed, world-dominating, British Empire, but to Roosevelt's alliance among the states that had won the war and which would now anchor a United Nations dedicated to peace. Attlee had told the Labour Party Conference that: "A new world organisation is being created, its foundation stone is the close and intimate cooperation of the British Commonwealth of Nations, the USA and the USSR. This cooperation will extend after the war; this is evidenced by the many declarations made by statesmen and the 20 years treaty made between America, G[reat] B[ritain] and the USSR. These three great nations, with France rising again, provide the rallying point for all the peace loving nations."[4] At this new dawn, the Labour Cabinet dreamed of a democratic socialist third way along which Britain would lead a revived Europe and a decolonized Commonwealth. Even such a mandarin figure as Orme Sargent, on July 11, 1945, "suggested Britain should 'not be afraid of having a policy independent of our two great partners and not submit to a line of action dictated to us by either Russia or the United States, just because of their superior power or because it is the line of least resistance or because we despair of being able to maintain ourselves without United States support in Europe.'"[5] The Macleans could only have cheered. For a few months it seemed that there would be three economic models available to the nations emerging from the devastations of war and colonialism, with Britain as the leader of the middle way of social democracy.

*Donald and Melinda Maclean*

The enormous changes in Britain brought about by as a result of the 1945 election transformed the context in which the Macleans, Burgess, Blunt, Philby and the others, including such as J. D. Bernal and his set, conducted their secret activities. Anthony Blunt, for one, decided that he had done enough and left both British military intelligence and the NKVD for the royal pictures and the Courtauld. (However, in the Bloomsbury fashion, he did not leave Burgess, which to him is what mattered.) And yet, for some of those who had followed Arnold Deutsch the struggle continued. The emerging American anti-Soviet policy became clear enough when in the last few months of 1945, "the Truman administration took an increasingly hard line—abruptly cutting off Lend-Lease, paring down the German reparation figures suggested at Yalta, and most important, ignoring Moscow's request for a reconstruction loan to rebuild Russia's shattered economy."[6] Many of those on the left wing of the Labour Party, and those to the left of the Labour Party, had come of age politically in the inter-war peace movement. The swift reversal of alliances in the middle 1940s appeared to them to be a return to a period when conflicts had been nurtured by business interests and a climate of opinion that equated the interests of big business with those of the nation and therefore would lead to an inevitable conflict between the Anglo-American powers and the Soviet Union.

The decision to continue their work with the NKVD was probably made easier for the Macleans by the atmosphere in Washington during the first years of the creation of the American national security state. Maclean had signed up with Deutsch "to work for peace" and an end to the social, economic and political systems that had brought the Hunger Marchers to Cambridge and Hitler to power in Berlin. He, and Melinda, had identified these goals with the Soviet Union as the chief opponent of a capitalist system that seemed to them irredeemably wedded to militarism and intolerant of social reform. It was not, at that point, that they were so much for the Soviet Union, about which they knew little, as that they were against the class system in Britain, the oppression of Empire, the excesses of

American capitalism. While Anglo-American postwar planning was predicated on the Soviet Union replacing Nazi Germany as the main enemy, in a mirror image, the United States was taking the place of Nazi Germany in the view from Moscow, in the view of those who identified their ideals with those professed in Moscow.

As we trace Donald Maclean's work at the Washington Embassy, we should keep in mind its doubleness: the effort made by all responsible British officials to retain British independence from Washington side-by-side with Maclean's personal effort to keep Moscow informed about Anglo-American agreements and disagreements. It made for long workdays.

The Macleans spent nearly four years in Washington, a period during which Donald Maclean was giving ever-increasing responsibility in the British Embassy until there hardly seems to have been any topic in Anglo-American relations in which he was not involved, or, at least, of which he was not aware. It seems better, then, to divide this account of their time in Washington, treating the various topics that are of obvious importance, and within those topical sections to proceed in chronological order, keeping in mind that during any given week Maclean would have discharged his responsibilities over a broad range of subjects of interest to the British, American and Soviet governments.

Maclean devoted much of his attention when he first arrived in Washington to the civil aviation matters with which he had been concerned in London. These were illustrative of what in Moscow would have been interpreted as the "contradictions" between the ambitions of the great capitalist powers. In the late Spring of 1944 it had seemed that an agreement would be reached in which American transport aircraft would be given to Britain in turn for concessions on routes and rules. Maclean appears in the record of civil aviation negotiations as "Mr. McLean"[*] in a Memorandum of Conversation, by the Chief of the Aviation Division of the State Department

---

[*] The FBI files use this spelling throughout. I have silently corrected it when quoting from those documents.

([Stokeley W.] Morgan) dated June 24, 1944: "Mr. [Paul] Gore-Booth called at his request and left a message for Mr. Berle from Lord Beaverbrook, which I immediately sent on to A[dolf]-B[erle]. He also brought in Mr. McLean, recently arrived at the British Embassy, to introduce him . . . We fell into a general discussion of the aviation situation . . ." Morgan and Gore-Booth aired a disagreement about the order of proceedings in the negotiations, Gore-Booth stating the British position that nothing permanent should be decided until the establishment of an international civil aviation authority, Morgan, the American position that bilateral agreements could be (and should be) put in place at once, to be absorbed into the structure of the international civil aviation authority when and if that were established. Maclean apparently did not contribute to the conversation. Perhaps he was the note-taker. The British and Americans had been discussing these matters for some months, discussions which included as well the British Dominions, particularly Canada; the Soviet Union, China and other nations. On the American side, the initiative seems to have come from President Roosevelt himself, involving from the beginning interested Senators and, in the background, Juan Trippe of Pan American World Airways. These were three of the four factors usual in American decision-making at the time: the executive, congress and corporate interests. As the discussions concerned civil aviation, the fourth leg of the stool, the military, was not yet involved.

By the fall of 1944 there were three quite different positions staked out by the British, American and Soviet governments. The American position was for regulated competition on international flights and exclusivity for national airlines for flights beginning and ending in given national territories. The British specified international flights by designated carriers regulated by an international organization and also generally wished to delay matters until Britain was in a position, especially in regard to aircraft, to compete with the U.S. (On the other hand, the British carrier, B.O.A.C. was beginning to negotiate bilateral agreements for routes and landing rights in areas where warfare had ceased, which was

188

making U.S. airlines nervous.) The Soviet government insisted on a closed system of civil aviation after the war, with all flights through Soviet airspace exclusively performed by Soviet carriers.

On September 9, 1944, President Roosevelt approved an international aviation conference for early November, in Chicago, to deal with these issues. Just before the conference the Soviet Union withdrew, citing the participation of "pro-fascist" Switzerland, Spain and Portugal. The Conference, which lasted until December 7, did not go smoothly, in spite of the Soviet withdrawal. On November 21 President Roosevelt wrote to Churchill: "The aviation conference is at an impasse because of a square issue between our people and yours.

> We have met you on a number of points, notably an arrangement for regulation of rates and an arrangement by which the number of planes in the air shall be adjusted to the amount of traffic. This is as far as I can go. In addition, your people are now asking limitations on the number of planes between points regardless of the traffic offering. This seems to me a form of strangulation.[7]

Churchill responded that an agreement had been reached on November 17, which had then been repudiated by the American negotiators, asking for the right to carry passengers between two other countries (e.g., between Britain and France). Churchill said this was unacceptable to the British Cabinet. Roosevelt threatened, in effect, to terminate Lend-Lease over the issue. Churchill accused the American negotiators of attempting to monopolize world civil aviation and suggested adjourning the conference. The last part of the conference continued to be characterized by bitter disagreements between the British and American delegations, the latter arguing for a "freedom of the skies" analogous to the freedom of the seas, the former arguing for, in effect, protectionism. This disagreement paralleled that over the terms of the British Loan and the Marshall Plan, between "free trade" and "Imperial Preference" with bi-lateral agreements between Britain and the Empire and Commonwealth. Negotiations to reach a general agreement in November, 1944, broke down and both countries began negotiating bilateral agreements, the

American negotiators seeking, by their lights, to maximize market openness, the British to regulate and protect their markets against American competition.

A resumed U.S.-U.K. Civil Aviation Conference ran from January 15th to February 11[th,] 1946,[8] at the Belmont Manor Hotel in Hamilton, Bermuda.[9] Donald Maclean was part of the British delegation. Melinda Maclean went with him to Bermuda rather than remaining in wintery Washington. The Bermuda Conference was intended to resolve the continuing disagreement between the United Kingdom and the United States over the right of airlines to collect passengers, mail and cargo in a second country and bring them to a third, e.g., American planes flying to England, boarding passengers there and taking them to France. The British viewed this as an American attempt to dominate world-wide commercial air services by virtue of the superior general economic position of the United States and its specific superiority in transport aircraft. (This last due, in their view, to a war-time "pooling" arrangement according to which the U.S. built transport planes and Britain built fighters.) The American negotiators viewed the British position as an attempt to prevent any American airline commerce beyond London. "American airlines . . . unlike the British, were well equipped with aircraft but lacked the range of airfields provided by the global extent of the British Empire.

A factor in the British agreement to talks at Bermuda in January 1946 was the hope that agreement would ease Congressional passage of the [British] loan . . . In general [Foreign Minister Ernest] Bevin was anxious to provide communications to help link Arab countries with Europe and maintain British influence . . . On 1 February Lord Winster, Minister of Civil Aviation, reported to the Cabinet that the British Delegation at Bermuda recommended accepting revised American proposals for an air transport agreement . . . the Cabinet, conscious of the loan agreement in the background, accepted the Air Transport Agreement on 11 February . . .[10]

In a memorandum of February 1, 1946, British Minister of Civil Aviation Lord Winster had noted that "The State Department . . . represented that whilst there was no intention on their part to link civil aviation matters specifically with the Loan Agreements it would greatly facilitate the task of securing the passage of the Agreements through Congress if the outstanding controversial issue of civil aviation could be settled, or at least be under negotiation, when the Agreements came before Congress." [11]

The Bermuda negotiations were a victory for the American side, especially in the matter of Fifth Freedom (transit) rights, about which the British gave way entirely. Maclean's reports to Moscow about the Bermuda negotiations would have been seen as confirming, in reference to civil aviation, the Soviet government's prediction of a conflict between the British and American economic interests.

Somewhat related to his work on civil aviation, Maclean also dealt in Washington, as he had in London, with the issue of joint US-UK military bases. [12] The agreement to exchange American destroyers for leases on land in some Western Hemisphere British bases had expressed and whetted the interest of the US military for a world-wide system of bases, seen at first as *facing out* from the United States, as it were, a first line of defense, later thought of as *facing in,* toward the Soviet Union, an instrument for preventing feared Soviet expansion. There was, in the summer of 1944, a clear difference between the stated policy of the President and that of the American military in regard to post-war arrangements. President Roosevelt was pursuing his war aim of dismantling the colonial empires, especially that of Britain. The military cared little about that, as long as they had a free hand to place bases on islands here and there in preparation for the next war. According to Verne Newton, on "August 29, 1944, Admiral William Leahy, Roosevelt's top military aide, and the senior officer of the Joint Chiefs of Staff (JCS), wrote a top-secret memorandum to Secretary of State Cordell Hull . . . [that] established that the [Southeast Asian] political spheres of influence would be decided by a Chinese-British-American committee . . .

The JCS had already concluded that "we should recognize, insofar as they are consistent with our national policies, the French desires concerning Indo-China." Similarly, the British were to be given the lead in their old colonial possessions . . . This was contrary to Roosevelt's stated intention of preventing the European powers from reclaiming their former colonies. The Joint Chiefs, however, were much more interested in constructing a chain of global air and naval bases as forward basing positions for their long-range bombers . . . within hours after [the memorandum] was written in the White House . . . it was in the hands of [Maclean].[13]

And from his hands to those of the NKVD and on to Stalin, who would understand that Roosevelt's strategy of a postwar global system of great power policing was giving way to a traditional spheres of influence formulation, excluding the Soviet Union except in areas already occupied by the Red Army.

Secretary of the Navy Forrestal took "it as a premise about all discussions of world peace that the United States is to have the major responsibility for the Pacific Ocean security, and if this premise is accepted there flows from it the acceptance of the fact that the United States must have the means with which to implement its responsibilities." By which he meant possession of the islands.[14] "America's aim to acquire a global system of bases was made public on 4 April 1945.

Maclean had access to the secret negotiations throughout 1945 and 1946. He saw detailed military information indicating the full extent of the Joint Chiefs of Staffs desires for bases in the Pacific, the Azores and Iceland, their location, facilities and operational control . . . He [also] knew there was to be an early warning aircraft station at Antigua.[15]

During the first months of 1946, British Foreign Secretary Ernest Bevin continued to "front run" American thinking about postwar arrangements. On May 1, 1946, the Military Adviser to the United States Delegation at the Council of Foreign Ministers meeting in Paris, Brigadier General George A. Lincoln, sent a "top secret" memorandum to the Secretary of State in which he expressed alarm that Foreign Secretary Bevin's statements at the meeting were giving "the Russians" the impression that the Pacific base negotiations were intended to lay the groundwork for the stationing of "considerable forces and weapons of war" there. This alarm was occasioned by a message to the State Department from Maclean concerning a set of Immediate, Top Secret summaries of the state of negotiations from Halifax to Bevin about the formulas governing the base agreements agreed by the Dominion Ministers.[16] General Lincoln argued that the United States only needed small numbers of technicians on the islands and to portray it as more than that "is a step accelerating the generation of two world regions—one Russia and one U.S.-British.

> You may wish to point out to Mr. Bevin the dangers inherent in his formula, that it seems premature and inadvisable, particularly when you can determine little military justification for such action at this time, that the grave precedents involved weaken the United Nations . . . [and] imply formal military collaboration between the United States and [the] British in peacetime.[17]

General Lincoln appeared to be unaware that "formal military collaboration between the United States" and the British Empire was exactly what Bevin wished to develop.

Later in the year Maclean was again concerned with the question of island bases. He visited John D. Hickerson, Deputy Director of European Affairs, at the State Department on the afternoon of October 17th, 1946, to discuss base rights in the Azores. Hickerson told him that the U.S. Government "would probably try to get the Portuguese Government to agree to extend [the existing agreement as to base rights in the Azores] for the duration of the occupation period for Germany and Japan . . .

> I [Henderson] told Mr. Maclean that we are fully conscious of the terms of the ancient alliance between the United Kingdom and Portugal and that I was sure he understood that we had no desire to undercut in any way the British position in her relations with Portugal . . . Mr. Maclean expressed appreciation . . . He added that we could, of course, understand that for security

193

reasons the British Government would welcome United States bases in the Azores but that they would not like to see any arrangement which would exclude British forces and thus worsen the present U.K. Security position.[18]

Relations between the British Empire and the United States in the period 1944 to 1946, as exemplified by the civil aviation and island bases discussions, were monitored by Donald Maclean, acting as a participant (for the UK) and observer (for the Soviet Union). From the perspective of the British Empire, this was an ultimately losing effort to maintain Imperial advantages, e.g., B.O.A.C. and its airfields, against American commercial interests, and a more complex set of interactions in which the British goal was to more deeply involve American military resources in, in effect, the defense of Britain and the Empire, without losing control of the network of bases that had connected that Empire since the eighteenth century. From the perspective of the Soviet Union negotiations displayed the emerging conflict between the two governments, as predicted by Marxist theory, and the gradually emerging determination of the American military, if not quite yet the American government, to surround the Soviet Union with bases suitable for use by B-29 atomic bombers.

## Civil Aviation and Island Bases: Notes

[1] See Costigliola, Frank. Roosevelt's Lost Alliances: How Personal Politics Helped Start the Cold War. Princeton: Princeton University Press, 2012.

[2] Forrestal, p. 58.

[3] Robson, Dorothy, Memoirs, volume 2, p. 619,

[4] Robson, volume 2, p. 625.

[5] Edwards, Jill. "Roger Makins: 'Mr Atom'" in Zametica, John (ed.). British Officials and British Foreign Policy: 1945-50. Leicester: Leicester University Press, 1990, p.8, citing FO371/50912 U5471/5471/70.

[6] Steel, Ronald. Walter Lippmann and the American Century. Boston: Little, Brown and Company. An Atlantic Monthly Press Book, 1980, p. 426. The abrupt termination of Soviet Lend-Lease, as well as that of British Lend-Lease, was contrary to the original understandings. "The first lend-lease agreement with the Russians throws some light on our general expectations of the course of events. It took the form of an exchange of letters between the President and Stalin by which we agreed to furnish aid up to a billions dollars which the Russians would repay without interest over a ten-year period beginning five years after the war's end." Acheson, Dean. Present at the Creation: My Years in the State Department. New York: W.W. Norton & Company, Inc., p. 34.

[7] FRUS, 1944, Volume II, p. 584.

[8] FRUS, 1946, Volume I, p. 1473-4.

[9] Verne Newton states that Melinda Maclean spent the week on the beach. Newton, Verne W. The Cambridge Spies: The Untold Story of Maclean, Philby, and Burgess in America. Lanham, New York: Madison Books, 1991, p. 111.

[10] Bullen, Roger and Pelly, M.E. Documents on British Policy Overseas, Series I, Volume IV. London: Her Majesty's Stationery Office, 1986, p. xiv.

*Donald and Melinda Maclean*

---

[11] Bullen, Roger and Pelly, M.E. Documents on British Policy Overseas, Series I, Volume IV. London: Her Majesty's Stationery Office, 1986, p. 75.

[12] Kerr, p. 125.

[13] Newton, Verne W. The Cambridge Spies: The Untold Story of Maclean, Philby, and Burgess in America. Lanham, New York: Madison Books, 1991, pp. 67-8, citing FRUS, Conference at Quebec, pp. 252-3. Newton somewhat overstates the importance of the Leahy letter, which according to FRUS was merely about military matters. There is nothing about bases in the text.

[14] Forrestal, p. 45.

[15] Kerr, pp. 163-4.

[16] "In a message to Mr. Mason in Washington telegram No. 2292 of 10 April Mr. D. Maclean, a First Secretary in H.M. Embassy, sought authority, given in telegram No. 3448 to Washington of 11 April, to give copies of Nos. 63-4 to the Canadian, Australian and New Zealand representatives in Washington, who had been kept informed of the progress of the talks." Bullen, Roger and Pelly, M.E. Documents on British Policy Overseas, Series I, Volume IV. London: Her Majesty's Stationery Office, 1986, p. 217, no 7.

[17] FRUS, 1946, Volume V, p. 35.

[18] FRUS, 1946, Volume V, pp. 1021-2.

196

*Post-Hostilities Planning, Turkey and Greece*

We next turn to plans that were formulated in London and Washington for the conduct of international affairs in the world coming into being after the defeat of Germany and Japan. This section also concerns Anglo-American relations with two countries in what was then called the Near East: Turkey and Greece.

Maclean was given documents from the British Post-Hostilities Planning (P.H.P.) Committee in the course of his work on the Civil Affairs Agreements for Europe.[1] This committee was a place where the Foreign Office and the military could, as the name implies, plan their efforts for the world that was coming into being with the defeat of the Axis powers. Its work was naturally of interest to Soviet leadership, which continued to be impressed by a vision of the strength and importance of the British Empire for some time after Britain had come to be viewed with a mixture of pity and contempt in Washington.

The Foreign Office and the British military had engaged in hypothetical postwar planning from as early as the Spring of 1942, when many might have thought that the prospects for the existence of an independent postwar British state were doubtful. Just after the Macleans arrived in the United States, the Anglo-Soviet alliance was, according to a Foreign Office paper of June 22, 1944, "at the base of our whole European policy and we should try to reinforce it by all means in our power. The formation of some Western European security system would, however, reinforce rather than detract from the Anglo-Soviet Treaty, more especially if the Russians, with our approval, constructed some similar security system in Eastern Europe—and they will almost certainly do so whether we approve it or not."[2] In early July, 1944, Christopher Warner, then Under Secretary of the Northern Department, stated that the Foreign Office view was that "the most important point in securing Russian collaboration after the war will be to convince Russia of our determination to go with her in holding Germany down and that only in the event of our appearing to play with Germany against Russia is Russia likely to try to get in first with Germany."[3] Also in July, 1944,

Foreign Secretary Anthony Eden wrote to Duff Cooper: "a Western group organized as a defensive measure against the possibility of Russia embarking at some future date on a policy of aggression and domination would be a most dangerous experiment which might well precipitate the evils against which it was intended to guard."[4]

So much for the views of the Foreign Office. On the other hand, according to Anne Deighton, "An anti-Soviet mindset can be detected in the intelligence community from 1943 onwards, with racist attitudes towards the 'semi-oriental' Soviet forces . . ."[5] The Secret Intelligence Service "along with certain military planners under the COS [Chiefs of Staff], and in contrast to the Foreign Office . . . was quick to embrace the concept of a future Soviet adversary, certainly no later than the summer of 1944 . . . these developments were observed by the Soviets with limpid clarity by virtue of Kim Philby's central role in the reform of SIS [M.I.6]." (By March, 1945, SIS had established a Soviet section under the direction of—who better?—Philby.[6]) Richard Aldrich has observed that "As the outcome of the war became increasingly predictable the COS [Chief's of Staff] called for strategic backgrounds against which to consider Britain's future commitments, and for this purpose the PHPS [Post Hostilities Planning Sub-Committee] identified the Soviet Union as the most likely post-war adversary. By July 1944 they had recommended that, if faced with a hostile Soviet Union, German help might prove 'essential' to Britain's survival."[7] Chief of the Imperial General Staff Alan Brooke recorded in his diary, 27 July 1944, "we must from now on regard Germany in a very different light.

Germany is no longer the dominating power in Europe—Russia is. Unfortunately, Russia is not entirely European. She has, however, vast resources and cannot fail to become the main threat in fifteen years from now. Therefore, foster Germany, gradually build her up and bring her into a Federation of Western Europe. Unfortunately this must all be done under the cloak of a holy alliance between England, Russia and America. Not an easy policy, and one requiring a super Foreign Secretary."[8]

Deighton underlined the point that "It was the military chiefs and intelligence officers who were the main driving force of Britain's future [anti-Soviet] Cold War strategy . . ."[9] A PHPS paper on "Security in Western Europe and the North Atlantic" of 15th September 1944 brought the conflict between the military and the Foreign Office to a head. Expressing the military point of view, it stated that "Much will depend on whether Germany is dismembered or any part of her territory is put under international control . . . we are unlikely to secure help from the <u>whole</u> of Germany against the U.S.S.R., and our interests are likely to be better served by dismemberment since we might hope eventually . . . to bring North Western, and possibly Southern Germany also, within the orbit of a Western European group, thereby reducing the likelihood of the whole of Germany combining with the U.S.S.R."[10] Reviewing this or a similar paper from the Chiefs of Staff, Foreign Secretary Anthony Eden wrote: "If we prepare our post-war plans with the idea at the back of our minds that the Germans may serve as part of an anti-Soviet bloc, we shall quickly destroy any hope of preserving the Anglo-Soviet Alliance and soon find ourselves advocating relaxations of the disarmament and other measures which we regard as essential guarantees against future German aggression."[11] Some of the Foreign Office mid- to senior-level staff (Christopher Warner, Gladwyn Jebb, et al) believed by the fall of 1944 that the Service Departments did not have "'the slightest faith in the Anglo-Soviet Alliance . . . the suspicion and even hostility of the Service Departments towards Russia are now becoming a matter of common gossip.'"[12] The Chiefs of Staff argued that they had to plan for any eventuality. The Foreign Office replied that the Soviets would learn of anti-Soviet planning, which would precipitate hostile action. The Foreign Office then withdrew from the PHPS over the military's anti-Soviet attitude.

The Foreign Office was correct in assuming that the Soviets would learn of anti-Soviet planning. During his first six months at the Washington Embassy, Maclean was able to keep Moscow abreast of both Foreign Office and military post-hostilities planning and the differences of opinion about post-war alliances between the military and M.I.6, on the one hand, and the Foreign Office, on the other. "Throughout the second half of 1944, a lively liaison had existed between the P.H.P.S. . . . secretariat and the British Joint Staff Mission in Washington, with the former furnishing copies of current papers to the latter on a weekly basis." However, "On 14 November [1944], [Committee Secretary Major Patrick] Davison regretfully informed [Brigadier Arthur] Cornwall-Jones that there would be 'no more games of Russian scandal for the J.S.M.', as papers or annexes on possible Soviet hostility were no longer to be supplied. This, in turn, put an end to the parallel practice whereby Cornwall-Jones had circulated copies of such material . . . to the British Embassy in Washington via its principal contact with the J.S.M. . . . Donald Maclean."[13] Soviet policy for the next ten or twenty years was guided, in part, by the idea that Britain and the United States wished to keep Germany divided, so that the more highly industrialized western section, in case of need, could be fashioned into a weapon against the Soviet Union.

As the end of the war in Europe approached, although Frank Roberts, George F. Kennan's opposite number at the British embassy in Moscow, "wished to see Britain's long-term strategy 'remain based upon the Anglo-Soviet Alliance and upon the necessity for avoiding conflict between Russia and the West,'"[14] some in the Foreign Office reversed course and began to agree with the military that it was time to change enemies. "On 31 March [1945] Robert Bruce Lockhart . . . told [Orme Sargent] that the time had come for some plain speaking with the Russians . . .

'I am sure . . . that the Anglo-American armies in the west could go through the Russian armies quite easily because of their enormous preponderance in armour and air power.' . . . Clearly impressed, Sargent returned to London and duly produced a long minute on 2 April, in which he made much of the military breakthrough in the West and called for a political 'showdown' with the Russians. Both Sir Alexander Cadogan, the Permanent Under-Secretary, and Anthony Eden, the Foreign Secretary,

200

found themselves in substantial agreement with Sargent."[15]

Eden, Cadogan, Sargent and Bruce Lockhart were not the only highly-placed British politicians and officials suddenly overcome by such ancient longings and fantasies of omnipotence. A few weeks earlier, "General Sir Alan Brooke, the Chief of the Imperial General Staff, had found it shocking that the Prime Minister [Churchill] was 'already longing for another war! Even if it involved fighting Russia!'"[16] The former KGB officer Oleg Tsarev, who depicted Stalin as personally reading raw intelligence reports, claimed that Stalin had seen "documents prepared by the UK Chiefs' Planning Staff in June 1945 on imperial defence which probably reached Stalin's desk thanks to Philby."[17] Or, perhaps, thanks to Maclean, whose responsibilities in Washington were as likely to bring such documents to Stalin's attention as those of Philby at M.I.6 in London.

John Balfour, Minister in charge of the Washington British Embassy, sent a telegram to Bevin, on August 9, 1945, which it is likely Maclean saw, giving an appraisal not of the Soviet Union, as George Kennan would six months later, but of the United States, and particularly of the attitude of Americans toward Britain and the British Empire. Balfour began by observing that "During recent months the concept has steadily gained ground in this country that Great Britain has come to occupy a position on the world stage which in terms of power and influence is inferior to that of the U.S.A. and the U.S.S.R." After a few pages, Balfour stated:

. . . the bulk of American commentators, who share the well nigh universal conviction of the public that armed conflict with the Soviet Union is an unthinkable expedient, have tended to relapse into a mood of baffled dismay whenever danger seems to threaten from unilateral Russian action. Their main theme on such occasions has been to bewail the ineffectiveness of their own diplomatic agents and, as often as not, to accuse them of allowing themselves to be dragged along in a campaign of bear-baiting 'at the tail of the British kite'.

Balfour speculated that "the United States is also now groping towards a new order of things in which Great Britain, whilst occupying a highly important position as the bastion of Western European security and as the focal point of a far-flung oceanic system, will nevertheless be expected to take her place as junior partner in an orbit of power predominantly under American aegis." He referred to the increase in American self-confidence from the use of the atomic bomb on Japan a few days earlier and on the complexities introduced into American views of Britain by the Labour Party victory.[18] The British Government had taken a sharp turn to the Left, to Socialism, just as the American Government was moving in the opposite direction toward a position from which "Socialism" was indistinguishable from "Communism," and the latter was anathema. Balfour's cable would have seemed to validate once again Stalin's prediction of a post-war falling out between the leading capitalist states.

In the final months of the war Soviet planners themselves had envisioned a post-war settlement along traditional spheres of influence lines and cooperation among Roosevelt's global "policemen" to keep the peace.[19] They had also predicted what would be in effect an Anglo-American cold war, as the United States moved to "remove British competition from the Western hemisphere and even from the British dominions." What the Soviet planners had not envisioned was that the British Government would choose, rather than "reaching an accord with the USSR" as Attlee wished, to allow the United States to strip it of much of its Empire and influence in return for protection against fears of possible Soviet military aggression in Western Europe.[20]

*   *   *

Donald Maclean had been promoted to Acting First Secretary in the British Embassy on December 27, 1944. By the end of the war in the West, in the Spring of 1945, Maclean was clearly a key liaison official between the U.S. Department of State and the British

Embassy and, through that, the Foreign Office itself. He had become one of the central personalities in the Embassy (or as much so as was reasonable, given his comparatively mid-level position). Thus, when Sir John Balfour, political Minister at the Embassy, "went to the State Department to concert plans for the meeting of [Canadian Premier] Mackenzie King and Attlee with Truman in mid-November 1945, it was Maclean whom he took with him."[21] In March 1946, Maclean was selected ("marked down") to become acting Head of Chancery, a position he held until the end of November, when the new permanent Head of Chancery, Denis Allen arrived.[22] During those months, "he had access to all the information in the Embassy, and he frequently deputised for senior officials.

> Maclean had become the administrative linchpin for all the British missions in Washington and thus had a commanding vantage point from which to report to the Soviets. He oversaw the work of the military attaches. He was responsible for Embassy security . . . He was responsible for codes and cyphers. He organised the division of work at the embassy and personnel matters.[23]

As is evident from this description, Donald Maclean's role in the Washington Embassy steadily increased in importance during his 1944 to 1948 tour of duty. His involvement with Anglo-American policies and programs increased as well, from the mundane list of initial responsibilities laid out by Wright: "all Near Eastern questions including India, all shipping questions, telecommunications . . . travel arrangements, trans-Atlantic passages . . . Spain and Portugal" to the greatest secrets of the alliance.

\*    \*    \*

The handoff of responsibility for the eastern Mediterranean from the British Empire to the United States began with Turkey and Greece. The Turkish aspect of the matter had deep roots, going back at least to the mid-nineteenth century. Turkey had been part of the

British sphere of influence since the Crimean War, if only to keep Russia from controlling the Straits.

> We don't want to fight, but by jingo, if we do,
> We've got the ships, we've got the men, we've got
> > the money too.
> We've fought the Bear before, and while Britons
> > shall be true,
> The Russians shall not have Constantinople.

Moscow, "the Third Rome," had strong cultural and political interests in Constantinople from at least the time of the father of Ivan the Terrible. The Tsars presented themselves as the protectors of Orthodox Christians in the Ottoman Empire and had ambitions to replace the Ottomans in the old Byzantine lands, ambitions which had some success. The collapse of the Ottoman Empire at the beginning of the twentieth century refocused Great Power attention on the Bosporus and Dardanelles Straits, the sole salt water access to the Black Sea, as important for the central European nations of the Danube basin as to Russia. The Straits were put under international control after the First World War, then more or less restored to Turkey by the Montreux Convention in 1936, with special privileges concerning the passage of war ships for states bordering the Black Sea, particularly the Soviet Union. Turkey's neutrality in the Second World War put it in a weak negotiating position after the war when Stalin resumed the southward ambitions of his predecessors.

The Soviet Union moved to terminate its treaty of friendship and neutrality with Turkey in March, 1945, then in June offered to renew it in exchange for the much disputed provinces of Kars and Ardahan in eastern Turkey, in addition to demanding a revision of the Montreux Convention such that the Soviet Union would control the Straits jointly with Turkey and have the right to place a military base there. Turkey did not agree to this and increased the degree of mobilization of its army. The Soviet Union formalized its demands for the revision of the Montreux Convention in a series of diplomatic notes to Turkey, Great Britain and the United States on August 7, 1945. This led to extensive Anglo-American consultations. The United States sent a naval task force to the area and proposed to take up the matter in the Security Council if the Soviet Union attacked Turkey. There was some ambiguity about the state of Soviet mobilization on the Turkish border, some reports of hundreds of thousands of troops, some of none.[24]

The State Department's Deputy Director of the Office of Near Eastern and African Affairs called Maclean in October, 1945, "to let him know that the American Ambassador at Ankara has been authorized, unless he perceives strong objections, to deliver to the Turkish Government our proposals concerning the revision of the Montreux Convention." The State Department and the Foreign Office had been working in the fall of 1945 to resolve their differences on that aspect of the Straits issue in regard to the passage of warships through the Dardanelles. In the course of the discussion a State Department official "mentioned the unfortunate article in the *New York Times* of yesterday, which implied that United States and Great Britain were formulating a joint policy on the Dardanelles question in order to face Russia with a common front.

> I pointed out that this story from London had undoubtedly resulted from our having consented to the British request to see our proposals in advance. Mr. Maclean expressed confidence that the "leak" had not occurred in the British Foreign Office and that if it did, strong disciplinary action would be taken because it was contrary to Mr. Bevin's policy to give the Russians any basis for feeling that they were being confronted by a united Anglo-American position.[25]

The irony involved in this exchange has received some comment, including the suggestion that the "leak" came from Maclean, but it was unlikely that Maclean would have risked being seen as untrustworthy over such a comparatively trivial matter. He was, on the contrary, always careful to be seen as scrupulous about security matters.

The following year, neither Britain nor the United States were any longer concerned about Soviet sensibilities in regard to a common Anglo-American front. On the contrary, the British Government was intent on drawing the United States into an active, visible, role in support of Britain in the Near East. Halifax had been replaced as Ambassador in Washington toward the end of May, 1946, by Lord Inverchapel (Archibald Clark Kerr), an Australian of progressive views and eccentric personality, who had been British Ambassador in China and the Soviet Union. Attlee wrote to Inverchapel in mid-October 1946, that he had been considering "how the United States and ourselves, with the means at our disposal, can further our common aim of arresting or reducing Soviet influence in the countries of eastern and southern Europe. There are certain possibilities of action in (the) economic sphere, but the scope of any measures we ourselves can take is severely limited by our financial position."[26] A few weeks later, "negotiations between the UK and the US began in regard to aid to Europe through some mechanism other than the UNRRA (the United Nations Relief and Rehabilitation Administration, to which the US objected as being an organization in which it had only one vote, although it supplied most of the funds).

Negotiations were conducted by Makins who delegated the allied question of aid to Greece and Turkey to Donald Maclean . . . [U.S. Secretary of State James] Byrnes at the instigation of the JCS asked for British appraisal of the military situation of both Greek and Turkish armies. He suggested that although it would be better if military assistance continued under British charge, the United States would be prepared to examine the possibility of helping and would "warmly welcome" any suggestions about economic assistance to Greece and Turkey. Since the UNRRA resolution [calling for a discussion of international aid at the next General Assembly] made secrecy imperative, Makins instructed that "a judicious report of this conversation will be sufficient". Retrospectively the futility of this caution and the implications of Maclean's access to the very heart of Anglo-American post-war planning have been made plain."[27]

Continuing these conversations, "Acheson told Makins his government still believed aid should at this stage be confined to Italy, Austria and Greece.

The British Government, therefore reluctantly followed the United States lead in suspending a deal currently being negotiated with Czechoslovakia until US policy was clarified. Makins led the conversations on the British side on 6 November, and emphasized the British "desire for harmony" of policy with the United States. The American team was led . . . by [Under Secretary of State William] Clayton . . . [who] remained adamant that "no, repeat no loans or credits from the Import Bank or other official U.S. sources were contemplated by the United States for Poland, Czechoslovakia, Roumania, Bulgaria or Albania", precisely those countries which ultimately remained outside Marshall aid.[28]

On August 30, 1946, Field Marshal Henry Maitland Wilson, representing the British Joint Chiefs of staff, lunched with his American counterparts to discuss the US plan, "PINCHER," for the use of atomic bombs in the event of a war with the Soviet Union over Turkey.[29] Given Maclean's responsibilities in the British Embassy, it is likely that he was familiarized with "PINCHER" at this point if not earlier. According to Vladislav Zubok and Constantine Pleshakov, "Stalin obviously learned about these plans . . . for he made a number of conciliatory gestures to dispel U.S.-Soviet tensions.

One KGB veteran believes that intelligence information on Truman's intentions "may have prevented the outbreak of war." Molotov later was of the same opinion: "It is good that we retreated in time," he recalled, "or [the situation] would have led to joint aggression against us."[30]

After the withdrawal of German forces from Greece, Churchill had added that country to the informal British Empire. The British Ambassador in Athens from 1943 to 1946, Reginald "Rex" Leeper, had a proconsular role. While a civil war of notable ferocity was underway within Greece, on September 14, 1946, Maclean called on

William L. Clayton, who was then the Acting Secretary of State, to discuss border incidents involving Greece and its neighbors. (That is, to discuss Bulgarian, Albanian and Yugoslav support for the Greek Communist forces.) In a memorandum of that date to the United States Acting Representative at the United Nations, Clayton described a conversation between himself and Maclean in which Maclean both presented and interpreted the British position that complaints from its neighbors about Greek provocations should be rejected.[31]

Two months later, on November 18th, John D. Jernegan, Assistant Chief of the Division of Near Eastern Affairs in the State Department, wrote a "Confidential" memorandum of a conversation with Maclean concerning a crisis involving Greek foreign exchange reserves. Responding to personal notes from the Greek Prime Minister, both Bevin and U.S. Secretary of State Byrnes had decided to reply first with their own personal notes of reassurance, then with a formal response scheduling economic missions to be sent to Athens. "When leaving, Mr. Maclean reiterated his remark that the Embassy would consult with the Department in due course regarding the answer to be made to the formal Greek note on the exchange situation. He seemed to want to make sure that this was understood."[32] The situation in Greece continued to be disordered, with significant gains against the British-supported government by the Yugoslav-, Albanian- and Bulgarian-supported Communist resistance. On February 21, 1947, Lord Inverchapel presented the American State Department with two dramatic documents, one describing the situation in Greece and the other that in Turkey. They stated that "The British could no longer be of substantial help in either. His Majesty's Government devoutly hoped that we could assume the burden in both Greece and Turkey."[33] Kerr believes that Maclean drafted the "letter to the American Secretary of State George Marshall, which informed him that on financial and manpower grounds Britain had to withdraw their troops from Greece and reduce those in Italy to five thousand. British economic weakness undermined the Western position in Greece . . .

This crisis was dangerous because Britain was about to withdraw and America was not yet ready to take over. Britain granted forty million pounds to Greece until the 31 March, and two million pounds to reorganise their armed forces. After that Britain trusted America to provide funds. Maclean handled [the] joint military talks concerning military requirements for Greece and Turkey and knew America intended to give Greece seventy million dollars of military aid, and a loan for military expenditure of between seventy five and one hundred million dollars.[34]

In this way Donald Maclean played a central role in the hand-over of responsibility for the Greek and Turkish situations, and that of the wider Eastern Mediterranean, from the British Empire to the United States. Later in the year, he "handled the cooperation agreement between British and American military missions in Greece."[35] In the course of these discussions Maclean would have seen a secret telegram from the Foreign Office to the Washington Embassy of September 12, 1947 describing a conversation between Foreign Secretary Ernest Bevin and the American Ambassador in London, during which the latter asked "whether the withdrawal of British troops could be delayed." Bevin replied that one of the four battalions would have to be withdrawn immediately, but the other three could remain until the end of the year.[36]

Given the template of Maclean's communications with the NKVD in the VENONA material, we can assume that Moscow was aware, at least week to week, in the finest detail, of British and American views of the situation in Greece, as they had been in the Turkish situation, their agreements and disagreements, and the developing hand-over of responsibility for the economic and military support of Greece from the British Empire to the United States.

On the 29th of September 1947, Maclean met with Jernegan, the Assistant Chief of the State Department's Division of Near Eastern Affairs "to discuss the Turkish Government's query regarding the advisability of reducing the size of the Turkish Army from 485,000 to 330,000 men. Maclean gave Jernegan an *aide-mémoire* setting out the joint position of the Foreign Office and the British military authorities, which was that the Turks should reduce the size of their army. The *aide-mémoire* noted that the United State had "now taken over the primary responsibility for assistance to Turkey." Jernegan, in turn, gave Maclean a paraphrase of a draft telegram, laying out a similar U.S. position. The processes and outcomes on both sides were nearly identical.[37]

Six months later, a secret State Department memorandum of March 2, 1948 concerned a Greek request for joint Anglo-American staff talks. William Baxter of the Division of Greek, Turkish, and Iranian Affairs reminded Henderson (then Director of the Office of Near Eastern and African Affairs) that the Greek Ambassador to the United States had recently suggested meetings by the American, British, and Greek military staffs to "clarify allied plans for the use of Greek forces or Greek territory in the event of large-scale hostilities." That is, World War Three. Baxter wrote that he has spoken with Maclean, who told him that the Greek Ambassador in London had said something similar to the Foreign Office and that the Foreign Office hoped that neither government would reply to the Greek communications before consulting with one another and that, in any case, the initial reaction of the Foreign Office was negative. Baxter assured Maclean that the State Department would not respond to the Greeks before discussions with the British Embassy. Baxter's analysis was that "many Greek officials are obsessed with the idea of getting the United States so deeply committed in Greece that it will be unable to withdraw." Baxter recommended a reply, coordinated with the British Embassy, stating that "all efforts of the Greek high command at the present time should be concentrated on the urgent problem of restoring internal security to Greece. If the guerrilla threat cannot be eliminated within the next few months it may be academic to discuss the role of Greece in any future major conflict."[38]

All through this period the Communist insurgency in Greece seemed on the verge of victory, assisted by either the governments of, or groups from, Albania, Yugoslavia and Bulgaria. However, when Tito broke with Stalin, the Greek Communists sided with the latter and Tito sealed the border, cutting off supplies to the insurgency. By September, 1949, the insurgent leadership had left Greece for a generation of exile in the Soviet Union. Those left behind were either killed outright or herded into island concentration camps to be swiftly shot or slowly starved. Maclean's reports to Stalin made Anglo-American activities, plans, agreements and disagreements in regard to the situation in the Eastern Mediterranean transparent to the Soviet leadership, which was no doubt helpful for Stalin and his advisors.

*Donald and Melinda Maclean*

## Post –Hostilities Planing, Turkey and Greece: Notes

[1] Aldrich, Richard J. The Hidden Hand: Britain, America and Cold War Secret Intelligence. Woodstock & New York: The Overlook Press, 2001, p. 57.

[2] Lewis, Julian. Changing Direction: British Military Planning for Post-war Strategic Defence, 1942-1947, Second edition. London: Frank Cass, 2003, p. 111.

[3] Lewis, Julian. Changing Direction: British Military Planning for Post-war Strategic Defence, 1942-1947, Second edition. London: Frank Cass, 2003, p. 116.

[4] Eden Dispatch to Cooper, No. 311 of 25 July 1944 in WP(44)409, quoted in Lewis, Julian. Changing Direction: British Military Planning for Post-war Strategic Defence, 1942-1947, Second edition. London: Frank Cass, 2003, p. 121. This idea of a Western European Regional Defence System and/or Western European Group, floated by the Foreign Office in July 1944 as a defense against a resurgent Germany, was to be picked up by Ernest Bevin as Foreign Secretary. See P.H.P. (44) 17 (0). Final, 20th July 1944, pp. 1,4, etc. signed by Gladwyn Jebb and others.

[5] Deighton, Anne. Britain and the Cold War, 1945-1955, in Westad, Odd Adne. The Cambridge History of the Cold War, Volume I: Origins. Cambridge: Cambridge University Press, 2010, pp. 115-6.

[6] Aldrich, Richard J. "Secret intelligence for a post-war world: reshaping the British intelligence community, 1944-51," in Aldrich, Richard J. British Intelligence Strategy and the Cold War, 1945-51. London: Routledge, 1992, p. 24; p. 25.

[7] Aldrich, Richard J. and Zametica, John. "The rise and decline of a strategic concept: the Middle East, 1945-1951" in Aldrich, Richard J. British Intelligence Strategy and the Cold War, 1945-51. London: Routledge, 1992, p. 237, citing PHP (44) 17 (0) (Revised Draft), 'Securing in Western Europe and the North Atlantic', 15 July 1944, U6791/748/70, FO 371/40741A.

[8] Cited in Lewis, Julian. Changing Direction: British Military Planning for Post-war Strategic Defence, 1942-1947, Second edition. London: Frank Cass, 2003, pp, 121-2.

[9] Deighton, Anne. Britain and the Cold War, 1945-1955, in Westad, Odd Adne. The Cambridge History of the Cold War, Volume I: Origins. Cambridge: Cambridge University Press, 2010, p. 115, citing Peter Hennessy, The Secret State: Whitehall and the Cold War (London: Penguin, 2002) and Richard Aldrich, The Hidden Hand: Britain, America, and Cold War Secret Intelligence. London: John Murray, 2001.

[10] P.H.P. (44) 17 (O) Revised, p. 9.

[11] Lewis, Julian. Changing Direction: British Military Planning for Post-war Strategic Defence, 1942-1947, Second edition. London: Frank Cass, 2003, p. 130, citing C13517/146/18.

[12] Lewis, Julian, p. 139 citing N5598/183/38.

[13] Lewis, Julian, p. 135.

[14] Zametica, John. "Three Letters to Bevin" in Zametica, John (ed.). British Officials and British Foreign Policy: 1945-50. Leicester: Leicester University Press, 1990, p. 48 citing FO371/47882 N4919/165/38 April 1945.

[15] Zametica, p. 43, citing FO 371/47881 N4281/165/38 2, 4 and 8 April 1945.

[16] Zametica, p. 49, cf. Project Unthinkable.

[17] Hennessy, Peter. The Secret State: Whitehall and the Cold War. London: Penguin, 2003, p. 16.

[18] Bullen, Roger and Pelly, M.E. Documents on British Policy Overseas, Series I, Volume III. London: Her Majesty's Stationery Office, 1986, pp. 10-22.

[19] Pechatnov, Vladimir O. The Big Three After World War II: New Documents On Soviet Thinking About Post War Relations With The United States And Great Britain. Working Paper No. 13. Woodrow Wilson International Center For Scholars, Cold War International History Project, p. 17. See Frank Costigliola, Roosevelt's Lost Alliances.

[20] "Ambassador Harriman . . . said that all through the British government there run these two main notes: a passionate desire for military and diplomatic cooperation with the U.S. coupled with the fear of our economic power." Forrestal, James. The Forrestal Diaries. Edited by Walter Millis. New York: The Viking Press, 1951, p. 185, 22 July 1946.

[21] Cecil p. 72.

[22] Cecil, p. 74.

[23] Kerr, pp, 152-3.

[24] See Gormley, James. From Potsdam to the Cold War, 1990, p. 182, and DeConde, Alexander. A History of American Foreign Policy, 1963, pp. 667-8.

[25] FRUS, 1945, Volume III, Turkey, pp. 1266-7.

[26] Edwards, Jill. "Roger Makins: 'Mr Atom'" in Zametica, John (ed.). British Officials and British Foreign Policy: 1945-50. Leicester: Leicester University Press, 1990, p. 20, citing FO115/4259, G275/4/46.

[27] Edwards, Jill. "Roger Makins: 'Mr Atom'" in Zametica, John (ed.). British Officials and British Foreign Policy: 1945-50. Leicester: Leicester University Press, 1990, p. 21, citing FO115/4259 G275/4/46; G275/8A/46.

[28] Edwards, Jill. "Roger Makins: 'Mr Atom'" in Zametica, pp. 21-2 citing FO115/4259, G275/35/46, 5 November 1946, G275/46/46, Inverchapel to FO. 11 November 1946.

[29] Walker, Jonathan. Operation Unthinkable: The Third World War: British Plans to Attack the Soviet Empire 1945. Stroud: The History Press, 2013, p.139.

[30] Zubok and Pleshakov, p. 93.

[31] FRUS, 1946, Volume VII, 217-8.

[32] FRUS, 1946, Volume VII, p. 264.

[33] Acheson, Dean. Present at the Creation: My Years in the State Department. New York: W.W. Norton & Company, Inc., p. 217.

[34] Kerr, p. 201.

[35] Kerr, p. 203. See, FRUS, 1947, Volume V, p. 32.

[36] TNA FO 800/468.

[37] FRUS, 1947, Volume V, p. 350. Maclean in *British Foreign Policy Since Suez* refers to a "diplomatic démarche in February 1947, inviting the United States to take over the cost of military and financial support for the anti-Communist régimes in Greece and Turkey, an example of the British Government "pushing the U.S. Government into the leadership of an anti-Soviet alliance, and of consolidating London's position as Washington's chief partner within it." Maclean, Donald. British Foreign Policy Since Suez. London: Hodder and Stoughton, 1970, pp. 54-5.

[38] FRUS, 1948, Volume IV, pp. 56-7.

*The Cold War Begins*

A year after the end of the Second World War Maclean's career was going well. The British Embassy was pleased with his work and was giving him ever-greater responsibilities, and the NKVD station had at least as great reasons to be pleased with his reporting. However, from the point of view of the Macleans themselves, a series of disquieting events were taking place in Washington. Elizabeth Bentley, a former Communist agent, had begun talking to the FBI in November, 1945. The FBI notified the head of M.I.6, Section IX (for Soviet matters), Kim Philby, who may well have communicated that information to Maclean, either directly, through the NKVD, or perhaps through Burgess. On February 15, 1946, the Canadian Prime Minister, Mackenzie King, released a statement making public "the disclosure of secret information to 'members of the staff of a foreign mission in Ottawa'." This was the Gouzenko affair. Igor Gouzenko, a clerk in the Soviet embassy in Ottawa, had defected the previous September, taking with him papers pointing to a large-scale Soviet espionage effort in Canada. Gouzenko's defection led to the arrest of Alan Nunn May in March, 1946, and Nunn May's sentencing to ten years in prison on May 1, 1946. (Nunn May was only one or two "hops" from Maclean, through Edith Tudor-Hart and Litzi Philby.)

There was a gradually intensifying campaign in the United States against Communists, Socialists, their sympathizers, and members of the Roosevelt Administration. Eventually thousands of people in public life or public employment were investigated in what Landon Storrs has called "the Second Red Scare." Those not denouncing others became themselves targets for denunciation. In July, 1946, the House of Representatives' Civil Service Committee appointed a subcommittee to concern itself with the loyalty of employees of the federal government and the McCarran rider to the State Department Appropriations Bill encouraged the Secretary of State to purge his department. These efforts joined those of the older House Committee on Un-American Activities (HUAC) and the Senate Internal Security Subcommittee.[1] Bentley began to tell her stories to the press in July,

1948. Whittaker Chambers, another former Communist agent, denounced Maclean's American colleague Alger Hiss to HUAC in August, 1948. Within a few years even such conservative figures as the (E. E.) Cummingses and (James Jesus) Angletons found the atmosphere oppressive, the former writing to Cicely Angleton that "Trumantown . . . must closely resemble Moscouw [sic] at this writing—everybody suspecting everybody without any time-off for a good honest hate." Mrs. Angleton replied that she had her husband, already a high-ranking C.I.A. official, had given up Wisconsin beer, as a gesture of disapproval of that state's junior senator, Joseph McCarthy.[2]

*        *        *

By the end of 1945 many members of the American Cabinet had concluded that if the Soviet Union was not quite an enemy, it certainly was not a friendly power.[3] This view was thought to have been confirmed by Stalin's February 9, 1946 speech announcing a new five-year plan "to guarantee our country against any eventuality." Stalin's speech was followed at the end of the month by Kennan's "long telegram," advising the American government to anticipate a long period of unfriendly relations between the United Sates and the Soviet Union. Churchill's "Iron Curtain speech," given on March 5, 1946 at a small college in Missouri, with Truman in attendance, is a customary marker for the beginning of the Cold War.[*] In his weekly political summary of March 10, 1946, Halifax had informed Bevin that "Tough-minded Conservatives in the [U.S.] War and Navy Departments talk about the inevitability of a showdown with the Soviet Union and hint that it may be better now than later."[4] Halifax's comments also indicated growing sentiment in the US for a US/UK anti-Soviet alliance. On the other hand, it seems

---

[*] One interpretation of the speech, and its American reception, is that it was an attempt by Churchill to counter Attlee's effort to "stay left," or, at least, to maintain the Grand Alliance.

that Halifax himself was "intensely irritated" by the Fulton speech. "Halifax had felt broadly sympathetic towards Russia since Hitler's invasion and had taken her side against the demands of the Polish and Baltic Governments-in-Exile . . . In July 1944 he had told Dalton how 'we must always treat the Russians with the greatest consideration, and never let them think we were having secrets with the Americans from which they were excluded.'"[5] The Foreign Office scrambled to assure the Soviet government that Churchill was not a member of the British Government, that he spoke only for himself.

The Soviet reply to Churchill came on March 14, 1946. Stalin, in a *Pravda* interview, "compared Churchill with Hitler and the Fulton speech with *the Fuhrer's* racial theories: 'The English-speaking nations are the only nations of full value and must rule over the remaining nations of the world.' Churchill was issuing 'an ultimatum saying "recognize willingly our domination, then everything will be all right!" . . . There is no doubt that the set-up of Mr. Churchill is a set-up for war, a call for war against the Soviet Union.'"[6] Kerr noted that "*Pravda* printed extracts from Truman's speech in which he distanced himself from Churchill. "This signaled to left wing circles that they should increase their attack on Churchill's policy.

In addition, by underlining Truman's position they were trying to split America from Britain . . . The Soviets did not believe British and American statements which tried to deny the importance of this speech. Perhaps this was due in part to the picture of the developing Anglo-American security alliance which Maclean's intelligence provided . . . Maclean attended Churchill's press conference and reported to London, it had been: 'as usual a roaring personal success. Churchill took a warmer tone towards Russia than in the Fulton speech, and went out of his way to disclaim he meant to advocate an alliance between Britain and the US.'"[7]

While observing increasingly anti-Soviet currents of opinion in British politics, Donald Maclean was also able to keep close tabs on anti-Soviet sentiments in Washington, and few sentiments were as anti-Soviet as those of the "Bourbon" Senator Eastland. On April 16th Maclean sent Paul Mason, head of the North American Department of the Foreign Office, a copy of a record of a conversation between his colleague Michael Tandy (British consul, Cincinnati) and Senator Eastland (Democrat, Mississippi) about Germany and the Soviet Union.[8] Maclean noted in his cover letter that "Eastland and his Mississippi colleagues, Bilbo in the Senate and Rank in the House of Representatives, are the nucleus of an extreme Russophobe and domestic reactionary group in Congress.

> They are notorious as such and what they say is, therefore, normally to some extent discounted. But there are other more moderate Senators and Representatives who are seriously worried about Communist 'infiltration' in America, especially into the Administration, and there are others, not necessarily the same people, who, without taking the rabid Eastland line, feel that Germany must somehow be won over to our side and made strong again 'just in case'. Both these groups, without actually supporting them, are inclined to tolerate Eastland than his kin, which makes the latter more influential than might otherwise be the case . . . We drew attention in our dispatch No. 201 of the 4th February to the danger of a revival of pro-German influence in the United States and in paragraph 4 stressed the part which fear and dislike of the Soviet Union could play in such a revival. As you will see Eastland provided Tandy with a classic example of this tendency . . . Incidentally we are not inclined to pay much attention to Eastland's allegation that Eisenhower had claimed that Germany would be America's only potential ally in Continental Europe in a war against the Soviet Union. It looks as though this remark, if made, had been reft from its context . . . We do not propose to encourage Eastland's interest in our German policy.

Yours ever,
D.D. Maclean[9]

\* \* \*

The United States, the Soviet Union and the British Empire had begun to demobilize their militaries as soon as the Second World War ended. British forces went from five to one million. The Soviet Union had discharged three and a half million soldiers by the end of September 1945 alone."[10] And much to the surprise of its Allies, the Red Army withdrew from Czechoslovakia in 1945. Although the United States suspended further demobilization in April, 1946, after Churchill's Fulton speech, by June the opinion in Washington was that "the Russians would not move this summer—in fact at any time."[11] As part of a Soviet "peace offensive," in the autumn of 1946 "the USSR placed on the agenda of the UN General Assembly a resolution requiring member states to declare the number and location of forces maintained on the territory of non-enemy states . . ." This seemed awkward in Washington and London, as while there were few Soviet soldiers in "non-enemy states," American and British forces were spread from the West to the East Indies, and beyond. Consequently, in an effort to get trans-Atlantic ducks in a row, there were extensive Anglo-American consultations on the matter, chiefly in order to decide what stance was to be taken in the United Nations. A "consultation followed between Maclean, representing the Embassy, and the Director of the State Department's Office of Special Political Affairs," Alger Hiss. "In September 1946 Hiss and Maclean exchanged statistics of overseas troops and discussed how to tackle the Soviet resolution . . ."[12] Late in the following month (October 21, 1946), Hiss wrote a memorandum of a telephone conversation between himself and Maclean concerning the American and British response to the Soviet initiative in regard to disclosing the troop strengths of the three powers in the occupied countries. This was a continuation of a conversation on this subject between Hiss and Maclean from the previous Saturday. The issue was whether to make a declaration of force strengths to the United Nations, which was of serious concern to Bevin, who, Maclean told Hiss, wished to have a delay in the matter until he had time to consider it and that he would then write directly to the U.S. Secretary of State. On October 23$^{rd}$ Maclean delivered to Hiss a telegram from Bevin, who passed it on to Acheson for Secretary of State Byrnes. Bevin strongly objected to disclosing overseas troop strengths to the United Nations, as to do so would establish a precedent favoring the Soviets, most of whose forces were within the Soviet Union, while those of Britain were scattered about the Empire.[13]

Hiss wrote a memorandum on October 30, 1946, concerning the "U.S. Position in the General Assembly on Soviet Proposal Relating to Information on the Disposition of Forces of United Nations Members." In that memorandum he described a series of telephone conversations and meetings in regard to the proposal at the United Nations by Soviet Foreign Minister Molotov that troop levels in foreign countries should be made public. The U.S. representatives at the United Nations told Hiss that "it was essential" that the U.S. accept the proposal if it were expanded to ex-enemy states. Hiss then called the Secretary of State, conveying to him the opinions of the U.S. representatives, who had Hiss pass his approval to the U.S. representatives at the U.N. Hiss "also called Mr. Maclean of the British Embassy at his house

> and asked him to inform the Ambassador promptly this morning of the fact that after the Secretary had seen the Ambassador last evening he had sent instructions to the Delegation along the lines he had discussed with the Ambassador . . . I [Hiss] added that subsequently, in view of statements on the subject in Mr. Molotov's speech, the Secretary had authorized the Delegation to make a statement in the General Assembly today or tomorrow of our willingness to support the Soviet proposal if broadened to include troops in ex-enemy states.[14]

All of which as likely as not demonstrates nothing at all about the vexed question of Hiss's relationship with Soviet secret intelligence, but does show the degree of access Maclean had to Anglo-American decision-making and presumably the information consequently available to Moscow. In this instance, Molotov might well have known from Maclean's information the reaction to his speech

221

planned by the American and British governments and be able to prepare accordingly.

As 1947 began, negotiations about the Anglo-Soviet Treaty continued in spite of the steadily deteriorating relations between the two countries. In a British Cabinet meeting on January 31, 1947, Bevin reported that "Marshal Stalin appeared anxious both to revise the existing treaty and, apparently, to draw up with us a military alliance." Bevin told the Cabinet on February 12th that he had been in touch with Stalin and that he was preparing "a fresh draft of the Treaty, which could then be sent to Marshal Stalin as a basis for discussion."[15] Jill Edwards has noted that early in 1947 "an exceptionally vituperative outburst in *Pravda,* in response to a speech by Bevin in December . . . [c]oinciding with negotiations for a revision of the Anglo-Soviet Treaty of 1942 . . . led to a sharp deterioration in relations . . .

> Offence had been taken at a reference taken out of context to the Anglo-Soviet treaty being "suspended in air". Perplexed at Stalin's response and not ready for an open break, Bevin tried to explain . . . Doubtless all would have been clear to Bevin had he known that secret policy discussions between the United States and Britain were being leaked. That Makins's assistant Maclean himself handled some of the negotiations, was privy to much else, and was able to keep Moscow informed is now clear. That the extent of United States determination to limit aid to Western and Southern Europe and to circumvent, if possible, United Nations agencies was known in Moscow helps explain Stalin's frustration. Whether it was also known that State Department post-war policy assumed that by giving "a strong lead in dealing with Russia Britain will follow" is less certain.[16]

As we have seen, on February 24, 1947, the British Foreign Office informed "the United States government that Britain could no longer be the reservoir of financial-military support of Turkey and Greece . . . [Secretary of State] Marshall said that this . . . was tantamount to British abdication from the Middle East with obvious implications to their successor."[17] President Truman presented

Congress with the Truman Doctrine on March 12, 1947, calling for an American global commitment against Communism, beginning with $400 million dollars in for Greece and Turkey. There was little talk of an Anglo-Soviet Treaty or military alliance after that.

\*    \*    \*

During the Macleans's time in Washington, while at first Prime Minister Attlee and much of the British Cabinet were working to dismantle the British Empire and hoping to maintain the Anglo-Soviet alliance, Foreign Minister Bevin had been pursuing the opposite policy, working to create an Anglo-American alliance such that American power—and funds—would be available to maintain the British role in the world and defend it against anticipated Soviet aggression. According to his biographer, "In the winter of 1946-7, Bevin felt keenly that he was being left to face as difficult a situation abroad as any Foreign Secretary had ever had to meet, with little understanding [or agreement] among his ministerial colleagues of what was at stake and even less disposition to come to his support against his critics in the Labour Party."[18] This situation was complicated by the acute European economic crisis. The delicate machinery of the internal economies of France and other western European states had ceased to function and showed no sign of revival. People in the cities had money, but the farmers had no reason to accept it in return for their products as there were no manufacturing products being produced which they could purchase. The people in the cities were beginning to starve, therefore, as the countryside, reverting to candles and sheepskins, grew fat. Keynes had thought he had saved Britain with a massive loan from America, but the Congress had removed price controls (as "Communist") and inflation had wiped out nearly half of the value of the loan. The conditions attached to the loan further aggravated Britain's fiscal crisis.

Bevin's anti-Soviet policy had crystallized during the second Moscow Foreign Ministers Conference, in April 1947, when he came to believe that the American Secretary of State, George Marshall, held views about the Soviet Union similar to his own. The implementation of that policy involved the creation of a set of Western European alliances, initially advertised as provision against German aggression, but soon enough turned around to face the Soviet Union, and then a larger military alliance including the United States with the same orientation. Both of these efforts ran in parallel with what became known as the Marshall Plan and developments in Germany. Donald Maclean had been a principal link between the State Department and the British Embassy, and thence to the Foreign Office, for the British Loan discussions.[19] He was therefore well-positioned to monitor the discussions that led to NATO, on the one hand, and the Marshall Plan, on the other.

In an oral history for the Truman Library, Sir Edmund Hall-Patch "cited some background to indicate that there was a good deal of development before the actual announcement of the Marshall Plan.

The first indication, he said, of the United States crystallizing its policy was in Dean Acheson's speech at Cleveland, Mississippi, in May of 1947 . . . He said that Bevin was frightfully conscious that the heart was knocked out of Europe, and that something was needed to provide a stimulus to get the Europeans to help themselves . . . Bevin was encouraged by the Acheson speech and from then on really expected some action such as the Marshall speech, although nobody knew specifically that Marshall was going to make that speech . . .[20]

On June 5, 1947, Secretary of State Marshall gave a short Commencement speech at Harvard University. After describing the breakdown of the European economies, he said, inter alia, "It is logical that the United States should do whatever it is able to do to assist in the return of normal economic health in the world, without which there can be no political stability and no assured peace.

Our policy is directed not against any country or doctrine but against hunger, poverty, desperation and chaos . . . Any assistance that this Government may render in the future should provide a cure rather than a mere palliative. Any government that is willing to assist in the task of recovery will find full cooperation, I am sure, on the part of the United States Government. *Any government which maneuvers to block the recovery of other countries cannot expect help from us. Furthermore, governments, political parties or groups which seek to perpetuate human misery in order to profit there from politically or otherwise will encounter the opposition of the United States . . .* It is already evident that, before the United States Government can proceed much further in its efforts to alleviate the situation and help start the European world on its way to recovery, there must be some agreement among the countries of Europe as to the requirements of the situation and the part those countries themselves will take in order to give proper effect to whatever action might be undertaken by this Government . . . The initiative, I think, must come from Europe . . . The program should be a joint one, agreed to by a number, if not all European nations.[21] (Emphasis added.)

Bevin jumped at this, telling "Hall-Patch the day after Marshall's speech to go to Paris and to ask Bidault if he would sponsor a conference in Paris on this subject."[22]

The European Recovery Program, as it was officially entitled, fit well with Bevin's plans, especially as it required joint, not bilateral, planning and agreements. The Soviet Union, not wishing to become part of the dollar zone, withdrew from the preliminary talks, taking with it those nations within its sphere of influence. Bevin, as anticipated, then took the lead in organizing the western European structures needed to implement the US initiative.[23] And yet some aspects Anglo-Soviet relations continued, for a time, to be closer than American-Soviet relations. In a Cabinet meeting on September 18th 1947, Bevin "said that he found it difficult to take an optimistic view of the international situation at the present time, particularly in the light of the attitude adopted by the United States Government towards the Soviet Government."[24] The divergence between American and British attitudes toward the Soviet Union at this point

225

is vividly indicated by the decision of the British Cabinet on September 24th to continue with an agreement to sell jet engines to the Soviet Union and to train Soviet engineers.[25] The very young Harold Wilson, Secretary for Overseas Trade, signed an agreement in Moscow on December 27th, exchanging British machinery and equipment for Russian grain. This sort of bilateral barter was exactly what the American negotiators of the British Loan and the Marshall Plan had sought to preclude. Be that as it may, Bevin seems to have ignored these activities of the Board of Trade (led by Cripps, for whom Wilson worked).

What Bevin wanted, like Chamberlain before him, was an anti-Soviet alliance with Germany. "After the abortive Conference of Foreign Ministers in December 1947, Maclean learned Bevin and Marshall were now determined to solve the German problem, if necessary without the consent or participation of the Soviets.

> Bevin was determined to halt the economic collapse of Germany by expanding the Western administration in Frankfurt, and co-ordinating the three Western zones more closely and by reforming their financial arrangements. Elections for a central German Government would also be necessary. Bevin wanted to "fit Western Germany into his plan for Western European Union" to stop Soviet expansion westward. Bevin and Marshall were cautious, believing the development of a German government should be evolutionary and, to some extent, dependent upon Soviet actions.[26]

Bevin's development of an anti-Soviet Western alliance continued to be a cause for disagreement between him and the Prime Minister. For example, "on the eve of the Foreign Secretary's notable speech on Western union in the Commons on 22 January, 1948, Attlee wrote to him urging a conciliatory note on Anglo-Soviet relations.

> Having read the notes to help Bevin in framing his speech, he minuted to him: "I suggest that you might include a passage stating that we believe that countries with different ideologies can cooperate. (I believe that Stalin said something to this effect which might be quoted)." Indirectly, this was a rebuke for

[Robin] Hankey who had prepared the notes in question, and whose constant message was that any Soviet pretence of belief that it would cooperate with countries upholding other ideologies was a sham.[27]

Attlee could write notes to Bevin, but could not, or would not, stop him. Nor could the traditional Imperialist opposition to the Labour Government: "As regards the Conservative Party . . . opposition to the special relationship came mainly from the ultra-colonialist lobby . . . they [gave] a particularly high priority to the preservation of the traditional British sphere of influence in the Commonwealth and colonial empire . . . [and] were peculiarly sensitive to American attempts to penetrate and undermine it . . . to many of its adherents the American drive towards domination of the capitalist world appeared to be an even more direct threat to British interests than Communism."[28] The commentator in this case being a Soviet political scientist, Donald Maclean, circa 1970.

*Donald and Melinda Maclean*

## The Cold War Begins: Notes

[1] See, inter alia, Caute, David. The Great Fear: The Anti-Communist Purge Under Truman and Eisenhower. New York: Simon and Schuster, 1978.

[2] Holzman, Michael. James Jesus Angleton, the C.I.A., & the Craft of Counterintelligence. Amherst: University of Massachusetts Press, 2008, p. 120.

[3] Forrestal, pp. 86 ff.

[4] Bullen, Roger and Pelly, M.E. Documents on British Policy Overseas, Series I, Volume IV. London: Her Majesty's Stationery Office, 1986, p. 153.

[5] Roberts, p. 295.

[6] Bullock, Volume II, p. 225.

[7] Kerr, pp. 168-9.

[8] Eastland had "expressed the view that the State Department contained a fair sprinkling of Communist sympathisers . . . For his part he was convinced that a war with the Soviet Union was inevitable and that it had better come now, rather than thirty years hence, when Russian industrial potential had been built up . . ."

[9] Bullen, Roger and Pelly, M.E. Documents on British Policy Overseas, Series I, Volume IV, No. 74. London: Her Majesty's Stationery Office, 1987, pp. 249-50.

[10] Dale, Robert. Re-Adjusting to Life After War: The Demobilization of Red Army Veterans in Leningrad and The Leningrad Region 1944-1950, dissertation, Queen Mary, University of London.

[11] Forrestal, James. The Forrestal Diaries. Edited by Walter Millis. New York: The Viking Press, 1951, p. 171. See also 16 July 1946, p. 182: General "Clay expressed it as his view that the Russians did not want a war and that we should find it possible to get along with them." 16 July 1946.

[12] Cecil, p. 75.

[13] FRUS, 1946, Volume I, pp. 960-2.

[14] FRUS, 1946, Volume I, pp. 978-9. Cecil wrote that Hiss visited Maclean at his home, but he may have confused Hiss's "called" with "called on."

[15] TNA CAB 131/5.

[16] Edwards, Jill. "Roger Makins: 'Mr Atom'" in Zametica, p. 23. See: Bohlen, Charles and Robinson, Gerold T. "The capabilities and intentions of the Soviet Union as affected by American policy," Diplomatic History, I (Fall, 1977), 389-99. December 10, 1945.

[17] Forrestal, James. The Forrestal Diaries. Edited by Walter Millis. New York: The Viking Press, 1951, p. 245.

[18] Bullock, Alan. Ernest Bevin: Foreign Secretary, 1945-1951. New York & London: W. W. Norton & Company, 1983, pp. 394-5.

[19] FRUS, 1946, Volume V, p. 45-6.

[20] Brooks, Philip C. Oral History Interview with Sir Edmund Hall-Patch, Chairman of the Executive Committee, Organization for European Economic Cooperation, 1948. Harry S. Truman Library & Museum, www.trumanlibrary.org/oralhist/hallpatc.htm accessed December 5, 2013.

[21] http://www.marshallfoundation.org/library/doc_marshall_plan_speech. html

[22] Brooks, Philip C. Oral History Interview with Sir Edmund Hall-Patch, Chairman of the Executive Committee, Organization for European Economic Cooperation, 1948. Harry S. Truman Library & Museum, www.trumanlibrary.org/oralhist/hallpatc.htm accessed December 5, 2013.

[23] William Hitchcock believes that "Europe had matched its prewar industrial production by mid-1948 . . . Since the ERP did not become law until April 1948, and since Marshall Plan aid did not start arriving in Europe until May and June of that year, Marshall aid cannot be said to have restarted European economic growth." What then was its purpose? "It may be too much to state that the Marshall Plan started the Cold War, whose many roots reached back across a wide acreage of wartime and postwar distrust and rivalry. But from

June 1947 on, the United States set a course for a western German state and a capitalist European economic revival that confirmed the division of Europe." Hitchcock, William I. The Marshall Plan and the creation of the West. In Leffler, Melvyn P. and Westad, Odd Arne (eds.). The Cambridge History of the Cold War, Volume I: Origins. Cambridge University Press, 2010, pp. 159; 168.

[24] CAB 131/5.

[25] CAB 131/5

[26] Kerr, 255.

[27] Rothwell, Victor. "Robin Hankey" in Zametica, John (ed.). British Officials and British Foreign Policy: 1945-50. Leicester: Leicester University Press, 1990, p. 170 citing Attlee to Bevin, 21 January 1948, and Hankey's notes for Bevin's speech, FO 371/71629/878 and 1141.

[28] Maclean, Donald. British Foreign Policy Since Suez. London: Hodder and Stoughton, 1970, pp. 47-8, citing Amery, Leo. The Awakening. London, 1948, p. xiv.

*Atomic Energy*

Donald Maclean's work at the British Embassy in Washington covered the full range of Anglo-American interests, from civil aviation to the details of relations with Greece and Turkey. The aspect of his work that brought him to the secret heart of the alliance was that concerning atomic energy matters. During their conference at Quebec in the August, 1943, Roosevelt and Churchill had signed "articles of agreement governing collaboration between the authorities of the U.S.A. and the U.K. in the matter of Tube Alloys." The agreement stated that "There shall be set up in Washington a Combined Policy Committee . . . The functions of this Committee, subject to the control of the respective Governments, will be:

(1) To agree from time to time upon the programme of work to be carried out in the two countries.

(2) To keep all sections of the project under constant review.

(3) To allocate materials, apparatus and plant, in limited supply, in accordance with the requirements of the programme agreed by the Committee.

(4) To settle any questions which may arise on the interpretation or application of this Agreement.

(b) There shall be complete interchange of information and ideas on all sections of the project between members of the Policy Committee and their immediate technical advisers.

(e) In the field of scientific research and development there shall be full and effective interchange of information and ideas between those in the two countries engaged in the same sections of the field.

(d) In the field of design, construction and operation of large-scale plants, interchange of information and ideas shall be regulated by such ad hoc arrangements as may, in each section of the field, appear to be necessary or desirable if the project is to be brought to fruition at the earliest moment. Such ad hoc arrangements shall be subject to the approval of the Policy Committee.[1]

It is interesting that at its first appearance the enterprise carries the

British name, Tube Alloys, rather than the later better-known American designation, the Manhattan Project.

As we shall see, little of the agreement held. According to Admiral Lewis Strauss, the first head of the American Atomic Energy Commission, "The British made a deal with us called the Hyde Park Agreement, and there's a strange story about that.

It was formalized between Roosevelt and Churchill. It had been signed at Hyde Park, from which it took its name, and it committed us to go pretty far in assisting the British in their atomic enterprise. But, of course, it was before the Atomic Energy Act had come into existence and the Congress knew nothing of it when the Act was passed. Certainly, Mr. Truman had never heard of it. There was a good deal of doubt as to whether there had ever been such an agreement because we had no copy of it. Mr. Churchill said he had a contemporary signed copy and exhibited it to friends who visited him at #10 Downing Street. The original counterpart—our copy of the Hyde Park Agreement, wasn't discovered until years later when, during a cleaning of the bookshelves in the Roosevelt mansion at Hyde Park, it was found. Someone had laid it on top of a row of books and it had fallen back behind them . . .[2]

The American government "misplaced" its copy of the agreement. Dean Acheson commented in his memoir *Present at the Creation* that he had come to believe "that our Government, having made an agreement from which it had gained immeasurably, was not keeping its word and performing its obligations."[3] As Machiavelli might have observed, international agreements are maintained for as long as they are useful to the more powerful party to the agreement.

The extensive FBI files on Burgess, Philby and the Macleans show that as soon as Burgess and Maclean disappeared from London in 1951 there was a scramble in Washington to learn how much Donald Maclean had known about atomic energy matters. Despite occasional chest-thumping about how easily "superior" Anglo-American airpower and armor would be able to defeat the Red Army, the exhilaration in Washington about what was seen as the purely American development of the atomic bomb and its seeming monopoly pointed to a realization that only the bomb would equalize the military correlation of forces. But this seemed more than sufficient and planning for the Third World War went forward on the premise that large numbers of atomic bombs would be available to destroy Soviet cities and industrial centers, while there would be no threat of equivalent retaliation. The initial complacency in that regard ended with the Soviet Union's test of an atomic weapon in the summer of 1949. It seemed unbelievable, to some, that the Soviet Union, burdened as it was with a Communist (or Socialist) economy and a large non-European population would be able to match the scientific expertise involved in the Manhattan Project. The "secret" must have been stolen.* But by whom? Had it been Maclean?

In June, 1951, J. Edgar Hoover, Director of the Federal Bureau of Investigations, was informed by Admiral Lewis Strauss of the AEC that Donald Maclean had been given a pass by the AEC general manager, Carroll Wilson, in November of 1947 "which required no escort and permitted Maclean to go anywhere in the Atomic Energy headquarters. Admiral Strauss stated that at the same time, high Army and Navy officials were required to have escorts in going through the building." Annoyed, Hoover annotated the memorandum: "I was always required to have an escort."[4] The FBI became very interested in Mr. Wilson, whom they extensively interviewed. "Wilson . . . stated that he first met Maclean in 1947 at a meeting of the Combined Development Trust, of which Mr. Wilson was Chairman. He said Maclean was not a member of the Trust but was an assistant to Sir Gordon Monroe, the United Kingdom representative.

> Maclean attended all meetings of the Trust from 1947 until he
> left the United States . . . Mr. Wilson said Maclean was also the
> United Kingdom representative on the Combined Policy
> Committee on which the Secretary of State was Chairman. This

---

* As a matter of fact, a range of engineering solutions *had* been provided to Igor Kurchatov and his atomic energy team by such as Klaus Fuchs.

Committee discussed policies in the field of atomic energy. Mr. Wilson also recalled that Maclean attended a three-day declassification conference held in October, 1947. The discussions at this conference were limited to atomic energy information held in common by the United States, Canada, and the United Kingdom during the war. A discussion did take place regarding atomic weapons. Mr. Wilson recalled that Dr. Klaus Fuchs also attended this conference. Mr. Wilson stated he never knew Maclean very well, although he met him occasionally at Washington cocktail parties. He also attended a farewell party for Maclean in the latter's home in Washington, D. C. in the summer of 1948, at which forty or fifty people were present. He recalled "Maclean as pleasant and easy going but not tense and not garrulous."

According to AEC logs, Maclean first visited AEC headquarters on August 6, 1947, and then on average twice each month until June, 1948, when his last visit occurred on June 11. The special meeting on declassification, with Fuchs in attendance, took place on November 14, 15 and 16, 1947. It is not yet known whether Maclean and Fuchs knew of one another's dual reporting activities. On the other hand, Fuchs's arrest, and his severe sentence on March 1, 1950, may have influenced Maclean's thinking about his future if he had remained in England.

Senator Eastland, whose views on prospects for peaceful co-existence with the Soviet Union were referred to above, on February 21, 1956, wrote a letter to the State Department asking: "'From 1944 to 1948 Maclean was Head of Chancery here and in that post was alleged to be fully acquainted with all the secrets of relations between the United States and Britain and with information regarding atomic policy. True or false?' . . .

The State Department replied: "In February 1947, Maclean was designated by his government to act as the United Kingdom's secretary on the Combined Policy Committee which was concerned with atomic energy matters and composed of representatives of the US, UK and Canada. In this position he had an opportunity to have access to information shared by the three participating countries in the fields of patents, declassification matters and research and development relating to the programme of procurement of raw material from foreign sources by the Combined Development Agency, including estimates of supplies and requirements. During the course of negotiations which resulted in the *Modus Vivendi* concerning atomic energy matters followed by the three governments after January 1948 Maclean in his official capacity had access to information relating to the estimates made at that time of ore supply available to the three governments, requirements of uranium for the atomic energy programmes of the three governments for the period from 1948 to 1952, and the definition of scientific areas in which the three governments deemed technical co-operation could be accomplished with mutual benefit."[5]

There is more detail now available.

The Minister at the Washington Embassy, to whom Maclean reported on his arrival in Washington in 1944, was Roger Makins, later Lord Sherfield. In July, 1945, Makins became Joint Secretary of the Combined Policy Committee on atomic energy. He "was the leading member of the very small group of Washington diplomats, including his successor, Donald Maclean, who knew anything about atomic matters."[6] If Makins was "Mr. Atom," as Jill Edwards called him, the keeper of the nuclear secrets, then Maclean, as his successor, had comparable knowledge, a comparable role in the vicissitudes of the Anglo-American atomic dialogue. Maclean became the United Kingdom's secretary on the Combined Policy Committee in 1947. The Combined Development Trust, subordinate to the Combined Policy Committee (CPC), was charged with accumulating and allocating world-wide supplies of uranium.[7] It was successful. "By the end of 1944 the Combined Development Trust (CDT), had achieved a virtual monopoly of atomic raw materials outside of the Soviet Union and areas occupied by the Red Army . . ." Donald Maclean's participation in the meetings of the CDT was also successful. Based on his knowledge of the activities of the CDT, "Maclean may also have had access to [reports concerning] the amounts of raw materials gathered and used. This intelligence would enable the Soviets to make a rough estimate of how many bombs were produced in 1944-45, and how many were being planned for the future."[8]

An early British move in the conflict between the British and American governments over the desire of the latter to monopolize the field of atomic energy came at a meeting of the Combined Policy Committee on October 13, 1945 (including Makins but not Maclean), when Lord Halifax announced that the "British Government proposes to set up a Research Establishment in the United Kingdom to deal with all aspects of atomic energy."[9] The American government thought this a very bad idea. Among other drawbacks, what would happen to this enterprise and its products if Britain were occupied by the Soviet Union? The British Government thought that if Britain were occupied by the Soviet Union the status of the atomic energy research establishment would not be high up on the list of important issues for whatever remained of the British Empire. The following month, as Admiral Strauss recalled, at "the time of the conference on atomic energy between Attlee and McKenzie-King [Prime Minister of Canada] and Truman . . .

> Mr. Attlee as he then was, came over—he was very much concerned, as indeed we all were, with the international control of the bomb. This was in November 1945. They had a conference about international control, which was the starting point for the negotiations which later took place on the Baruch plan; and they also discussed the continuance of the collaboration in the atomic energy field between the United Kingdom and this country. Indeed it was thought that Mr. Truman had agreed to continue collaboration, but it finally broke down in the following year with the passage on the McMahon Act . . . I don't think [Truman] did grasp the atomic energy point about collaboration. I don't think he quite realized what the

underlying issue was there, but then he'd only been in office for a week or so—a very short time . . .[10]

Discussions concerning the regulation and control of nuclear energy matters had begun in the American Congress shortly after Truman became President. On the issue of the allocation of materials, the US representatives to the Combined Policy Committee stated that the United States had no reserves of materials and would soon have to start shutting down the operation of its plants. To avoid this, the US began to make large demands on Britain, which, with Belgium, *did* hold significant stocks of uranium. At the Combined Policy Committee meeting on April 15, 1946, the refusal of the US to continue full cooperation with the UK and Canada became clear.[11] On April 17, 1946, Sir James Chadwick in Washington wrote a top secret letter to Sir John Anderson in London that "negotiations with the U.S. for a new agreement on co-operation are completely blocked . . .

> My view that the present position is extremely serious . . . is confirmed by my reading of the new draft of the McMahon bill for the control of atomic energy . . . As I read it . . . the bill seems almost to exclude the possibility of collaboration with us except by the expressed approval of Senate or Congress . . . to prevent the transmission of information which we require . . . to prevent our acquiring material from the U.S. . . . and the position with regard to patents and invents . . . seems to bristle with difficulties."[12]

Chadwick's reading of the situation was correct. Truman cabled Attlee on April 20, 1946, declaring that he had not meant to allow Britain to be provided with information necessary to build a nuclear reactor, even though he had signed a document saying so.[13] Further discussions were held in which the U.S. asserted rights to all obtainable uranium and thorium (a naturally radioactive mineral). Frustrated by the American government's growing reluctance to continue atomic cooperation, the British Government secretly began work on a nuclear reactor and research program at Harwell in April, 1946.[14] On May 2, 1946, a cable from the British Joint Staff Mission in Washington to Sir John Anderson gave estimates of supplies of uranium in a proposed UK compromise: US, 2,757 tons; U.K., 1,350 tons.[15] The numbers were likely to have been seen by Maclean and, and if so, to have reached Moscow.

The McMahon Bill was passed by the Senate of on June 1, 1946, by the House of Representatives on July 20, and signed by the President as the Atomic Energy Act of 1946 on August 1, 1946. In addition to setting up the Atomic Energy Commission as the successor to the Manhattan Project, it included the draconian provisions against the dissemination of information in regard to the construction of nuclear reactors and atomic bombs feared by Chadwick, effectively banning US cooperation with Britain and Canada. Attlee sent a strong message to Truman on June 6, 1946, laying out the history of nuclear cooperation and implicitly accusing the US of breaking a series of agreements and understandings and coming close to stating that Truman had lied to him about the issues.[16] There was no reply from Truman. On October 28, 1946, the war-time Manhattan District became the Atomic Energy Commission. Admiral Lewis Strauss, first head of the AEC, recalled that "it was a smooth transfer, with one minor exception.

> From the point of view of the transfer of property—and by property I also include uranium and bombs—*there were no bombs*...[a] particular surprise in view of the statement that had been made after the second bomb had been dropped on Nagasaki. The President gave the Japanese to understand that if they did not surrender, there would be more of the same . . . [t]he people who made the bomb, both the Army and the navy, and the scientists were pretty well convinced that the last war had been fought and won and that there was no more need to spend any money[17] (Emphasis added).

The first meeting of the Combined Policy Committee for which Maclean's presence is noted in the Foreign Relations of the United States (FRUS) was that of February 3, 1947, Maclean substituting for Roger Makins. An indication of the importance of these meetings is the level of the others present: James Byrnes, the Secretary of

State; Robert Patterson, the Secretary of War; Dr. Vannevar Bush, Director of the Office of Scientific Research and Development; the British (Inverchapel) and Canadian (H. H. Wrong) ambassadors; Field Marshal Lord Wilson; Dean Acheson and members of the Committee staff. There was no more senior group in Washington. At the February 3$^{rd}$ meeting Acheson made an official announcement of the establishment of the Atomic Energy Commission. There was discussion of thorium supplies and a review of procedures about sharing patents, when and if that became possible, given security concerns.

Two days later the United States Ambassador in Belgium (Kirk) sent to Undersecretary Acheson a translation of a memorandum from Spaak, the Belgian Prime Minister, stating that "the uranium question" was being increasingly discussed in the press and in political circles and that the Belgian public were aware that the entire uranium production of the Belgian Congo was sold to the United States. Spaak was sure that he would soon be asked about the matter—whether there was a secret treaty covering it and what were its terms—and wished to have guidance on what he should say, if asked. (A complicating issue was that the Belgian government included Communist ministers.) Spaak also referred to the desire of the Belgian government to have the United States facilitate atomic research by Belgian scientists. Secretary Marshall replied, in regard to the research issue, that this could only be done when and if control of nuclear matters was assumed by the United Nations (which, of course, never happened). Apparently as part of an attempted compromise, a message of January 31 from Maclean to his usual American contact on atomic energy matters, Edmund A. Gullion, Special Assistant to Acheson, stated in part that "in the event of the two Governments [U.S. and U.K.] deciding to utilize as a source of energy for commercial purposes, ores obtained under the Agreement, they would admit the Belgian Government to participation in such utilization on equitable terms . . ."[18] Continuing this exchange of messages concerning Spaak's initiative, Gullion wrote a top secret memorandum to Acheson on February 18, 1947, describing a

239

meeting with Maclean. At the meeting Maclean conveyed the Foreign Office's thought that it was "unfortunate" that the State Department had cited the McMahon Act when turning down Spaak's question about Belgian participation in atomic research: "The British felt that this might cause the Belgians to question our good faith in making the Belgian accord." Gullion "took the occasion to point out that this same restriction which prevented us from complying with the Belgian request was also one which appeared to prevent our transmitting to the British certain information requested by them."[19]

On March 10th, Gullion provided to Maclean the American rejection of French participation in a "patents' pool," as suggested by Professor Joliot-Curie, France's High Commissioner for Atomic Energy, once again citing the McMahon Act.[*] In a related issue, Gullion informed Acheson in a top secret memorandum of June 5th that, "As he does at frequent intervals, Mr. Maclean asked me if any progress could be reported on the British desire to secure from this country information relating to the construction of a large-scale atomic energy plant in Britain . . . I said nothing to give Mr. Maclean any impression as to whether we would or would not have resolved the problem by September."[20]

By mid-1947, the war plan "PINCHER, already a year old, assumed an availability of fifty atomic bombs. 'However . . . there were still only thirteen.

> By then members of the joint Congressional Committee on atomic energy were hot on the trail of the secret agreements, and Donald Maclean . . . was warned that these could be contained no longer. Acheson's revelations to the Senate Joint Committee on 12 May were humiliating: not only did the British know how to make the bomb, but half the supplies of uranium essential for production were legally going to Britain under arrangements hitherto concealed from Congress. Worse, the British had the

---

[*] Joliot-Curie's suggestion, given his loyalty to the French Communist Party, likely would have resulted in the de facto inclusion of the Soviet Union in the patents pool. See TNA file: KV 2/3686.

reciprocal right under the wartime agreement to veto American use of the bomb . . . The reaction of powerful senators, Hickenlooper, Vandenberg and Connolly, was immediate and predictable: in return for financial assistance Britain must renounce her 50 per cent share of Congo ore . . . This was to remain policy until September [1947]."[21]

A September 11, 1947 meeting between the leading members of the American Cabinet and important Department of State officials, including Lovett, Bohlen, Kennan, Gullion and Rusk, discussed whether aid to Britain and Belgium should be used as a lever to ensure cooperation over uranium supplies. Kennan and others argued against doing so. Those present at the meeting also favored continuing cooperation on atomic energy matters with Canada and the United Kingdom.[22] Nonetheless, in November 1947 there was a "rising crescendo of 'hints' from the Americans that unless the British concluded an agreement quickly, atomic energy negotiations would be 'caught up' in Congress in the ERP ["Marshall Plan] debate."

> The administration would then be unable to prevent Congress demanding heavy uranium penalties as a quid pro quo for aid . . . [on December 4, 1947] Maclean briefed Makins on the strategic element believed to be on the agenda and the inclusion in the talks of George Kennan . . . regarded as well disposed to Britain . . . but it was all too clear the Authorization Bill on which Marshall Aid depended meant British acquiescence on uranium.[23]

In November 1947 Maclean was given the pass allowing him to enter the Atomic Energy Commission (AEC) building and move about unescorted, presumably on his way to meetings with with AEC officials.

Maclean participated as a member of the Secretariat (that is, he helped keep the minutes, probably in two copies) in the meeting of the Combined Policy Committee on December 10th, 1947, occasioned by the Atomic Energy Act's change in the nature of the relationship among the U.S., the U.K. and Canada. The Americans having called the meeting, Acting Secretary of State Robert Lovett began by outlining three areas of interest: the exchange of information, as limited by the United States Atomic Energy Act; raw materials, and a public announcement of the resumption of U.S.-U.K.-Canada talks on atomic energy matters.[24] A couple of days later, on December 12th, 1947, Maclean gave Carroll Wilson, Chairman of the Combined Development Trust, "Notes on Conversation Between the British Prime Minister (Attlee) and the South African Prime Minister (Smuts)," with the comment that the conversation had occurred "two weeks ago." The document is marked top secret. The conversation had concerned extraction of uranium on a commercial scale in South Africa, which, it seems, was soon to begin in conjunction with gold mining operations.[25] Another meeting of the Combined Policy Committee occurred on December 15th, 1947, again with Maclean as part of the Secretariat. The Committee discussed progress in the exchange of information; reports on the supply and requirements situation of materials, among which uranium was significant; standards of security, nomenclature and the basis of future cooperation. In the course of the discussion of materials, Secretary of Defense Forrestal "pointed out that as a result of the military planning of the United States, the Joint Chiefs of Staff have put demands on the Atomic Energy Commission for increased production . . ." During a discussion of the basis for future cooperation Maclean was appointed to the drafting committee for a paper setting out the intent and purpose of the Committee.[26]

The Combined Policy Committee met again on January 7, 1948, with the usual high-level participants, as well as Roger Makins, now Assistant Under Secretary of State, British Foreign Office, Kennan and Maclean. In his concluding remarks to this meeting, Lord Inverchapel "said that the declarations made and decision taken at the meeting inaugurated a new and hopeful chapter in the association of the three countries [U.S., U.K. and Canada] in atomic energy development.

He expressed appreciation of the frank and helpful attitude which had been shown during the discussions and said that the

U.K. members were deeply impressed by Mr. Forrestal's statement at the Committee's last meeting [December 15, 1947] that he regarded the United Kingdom and Canada as partners in the field of atomic energy . . . The United Kingdom expected this partnership to develop and extend rapidly.[27]

The declarations and decisions referred to were in a draft proposal decided on at the CPC meeting of December 15th. The drafting group included, among others, Gullion for the US, Maclean for the United Kingdom and George Ignatieff for Canada. The agreement stated that the CPC would continue as the group for dealing with atomic energy problems of common concern. It stated that the "Committee shall *inter alia:*

(a) Allocate raw materials in accordance with such principles as may be determined from time to time by the Committee, taking into account all supplies available to any of the three governments.

(b) Consider general questions arising with respect to cooperation among the three governments.

(c) Supervise the operations and policies of the Combined Development Agency . . .

The agreement continued the Combined Development Trust agreed to by Roosevelt and Churchill on June 13, 1944, renaming it the Combined Development Agency. Under the new agreement the United States, the United Kingdom and Canada would "use every effort to acquire control of supplies of uranium and thorium" in their territories and that the United Kingdom would facilitate this with the Governments of the British Commonwealth. The agreement listed policies concerning, and amounts of allocations of, supplies. In 1948 and 1949 all supplies from the Belgian Congo would go to the U.S. If these were insufficient to maintain the U.S. "minimum program," they will be topped up from the supplies then in the United Kingdom. The U.S. requirements were listed as 2,547 tons in each year. The United Kingdom's requirement was listed as 2,030 for the two years together.[28]

The agreement also included security measures.

Kerr summarizes these matters as follows: "In August the AEC restored cooperation on the declassification of information, culminating in a conference in November . . .

In December, they concluded a new arrangement, the "modus vivendi". The modus vivendi cancelled all of the wartime agreements except for the agreement on raw materials . . . Maclean was present at the CPC in February when they examined the figures of the raw materials programme, between 1946 and 1948. From these figures the Soviets could calculate the numbers of atomic bombs in the American arsenal . . . We now know that America had thirteen nuclear warheads at the end of 1947. Not all of these were ready for use, and neither were the delivery vehicles, modified B-29 bombers.[29]

Maclean knew, and therefore presumably Stalin knew, that as 1948 began the American atomic big stick was not big enough to be a deciding factor in the event of a military conflict.

On March 19, 1948 Gullion sent a top secret memorandum to Lovett, the Under Secretary of State, of a conversation with Maclean. It must have come as an unpleasant surprise to Lovett: "He states that he was directed to inform the Department that since the beginning of last year United Kingdom had been engaged on research and development work in atomic weapons . . . by a special section of the Ministry of Supply under Lord Portal." Maclean told Gullion that the British were about to make this publicly known, as it was becoming increasingly difficult to keep it completely secret and the secrecy was interfering with the work. The Foreign Office was not asking for State Department comment. The announcement was made on May 12. It was a declaration of British nuclear research independence from the United States. That independence pertained only to research. Otherwise, Britain remained dependent on American atomic weaponry.

Soon after Maclean's departure from London in the Spring of 1951, Hoover asked the Atomic Energy Commission for a description of "the extent of damage done through Maclean representing the British Embassy during 1947 and 1948 on matters dealing with the political aspects of atomic energy and through his work on the Combined Development Agency." Mr. Algie Aaron Wells, an attorney in the office of the General Counsel of the Atomic Energy Commission, assured the FBI "that generally Maclean had in is possession all information concerning atomic energy of a political nature which was made available by the Atomic Energy Commission to the British Embassy. Mr. Wells did not feel that Maclean had scientific information concerning atomic energy matters." Not that it mattered. Admiral Strauss recalled that "We had a number of meetings on the subject of Anglo-American cooperation and finally worked out a *modus vivendi*, which was to give the British the kind of information that they would need for defense (so-called weapons effects), and non-weapons applications.

> But they had their own scientists here who had worked in our laboratories and who knew nearly everything about it. One of those scientists was a naturalized British subject by the name of Klaus Fuchs. So not only did the British know, but Dr. Fuchs, when he confessed, said he had given everything to the Russians as fast as he got it. So the whole question of sharing information with the British turned out to be academic.[30]

A letter from the Atomic Energy Commission to Hoover, date-stamped July 1, 1951, stated that, "assuming that Maclean was either a Soviet agent or has defected to the Soviet Union . . . as the United Kingdom's Secretary of the Combined Policy Committee concerned with atomic energy matters . . .

> Maclean's duties involved the handling with his Canadian and American counterparts of those atomic energy matters of concern to his Government . . . In connection with those duties, Maclean had opportunity to have access to the information shared by the several countries in the fields of patents, declassification matters, and the research and development relating to the procurement and beneficiation [       ] materials from foreign sources by the Combined Development Agency . . . In his capacity as UK Secretary of the CPC he took part in the negotiations which resulted in the Modus Vivendi which governs

the atomic energy relations about the three governments since January 1948. During the course of these negotiations, Maclean had access to information relating to the estimates made at that time of ore supply available to the three governments through 1952; requirements of uranium for the atomic energy programs within the three governments during that period; and the definition of scientific areas in which the three governments deemed technical cooperation could be accomplished with mutual benefit . . . Some of the information available to Maclean in 1947-48 was classified Top Secret and would then have been of interest to the Soviet Union . . .

The AEC's letter concluded: "we do not believe that the information available to Maclean in 1947-48 would now be of any appreciable aid to the Soviet Union because of the changes in the rate and scale of the United States program which have taken place in the intervening years." Hoover commented in ink on another memorandum that "It is obvious that AEC is not particularly cooperative in this matter."

The "information available to Maclean in 1947-48" would have interested the Soviet leadership in various ways, to some extent confirming Stalin's prediction of a postwar falling-out between the U.S. and the British Empire and providing some indication of the scale of the U.S. atom bomb construction activities. Pavel Sudoplatov (or his collaborators), an occasionally informative source, claimed that "The information Fuchs gave us in 1948 coincided with Maclean's reports from Washington on America's limited nuclear potential, not sufficient to wage an all-out and prolonged war."[31] It is hardly coincidental that there were, for example, notable Soviet activities in the Belgian Congo (the chief uranium source) at that time as well as Communist Party agitation in Belgium, which controlled the uranium exports from the Congo. Maclean's information provided Stalin with an important view into British and American policy that was not paralleled by information about the Soviet Union available—as far as we know—to London or Washington planners and policymakers. It is therefore likely that some of Stalin's decisions, concerning, say, Berlin, were facilitated by this superior information source, while the decisions of planners and policymakers in Washington and London proceeded more or less in the dark as to Soviet capabilities and intentions.

## Atomic Energy: Notes

[1] http://avalon.law.yale.edu/wwii/q003.asp

[2] Oral History Interview with Admiral Lewis L. Strauss. Harry S. Truman Library & Museum, http://www.trumanlibrary.org/oralhist/strauss.htm, accessed December 5, 2013.

[3] Acheson, Dean. Present at the Creation: My Years in the State Department. New York: W.W. Norton & Company, Inc., p. 164.

[4] According to an FBI document of 11/7/55, the Joint Commission on Atomic Energy met in the AEC building, hence Maclean's pass.

[5] Page, Bruce, Leitch, David and Phillip Knightley. Philby: The Spy Who Betrayed a Generation. London: Andre Deutsch, 1968, pp. 182-3.

[6] Edwards, Jill. "Roger Makins: 'Mr Atom'" in Zametica, p. 13.

[7] Cecil, p. 71.

[8] Kerr, pp. 111-2.

[9] FO 115/4232.

[10] Brooks, Philip C. Oral History Interview with Sir Roger Makins. Harry S. Truman Library & Museum, http://www.trumanlibrary.org/oralhist/makins1.htm, accessed December 5, 2013.

[11] FRUS 1946, vol. I, pp. 1227-31.

[12] Bullen, Roger and Pelly, pp. 250-1.

[13] Bullen, Roger and Pelly, pp. 260-1.

[14] Edwards, Jill. "Roger Makins: 'Mr Atom'" in Zametica, p. 15.

[15] Bullen, Roger and Pelly, p. 273.

[16] Bullen, Roger and Pelly, pp. 339-43.

[17] Oral History Interview with Admiral Lewis L. Strauss. Harry S. Truman Library & Museum, http://www.trumanlibrary.org/oralhist/strauss.htm, accessed December 5, 2013.

[18] FRUS, 1947, Volume I, pp. 792-4

[19] FRUS, 1947, Volume I, pp. 795-6.

[20] FRUS, 1947, Volume I, p. 817.

[21] Edwards, Jill. "Roger Makins: 'Mr Atom'" in Zametica, p. 17.

[22] FRUS, 1947, Volume I, pp. 838ff.

[23] Edwards, Jill. "Roger Makins: 'Mr Atom'" in Zametica, pp. 30-1, citing FO371/62802 UE12106/1830/50, Maclean to Makins, 4 December 1947.

[24] FRUS, 1947, Volume I, p. 889ff.

[25] FRUS, 1947, Volume I, pp. 895-6.

[26] FRUS, 1947, Volume I, pp. 897-903.

[27] FRUS, 1948, Volume I, pp. 679 ff. Forrestal was eager to complete revised agreement in order that the United States would be free to step up atom bomb production. Forrestal, James. The Forrestal Diaries. Edited by Walter Millis. New York: The Viking Press, 1951, p. 339.

[28] FRUS, 1948, Volume I, pp. 683-7.

[29] Kerr, pp. 213-4.

[30] Oral History Interview with Admiral Lewis L. Strauss. Harry S. Truman Library & Museum, http://www.trumanlibrary.org/oralhist/strauss.htm, accessed December 5, 2013.

[31] Sudoplatov, Pavel and Anatoli Sudoplatov. Special Tasks: The Memoirs of an Unwanted Witness—A Soviet Spymaster. Boston: Little, Brown and Company, 1994, p. 209.

We have now reviewed much of Donald Maclean's activities on behalf of the British, American and Soviet governments during the time that he and Melinda Maclean spent in Washington: civil aviation, island bases, Greek and Turkish affairs, post-hostilities planning, the first moves in the Cold War, atomic energy. The last few months of the Macleans's time in Washington were dominated by the Berlin Crisis and the formation of NATO, which froze in place the European map of the Cold War.

Having secured the American administration's commitment to economic support for Western Europe,[1] Bevin, without waiting for the Congressional approval of the Marshall Plan that would not come until April, 1948, moved toward a military alliance. According to Peter Boyle, "Bevin was endeavouring, in 1948, to influence the main lines of American foreign policy, setting the United States on a course of international involvement to deter Soviet expansion."[2] The December, 1947, meeting of the Council of Foreign Ministers (of the United States, the United Kingdom, France and the Soviet Union) had failed to reach agreement on a joint policy for Germany. The day of the breakdown of the Conference, December 15th, Bevin proposed "the formation of some form of union, formal or informal in character, in Western Europe backed by the United States and the Dominions."[3] The "Western Union" was to be "a sort of spiritual federation" of the West.[4] This was put into writing in a summary sent to Marshall by Inverchapel on January 13, 1948. It called for a mutual assistance treaty—against possible *German* aggression—between Britain and France, Belgium, Holland and Luxembourg, envisioning expansion to include Italy, "other Mediterranean countries, and Scandinavia. "In this way Mr. Bevin plans to link together the non-communist countries of Western Europe with the Middle East."[5] Bevin's memorandum added that: "As soon as circumstances permit we should, of course, wish to include Spain and Germany, without whom no Western system can be complete."[6] Spaak, the Belgian premier, immediately saw the proposal as a screen for an anti-Soviet alliance, while the American Department of

State was puzzled by the anti-German format. On January 27, Inverchapel summarized Bevin's position in a letter to Lovett, the Under Secretary of State: "Mr. Bevin's basic conception is briefly to achieve economic consolidation of the West through the European Recovery Programme [the Marshall Plan] and at the same time to call into being a Western political system founded upon the common way of life of the Western democracies and reinforced by the efforts which will be made to combat Communism in the territories concerned . . . But the treaties that are being proposed cannot be fully effective . . . unless there is assurance of American support for the defence of Europe."[7] He then quoted Bevin as calling for secret talks in Washington between representatives of the State Department and the Foreign Office and their respective military staffs.

The State Department thought that Bevin was going too fast, particularly as the ERP had not yet been approved. However, on February 21, 1948, the non-Communist ministers in the government of Czechoslovakia submitted their resignations to the Communist Prime Minster, Gottwald, over the issue of the staffing of the police with Communists, initiating a crisis. Gottwald declared that there was a plot against the state, setting off massive pro-Communist demonstrations. President Bênes accepted the resignations of the non-Communist ministers. The Social Democrats and others agreed to serve as minority members of a government in which the Communists held the key ministries. The country was declared "a people's democracy" on May 9, 1948. "On February 27, the day after the Prague coup, Stalin demanded from Finland the conclusion of the same kind of mutual defense treaty that tied to the Soviet Union its already subjugated Eastern European dependencies; in the next few days, Norway received warnings that a similar request might be forthcoming.

> Yet when the time came for the Finns to discuss the treaty in Moscow at the beginning of April, they were surprised to find Stalin satisfied with a much more benign document, merely obliging them to consult in case of a foreign threat to their country and defend its integrity. In changing his mind, Stalin

251

may have been influenced by his awareness of the secret proposal, prepared in the Canadian foreign ministry by Assistant Undersecretary of State Escott Reid, to include Finland in the planned Western military alliance—a bit of information that Maclean was in a position to relay to his Soviet paymasters [sic]. In any case, the impetus that the communist seizure of power in Prague had unwittingly given to Western alliance-building was a sufficient reason for abstaining from an action likely to encourage the process.[8]

After the Communist coup in Czechoslovakia, sentiment in the State Department, which had been cool toward Bevin's proposals, changed. On March 8, Hickerson, Director of the Office of European Affairs, recommended to the Secretary of State consideration of "The possibility of U.S. participation in a North Atlantic-Mediterranean regional defense arrangement." A few days later Bevin used rumors of a Soviet move on Norway to press for an Atlantic military alliance. On March 12, 1948 Marshall wrote to Inverchapel that he should "inform Mr. Bevin that . . . we are prepared to proceed at once in the joint discussions on the establishment of an Atlantic security system . . . I suggest the prompt arrival of the British representative early next week." [9] Bevin accepted on the 14th. The Treaty of Brussels, creating an alliance of Britain, France, Belgium, Luxembourg and the Netherlands, ostensibly as a defense against any revived German aggression, was signed "on 18 March [1948] and it was warmly welcomed by Truman.

This was an important signal to the Soviets as they were convinced that the strength of Western Europe depended upon American economic and military support. On 13 March, Maclean knew Marshall had agreed to discuss, in secret, an American military commitment to West European security with the British and Canadians. At the Pentagon talks, 22 March to 1 April, Maclean learned that, if the alliance was formed, its composition, and the conditions in which it would fight, would radically alter the balance of power in Europe to the advantage of the West.[10]

The top secret "Minutes of the First Meeting of the United States-United Kingdom-Canada Security Conversations" of March 22, 1948, listed as present for the U.S. Ambassador Lewis Douglas and Major General Alfred Gruenther, Joint Chiefs of Staff, among others; the British were represented by Ambassador Inverchapel, Gladwyn Jebb, Robert Cecil, Donald Maclean and two generals; Canada by Ambassador Pearson and others. Inverchapel and Jebb stated that a firm commitment "on the part of the US to aid militarily in the event of any aggression in Europe" was necessary before talks got go any further. The Americans replied that this would necessitate Congressional action, which was problematic and discussions had not yet begun, but that "US full support should be *assumed.*" Ambassador Douglas stated that it would be useful to begin by discussing "the various types of defense pacts which might be adopted to extend resistance to the Communistic threat": an extension of the Brussels pact, an Atlantic pact, and a world-wide pact. "It was agreed that the first order of business would be to explore the pros and cons in connection with the various types of common-defense pacts."[11] A cover plan for the meetings was improvised. Jebb was to said to be in the U.S. for meetings of the United Nations in New York and would make occasional appearances there. Ambassador Douglas proposed that the conversations should be based on the assumption of U.S. military support. This first conversation was in the main concerned with the type of alliance (regional or world-wide) that was to be devised.[12]

The group met on the 23rd of March in the absence of the American and British ambassadors, again wrestling with the nature and extent of the military pact contemplated, and yet again on the 24th, by which time a drafting committee had been created for a "Security Pact for the North Atlantic Area." The Canadian, British and American ambassadors were back for the fourth meeting on March 29, 1948, which solidified the concept of a pact to resist the expansion of Communist influence. There was another drafting meeting on the 31st (considering such questions as "should

*Spitzbergen* be included in the pact?") and a final meeting on April 1, 1948, which approved the Final Draft of a paper laying out "a collective defense agreement for the North Atlantic Area."[13] The main thrust of the paper was that the President would consider an armed attack against any signatory as an attack against the United States.

The motivation for the NATO treaty was to counter the *political* offensive of the Soviet Union, such as the Czechoslovakian ministerial coup and the Finnish treaty, with *military* power. In retrospect, this was a nearly inexplicable asymmetrical response. The Red Army had withdrawn from Czechoslovakia in December 1945.[14] According to Russian historian Vladimir Pechatnov, by "1948, the Red Army was reduced to one-quarter of its 1945 strength, and the military budget of 1946-47 was only half of its wartime peak . . . contrary to American assumptions, Soviet contingency plans did not envision any offensive operations in Western Europe, concentrating instead on holding the line of defense in Germany."[15] Was this known to British and American planners at the time? Perhaps. Perhaps Secretary of State Marshall agreed with the opinion expressed by one of his successors: "I don't see why we need to stand by and watch a country go communist due to the irresponsibility of its people. The issues are much too important for [those] voters to be left to decide for themselves." In that case Henry Kissinger was referring not to Italy (or Greece or Spain), but to Chile. The sentiments in Washington in 1948 were similar.

On May 18, 1948, Maclean called on the Chief of the Division of Western European Affairs, Achilles [sic], saying "that the Embassy had received another message from Bevin to the Secretary but had discretion as to whether or not to present it." Bevin was again urging the United States to negotiate a treaty "for the security of the North Atlantic Area." The hesitation was because Bohlen and Kennan had told "Jock" Balfour that a treaty was not desirable and that a query would result in a reply that the United States was not willing to conclude such a treaty. Achilles repeated the advice of Bohlen and Kennan. That morning Maclean and John Henderson, Second

Secretary at the British Embassy, met with Donald Blaisdell, Assistant to Dean Rusk, then Director of the Office of United Nations Affairs. Blaisdell brought Gullion and two of his colleagues into the meeting. Maclean and Henderson gave Blaisdell an aide-mémoire from the Foreign Office recommending the suspension of the work of the United Nations Atomic Energy Commission, the Commission for Conventional Armaments, and the Military Staff Committee. The aide-mémoire gave as Bevin's view that no progress had been made by the three groups, implicitly because of Soviet obstructionism. It stated, *inter alia,* that

> His Majesty's Government must of course be ready to counter vigorously accusations by the Soviet Government that the machinery as well as the atmosphere of peace is being destroyed by an organized conspiracy. His Majesty's Government's general line on this might be ... that they are most anxious to make progress, that no one disputes the right of the Soviet Government to its own views, but that they have so far shown themselves quite unwilling to try to adjust those views to the views of other governments.[16]

Kerr found that "Gladwyn Jebb, who led the British team in the Atlantic Pact negotiations described Maclean as his chief embassy advisor who took the minutes of all the meetings in March and April.

> It is evident that Maclean had access to all the documents as the records show that his signature authorised telegrams which were sent to London coded in the highest classification. Maclean knew everything about these discussions . . . He also attended the first meeting of the Washington Exploratory Talks, in July, and probably followed their progress until he left in September. Maclean's most important function was to liaise with State Department officials: Maclean was considered to have excellent political sense, especially about the Americans, and had a reputation as a shrewd and skilled negotiator.[17]

\* \* \*

That summer the Berlin Crisis appeared to bring the world to the verge of war. In a Cabinet meeting on 27 July, 1948, Bevin "said that the main problem was how to improve our state of preparedness against the possibility that an emergency might arise in the course of the next two to three months . . . The United Kingdom could not contemplate embarking single-handed on a war against the Soviet Union. It was therefore essential that all concerned, and particularly the United States, should realise that such a war would be primarily a United States undertaking and that the role of the United Kingdom would be bound to be subsidiary." Releases from the British armed forces were suspended. Civil defense arrangements were moved to a war footing.[18] In a Cabinet meeting on July 30, 1948, "The Chief of the Air Staff [Lord Tedder] said that the possibility that war might break out in a matter of weeks must be faced." That was the most intense point of impending conflict. The sense of emergency then gradually ebbed, for a time.

The occupation regime in Germany following the war combined a territorial division—the British in the northwest, the Americans in the south, the Soviets in the east (and eventually a smaller French presence in two areas on the west), with a set of joint arrangements, governing, at first, reparations, and, of great symbolic importance, the occupation of Berlin. None of this was stable. The great German industrial machine was idle, entire factories from the Soviet zone dismantled and shipped east (and others dismantled and shipped west); the shrunken country filled with refugees from areas now Polish or Czech, housed in displaced persons camps side by side with former slave laborers and survivors of the Holocaust. The currency of the Third Reich, plentiful enough among a population that had battened on the spoils of war, was worthless. At the beginning of 1948 Bevin was in favor of introducing a new currency in all four occupation zones of Germany and "was strongly opposed to American pressure to end dismantling and with it the payment of reparations, including reparations to the Soviet Union."[19] On the other hand, a statement by the British and American military

256

proconsuls at a meeting in Frankfurt on January 7-8 seemed to point toward an Anglo-American plan for a separate government for West Germany. The Soviets objected, citing their proposal the previous month for a central German government, which had been rejected by the Americans, British and French.[20] The French also objected, Bevin denied any knowledge of the plan, and the Military Governors implemented the framework for quasi-governmental mechanisms in West Germany on February 9.

The Soviets proposed at a meeting on February 11 of the Allied Control Council (ACC) to begin steps for a new currency for all of Germany, which was agreed to by the other members. Frank Wisner, then Deputy to the Assistant Secretary of State for Occupied Areas, later director of covert operations for the C.I.A., sent a memorandum to Lovett on March 10, stating that "we may be approaching agreement in the ACC on quadripartite currency reform for all of Germany." But, he went on, "The question arises whether this is desirable from a US standpoint . . . It is considered that the institution of currency reform on a bizonal (or tripartite) basis . . . would represent a very definite move toward recognition of the East-West partition of Germany . . . A decision in this regard is one which should be taken at the top level within the [State] Department." Lovett approved the change in policy from quadripartite to bizonal currency on March 11.[21] "Analyzing developments, the Soviet Foreign Ministry concluded that 'the Western powers are transforming Germany into their stronghold and including it in the newly formed military-political bloc, directed against the Soviet Union and the new democracies."[22]

The substitution for the Reichsmark of a new currency, only valid in the American and British zones of occupation, likely would have resulted in a flood of the old currency into the Soviet zone of Berlin, where it remained valid, if increasingly worthless. For that and other reasons Stalin decided to blockade the non-Soviet occupation zones of Berlin. "The first steps to cut off Berlin from the West were taken in March 1948 but were described as temporary interruptions due to the need for repairs. The blockade of the

Western sectors was not complete until August. Each step was followed by a pause to assess the danger of war which the Russians correctly concluded no one in the West wanted to risk any more than they themselves did."[23] Kerr observed that "Before the blockade began, Maclean could give the Soviets a clear indication of Western plans and an accurate assessment of Western capabilities.

> During the crisis Maclean continued to provide the Soviets with crucial information. Britain and America expected the Soviets to take counter-measures against the currency reform. Western leaders announced they would stay in Berlin, but their projected image of determination was partly undermined by Western officials publicly airing their doubts about whether staying was in fact desirable or possible.[24]

On April 1, the United States Political Adviser for Germany (Robert D. Murphy) predicted that the "Soviets may move obliquely endeavoring [to] make it increasingly impossible or unprofitable for western powers to remain on, for example, by interfering with slender communication lines between Berlin and western zones . . ."[25] That same day the Soviets began making demands for increased control of train traffic. On April 5 a British civil passenger aircraft attempting a landing in Berlin was struck by a Soviet fighter. Both aircraft crashed. It was apparently accidental.

Churchill, out of office, told the American Ambassador in the United Kingdom in mid-April that he thought that the U.S. should "tell the Soviet that if they do not retire from Berlin and abandon Eastern Germany, withdrawing to the Polish frontier, we will raze their cities."[26] On April 27th, US and UK representatives in London discussed whether, or at what point, either would either use force or go to war to preserve the status quo in Berlin. Both governments took the position that force would be used, but not necessarily to the point of going to war.[27] Attlee was still Prime Minister.

By the beginning of June the American government had decided on a financial reform for the Western occupation zones (but not Berlin) to begin on June 20 with the substitution of new currency for old, with the Soviet occupation authorities to be informed on June

18. The Soviet reaction was to institute a blockade of ground traffic to Berlin from the Western zones to protect Soviet zone from inflows of old currency.[28] Bevin, fetched back from a holiday, met with Douglas, the American Ambassador in London on June 26th. He proposed to consolidate communications about the crisis in London.[29] A British officer, Air Commodore Waite, had come up with the idea of supplying the civilian inhabitants of Berlin, as well as the Allied garrisons, by air. He persuaded the British Military Governor in Berlin, General Robertson, and they then convinced the American Military Governor, General Clay. Kerr: "The western supply position was a paramount question for Stalin. The Washington Embassy was informed of the supply position on 29 June. The Soviets showed that they knew the supplies for Berlin were sufficient for several weeks on 30 June."[30] The implication is that Maclean was closely monitoring the Berlin situation from the Washington Embassy, as Burgess was doing from the Foreign Office itself.

On June 26, General Lucius Clay, head of the Office of Military Government, United States, OMGUS, gave orders for the organization of air lifts between the Western Zones and Berlin.[31] On June 27, Secretary of State Marshall told the American Ambassador in London to "inform Bevin there is possibility we may wish to send 2 or 3 B-29 bomber groups to Great Britain. Please ask him for clearance."[32] The suggestion of sending the atomic capable bomber groups to Europe was at Bevin's initiative.[33] The request to send one to Britain was apparently an American idea. Sixty planes reached Britain on the 17th of July. Those, the RAF, a couple of American Army divisions and the British forces in Germany were the available counter to the Red Army in case of war. American atomic bombs were envisioned by some as evening things out, but the B-29s in Europe had none and there were few enough ready in the United States.

On July 1 the Soviets ended their participation in the Allied Kommandatura, the joint command in Berlin. Clay met with the Soviet Military Governor, who confirmed "that the technical difficulties would continue until we had abandoned our plans for West German government."[34] The technical difficulties continued, as did the airlift, until the following May. In 1979, Lord Gladwyn wrote that he thought Maclean's transmission of the proceedings that initiated NATO might actually have been helpful to peace: "Looking back, I can only assume that the likelihood . . . of the Americans coming into a powerful Western Alliance may well have exercised restraint on an Russian 'hawks'. In other words, but for Donald, there might have been a different issue to the subsequent grave crisis over Berlin."[35]

Kerr concludes that "During the crisis Maclean made the low-risk, high-gain strategy a no-risk strategy for the Soviets.

He could constantly reassure the Soviets that the mixed signals emanating from the West of determination and panic, sabre-rattling and military restraint were not an elaborate charade behind which the West was planning to attack the Soviet Union. This explains why the Soviets were confident that the West would not resort to force. Maclean knew where the threshold of military force lay, and the Soviets were able to pursue their goals vigorously up to this point, not pausing when the B 29s arrived.[36]

\*     \*     \*

Kerr, who received much of her information about Maclean from Robert Cecil, Maclean's assistant in Washington and London, summed up this phase of Donald Maclean's careers as follows: "Maclean was a successful Acting Head of Chancery.

He contributed to re-establishing and deepening the wartime habit of "consultation, cooperation and coordination". In serving British policy, he increased Soviet access to American information in particular to military and atomic secrets. The quantity and quality of the intelligence Maclean could gather was impressive. The importance of Maclean's knowledge of British and American personnel is more difficult to assess. He had good, friendly relations with American officials. That said, these official contacts appear to be important as sources of information rather than targets for influence operations. Although Maclean was responsible for embassy security and codes and cyphers his full knowledge is unknown.

Maclean's espionage had the potential to damage British and American efforts to achieve their policy goals. Through Maclean they lost control of two important tools of statecraft—information and secrecy. They could not control their external image because Maclean was providing inside information to the Soviets, thus their hopes, fears, and their postwar plans were laid bare to Soviet view. Moreover, they lost the option to bluff the Soviets."[37]

Not a good situation in the card game of the emerging Cold War.

\* \* \*

It was time for the Macleans to leave Washington. The Atomic Energy Commission gave Donald Maclean a farewell lunch at the Hay Adams Hotel, across from the White House.[38] The Macleans, in turn, "gave a farewell cocktail party for about fifty of his American friends and colleagues on the CPC and CDT. Then they packed up and went together for the last time to New York." The Macleans left from New York for England on September 1, 1948. The anti-communist purges were well underway. "It seemed to [Maclean] that the fascist monster had lifted its ugly head and that in its hand was the atom bomb."[39]

*Donald and Melinda Maclean*

## Berlin and NATO: Notes

[1] The term "Western Europe" was little used until 1945, usage peaking in the early 1960s and then again in the mid-1980s, before dropping precipitously. It was a Cold War phrase.

[2] Boyle, Peter G. "Oliver Franks and the Washington Embassy, 1948-52," in Zametica, John (ed.). British Officials and British Foreign Policy: 1945-50. Leicester: Leicester University Press, 1990, p. 193.

[3] Wiebes, Cees and Bert Zeeman. "The Pentagon negotiations March 1948: the launching of the North Atlantic Treaty," International Affairs (Royal Institute of International Affairs, Vol. 59, No. 3 (Summer, 1983), p. 352.

[4] Bullock, Alan. Ernest Bevin: Foreign Secretary, 1945-1951. New York & London: W. W. Norton & Company, 1983, p. 499.

[5] FRUS, 1948, Volume III, p. 4.

[6] FRUS, 1948, Volume III, p. 5.

[7] FRUS, 1948, Volume III, p. 14.

[8] Mastny, Vojtech. NATO in the Beholder's Eye: Soviet Perceptions and Policies, 1949-56. Washington, D.C.: Woodrow Wilson International Center for Scholars, Cold War International History Project, Working Paper No. 35, March, 2002.

[9] FRUS, 1948, Volume III, p. 48.

[10] Kerr, 257.

[11] FRUS, 1948, Volume III, pp. 59-61.

[12] FRUS, 1948, Volume III, p. 61.

[13] FRUS, 1948, Volume III, p. 73.

[14] Pechatnov, Vladimir O. The Soviet Union and the World, 1944-1953, in Leffler, Melvyn P. and Westad, Odd Adne. The Cambridge History of the Cold War, Volume I: Origins. Cambridge: Cambridge University Press, 2010, p. 98.

[15] Pechatnov, p. 103-4.

[16] FRUS, 1948, Volume I, pp. 342 ff.

[17] Kerr, 236-7.

[18] CAB 131/5.

[19] Bullock, Alan. Ernest Bevin: Foreign Secretary, 1945-1951. New York & London: W. W. Norton & Company, 1983, p. 514.

[20] FRUS, 1948 (2) p. 868.

[21] FRUS, 1948, (2), pp. 879-80.

[22] Pechatnov, p. 106, citing A. Smirnov to V. Molotov, March 12, 1948, in G. Kynin and J. Laufer (eds.), SSR I germanskii vopros, 1941-1949 [The USSR and the German Question], vol. II (Moscow: Mezhdunarodnye otnosheriia, 2000), 601.

[23] Bullock, Alan. Ernest Bevin: Foreign Secretary, 1945-1951. New York & London: W. W. Norton & Company, 1983, p. 571.

[24] Kerr, p. 261.

[25] FRUS, 1948 (2), p. 885.

[26] FRUS, 1948 (2), p. 895.

[27] FRUS, 1948 (2), pp. 899-900.

[28] FRUS, 1948 (2), p. 910.

[29] Guy Burgess, working then in Bevin's assistant Hector McNeil's office, would have been the NKVD source on developments in London. Burgess drew a cartoon of Bevin responding to McNeil's summons back to London from his vacation.

[30] Kerr, Sheila. Secret Hotline to Moscow in Deighton, p. 79.

[31] FRUS, 1948 (2), p. 918.

[32] FRUS, 1948 (2), p. 927.

[33] Bullock, Alan. Ernest Bevin: Foreign Secretary, 1945-1951. New York & London: W. W. Norton & Company, 1983, p. 576.

[34] FRUS, 1948 (2), p. 947.

[35] Cecil, pp. 85-6.

[36] Kerr, Sheila. Secret Hotline to Moscow in Deighton, p. 83. This is similar to Cecil's appraisal: Cecil, p. 87.

[37] Kerr, p. 187.

[38] Cecil, p. 84.

[39] Cecil, pp. 89-90.

# Chapter Eight

## *Cairo*

The Macleans arrived in London from Washington early in September, 1948. Donald Maclean, promoted to the rank of Counsellor and assigned to the Cairo Embassy, was briefed for his new posting by George Clutton, the head of the Foreign Office department responsible for Egypt, and by Bernard Burrows, head of the Eastern Department, which dealt with Palestinian affairs. Maclean would have been told by Clutton that the Cairo Embassy's main occupation was the renegotiation of the 1936 Anglo-Egyptian defense treaty, which, among other things, gave the British Empire the right to maintain large bases in the Suez Canal Zone. Aside from the Egyptian wish to terminate that right, the other main cause of friction was the Sudan, which was governed under a "condominium" between Britain and Egypt, but which was, in effect, a British colony. Egypt wanted to annex it, while Britain wished to move the Sudan toward self-government as part of the informal Empire. However, the Sudan was a minor issue. The major point was that of the Canal Zone bases and their role in Prime Minister Bevin's grand plans for continuing British dominance in the Middle East and their use as forward strategic bases for American bombers in the thought-to-be-imminent war with the Soviet Union.

Egypt was, as was often said in Whitehall, "the lynchpin" (sometimes "the hinge") of what remained of the British Empire after Indian independence. According to David Devereux: "The Middle East was considered to be of vital importance to Britain by both the Labour and Conservative governments of the postwar decade . . .

> British interests were above all strategic, the Middle East . . . was thought to be a necessary bastion for the defence of British Africa and the Far East sea routes. The independence of India in 1947 enhanced the Middle East's importance; Egypt replaced India as the main British garrison between Britain herself and Singapore.[1]

The United States and the United Kingdom had held talks in Washington between October 16 and November 7, 1947, in order to coordinate Middle Eastern strategy. Although Maclean is not listed as a participant, it is highly likely that he had been able to follow the discussions, if only by means of the documents exchanged with London. One of the Top Secret summary statements concerned, "Retention of British Military Rights in Egypt," began: "It was the consensus of both the American and British groups that it was extremely important in the interest of the maintenance of the security of the Middle East and of the preservation of world peace that the British have certain strategic facilities in Egypt.

> The British should have the right to maintain these facilities during peace time in such a condition that they could be effectively and speedily used in case of an immediate threat to the security of the Middle East and right of reentry in order to make full use of these facilities in accordance with the provision of the Charter, and with the principles of the United Nations in case of such a threat . . . In order to ensure such rights, it is necessary to negotiate a satisfactory agreement with Egypt . . .[2]

Between sometime in mid-1947—say, the day of Indian Independence, August 15, 1947—and the end of the year, the purpose of the bases in the Canal Zone changed from the defense of the British informal empire in the Middle East to facilitating an atomic attack on the Soviet Union by the United States. Peter Hahn observed that "American contingency war plans conceived in 1947 underscored the importance of maintaining British military rights in Egypt . . . In the event of war with the Soviet Union, American strategists still planned to 'initiate a powerful air offensive against vital strategic elements of the Soviet war-making capacity,' particularly petroleum production." As during the run-up to the Second World War, the Baku area was to be targeted. The idea was to place B-29 bombers at British bases in the Canal Zone readied for this purpose.[3] Much of Maclean's work in the Cairo Embassy was devoted to negotiations about those bases.

British forces had first surveyed Egypt when Nelson defeated Napoleon at the Battle of the Nile in 1798. Ninety years later Egypt was added to the informal Empire and the British gradually established the apparatus of indirect rule. The Suez Canal provided an efficient passage to India, while Cairo functioned as a subordinate coordinating center between New Delhi and London. (The Foreign Office records of the activities of such as St. John Philby and Colonel T. E. Lawrence in the Arabian peninsula, for example, preserve reports and directives flowing alternately from the military and intelligence commands in Cairo and New Delhi.) Between the World Wars, Mandate Palestine (including what is now Jordan) on the east and the Sudan to the south were the responsibility of the British Ambassador in Cairo working with the military and intelligence Middle East headquarters. During World War Two Cairo was, after London itself, the British Empire's most important coordinating center, overrun with British and Commonwealth troops and the military units and officials of governments in exile. Churchill said, in one of his colorful images, that any attack on Cairo would be thrown back by the sheer weight of British officers on the terrace of Shepheard's Hotel. "Chips" Channon, Conservative Member of Parliament, flaneur and diarist, touring the Middle East in 1941, thought Cairo still a colonial paradise: "Sun, oranges, ease, bad taste, heat, dazzling shops—how I love Cairo. It is the occidental-ised East, without the dirt of the usual Eastern town."[4]

In 1948, British soldiers and officials remained much in evidence in Cairo, although the military command itself had been moved to the Canal Zone after repeated complaints from the Egyptian government about the colonial appearance of the city. The Middle East operations of M.I.6, under the cover name of the Combined Research and Planning Organisation, were housed with the Foreign Office's British Middle East Office (BMEO), which had been created by Bevin "to secure Britain's long-range foreign policy interests in the Middle East," in the Sharia Tolumbat compound (just off Tahrir Square).[5] The Ambassador, Sir Ronald Ian Campbell, who oversaw the Imperial presence in Egypt, was not the proconsular figure that his predecessor, Sir Miles Lampson had been, but the British representative's role was still central to Egyptian politics. No one, least of all the King, had forgotten how close Lampson had come to deposing Farouk six years earlier.

What were those "long-range foreign policy interests" that were to be supported by the Foreign Office's establishment in Cairo, the Embassy and the BMEO? Until Attlee's great achievement of Indian independence, that policy had been to hold the Middle East to protect the Indian Empire. After the Midnight Hour of Indian Independence, dominating the Middle East became an end in itself, a policy in search of a raison d'être. It found its first justification in Bevin's "certain idea of Britain": a great power manipulating the greater power of the United States against the Soviet Union. This policy required holding what the Empire had possessed before the war (except India) and what had come into its hands during the war—that is, everything from Tripoli to Baghdad and both coasts of the Persian Gulf. With the mainland of Greece, practically, and many of its islands, actually, British possessions and Turkey under joint Anglo-American protection, the Mediterranean was for all practical purposes a British lake. Bevin aimed to keep it that way.

The Eastern Department's Bernard Burrows was an Arabist who had spent the Second World War in Cairo. In the Fall of 1948, when he briefed Maclean, he had his plate full with Palestinian issues that Maclean would be responsible for dealing with from the Cairo Embassy. Some of those issues were indigenous: aspects of the complexity of relationships between the political situation within Egypt and its British-dominated foreign affairs. Others were part of the wider policy issues involving the Atlantic Alliance and preparations for the Third World War.

Britain had assumed control of "Mandate" Palestine after the First World War, governing it under a League of Nations mandate as if it were a colony, along lines familiar from Imperial practices in India. This effort came under increasing strain between the wars as the Arab population sought independence, or, at least, an end to the Mandate, and the Jewish population organized state-like structures within the Mandate and sought an end to restrictions on immigration under the rationale of the Balfour Declaration's promise of a homeland for the Jewish people in Palestine. Some in the Arab leadership sided with the Nazis during the war, cheering on the Final Solution and adopting it as their own. The Jews created an increasingly formidable set of armed units, some in military formations, some in terrorist cells. British efforts to maintain a population balance had not pleased either party and soon after the war the Jewish self-defence efforts morphed into a revolt against the British Empire, a conflict which was portrayed as a civil war between the Jews and the Arabs. It was that, but not only that. Bevin had his thumb on the scales. The Arab armies were in many ways typical British colonial forces, armed, trained and officered by the Empire. Bevin was determined to use them to hold Palestine for the Empire.

Wm. Roger Lewis reminds us that "It is important to note that in mid-1946, when it became clear that British military, air, and naval forces might be withdrawn from Egypt, the Chiefs of Staff attached emphatic importance to the retention of strategic rights in Palestine. Haifa would be substituted for Alexandria as the linchpin of British defence in the eastern Mediterranean."[6] This position of the Chiefs of Staff manifested politically in late 1946, when Attlee and Bevin decided that "If there could be no agreement [in Palestine], then the British government would continue to play the same hand at the United Nations where a showdown could not be avoided.

> The British would appear to assume an impartial position, but in fact they would allow the pro-Arab majority of the General Assembly to decide the issue for them . . . The United Nations would determine the issue in favour of a unitary state, which in turn would conclude a treaty securing the strategic and economic benefits of Britain's traditional informal empire in the Middle East.[7]

The creation of a unitary Palestinian state was to be accompanied by a military alliance with the British Empire. "A treaty with a Palestinian state similar to the one with Transjordan might also grant strategic rights for air transit of troops and the protection of pipelines.

The Chiefs of Staff presented their case for these demands in a Cabinet meeting of the 15th of January 1947: 'It was essential to our defence that we should be able to fight from the Middle East in war . . .

> In future we should not be able to use India as a base for . . . deployment of force: it was the more essential, therefore, that we should retain other bases in the Middle East for this purpose . . . Palestine was of special importance in this general scheme of defence. In war, Egypt would be our key position in the Middle East; and it was necessary that we should hold Palestine as a screen for the defence of Egypt . . .

Far from wishing to relinquish Palestine for mere reasons of political discontent, the Chiefs of Staff wished to retain it as a permanent possession. A naval base at Haifa, a few military garrisons scattered throughout the territory, and a strategic air base in the interior would satisfy British strategic requirements.[8]

The planning for an anti-Soviet war entailed the identification of places from which to launch an attack. Post-hostilities planning exercises had established the futility of a land offensive across Germany. The alternative was an air war, an alternative seemingly made practical by the atomic bomb.[9] The map rooms depicted the deployment of atomic bomb-laden aircraft, based in the Middle East, targeting the Soviet Union's chief cities along flight lines laid down by J. D. Bernal, who, perhaps, sent copies of those maps to Moscow.[10] The bases from which the RAF was to threaten the Soviet Union were those located in Egypt itself, but when the political situation in Egypt became increasingly uncertain and there was a possibility that British forces might have to withdraw to the Canal Zone, the planners turned to Palestine where some facilities were in place and more, it was thought could be built, particularly in the southern part of the country: the Negev.

Ilan Pappe tells us that for the exercise "Intermezzo," in a classic

269

case of mirror-imaging, Palestine "was perceived as a battleground in case of a Third World War and the Transjordanian army [the Arab Legion, which Walter Lippmann called a "British satellite army"[11]] was regarded as the main local ally that would fight alongside the Western forces in a possible confrontation with the Russians. In order to prepare the Arab Legion for this task, Britain had immediately as the Second World War ended strengthened this force by adding new and substantial numbers of British officers to its core."[12] We are to imagine fifty or more Red Army divisions marching through Armenia, say, down through the Kurdish areas of eastern Turkey and heading to the Canal, only to be stopped by the Arab Legion, perhaps assisted by Polish cavalry, Sikh artillery, the battle-hardened troops of the Nigerian brigades.

The "British decision in February 1947 to refer the Palestine issue to the United Nations . . . was not intended as an abandonment of the mandate but rather as an attempt to win international endorsement for a binational [a single state including both Jews and Arabs] solution."[13] But on November 29, 1947, much to the astonishment of the British Government, the U.S. government and its Latin American allies joined the Soviet Union and its allies to out-vote the British Commonwealth and the Arab countries in the United Nations, bringing the Mandate to an end. The British-trained and equipped (and sometimes led) armed forces of the surrounding countries attacked the new State of Israel, Bevin anticipating either a victory by those forces or a stalemate that would leave Britain with a predominate role in the region: sufficient to secure bases in the Negev.[14] Bevin was supported in this by the British military leadership. "The Chiefs of Staff could not envisage the exclusion of Palestine from the British sphere of influence. Their committee ruled in January 1948 that one of the basic and essential British requirements was the maintenance of strategic rights in Palestine."[15] In February 1948 "The revised [Anglo-Transjordanian] treaty served to strengthen British control over Transjordan . . . Direct British control over the Legion was replaced by a joint board of defence . . . Its chairman was . . . a British officer . . . the board was incorporated in the British military organization in the Middle East . . . it had become subordinated to the British Middle East Forces."[16] That is, the intervention Transjordan's Arab Legion in Palestine was, for all intents and purposes, an intervention by Britain itself.

Israel had been proclaimed in May 1948, while the Macleans were still in the United States, and was immediately recognized by both Moscow and Washington.The intensified war that followed was essentially one between the new Israeli government, with strong support from the Diaspora, and Britain's Arab allies, especially Iraq, Jordan and Egypt.[17] The Arab Palestinians, the Iraqis, and the Egyptians sought to eliminate the Jewish presence from Palestine. Abdullah of Transjordan simply wished to expand his realm westward, to Jerusalem. At this point "British policy aimed at detaching the Negev in order to provide a common frontier between Transjordan and Egypt."[18] The Egyptian Air Force used RAF pilots and their Spitfires in its battles with the Israelis, while the Israelis also used Spitfires as well as other aircraft, including American bombers, piloted and maintained by an International Brigade of veteran air personnel.

Clutton and Burrows gave Maclean two wars to watch from his new post in Cairo: the big war with the Soviet Union, just around the corner, as they thought, and the little war, in Palestine, momentarily on the back burner, but bubbling away. Burrows would have explained to Maclean that the British minimum aims in Palestine in the Fall of 1948 were to maintain control of the southern Negev desert, connecting Transjordan and Egypt; to restrain Israel; and to prevent a war against Transjordan by the other Arab countries, which did not approve of the occupation of the eastern part of Palestine (now known as the West Bank) by King Abdullah.

As was the custom, in addition to Donald Maclean's two weeks or so of official briefings, the Macleans were invited as a couple to less formal occasions, to meet and to be met. Burrows, for example, gave a dinner party, where they first met Geoffrey Hoare and Clare Hollingworth, journalists and old Near Eastern hands.[19] Hoare recalled: "It was a party of twelve people, and we all knew one another, were almost old friends—except Melinda

At dinner I sat next to this delicate-complexioned, soft-voiced little American girl and sensed that in this Christian-name gathering of people who had been in or had had some connection with or special interest in the Middle East, Melinda felt herself rather out of her depth. She was thrilled at the thought of going to Cairo, and I told her all I could about that large, dusty, perversely attractive city. I found her utterly charming, and possessing the kind of fragility and defencelessness that made nearly all men feel they wanted to protect her, although against what one had no idea . . . After dinner Melinda, Donald and I sat together and continued to talk about Egypt. Although Donald showed no marked enthusiasm, I felt that he too was pleased with his new appointment. They seemed a harmonious couple, and later Clare and I expressed our happiness at the thought that we had made two extremely pleasant new friends.[20]

Hollingworth, separated from but not then yet divorced from her first husband, was a famous war correspondent. She had survived the German invasion of Poland, which she was the first to report, and, more recently, the bombing of the King David Hotel in Jerusalem, headquarters of the British administration, by the Irgun. Perhaps it was her stories about the latter that dampened Donald Maclean's enthusiasm for his new assignment. The perception of Melinda Maclean was typical—fragile, innocent, out of her depth. Sexism projects its own deceptions, needing no great effort from its objects.

The Macleans reciprocated the hospitality of the London diplomatic/journalist set, as would have been expected. Cyril Connolly remembered that their dinner party "was a delightful evening; he had become a good host; his charm was based not on vanity but on sincerity, and he would discuss foreign affairs as a student, not as an expert. He incidentally enjoyed the magazine that I then edited . . .'[21] Incidentally. In Malcolm Muggeridge's diary for September 23-30, 1948 we find "Dined with Philip Jordan[22] and his wife at a flat they have now got in Long Acre.

Also present, Donald Maclean who was in the Embassy in Washington and his American wife, rather pretty, well off. Discussed everlasting question of Russia and the possibility of war. Philip is quite certain that there was no question of appeasement. He expected that the Americans would act, but not for some months, since they wouldn't be sufficiently armed. Thus, it really does begin to seem as though the inconceivable must happen, and that an atomic war with Russia is almost a certainty."[23]

It was, then, assumed in British governing circles and among the chattering classes that the United States was on the verge of launching "an atomic war with Russia." Donald Maclean would not have been surprised by this gossip. However, it would have been something to add to his reports to the NKVD, another factor for consideration in Moscow, along with his accounts of his briefings on current British and concerns in the Middle East.

There is an implication in Connolly's comments that he had known Donald Maclean earlier, perhaps through, or with, his wife Barbara Skelton. (There is a similar implication in Hoare's "we all knew one another, were almost old friends.") Melinda Maclean, the American wife, was analyzed by Muggeridge, the former intelligence officer and journalist, as "pretty" and "well off," nothing more. Nothing to see there. A nearly impenetrable cover. A few years later, Connolly and Muggeridge threw as much mud as possible at Donald Maclean—as would be expected of them.

A week or two after the dinner party at the Jordan's flat, the Macleans were in Cairo, the de facto capital of the part of the British Empire that then covered much of North Africa to the west, Africa to the south all the way to the Cape, and much of the land to the east to the borders of the newly independent successor states of the Indian Empire. The 1949 Foreign Office List for Egypt shows Maclean in the third place in the Cairo Embassy after the "Ambassador Ex. and Plen." Sir R. I. Campbell and the Minister, E. A. Chapman-Andrews. The Head of the British Middle East Office, Sir John M. Troutbeck, was listed after Maclean. Donald Maclean's "new seniority meant that a fine house in Gezira, originally built for British servants of the Egyptian Government, was at his disposal.

> It was furnished by the Ministry of Works, who also kept up the garden, where mimosa and jacaranda bloomed. His higher allowances enabled them to employ an English nurse for the two boys and four well-trained servants. Relieved of most of the cares of being a mother and a housewife, Melinda began for the first time to enjoy entertaining in her home. The Ambassador was a bachelor and she soon found herself in demand as a hostess.[24]

This description follows the usual narrative about Melinda Maclean. In fact, she had had a nurse for the children and always at least one and sometimes two servants in Washington. There were a range of reasons why in Cairo, with Donald Maclean's promotion, it was advantageous and possible for them to entertain, to oblige the Ambassador. The novelty of servants was not among them.

In addition to a large house and a tropical garden, "Maclean's promotion increased his access to secrets.

> He oversaw all incoming and outgoing messages. The Cairo Embassy was the nerve centre of British power in the Middle East. The Embassy received news and issued instructions to British officials in the Sudan. It liaised with the British Middle East Office (BMEO) and Security Intelligence Middle East (SIME) . . . the Embassy reported on Egyptian communism and the Soviet and satellite legations in Cairo to [British secret intelligence], and received [their] reports from London. Maclean was thus closely connected to the British and American military and to British intelligence and security. Cairo also received most of the telegrams that were sent home to London from Washington, Moscow, Paris and Berlin. It also routinely received, Foreign Office Print, Cabinet decisions, Chiefs of Staff minutes, information policy guidance and propaganda material from the Information Research Department, (IRD). Given the subordination of diplomacy to military-strategic goals, much of the information in the Embassy was military.[25]

In other words, during this crucial period at the beginning of the Cold War, Maclean was able to continue making the diplomatic, intelligence and much of the military activities of the British Empire known to Moscow. Additionally, Maclean was able to continue providing information and analysis about American activities that were shared with Britain, especially in the Middle East.

Egypt was the ribbon of fields beside the Nile. In 1948 two-thirds of the population were employed as farm laborers or farmed their own half acre of land or both, while two thousand families owned twenty percent of the country. When the state sold some of its land, beginning in 1934, ninety percent went to big landowners.[26] "A donkey cost more to hire than a man.

> In the cotton mills, children aged seven to thirteen laboured under the blows of European taskmasters. Only the foremen had masks to protect them against the choking dust. Every year a third of the children died of consumption. Malaria carried off whole villages. Ninety five per cent of the peasants had bilharzia. Trachoma gave Egypt the world record for the numbers of blind. Average life-expectancy was twenty seven, excluding children who died within a year of birth.[27]

But Egypt itself was not well differentiated in the Imperial mind from other sandy bits between London and Delhi. What was meant by those hardware store metaphors of hinges and the like was the Canal, of course, and Cairo. "Cairo was the most densely populated city of Africa. Plague accompanied poverty; one year before the Macleans arrived, cholera had broken out and, in a single day in October 1947, 175 deaths were registered . . ."[28] Cairo then had a population of two million, doubling in a generation. Having been, if to a steadily diminishing degree, a provincial Ottoman city for four hundred years, there remained a layer of aristocratic Ottoman families among the local rentiers, and a complexity of Copts, Jews, Greeks, Armenians and so forth, each with its own dominant and subordinate families, religious institutions and schools: this between the vast poverty of the city's Muslim slums, the bazaars and the remnants of the British forces of occupation.

275

In Cairo, Alexandria and the other Egyptian cities there was a working class, incredibly oppressed and impoverished. "The circumstances of the Egyptian worker were in fact so shocking that even such outsiders as the British Embassy labor counselor were compelled to comment. In his words:

> The Egyptian workers live in unhealthy and overcrowded dwellings—they are so overcrowded in many areas that the workers occupy the dwellings in shifts as in a factory; they sleep in the streets and in any odd corner, servants and their families sleep under staircases, in sheds and in gardens or in quarters in the more modern buildings which are often not sanitary. Their nutrition is usually inadequate and lacking in food values. Their health conditions are appalling and the provisions for dealing with diseases are totally inadequate. . . . There is no unemployment insurance, no provision for old age and similar state benefits.[29]

This after more than half a century of effective Imperial responsibility.

The unstable political situation in Egypt shortly after the Macleans's arrival was dramatically laid out in a Secret message from the American Embassy in London to the Secretary of State, sent on January 7, 1949:

> In a private and personal conversation recently a responsible official in the British Foreign Office, who deals directly with Egyptian affairs [Clutton?], remarked to an officer of this Embassy in a mood of deep gloom that "from the way things are going from bad to worse in Egypt it seems to me that a revolution there is inevitable." . . . the official said that the economic and social problems of Egypt, which were already bad, had been aggravated by the war in Palestine and that instead of Egyptian leaders endeavoring to take remedial steps they seem to be vying with one another to scramble to the top of the manure pile out of reach of the rising sea of discontent, hunger and despair . . . The official did not know how long the patient "have-not donkey" would support the heavy burden of the

unenlightened "haves" but he "imagined that it would kick before long."[30]

*   *   *

By the time the Macleans arrived in Cairo, the easy victory that the Egyptian military had anticipated in Palestine was slipping away. During the two or three months either side of the New Year of 1949 there were deluges of communications between the Embassy and the British Middle East military authorities, between each and their London masters, between each and their Egyptian counterparts, and between each and their American counterparts, all flowing across Maclean's desk. Israel had again attacked Egyptian forces on December 22 and soon the Egyptian army was close to disaster along the border between Palestine and Sinai, much of it pushed into the Gaza strip, other units more or less under siege in the Negev desert. In an attempt to accomplish a classic encircling movement, the Israeli army apparently crossed the Egyptian/Palestine border to attack Rafah (now the site of a famous crossing point and tunnel complex between Egypt and Gaza). Egyptian aircraft and ships shelled and bombed Tel Aviv and Jerusalem. Worryingly, there were a series of air battles between Israeli and *British* aircraft. Four RAF Spitfires were shot down near Rafah, one by ground fire, the other three by Israeli Air Force Spitfires. Another RAF airplane was shot down later in the day. (As the pilots of the Israeli planes were North Americans, this was the first battle between Americans and British military men since the early 19th century.[31])

When on January 7, 1949, the Israeli government informed a U.S. representative of the fight between Israeli and British aircraft, it stated that the British aircraft had strafed Israeli troops on the Israeli side of the border, near Rafah.[32] The British Government denied strafing Israeli troops, stating that theirs were unarmed aircraft, which had been on a reconnaissance flight to verify Egyptian claims that the Israeli army had crossed the border. On January 10, 1949, the Special Representative of the United States in Israel sent a secret, priority, telegram to the President and the Acting Secretary of State: "All political officers and service attaches of Mission are of opinion that British actions are destroying chances of peace.

Official explanation of RAF reconnaissance flights over battle area at moment Egypt accepted US-inspired UN order cease-fire and armistice negotiations and subsequent British troops landing Aqaba while Transjordan negotiations were proceeding satisfactorily are unconvincing. To us such provocative moves appear to be determined efforts forestall direct negotiations Israel-Egypt and Israel-Transjordan which might deprive Britain effective control Southern Negev.[33]

Egyptian-Israeli negotiations began on Rhodes on January 12, 1949. On January 12th the British Consul in Jerusalem told his American colleague that the British Government "considered at least corridor linking Transjordan and Egypt or Transjordan and Gaza vital for defense needs . . . UK would use force if necessary obtain route."[34]

In early March the Israeli army began a march on Aqaba to sever that corridor and secure the entire Negev for the new state. Britain sent a battalion of troops into the town, anticipating that Transjordan might invoke its treaty with Britain, and readied heavy bombers.[35] For a few days it appeared that regular British forces would attack Israel. It is unpleasant to contemplate the counter-factual of an Anglo-Israeli war, in which the U.S. might well have at least supported the Israeli side, if not intervened. In any case, the willingness of Bevin to use British-piloted RAF aircraft (as opposed to Egyptian British-supplied aircraft with British pilots) to engage the Israelis in early 1949, and his apparent willingness to launch a full-scale, overt, intervention, underlines the centrality of Palestine to his long-range foreign policy objectives. It was not a matter of the respective rights and injuries of Arabs and Jews. It was about airbases in the Negev, the naval base and pipelines at Haifa.

The Egyptians were demanding British intervention; the Americans were strongly against it; the attitude of the Soviet Union was unclear. If Britain went beyond sending troops into Aqaba and reconnaissance flights over the battle lines, would the Soviet Union intervene on behalf of Israel? No one knew. And no one in the British or American governments knew that British plans and actions and Anglo-American discussions were immediately sent to Moscow, courtesy of Donald Maclean, who was, in fact, drafting some of those plans as well as participating in those discussions.

\*   \*   \*

Donald Maclean's duties as Counsellor and head of Chancery in the Cairo Embassy fell into four areas: administration (including security and the code room); Egyptian domestic affairs; Egyptian international affairs (chiefly the war with Israel), and planning for the role of Egypt and the former Palestine Mandate areas in the anticipated war of the British Empire and the United States with the Soviet Union. Egyptian domestic affairs were complicated and violent. The various activities arising from the permutations of power between the court and the parliament were closely followed by the British Embassy and the Foreign Office, when not instigated by them. King Farouk had repeatedly attempted to establish a dictatorship, while the British insisted on the façade of parliamentary democracy. Parliament was dominated by the Wafd party, more anti-British than the King, but considered too accommodating by more nationalist or radical groups, the most prominent of which was the Muslim Brotherhood. In December, 1948, just after the Macleans moved into their new home among the mimosas and jacarandas, the Muslim Brotherhood was outlawed by the Egyptian government. The Prime Minister, Mahmud al-Nuqrashi, who was associated with the Wafd party, was murdered by a member of the Brotherhood and shortly thereafter the Brotherhood's founder, Hasan al-Banna, was assassinated. The Wafd party itself would come to power in the general election of January 1950. Various groups were positioning themselves for a time when both the British and the king were gone. The army, the strongest institution in the Egyptian state, then and now, had been humiliated in the war in Palestine. Even before the fighting ended, junior officers like Gamal 'Abdel Nasser had begun

279

"recruiting officers to the clandestine Free Officers Organization, which planned and eventually carried out the coup that overthrew the monarchy in 1952."[36]

Bridging British interests between Cold War and Imperial concerns, Maclean followed "Egyptian officials' perceptions of the threat from the Soviet Union at [both] the international and national level."[37] Communism in Egypt was highly marginalized and splintered. The initial Communist formations, founded after World War I, were soon destroyed by the government. The groups that formed in the 1930s were created by young intellectuals from wealthy families—the two largest by Jews: Henri Curiel and Hillel Schwartz. Neither those nor other competing Communist groups were able to form mass parties or recruit significant numbers of workers or farm laborers.[38] Around 1949 there were perhaps one thousand, perhaps two thousand, members of the Egyptian Communist Party(ies). Curiel was arrested and deported on August 26, 1950, having spent the previous eighteen months in the detention camp of Huckstep, in the desert north east of Cairo.[*]

When important visitors came to Egypt, the Macleans, having as a matter of course made a study of these things, would show them the classical sites, take them out to the desert oases or to Luxor for culture and to the Grand Bazaar for trinkets. In the summer the Embassy packed up and moved to Alexandria, an annual logistical tour de force which Donald Maclean had some role in supervising, Melinda Maclean in implementing. Hoare visited the Macleans in March, 1949. "I was there at cocktail time, curious to discover how Melinda was getting on in Cairo.

Physically, Gezireh, the European residential district where they lived, was attractive. The wide, quiet streets were lined with beautiful flowering trees—delicate mauve jacaranda, bursting orange and scarlet flame trees, woolly yellow mimosa, and, all over walls and hedges, deep purple and rusty red bougainvillaea.

---

[*] He was a cousin of George Blake, a Foreign Office official and Soviet spy who was later a friend of Donald Maclean in Moscow.

The house had a certain dignity and spaciousness, and their gardens, in which green-fingered Egyptian gardeners produced an extraordinary profusion of common and exotic flowers and plants, were cool and fresh oases in the prevailing dusty heat.

So much for scene-setting. On to character sketches. "I found Melinda on top of the world.

She still adored Cairo, was delighted with her life, had made dozens of friends, and had probably for the first time in her married life emerged from her protective shell. Donald, after about six months in Egypt, was doing exceptionally well at the embassy, and he too appeared at this time to be enjoying his new post. It was an excellent party, and I went back to my hotel marveling at the change Cairo had wrought in Melinda. She was as charming as ever, but I no longer felt any great need to protect her![39]

That summer she gave a highly successful "young-people's party" for the visiting Duke of Edinburgh. The talk and laughter must have been heard all the way to Moscow.

Hoare felt that early in his Cairo assignment, Donald Maclean "was developing a deep antipathy for...the contrast between the quite shocking poverty of ninety-five per cent of the population and the arrogant, ostentatious wealth of the small, ruling-class minority . . .

British policy at that period was also the traditional one of doing nothing, of sitting back and seeing what would happen, of "non-interference." This policy was tainted by the fact that British diplomatic influence and the presence of our troops in the Canal Zone constituted at least a passive interference . . . Donald [Maclean] objected strongly to this policy. He felt that as we could not escape from the predominant position in Egypt that our previous status there had given us, we should accept our responsibilities and try to persuade the rulers of Egypt to institute the reforms that alone, in his opinion, could save the country from communism.[40]

Hoare's "Donald" was concerned with saving Egypt from Communism. A liberal, no doubt, in his family tradition, but no more liberal than was suitable for the Embassy's Counselor. So, apparently, he seemed to a visiting journalist.

The Macleans settled into diplomatic society with its outer ring of expatriates and the Europeanized, or partially Europeanized, wealthy Egyptian, and remnants of multinational Ottoman, society. They went to the parties of the King's "fun-loving" sister, Princess Faiza.[41] The FBI later reported that Donald Maclean was said also to have attended "parties given by King Farouk . . . it was general knowledge [in American diplomatic circles, from which this tid-bit came] that Farouk's parties were of the most immoral type, for which Farouk was notorious."[42] It would be interesting to know in what ways those parties were "immoral." Given the morality codes of the FBI, perhaps there was dancing. Perhaps coffee was served. In any case, it would be expected that Maclean, as well as the Ambassador and Minister at the Embassy, and their colleagues at the American Embassy, would attend the King's parties as part of their diplomatic duties, dancing and even drinking coffee, if required.

We have a portrait of Maclean on duty during office hours from an American diplomat who was in Egypt during Maclean's time there. He told an FBI interviewer in 1951 that "the 'heart' of a British Embassy is its Ambassador and the 'keystone' of a British Embassy is the head of its Chancery to whom the Ambassador looks for aid in administering the many diverse activities of the Embassy.

He stated that Donald Maclean, while head of the Chancery in Cairo, had the ability to handle the position, and that from the moment Maclean had arrived there in September, 1948, he had formed the highest opinion of Maclean's intelligence and ability to quickly grasp the many factors involved in connection with the work of the Embassy. [He] stated that he would "have to confess" that on one occasion he went home from the Embassy and mentioned to his wife that Maclean's physical condition while at his desk dispatching Embassy business was that of a person who had been thoroughly intoxicated on the previous night. [He] stated that he "had to almost admire" Maclean's ability to hold up under the work of the Embassy while having the obvious appearance of one who was quite "loaded".

The American diplomat also told the FBI that "Maclean had been hospitalized on about four occasions in Cairo because of an illness that he had picked up while on duty in Cairo . . .

It was [his] belief that although Maclean was a heavy drinker, in matters of high secrecy and military matters he did not believe Maclean would have willingly or even inadvertently disclosed a "single piece of information" . . . Both [he] and his wife stated that they had no reason whatsoever for believing that there were any Soviet angles involved in the disappearance of Maclean, and had never heard him make any remarks concerning the Soviet Union.[43]

In other words, the Macleans managed to maintain their cover in diplomatic circles, in spite of Donald Maclean's increasingly heavy drinking and Melinda Maclean's possible lack of popularity among the Embassy wives (some of whom said, as they do, that she did not manage the household servants well).

It was Maclean's responsibility, under the Ambassador and Minister, to persuade the King and the Egyptian government to reach a new military alliance with the British Empire, retaining the British bases in the country and in the Canal Zone, as well as, if possible, the right to, in effect, re-occupy Egypt in case of war. Within six months of the arrival of the Macleans in Cairo there was a major war scare. Maclean found himself responsible for plans to evacuate Cairo (as had nearly happened just before the Battle of El Alamein). On March 20, 1949, the Embassy received a top secret cable from Field Marshal Montgomery: "In the event of the outbreak of a war, whether Egypt were directly involved or not, it may be desirable in the interests of efficiency, and will certainly be desirable in the interests of individuals, for non-essential personnel of His Majesty's Embassy in certain cases to be evacuated as soon as war becomes inevitable or has actually broken out.

> It is therefore desirable to prepare plans for the phased evacuation of non-essential staff in the event of a state of emergency becoming critical, and I should be grateful to have lists of any non-essential personnel in your Department who could in cases of emergency be evacuated, together with their families or dependents.

Maclean minuted: "We have a plan for emergencies of a civil (Egyptian) kind which . . . involved the British, and other foreign communities, staying put. We have as far as I know, no plan for the event of war, e.g. an attack by Russia . . . planning might well be coordinated with the Americans as proposed . . . I suggest that we reply agreeing . . . but pointing out the differences between these two problems."[44] Discussions about actions to be undertaken in the event of war continued later in the year, with less sense of urgency.

Not quite half a year into his tour of duty in Cairo, Maclean was deep into Anglo-American planning of Middle East strategy for World War Three. In January, 1949, Bevin, hoping to bring the United States into the negotiations over the Canal Zone bases, had U. S. Admiral Richard Conolly, Commander of U.S. Naval Forces Eastern Atlantic and Mediterranean, invited to discuss Middle East defense at Fayid, the British Canal Zone headquarters.[45] Maclean became involved when Bevin explained this strategy in a cable to the Cairo Embassy, if not before.[46] The State Department eventually rejected the invitation (on May 2), not wishing to give the Egyptians the impression that the United States, rather than Britain, was their primary protector. This was partly to conceal from the Egyptian government U.S. plans for the Canal Zone airbases and the construction at one of them, Abu Sueir, to make it suitable for use by B-29 bombers. Nonetheless, late in January, 1949, King Farouk, who appears to have had rather good sources of secret intelligence, "during a . . . call at the British Embassy, had expressed discontent over his understanding that the British and Americans in Egypt were consulting together regarding the role Egypt might play in case of hostilities. The King indicated his dissatisfaction over being thus by-passed."[47]

Basically, the American and British governments were discussing plans for the defense of the Middle East in anticipation of a Soviet invasion of the area during World War Three, penciled in for sometime in the early 1950s, as well as plans for the use of Middle Eastern bases for offensive warfare against the Soviet Union. Perhaps that distinction is simply rhetorical. The British intended to occupy Egypt, as they had during World War Two, and the Americans wished to have airbases ready for their own use in the "Cairo-Suez area." The British wanted to coordinate this planning with a renewal of their military alliance with Egypt, which, therefore meant including the Egyptian military in the planning process. The American government and military were adamantly opposed to tri-partite planning, fearful of Egyptian "leaks" to the Soviets. Further, the American government wished the talks to remain secret from the Egyptian government and towards that end suggested that they might be held somewhere outside Egypt. [48] Therefore there were elaborate and, in retrospect, useless efforts, given the flow of information from Maclean to Moscow, to keep the Egyptians from learning about the Anglo-American meetings.

The British Middle East Command suggested that a number of American officers on the staff of Admiral Conolly, in lieu of the Admiral himself, travel to British General Headquarters (GHQ) Fayid.[49] A three- to four-week visit was proposed. On February 3, Maclean was copied into a set of telegrams between Conolly and General Sir John Crocker, Commander in Chief, Middle East Land Forces, by the British Middle East Office, Military Division, "To keep you in the picture."[50] Five days later Maclean noted: "The Foreign Office seem to be influenced in favour of our original scheme by their belief that the Egyptians would prefer the Americans to be associated with Anglo-Egyptian talks and by the importance which they attach to getting the Americans' feet wet in this part of the world.

> They seem to fear that if we abandon the proposed "high-level tripartite talks" as stage one, the Americans will drop out. But this does not necessarily follow. There is no reason that I can see

why the Americans should not be associated with stage three, i.e. the technical talks with the Egyptians about the defense of Egypt (and our consequent military requirements in Egypt), if it is decided as a matter of policy that an attempt to include the Americans at all should be made.

No consideration has yet been given to who the participants in the "high level tripartite talks" at stage one should be, but I suppose in any case General Crocker, Haidar Pasha [Egyptian Defense Minister] and Admiral Bolger would take part. I cannot see such a conference being successful unless the way had been cleared by a talk between H.E. [the British Ambassador] and the King and possibly between the U.S. Charge d'Affaires and the King also i.e. it looks as if our modified stage one would have to take place in any case. It might well be better if it were substituted for the "high-level tripartite talks" which, bearing in mind the nature of Haidar Pasha, might do more harm than good, even if he has had his marching orders from the King.

In short, the arguments produced by London in favour of adhering to the original plan do not seem to be sound even on their own premises. On the other hand, they were no doubt influenced by the fact that the British Joint Planning staff in Washington had already started to put across the original plan by the time our modifications arrived, and I suppose it is true that confusion would have resulted by changing course. I hope however that Sir O[liver] Franks will produce our modifications out of his hat if the Americans hesitate over the plan as put to them. I do not think that there is any action which we could usefully take at present.[51]

There were various schemes put forward about how members of Conolly's staff could travel to Fayid without the Egyptians learning about it, but these were soon judged to be futile and it was decided to hold the talks at Tobruck, the great British base in Libya. On February 12th, Maclean wrote a "top secret" communication on Middle East Defence, continuing to argue the British case for at least partial Egyptian involvement in the talks: "Colonel Jenkins, the

Secretary of the Commanders-in-Chief Committee at Fayid told me yesterday that, subject to any last-minute hitch, it had now been arranged that the Anglo-U.S. planning talks, originally proposed for Fayid, will take place at Tobruk, starting on February 16th, and that the U.S.S. "Columbus" will arrive there on that date with the American planning committee on board.

The Commanders-in-Chief themselves would meet Admiral Conolly at Tobruk on February 22nd, as originally arranged, to consider the results of the planning work. The "Columbus" would stay at Tobruk throughout the whole conference . . . It seems to me to be probable that King Farouk will either learn or guess about the forthcoming Tobruk conference, particularly as the "Columbus" will be there for an abnormally long time and as the Commanders-in-Chief will be missing from Fayid. Ideally, it would be best if we could inform him of the conference beforehand or at least while it is going on and go through with our proposed approach about Anglo-American staff arrangements in general, Egyptian participation therein etc. He is ripe for such an approach now . . . If we wait too long he may be soured by his isolation or the tide of goodwill towards us may be re-set against us by some advantageous incident as frequently seems to happen in these parts . . . I think we should express the hope to both London and Washington that the proposed approach to King Farouk will not be dropped merely because it has been possible to make alternative arrangements at Tobruk for the present planning conference. There are three main reasons why this is so. First, the continuing military requirements referred to above. Second, the danger of missing the boat with King Farouk also referred to above, and thirdly, the advantage which we hope to gain by such an approach i.e. the eventual satisfaction of our own military requirements in Egypt . . .[52]

A minute by Maclean of April 7th, 1949, analyzing the understandings—and misunderstandings—concerning the joint staff talks is annotated by the Ambassador: "Many thanks," a comment of a kind cherished by any bureaucrat.

These exchanges included a reference to "American plans in Middle East under Trojan."[53] Trojan was an early (December, 1948) script for nuclear war, which included a plan for 133 atom bombs hitting 70 Soviet cities, with an expected loss of 2.7 million lives.[54] (Ironically, the US stockpile of atomic bombs at that point amounted to a total of 50.) Maclean, then, had been indoctrinated into Trojan, which meant, no doubt, that it was known in Moscow as well. At this time concern about World War Three had overtaken all other considerations for the British Government. For example, on February 21, 1949, Michael Wright, Superintending Under Secretary in the British Foreign Office, told Admiral Conolly "that Britain's primary interest in the Middle East is strategic and that British Foreign Policy in that area is only the handmaiden of British strategic planners."[55] The British and American governments had decided that in event of war their main bases for the Middle East, including bomber bases, would be in Egypt, Palestine fading from the equation. Negotiations between the British Government and the Egyptian government, on the one hand, and between the British and American governments, on the other, continued through the Spring of 1949, the British Government attempting to renew, and, if possible, to extend the alliance with Egypt, the American government attempting to secure airbases in the Canal Zone to support attacks on the Soviet Union without consulting, or even notifying, the Egyptian government.

Running on a parallel track, there were talks in mid-March between Field Marshal W. J. Slim (CIGS), King Farouk and members of the Egyptian Cabinet concerning U.K.-Egyptian defense cooperation. "Farouk said he was convinced that the USSR would not only attack Europe but that it would also attack the Middle East and agreed with Slim that Egypt would be the main target . . .

> Farouk on several occasions mentioned his intelligence sources which, among other things, had made him aware of US defense preparations in the Middle East such as "underground US airfields in Saudi Arabia" . . . Farouk also mentioned the threat of Israel to Middle East security and expressed pleasure at the decision of the British Government to send troops to Akaba

[Aqaba, to block an expected Israeli attack on Transjordan] . . . Farouk mentioned the fact that his "counter-espionage sources" had given him complete information regarding UK's military and strategic needs in Egypt in the event of war . . . Slim spoke of desirability of advance talks to prevent clashes between Egyptian forces and arriving British forces in the event of war.

Slim also had a meeting with the chief members of the Egyptian Cabinet during which the Egyptian Prime Minister asked for an account of British planning of activities in Egypt in the event of war with the Soviet Union. Slim agreed to give the Prime Minister a paper describing British requirements "now" and "when war becomes imminent."

Apparently drafted by Maclean, "The completed paper covered the following:

(1) The strategic aspects of the Middle East in the event of war with Russia. The strategic importance of Egypt would be emphasized. It would be pointed out that Russia in the event of war would undoubtedly strike for the Delta, the control of which would be essential to Russia. It would be thus indicated that the presence of the British in the Canal [Zone] would not be the reason for Russian attack, but that on the other hand, the presence of the British in Egypt would be an asset in its defence.

(2) The role which Egypt should play in the defence of Egypt. This section concerned itself with suggesting the needs for training and organization of the Egyptian forces, together with proposals as to how this might be accomplished.

(3) Requirements of Great Britain now and in the imminent threat of war. The number of troops would not be stressed but rather the organizational set-up. Thus, a headquarters staff, probably rather large, would be required; a certain amount of troops, organized on a skeleton basis with adequate administrative staff; certain technical troops, by which it was understood he [Maclean] meant technicians in radar, radio, and other fields. There would also be an

expanded RAF installation with enlarged administrative set-ups. Expansion of installations slightly outside of the Canal Zone might be asked in order to provide for the new arrangements. The creation of airfields outside would also be suggested.

(4) The creation of a liaison group of Egyptian and British officers to carry out any program which might be agreed upon, to discus differences of opinion and to plan in case of future developments, including war.[56]

When asked by the Americans about negotiating with the Egyptian Prime Minister, "if British Embassy was not afraid to push conclusion of such arrangements with [Prime Minister] Abdul Hadi lest it be repudiated by Wafd if it came into power after elections . . . [Maclean] replied that important fact was now that King and Prime Minister were in agreement. Believed this advantage should be pressed home. He promised to keep [American] Embassy informed."[57]

The details of these meetings and communications are not as important for our purposes here as the realization that Maclean was central to joint UK/Egyptian military planning for the defense of Egypt, and, by extension, the Middle East well as for UK/US planning, both offensive and defensive, in the area. He not only saw the documents, he drafted some of them. He was in continual communication with the American Embassy, with the leaders of the Egyptian government and with the British military command, as well as with the Foreign Office in London. The contacts with the American Embassy staff, including the Ambassador, were informal as well as formal. It is often the case that information as valuable as that obtained through official channels is obtained casually, standing about in an outer office waiting for a meeting, walking from one room to another, over lunch. However, the official documents are clear enough on their own. There was little, if anything, of interest in Moscow known to the British and American diplomatic and military staffs in Egypt that was not known by Maclean.

Egypt agreed to a new Suez Canal agreement, continuing the Suez Canal Company's extra-territorial status, on March 8, 1949. In the wider world, the NATO pact was signed on April 4, 1949. On April 18, 1949 President Truman directed the Secretary of State to undertake negotiations with the British Government to construct airfields suitable for American bombers in the Cairo-Suez area.[*] The Anglo-Egyptian military talks scheduled to begin on June 6, 1949, were delayed for about three weeks. Once begun, the "British wished to dissuade the Egyptians 'from idea large land army' [sic] and to convince them that 'their principal functions defense Egypt should be anti-aircraft, radar and fighter defense' and 'water works'."[58] The British Government wished to discourage the development of a large Egyptian Army because, among other things, they wished to have a rationale for the permanent stationing of large British forces in the Canal Zone. By July, 1949, the Egyptians had "accepted British estimate as to probable time-lag between outbreak of war and Soviet attack on Egyptian territory . . . [meaning] that Egypt would have to accept presence British troops to man bases and installations in order cope with attack at that time."[59] These talks had become entangled in the political maneuvering for the forthcoming Egyptian elections, which were anticipated in October.

Late in August Maclean was once again working on plans for the evacuation of British official personnel as well as others in the event of war with the Soviet Union, which was viewed as likely at any moment.[60] On August 27th, 1949, he drafted a telegram to the Foreign Office (Top Secret. Priority) concerning "Evacuation in case of war." Evacuations planning continued into 1950, with somewhat decreasing urgency, as evident from a letter from the Foreign Office to Maclean, June 13, 1950:

---

[*] Between those dates, the American Secretary of Defense, James Forrestal, resigned or was fired by President Truman, suffered what seems to have been a psychotic breakdown and convinced that "the Russians" were after him, committed suicide. The policy implications of Forrestal's mental condition in the previous years are of interest.

I am afraid it has been a long time since you received Foreign Office telegram No. 1344 of the 29th July 1949, about evacuation in the even of war, and I hope you have not come to the conclusion that the Foreign Office has lost sight of this matter.

Plans are to be coordinated, but not combined with, those of "your American colleagues," as theirs were likely already to have been completed and call for earlier evacuations than the UK would. The letter (from C. G. Kemball) concludes:

I should like to add that the fact that we are now asking you to send plans to the B.M.E.O., does not mean that the danger of an outbreak of hostilities is greater now than it was when our telegram was sent to you last year. Similar letters are being sent to all Levant and Middle East posts and are being copied to B.M.E.O.[61]

A November 4th, 1949, cable to the Foreign Office on Middle East Policy, with an appreciation of possible areas of Anglo-American conflict, provides an idea of Maclean's analytical drafting at a time when he was coming under increasing pressure in the espionage realm. (Philby may have learned of the efforts to identify "Homer" as early as August of 1949.)

I had the impression by the time I left Washington and also from the current exchanges between the Foreign Office and the State Department that the disadvantages of rivalry between the United States and Great Britain in the Middle East, other than the so-called healthy competition in the "free trade" sense, were well appreciated in the State Department itself and one would think in the upper circles of the United States Government and Army and Navy, but this does not of course mean that there will not be rivalry particularly if it is caused by non-Government factors. There are at least three large nuclei of American interests in the Middle East –

(1) The oil companies whose wars, truces, peaces and alliances with the British oil companies follow an esoteric course of their own. So far as I know, we are in a period of peace and

even alliance, but obviously "rivalry" might break out again some time.

(2) The American military aviation interest in Dahren and their strategic interest in the area generally. The Combined Chiefs of Staff would be able to prevent any serous trouble in this field.

(3) Palestine where American Jewry has so large a stake. It is very possible that rivalry between the interests of Israel backed, perhaps reluctantly, by the United Sates Government and interests of the Arab States backed by H.M. Government might clash with resultant Anglo-American (in a rather special sense) rivalry.

The Commercial Minister has already commented on commercial and economic activities. I only venture to add that where it is a question of loans for purposes of which we approve, e.g. Nile Waters and development generally, we are entirely to welcome American aid if we cannot, as we probably cannot, give it ourselves; the word "rivalry" hardly applies in this field. In other words, I doubt if we should want to prevent American assistance under President Truman's point 4. It is of course a different matter when it comes to straight competition for business, e.g. in tendering for the construction of a bridge or a dam. One can imagine situations in which America would put up the money and the contract would go to a British firm, which the Egyptian Government could not otherwise afford to employ at all. If the Americans try to insist on American firms getting such contracts, they would indeed be pinching us out.

I am afraid that all this is mere speculation.

D.D. Maclean[62]

Diplomatic relations between the British Empire and Egypt included the very important negotiations, still continuing in February 1950, concerning British World War Two debts to Egypt, which amounted to about one billion dollars and the status of the Sudan. American State Department observers believed that "The British would like to see a part of this debt canceled by the Egyptians or to arrange for a long term funding program supplemented by the inducement of an exchange of U.S. dollars by the U.S. for a portion of the Egyptian held sterling."[63] The Egyptian government, on its side, wished to take over the Sudan from Britain. Both sets of negotiations were complex and lengthy. "Finance was an 'incubus' on Anglo-Egyptian relations and any occurrence of haggling always brought in the question of Britain's presence in Egypt. Financial talks stalled, and by March Maclean was preparing to ask for a postponement of the talks if he could not get them back on track. This problem outlasted Maclean's sojourn in Egypt and continued to trouble Anglo-Egyptian relations."[64] Nonetheless, Bevin was optimistic that British forces could remain in Egypt for twenty to thirty years.[65]

Peter Hahn found that "American policy toward Egypt between January and June 1950 followed two distinct but interwoven themes. First, American officials reaffirmed their traditional willingness to cooperate with Britain on matters pertaining to Egypt, fully supporting the ongoing negotiations on the base and Sudan issues. Second, for the first time, the United States accepted a small responsibility for preserving stability in the Middle East."[66] When in March, 1950, Chief of the US Joint Chiefs of Staff, General Collins, visited Cairo "he spoke to King Farouk . . . to impress upon the Egyptians it was necessary for British troops to stay in the Canal Zone, and that the Americans would support the British position in Egypt . . .

Maclean participated in high-level Anglo-Egyptian military discussions held in Fayid . . . Patterson, the American Charge-d' Affaires, was uneasy about these talks, it seemed as if Britain was going ahead with Anglo-Egyptian military talks whether or not American assent was obtained. Chapman-Andrews [the British Minister] explained that, in a sense, Britain was acting as America's agent in the Middle East. Maclean later kept Patterson informed of progress in the talks. He emphasised the necessity for Anglo-American planning and to keep the Egyptians in a favourable mood . . . By May 1950, Anglo-Egyptian and Anglo-American defence relations were steady and productive.[67]

*       *       *

We can, then, give the main headings of Maclean's work at the Cairo embassy:

- He supervised the embassy's own administration, including security and the code room;
- Under the Ambassador and Minister, he maintained contact with the Egyptian government, reporting on internal Egyptian politics;
- He worked with the British Middle East Office on broader area policy and military matters;
- He worked with the British military command and secret intelligence services for the area;
- Under the Ambassador and Minister he maintained contact with the American embassy;
- He worked with the Foreign Office and American authorities on planning for a war with the Soviet Union.

These duties no doubt were sufficient to occupy him during office hours. After office hours, he and Melinda Maclean attended receptions at the various embassies and ministries in Cairo, hosted receptions and dinners, went to the parties of important local individuals, toured the country on their own and with such dignitaries as fell to their lot to entertain.

It is good to keep this work-load and rounds of more or less official activities in mind when considering the depiction of the Macleans, in the popular spy books and, indeed, in the files of organizations like the FBI. There are standard stories in the espionage literature having to do with the personal habits of spies. Many such stories are homophobic—*if Burgess and Blunt were homosexual, then it is no wonder that they were spies.* (Which does not explain Philby or Cairncross, but that is hardly the point.) Some have to do with hygiene, especially that of Burgess. *His fingernails*

295

*were not clean, therefore he was a spy.* Many have to do with alcohol. Stories of this type about Maclean are chiefly about alcohol, with an occasional reference to homosexuality, none to his fingernails. From early during his time in Egypt there is a story about a trip up the Nile that resulted in a drunken struggle with one of his colleagues. In February 1950, there were more stories that Donald Maclean had begun to drink too much.[68] Robert Cecil, who was not on the spot, but would have been in a position to pick up Foreign Office gossip, wrote that "Away from the city for a few days' local leave at Luxor or Assouan he seemed to be his old self, playing family bridge and tennis and showing his affection for his small sons; but back in Cairo it was another story.

> More and more frequently he would set out with Melinda on the nightly round of cocktail parties, followed by a dinner engagement, which Melinda alone would keep . . . word reached the Foreign Office through the Embassy Security Officer . . . that all was not as it should be and early in 1950 George Middleton (Sir George), head of Personnel Department, wrote to [Ambassador] Campbell to enquire. Campbell . . . replied . . . that he disliked hearing tittle-tattle about an able officer like Maclean . . ."[69]

It is not that the stories are all untrue. Maclean was indeed an alcoholic. It is just that he was not only an alcoholic. He was, as the Ambassador said, "an able officer," and a spectacularly successful spy.

Isis Fahmy, a Coptic socialite and journalist, who in her memoirs describes herself as a neighbor of the Macleans in Cairo and a confidante of Melinda Maclean, recalled: "Work over for the day Maclean, who was a keen tennis player and swimmer, would be off in the afternoons to the Guezireh Sporting Club.

> Maclean began to invite his Soviet counterparts and went on to meet them more and more often, quite openly. In addition his secret night meetings with the Russians became more frequent . .
.

In is not clear how Isis Fahmy knew about "his secret night meetings with the Russians." In any case, she speculated that

He used Princess Fayza's parties as a cover, going on from them late at night to meet the Russian diplomats. Melinda, who was still in love with him, cried because she was convinced he as seeing another woman. I did what I could to calm her down, but to no avail, because it was true that Fayza was attracted to him and danced regularly with him at her parties.

Princess Fayza (or Faiza) "was married to a tolerant Turkish prince, [Mohammed] Ali Raouf [Bulent], and liked her friends to organize parties and dances for her on an almost daily basis.

Most of the foreign diplomats who enjoyed night-life were invited, bachelors mostly, but some couples. To be admitted into this exclusive circle one had to be refined, handsome and charming. Maclean had all the qualifications. No one could dispute that he was smart, tall, and slender, with delicate features; the man-about-town par excellence. Thanks to his physical qualifications, his approachable nature and ease in conversation, he had no difficulty in gaining access to the best circles. All fell under the spell of his charm.[70]

Elsewhere in her memoir, Fahmy writes about quarrels she had with Maclean, whose political views, she felt, were to the left of hers and those she had expected of a British diplomat.

There are stories in the spy literature that the good relationship Maclean had with his Soviet contacts in Paris, London and Washington were not replicated in Cairo. According to Yuri Modin, who, it must be said, was not there, "as soon as Maclean arrived [in Cairo] his KGB contact started trying to order him around . . .

Maclean's reaction was to suggest that all communication between him and the handler should cease, and that two liaison agents should take his place: namely, Melinda Maclean and the wife of the Soviet resident. The two women could meet at the hairdresser's, for example. Melinda was quite prepared to do this, but the Cairo residence categorically rejected the idea . . . It was at this crucial juncture that Donald Maclean wrote a letter to the Center via the Cairo KGB residence. The letter was short, a kind of SOS: in it he declared that he had always wished to work in Russia and felt that it was the best place for him to carry on his struggle against American and Western imperialism . . . I am quite sure that nobody looked at it. Had the Cairo resident had the sense to act immediately to get Donald Maclean and his family to the USSR—Melinda was perfectly prepared to go . . . our Cambridge network might never have been dismantled at all.[71]

It is quite possible that the Soviet resident in Cairo was this clumsy. On the other hand we have Isis Fahmy's story about Maclean bringing Soviet officials to his club. Although Modin's memoir is useful when recording events in which he was involved, it is often unreliable concerning events and personalities with which he was not directly acquainted. Perhaps his account of KGB clumsiness in Cairo was a way to conceal the communications routes used by Philby to warn Maclean about the progress of the Venona project. In any case, the reference to Melinda Maclean's willingness to work as a linking agent is of interest.

Kerr conjectures that Maclean may have learned of the Venona investigation early in 1950 and decided then to leave Cairo.[72] London might have seemed a better place to track the progress of "the hunt for Homer," so-called, and an easier place from which to disappear. (Some years later, Philby was to have had some difficulty making the jump to Moscow from Beirut.) In any case, according to Kerr, although "Maclean's work towards the end of 1949 and 1950 may have been overshadowed by the knowledge that MI5 was hunting for a Soviet agent in the Foreign Office. However, there is very little evidence to suggest this affected his work."[73] For much of his life Maclean would occasionally engage in bouts of drinking, occasionally becoming violent. These episodes, also, did not seem to have affected the quantity or quality of his work. That work in the Spring of 1950 continued to involve both relations with Egypt and those with the United States. These had a considerable overlap, as Anglo-Egyptian relations were focused on the renewal of the Anglo-

Egyptian treaty, governing the British forces and bases in Egypt in peacetime and preparations for expansion in the event of war, while those with the United States were especially concerned with planning for war, including the preparation of airfields for American B-29 bombers to use against the Soviet Union in the event of war.[74] The Foreign Office files from this period have been thoroughly "weeded"; there are none from Cairo bearing Maclean's signature. On the other hand, there are many from "Chancery," signed with illegible initials that are likely those of Maclean, showing his usual expertise in drafting, in this case, accounts of Egyptian politics and the successful efforts of the Egyptian government to suppress the Egyptian Communist Party. These run through the events described below to the end of his time in Cairo.

\*     \*     \*

On April 9, 1950, Maclean's old friend Philip Toynbee, separated from his first wife, and drinking heavily, arrived in Cairo as a reporter for *The Observer*. Here begins another twice-told tale. It may be that Toynbee's appearance precipitated or facilitated an alcoholic binge. It may be that the Macleans decided that Toynbee's appearance provided the opportunity that they needed to persuade the Foreign Office to cut short Donald Maclean's tour of duty in Cairo.[*] In any case, by the 21st of April Toynbee had moved in with the Macleans. Harriet Marling was also staying with them. (She was often present at key moments of her sister's life.) The following are excerpts from Toynbee's diary: "Suddenly Donald arrived, called me "Philippo", his old private nickname.

Tall, graceful, delightful old friend! With his pretty little son. Then I was at a roof party, among bougainvillaea, military attachés, thin colonial women ... Whirling into a wilder and wilder world. Dinner with Donald on Sunday, then both to the

---

[*]  As will be evident, Toynbee was too far into an alcoholic episode to realize how he was being used, if that was indeed the case.

Izzards [Daily Mail]. Very drunk. Relax! As Melinda sweetly and often said to me ... Delightful to have moved to Donald's where I have my own little white flat at the top of the house... It even seems cooler (yesterday 105°!) ... "extraordinary conversation with Donald [22 April] I find him more and more fascinating and delightful. His extreme gentleness and politeness–the occasional berserk and murderous outbursts when, so to speak, the pot of suppressed anger has been filled ... Donald told me he wished, still, for the death of his wife.[75] He was in a queer and terrifying condition ...

*Relax, said Melinda. Have another drink.*

More from Toynbee's diary: 26 April "Donald and I tumbled into a two-day trough together ...

I was back in bed by midnight, but Donald rushed out again to disaster after disaster, ending by hitting Eddie [Gathorne-Hardy] and throwing glass after glass against the wall ... [the next morning] Donald was still rather drunk, but I forced him out of bed, sobered him with talk and took him all the way to his room at the Embassy. Somehow, once there, he managed to heave on his armour and become a good semblance of a Counsellor. I admired it ...

Gathorne-Hardy was a minor Bloomsbury figure, brother of Lady Anne Gathorne-Hardy, who married the bookseller Heywood Hill; sometime roommate, as it was said, of Brian Howard, and so on. In Cairo he was working, if he was working, with the British Council.

[May 4] an evening of Rabelaisian exhibitionism ... wilder and wilder attempts to shock [the Marling sisters]. Failure. They retired in good order long before we did. Donald began to become aggressive [Eventually MacLean went out with one of the guests, "a known homosexual," perhaps Gathorne-Hardy, and did not reappear that night. The next day was Saturday] ... All that day I was affected by Donald's gigantic grief. When he came back for lunch, Melinda was upstairs in her bedroom. I told him the headmaster was waiting in his study ... [Monday morning] Donald came down with those terrible, tell-tale bleary eyes and told me that he had gone wild again last night, publicly insulted Harriet, hit Melinda ... "I really am getting near to the point where I shall have to be shut up." I tried to say, "How absurd!", but of course it's terrifyingly true ... I am now convinced that he must at once, and at whatever cost, be analysed—even if it means asking for two years' medical leave from the foreign service. It can't go on ... [Some days later? At British Embassy official John Wardle-Smith's home. Wardle-Smith would succeed Maclean as Counsellor.] All yesterday we drank and drank, mostly sitting on a balcony in the sun, very happy for several hours and very certain that what we were doing was the best thing we could possibly be doing. The snarling hog's head on the gin bottle, whom we named Gordon and whom we emulated by drinking, in all six bottles [among three men?] ... Then, girl-hounding, we went to another flat and, finding nobody, smashed it to pieces.

In Paris, ten years earlier, it had been Toynbee who was given to smashing up his friend's apartment when drunk.

At this point the received narratives become somewhat confused. There is a story of Maclean smashing a bathtub with a mirror, a story not in the diary, but canonical as published by Toynbee many years later. Other accounts mention a mantelpiece, dishes or a marble shelf. The FBI interviewed an American diplomat who had been stationed in Cairo during Maclean's time there. He told the FBI about the room-wrecking incident in less dramatic terms, having heard that one of the young women occupying the apartment had slept through the entire incident.[76] In any case, after the room-wrecking, Toynbee and Maclean were somehow gathered up by Melinda and Harriet and taken home. Melinda told Philip that he should move to a hotel. The next day Maclean sent a written apology to the American young women whose flat he and Toynbee had wrecked, saying that he was going to obtain medical help, and offering to pay for the damage.[77] Harriet[*] called on the young American women and apologized for the actions of Maclean and Toynbee. According to Cecil, "On the same day Melinda, white-faced, but resolute, went to see the Ambassador and demands that Maclean be sent to England for [medical] treatment." He was.

"In the early morning of Friday, May 11, I [Geoffrey Hoare] drove out to Farouk Field on my way back to England ...

At the airport I met Donald and found he was going on the same plane. A rather strained and unhappy Melinda, with Harriet and the British minister, was there to see him off. I asked Donald why he was flying to London, and he replied merely that he was going home on private business for a few days ... Although I knew Donald fairly well by then, I noticed nothing wrong with him in any way except possibly that he was rather more silent than usual. He had none of the external signs of a person suffering from a severe nervous breakdown.[78]

Some stories point one way; others point another way.

After Donald Maclean left Cairo for London, Toynbee traveled to Palestine, apparently having seen no more of Melinda Maclean and her sister. Perhaps they felt he had been a bad influence on Donald Maclean. Perhaps they felt he had served his purpose. Perhaps he was ashamed of himself.

Having followed Toynbee this far, from Castle Howard, through his Communist student days and his intermittent friendship with Donald Maclean, whom it seems he hardly knew at all, we can follow him a bit further before later noting the role that he, with Muggeridge and Cyril Connolly, played in characterizing Donald Maclean (and Guy Burgess) for the popular press.

Toynbee had become the Middle East correspondent for *The Observer* in the usual way: connections. When Toynbee's wife Anne

---

[*] Or possibly Mrs. Dunbar, the accounts are unclear and there is some ambiguity about the date of Mrs. Dunbar's arrival in Cairo.

left him for Richard Wollheim,[*] Toynbee's historian father had asked the publisher of *The Observer,* David Astor, to give his son a job. Philip Toynbee's frequent articles in *The Observer* were also syndicated to other Commonwealth papers. On Friday, June 23, 1950, *The Mercury* of Hobart, Tasmania, carried an "exclusive": "Arab States Have Legitimate Sense of Injury." Toynbee begins with the observation that "The tragedy of the Palestine problem is that both sides think and argue on quite different levels and that both are right on their own level." The article is based on a conversation with "an Arab friend," who describes Israel as a plot by American Jews to build "a little America" in the Middle East.[79] On Sunday, June 25, Toynbee reported that Arab peasants, who had been allowed to sow their fields near the Dead Sea, were being turned away by Israeli border officials, resulting in violence on both sides. Toynbee "interviewed some of the Arab victims."[80] On June 29th he reported the conditions in a refugee camp on the east bank of the Jordan. On the 17th of August he reported, from Tel Aviv, about issues around the definition of who is a Jew (noting that hardly any Jews in the new state were religious). And on September 5th, again from Tel Aviv, Toynbee wrote about the paradoxes of a then largely communistic (small "c") country that was careful not allow the growth of a significant Communist Party presence, which Toynbee characterized as essentially anti-Zionist and in the end determined to make Israel a part of the Soviet Union:

> Israeli Communists are no more Israeli in their loyalties than English Communists are English, or Rumanian Communists are Rumanian. They are at best indifferent to Jewish immigration, and they regard the building up of the State as a dangerous waste of time, since they believe that the independent State of Israel must eventually become a republic of the Soviet Union.[81]

Despite his journalistic responsibilities and remarkable alcohol consumption, Toynbee managed to make a comprehensive survey of

---

[*] Toynbee's anguished diary entries from the period when his marriage was coming apart are heartbreaking.

sexually available women in Israel—Arab, Jewish, neither—eventually deciding to give the palm to a secretary in the American Embassy, Sally (Francis Genevieve Smith), whom he married. She, like Melinda Maclean, was the daughter of an American oil company executive.[82]

It is evident from his newspaper stories that Toynbee was not only no longer a Communist, but that he was moving toward, if he had not already arrived at, anti-Communism. And during his weeks in Cairo he had rarely been sober. These matters should be factored into a consideration of his account of the end of the Macleans's time in Egypt. His political views, if expressed, would have severely limited any confidences he received from the Macleans and his drunkenness was likely to have affected his perceptions and memory. As Toynbee was the only witness to much of Maclean's reported alcoholic breakdown the details of the received narrative of the events of those weeks should be treated with caution. Kerr, who may have gotten the idea from Cecil, suggests that the scenes with Philip Toynbee could have been deliberately staged. Toynbee would have been a useful audience for this act. He was often, if not usually, nearly insensible with drink, worshipped Maclean, and was disoriented by his sudden transfer from his English context to Cairo. If we follow that line of thought, a story could be composed in which Toynbee's sudden appearance in Cairo was seized upon by the Macleans as a way of making it necessary for the Ambassador to send Donald Maclean home. This would have been facilitated by Melinda Maclean's role as the Ambassador's hostess. It is suggestive that after "his return to London, [Maclean] wrote to Toynbee ... "It would be no use concealing it. After all, we broke up that room in order that it shouldn't be concealed."[83]

*   *   *

After seeing off her husband at the Cairo airport, Melinda Maclean, reinforced by her sister and mother, considered her options. She cancelled their usual summer rental of a house in Alexandria and decided to spend the summer in Spain, away from the diplomatic community. Melinda and Harriet and Mrs. Dunbar visited an American diplomat at the American Embassy in Cairo (perhaps Patterson), who later told the FBI interviewers that Mrs. Dunbar and the Marling sisters had "officially requested his aid in securing visas for them to go to Spain," which he did.[*] Mrs. Dunbar paid the bills, supervised the packing and other preparations, and on June 18 she, Melinda Maclean and the children sailed from Alexandria for Spain. "The morning before they sailed from Alexandria to Spain, she [Melinda, but surely not alone] went out for the evening for "dinner in Alexandria's leading restaurant, followed by the usual round of night clubs."[84] Thus so far Hoare's account. What he does not report, what Melinda and her mother may not have told him, is that they were accompanied to Spain by her lover, Prince Ismail Daoud. Perhaps Prince Daoud had a castle, or apartment, in Spain. If Donald Maclean had in fact been the lover of Farouk's sister Faiza and Melinda Maclean the lover of Farouk's cousin Ismail Daoud ... matters in Cairo had been complicated.[†]

---

[*] This diplomat was quite sure that Maclean had not had any contact with Russians in Cairo, as "he undoubtedly would have heard of it inasmuch as Cairo was considered a small settlement in this respect and the news of such a contact would have reached him rapidly."

[†] See, for further such local color, inter alia, Lawrence Durrell's *Alexandria Quartet.*

## Chapter Eight: Notes

[1] Devereux, David R. Britain and the Failure of Collective Defence in the Middle East, 1948-53. in Deighton, Anne (ed.) Britain and the First Cold War. New York, St. Martin's Press, 1990, pp. 237-8.

[2] FRUS, 1947, Volume V, p. 584.

[3] Hahn, Peter L. The United States, Great Britain, and Egypt, 1945-1956. Chapel Hill and London: The University of North Carolina Press, 1991, p. 53.

[4] Channon, Sir Henry. 'Chips': The Diaries of Sir Henry Channon. Ed. Robert Rhodes James. London: Orion, 1996, p. 290.

[5] Dorril, Stephen. MI6: Inside the Covert World of Her Majesty's Secret Intelligence Service. New York: Free Press, 2002, p. 534.

[6] Louis, Wm. Roger. The British Empire in the Middle East 1945-1951: Arab Nationalism, The United States and Postwar Imperialism. Oxford: Clarendon Press, 1984, p. 446.

[7] Louis, pp. 459-60.

[8] Louis, p. 457, citing CM (47) 6th Conclusions, Minute 3, Confidential Annex, 15 Jan. 1947, CAB 128/11.

[9] Cecil, p. 83.

[10] Brown, Andrew. J. D. Bernal: The Sage of Science. Oxford University Press, 2005, p. 269; 272-3.

[11] Steel, Ronald. Walter Lippmann and the American Century. Boston: Little, Brown and Company. An Atlantic Monthly Press Book, 1980, p. 454.

[12] Pappe, Ilan. "Sir Alec Kirkbride and the Anglo-Transjordanian alliance, 1945-50," in Zametica, John (ed.). British Officials and British Foreign Policy: 1945-50. Leicester: Leicester University Press, 1990, p. 126, citing FO 371/68378 E4319, notes on Intermezzo, an exercise on Russian invasion of the Middle East.

[13] Louis, p. 395.

[14] A 1944 P.H.P. document stated that "Palestine and Transjordan . . . are at present under British mandate and a force stationed in this area would be on the right side of the Canal for dealing with the most probable land threat. Such a force would also act as a deterrent to

any threat to internal security resulting from the Palestine partition scheme." P.H.P. (44) 16 (0) Annex. September 1944.

[15] Pappe, p. 137, citing [perhaps mistakenly], FO 371/68864, Kirkbride to Burrows, 21 October 1948. But see DEFE 4/12, CoS (48)48, 1 April 1948.

[16] Pappe, pp 134-5.

[17] The new Israeli state also had a certain amount of support from the Soviet Union, which influenced Czechoslovakia to allow arms purchases by the Jewish Agency: "From December 1947 to 15 May 1948, the Jewish Agency purchased about $13 million of heavy and light arms from Czechoslovakia. For the second half of 1948, Prague granted Israel $12 million in credit to pay for the arms, of which Israel used only $9 million. In all, the Jewish Agency and the Israeli government purchased about $22 million worth of military supplies from Czechoslovakia, which also organized the training of Israeli pilots and paratroopers. This military cooperation continued until 1951." Rucker, Laurent. "Moscow's Surprise: The Soviet-Israeli Alliance of 1947-1949. Woodrow Wilson International Center for Scholars, Cold War International History Project, Working Paper #46, p. 27. The entire article is of great interest.

[18] Louis, p. 376.

[19] Cecil, p. 92.

[20] Hoare, Geoffrey. The Missing Macleans. New York: The Viking Press, 1955, pp. 75-6.

[21] Connolly, Cyril. The Missing Diplomats. London, Queen Anne Press, 1952, p. 27.

[22] Maclean's former colleague in Washington, who was then Press Officer at No. 10 Downing Street. His wife was related to Beatrice Webb.

[23] Muggeridge, Malcolm, Like It Was: The Diaries of Malcolm Muggeridge. London: HarperCollins Publishers Ltd, 1981, p. 299.

[24] Cecil, p. 95

[25] Kerr, p. 282-3.

[26] Botman, Selma. Egypt from Independence to Revolution, 1919-1952. Syracuse, New York: Syracuse University Press, 1991, pp. 73ff.

[27] Perrault, Gilles. Henri Curiel, Citizen of the Third World. Le Monde Diplomatique, English Edition, April, 1998, http://mondediplo.com/1998/04/13curiel.

[28] Cecil, p. 95

[29] Botman, p. 104, citing FO 371/46003 J2962/440/16, September 1, 1945.

[30] FRUS, 1949, Volume VI, p. 187.

[31] Morris, Benny. 1948: The First Arab-Israeli War. New Haven: Yale University Press, 2008, pp. 369-71.

[32] FRUS, 1949, Volume VI, p. 627.

[33] FRUS, 1949, Volume VI, p. 639.

[34] In opinion of British Consul Jerusalem. FRUS, 1949, Volume VI, p. 670.

[35] TNA CAB 131/8.

[36] Morris, p. 275.

[37] Kerr, p. 283-4.

[38] The British secret police eavesdropped on a conversation in Pollitt's office in January, 1945, when it was mentioned that Klugmann, then in Cairo, had judged the Curiel Group to be "completely unreliable," with little contact with "the Arabs." KV 2/788.

[39] Hoare, pp. 76-7.

[40] Hoare, pp. 78-9.

[41] The FBI interviewed an American diplomat in 1951 who had been stationed in Cairo during Maclean's time there. He "described this group as not particularly immoral, but merely fun-loving." FBI, Cambridge Five Spy Ring, Part 2.

[42] FBI, Cambridge Five, Part 5

[43] FBI, Cambridge Five, Part 5

[44] TNA FO 141/1345 March 20, 1949.

[45] Admiral Conolly had been the British choice for the chief planner of Mediterranean strategy. Forrestal, James. The Forrestal Diaries. Edited by Walter Millis. New York: The Viking Press, 1951, p. 526.

[46] Hahn, p. 78, citing Bevin to Campbell, 5 Feb. 1949, FO 800/457, Eg/49/6.

[47] FRUS, 1949, Volume VI, p. 190.

[48] FRUS, 1949, Volume VI, pp. 203-4.

[49] FRUS, 1949, Volume VI, p. 188.

[50] TNA FO 141/1365.

[51] TNA FO 141/1365 Minute by Maclean, February 8, 1949.

[52] TNA FO/141/1365 TOP SECRET Middle East Defence, February 12, 1949.

[53] For an account of American war plans during the immediate post-World War Two period, see, inter alia, Borowski, Harry R. "A Narrow Victory: the Berlin blockade and the American military response." Air University Review, July-August 1981.

[54] Mastny, Vojtech. NATO in the Beholder's Eye: Soviet Perceptions and Policies, 1949-56. Washington, D.C., Woodrow Wilson International Center for Scholars, Cold War International History Project, Working Paper No. 35, March 2002. Other sources mention 300 atomic bombs.

[55] FRUS, 1949, Volume VI, p. 195.

[56] Airgram 373, March 30, from Cairo, 883.20/3-3049. FRUS, 1949, Volume VI, pp. 199-201.

[57] FRUS, 1949, Volume VI, pp. 199-202.

[58] FRUS, 1949, Volume VI, p. 219.

[59] FRUS, 1949, Volume VI, p. 220.

[60] A reading of the Cabinet papers under CAB 131/8 shows a level of concern and conviction of inevitability now forgotten.

[61] TNA FO 141/1402.

[62] TNA FO 141/1377 Middle East Policy

[63] FRUS, 1950, Volume V, pp. 284-5.

[64] Kerr, p. 304.

[65] CAB 131/8.

[66] Hahn, p. 94.

[67] Kerr, pp. 305-6.

[68] Hoare, p. 80.

[69] Cecil, pp. 99-100.

[70] Fahmy, Isis. Around the World With Isis. London: Papadakis, 2006, pp. 27-8. There is an interesting footnote to these stories of the Egyptian/Ottoman aristocracy. During the events leading to the 1952 coup that overthrew King Farouk, Princess Faiza and her husband Bulent Raouf decided to pass the time by making a film. Princess Faiza played herself, while her husband and friends took other roles in "Oil and Sand." The film "takes place in a fictional desert kingdom in the Arabian Gulf, where a military coup d'état had just taken place.

A modern General was now the new republican ruler, and his rival, the deposed Sheikh was fighting a hit-and-run war from his desert stronghold. Into the fold come two competing Oil companies—one British, one American-both intent on signing a drilling concession. The British back the traditional desert King while the Americans support the new military dictator. In reality, the British agent in the film was the Oriental Secretary at the British Embassy, while the US Agent was acted by Bob Simpson, in reality the special assistant to the US ambassador in Cairo. It later turns out that Mr Simpson was the contact man between the Embassy and the Free Officers led by Gamal Abdel-Nasser—the group behind the real coup in July '52.
http://middlewestfilms.com/oil&sand/press.phpBri

[71] Modin, p. 164.

[72] Kerr, p. 278.

[73] Christopher Andrew concurred: "Philby had been 'indoctrinated' into Venona in September 1949, on the eve of his posting to Washington as SIS liaison officer, and had passed on an urgent warning . . . Donald Maclean reacted as badly as Burgess to news of the threat posed by Venona . . . Though his work remained highly

professional, his drinking out of hours slipped out of control."
Andrew, Christopher and Gordievsky, Oleg. KGB: The Inside Story.
London: Hodder & Stoughton, 1990, p. 325.

[74] See CAB 131/9 for British mobilization plans, contributions to
Allied Defence and related matters preparatory to either a
continuation of the Cold War or the beginning of a hot war.

[75] Cecil seems to attribute Maclean's wish "for the death of his wife"
to Melinda Maclean's affair to the "princeling of the royal house."
The use of the term "princeling" Prince Ismail Daoud is a
colonialism on Cecil's part. Daoud was a descendent of Muhammad
Ali, founder of modern Egypt, and brother-in-law of King Fuad,
King Farouk's father. He had been head of the Egyptian Red
Crescent during the Italian war against Ethiopia. Daoud served in the
Egyptian army during World War II and was recommended for the
award of Commander of the Most Excellent Order of the British
Empire.

[76] FBI, Cambridge Five Spy Ring, Part 2.

[77] FBI, Cambridge Five Spy Ring, Part 4, Interview Report August
12, 1951.

[78] Hoare, p. 87-88.

[79] Toynbee, Philip. Arab States Have Legitimate Sense of Injury. The
Mercury, Hobart, Tasmania, June 23, 1950, page 3,
http://trove.nla.gov.au/ndp/del/article/18478215?searchTerm=%22Ph
ilip%20Toynbee%22&searchLimits=sortby=dateAsc, accessed
November 11, 2013.

[80] Toynbee, Philip. A Tale of Terror. The Sunday Herald, Sydney,
NSW, June 25, 1950, page 8,
http://trove.nla.gov.au/ndp/del/article/18478215?searchTerm=%22Ph
ilip%20Toynbee%22&searchLimits=sortby=dateAsc, accessed
November 11, 2013.

[81] Toynbee, Philip. Communism Plays a Paradoxical Role in Israel.
The Mercury, Hobart, Tasmania, September 5, 1950, page 3,
http://trove.nla.gov.au/ndp/del/article/18478215?searchTerm=%22Ph

---

ilip%20Toynbee%22&searchLimits=sortby=dateAsc, accessed November 11, 2013.

[82] Oxford Dictionary of National Biography, Philip Toynbee article. When Donald Maclean disappeared from England, the British secret police immediately tapped Toynbee's telephone in London, eliciting much gossip from Cyril Connolly and friends. See: TNA KV 2/3436.

[83] Cecil, p. 107.

[84] Hoare, p. 49.

# Chapter Nine

*London, Once More*

The evening after his arrival in London, Maclean, who was staying with his mother, wrote to Melinda: "Dear Lin,

I got in late last night after a good trip ... I sent you a telegram this morning which I hope reached its objective alright. I am tucked away in the womb very comfortably ...

I lunched with George Middleton [then head of the Foreign Office Personnel Department] today and told him the score. He was very understanding and has fixed for me to see a Dr. Wilson tomorrow morning, who is said to be a leading psychiatrist and who the F.O. employ as a consultant when their employees psyches miss a beat. I still have my lid off and I am prepared therefore to ask help; if he says I need more exercise I shall go round the corner to ... [first name of a woman psychoanalyst] (Harley to Wimpole not far). I see no point in resisting George's offer to start me on this path anyhow; but also if it looks like being what I need I should get an analysis for nothing—but I promise to be expensive and go to ... or elsewhere if it don't look any good. Anyhow George has been extremely decent and I am very grateful to him and still [more] to Andrew at his end ...

I am grateful to you my sweet for taking all you have had to put up with without hating me. I am still rather lost, but cling to the idea that you do want me to be cured and come back. I am leery of making promises of being a better husband, since past ones have all been broken; but perhaps if some technician will strengthen my gasket and enlarge my heart I could make a promise which would stick. Anyhow you have been very sweet to me and I will try to give you something in return. I was overwhelmed with sadness at leaving the boys; I suppose it affects one particularly because they expect one to be there and have no means of understanding why one goes away; it is, however, I suppose bathetic rather than pathetic so long as they are happy; I know you will keep them so. I hate having left you with all the responsibility for the house, family, car, servants;

and long to hear that you are managing all right. Please say a special word of thanks to Harry [Harriet] for me if this reaches you in time. She was so kind when she had much reason not to be and I shall try never to forget her sweetness any more than I shall forget yours.

I saw the Italian film about the bicycle thief today. It was very good, but too sad for you my chickabid! I will try to keep you posted. I think very much of you my darling, miss you badly and love you. Don't feel sad about me as I will come back a better person and we can be happy together again I am sure. D.

The status of this and the other letters quoted by Hoare is unclear. They were apparently given to him by Melinda Maclean or Mrs. Dunbar. He does not explain their motives for so doing. This letter certainly fits with the public story of Donald Maclean's breakdown under the strain of work and alcohol. The strong sentiments of love and affection for "Lin" (and "chickabid") are somewhat at odds with Toynbee's account, but do not contradict it: loving spouses, when drunk, sometimes do behave badly to one another. It does not, on the other hand, read much like a communication from a spy who believes himself on the verge of exposure. Of course there are not many of those at hand for comparison.

Middleton, with whom Maclean had played tennis at the Washington Embassy, had given Maclean a six-month sick leave, on the assumption he would be treated for his breakdown and, presumably, for alcoholism. Maclean at first visited the Foreign Office's psychiatrist, who recommended that he go to a clinic for the period. Maclean refused and decided instead to be treated by Dr. Erna Rosenbaum, a Jungian psychoanalyst who had been recommended to him (he does not say by whom). There is some implication in the espionage literature that she was a Communist Party nominee. This seems unlikely. Rosenbaum, a founder of the Society of Analytical Psychology in London, early in her career had been held in sufficient regard by Jung as to be delegated to treat the physicist Wolfgang Pauli, which does not seem like a Communist Party profile.[1] Klugmann, for example, probably would have used his

Austrian Center contacts to nominate a Freudian. In any case, Rosenbaum treated Maclean for six months, diagnosing overwork, marital troubles and repressed homosexuality.[2]

Maclean soon moved into a hotel. His activities during this period are difficult to trace except those with members of his old social milieu at the intersection of the Liberal aristocracy and the Gargoyle Club. Cressida Ridley, née Bonham Carter, invited him for a country weekend in Stockton, Wiltshire; her sister Laura Grimond and her husband the MP Jo Grimond had lunch with him. Laura Grimond told Cecil that "There was nothing wrong with his memory, nor with his grasp of the international situation. He made light of his own troubles too, even suggesting that he might soon be going back to rejoin the Embassy staff in Cairo."[3] Others found him less well, given to fits of delirium tremens and paranoid hallucinations about "the Russians." He again frequented the Gargoyle, becoming himself a member that summer if he had not been before, drinking heavily. On one famous occasion, according to Goronwy Rees, not always reliable, Maclean accused Rees of betraying the cause: "You used to be one of us, but you ratted," which was probably true, even if the story is not.

Concerning "the international situation," on June 25th, 1950, on June 25th, 1950, on June 25th, 1950, after consultations with Stalin and Mao, Kim Il Sung had sent his army across the 38th parallel, routing the South Korean and American armed forces. The British Joint Intelligence Staff immediately began providing the Cabinet with frequent situation reports, while the Chiefs of Staff surveyed the "order of battle" of the Empire for resources that could be applied in Korea. The American government obtained a condemnation of the invasion in the United Nations and reinforced its occupation units, who were, nonetheless, forced rapidly south into the Pusan Pocket, a comparatively small defensive perimeter in the southeast corner of the peninsula, which was set up on August 4th. The imperious American proconsul in Japan, General MacArthur, who was at first confident that the invasion force would be crushed, was then convinced that his army would be pushed into the sea. President

Truman ordered the Seventh Fleet to take up a position between mainland China and the Nationalist Chinese refuge on Formosa, to prevent either from invading the other. Many in Washington and London were certain that Stalin would at any moment make a parallel move in the West, using nominally East German units. As the British Joint Intelligence Committee estimated the military strength of the Soviet Union at 215 army divisions, 18,000 aircraft, and 20 atomic bombs, planning began for stay-behind units to operate after the Red Army occupied Western Europe and ideological rehabilitation measures to be taken if, by some chance, that occupation came to an end.

American Secretary of State Dean Acheson "in mid-September, 1950, finally confirmed what many had long suspected by calling for a ten-division German Army. [Walter] Lippmann, after talks with German leaders, recorded in his private notes that 'nothing could be plainer or clearer than that the German army is thinking of a war of revenge and not of the defense of Europe at the Elbe river.'"[4] The British Government were notably cool about the prospect of a German army and the French government were, as would be expected, strongly opposed.[5]

Early in September Donald Maclean sent his wife a letter that was very depressed and self-critical. Melinda Maclean, who was still in Spain with her children, mother, and Prince Ismail Daoud, apparently consulted someone from the Foreign Office, perhaps Middleton. Perhaps she consulted someone from the Soviet foreign intelligence service. In any case, she went with her household, including Daoud, to Paris and then flew alone to London. She stayed there for two weeks, at the end of which she was again pregnant. Harriet Marling (now Mrs. Sheers) had returned to New York, where Melinda Maclean wrote to her: "Donald had grave doubts at first about our ability to be happy together but we decided to try it again.

To me it was the only decision to take on account of the children, and I think Donald has already benefited tremendously. He realizes many things which he never allowed himself to think before. We have both, alas, developed in opposite directions. I

316

have become more extroverted and enjoy gayer and simpler people, but Donald will have none of that at all. However if we are frank and above all don't repress our feelings perhaps we will work something out. He is going back to the F.O. on November 1 poor lamb![6]

Not apparently under any sort of official cloud, Donald Maclean was going back to the Foreign Office as head of the American Department, reporting to Under-Secretary Sir Roger Makins, with whom he had worked at the Washington Embassy.[7] Just like old times.

After a month or two, Prince Daoud having been abandoned, the Macleans found a house ("Beaconshaw") in the Surrey village of Tatsfield. Tatsfield is reached by train from London to Oxted (Lady Maclean's family home), then by taxi for the last four miles: perhaps two hours from Maclean's desk to his front door. The house was, as described in a recent (2013) advertisement for half of it (guide price £850,000) "Located in a highly popular village ... This attractive and large property forms one half of a former manor house built in 1918 ...

The accommodation is well proportioned throughout and arranged over three floors. There are four good size bedrooms each serviced by either a bathroom or shower room. Externally the property is found at the end of a private drive and occupies beautiful and private grounds extending to approximately 1.8 acres. There is a large lawn area and a wonderful raised patio overlooking the garden, which is accessed by double doors opening from the family room. There is ample parking which includes a large detached garage and the property also benefits from two extensive outbuildings currently used as a gymnasium and a home office with library.[8]

The advertisement mentions the Macleans, who had acquired the entire property for £7,000.[*]

---

[*] The equivalent of perhaps £700,000 in 2014.

Hoare found that "There is ample evidence at least of [Maclean's] early interest in Russia to be found in the extensive library he left behind at Beaconshaw.

> For there … are row after row of works on Russia. They are all dated in the early thirties—when he was in his late teens and early twenties—on the flyleaves. They extend from complete sets in English or in German of all the classical Russian novels—by Tolstoy, Dostoevski, Gorky, Turgenev—and Russian histories, to much more specialized and recondite works of the Russian revolutionaries, including Marx, Lenin, Trotsky, and Stalin, down to the propagandist outpourings of the Soviet Union. The latter writings include not only massive volumes on politics and economics; Donald appeared interested in every aspect of life under the Communists and had a great number of books on Soviet architecture, music, literature, the theatre, and the ballet. There are even such exciting masterpieces as "How Beautiful It Is to Live on a Collective Farm"! All appear to be much read, and all are inscribed neatly with his name and the date of acquisition. It is the kind of library one might expect to belong to someone who was or who planned to become an expert on Russian affairs …[9]

Ironically, once he was in the Soviet Union, Maclean made his academic reputation as an expert on *British* affairs.

The American military had begun a counter-attack in Korea with a landing at Inchon, a port near Seoul, on September 15th. By September 26th American forces moving north from Pusan had linked with those moving east from Inchon, encircling and destroying the North Korean army. The North Korean capital of Pyongyang was captured on October 19th. MacArthur's reputation was vindicated. Intoxicated with victory, he pushed his units on toward the Chinese border. Then: Nemesis. On October 25th Chinese "volunteers" crossed the river and the UN forces were retreating in disarray. Many in the British Government, and perhaps more in the American, were convinced that this was the equivalent of the German invasion of Poland at the beginning of World War Two: the opening act of World War Three, to be followed at any moment by a Soviet, or East German, attack on West Germany, which in turn would be followed by Armageddon.

However, as Katheryn Weathersby has found, Stalin was as fearful of an American initiated world war as British and American planners were of a Soviet initiated world war.[10] The Soviet Union did not intervene with its own forces in Korea; China did not attack Hong Kong; no Soviet tanks crossed the Elbe. On the other hand, the Soviet Union continued to devote a highly disproportionate amount of its budget to the military and the British Government redirected its budget and planning from domestic social democracy to military uses: taxing medical prescriptions, eyeglasses and dentures to pay for atomic bombs. The American economy became addicted to vast expenditures for a military industrial complex. Each fearing the other, the United States and the United Kingdom, on one side, the Soviet Union, on the other, spent most of the next forty years preparing for war.

The promotion of Donald Maclean to head of the American Department, surely the most important Foreign Office position at his level, would have taken place after extensive consultations between Middleton and Makins. Ambassadors Franks and Chapman-Andrews would also have been consulted. The appointment was an endorsement of Maclean's record in the strongest terms. Given the position's importance, briefings would have started some time, perhaps a week or two, before November 1st. They would have included meetings with Makins and Sir Andrew Noble, as well as with the intelligence services, the American Ambassador or his deputy, etc. The Korean operations would have been a central topic of conversation, both the facts on the ground (order of battle and so forth) as well as the exchanges of information and opinion that had been taking place between London and Washington. This was also a period of continuing difficult conversations between London and Washington in regard to atomic energy matters and complicated multi-national negotiations in regard to the Marshall Plan.

Kerr has defended Maclean against MacArthur's charge that the Chinese went into Korea because they knew from Maclean that MacArthur had been forbidden from crossing the Yalu River and that Truman had promised Attlee not to allow the use of atomic bombs in Korea. Her argument rests on a chronology that assumes Maclean had no access to Foreign Office documents between the time he left Cairo and November 1st, 1950, when he assumed direction of the American Department.[11] MacArthur's defeat was caused by his own hubris, but that does not mean that Maclean was not briefed about MacArthur's planning and the discussions in Washington in late-October when Maclean was preparing to take over the American Department and that he did not convey those briefings to Moscow, which, in spite of Kerr's doubts, we now can be confident would have forwarded that information to Beijing. Modin, believed that "it may well have been on account of a piece of news brought to us by [Maclean] that East-West tension finally began to relax. As soon as the decision had been made, he informed us that Washington had forbidden General MacArthur to invade Manchuria."[12] Not that, in the final analysis, it would have mattered. Mao was not afraid of the American army, nor of atomic bombs.

When Maclean took up his duties in the American Department he received the usual messages distributed to department heads. "Each day Maclean would receive the 'Departmental Float' which contained telegrams which had been received and sent out, together with any other important papers or instructions which were being circulated.

> He would also receive Cabinet papers, the Foreign Office Print, and the monthly digest of Soviet tactics from the Information Research Department (IRD). The department also received a wide range of information from the Washington Embassy. Amongst these, the weekly political summary was the most important report as it assessed political developments in America and formed the basic information on America within Whitehall. There were also important letters from the Ambassador, economic reports, British Information Services reports, and

reports from the three service attaches. From these routine sources Maclean had an accurate picture of the political fortunes of the administration, and its opponents, the aims and tactics of American foreign policy, their economic strengths and weaknesses and a detailed picture of American military power.[13]

In addition, there was the "'Korea Distribution' which kept the main departments concerned with Korea up to date, this included the Far Eastern Department, the American Department, the Commonwealth Relations Office, the Information Research Department, the Foreign Office Research Department, and the Director of Intelligence."[14] If Maclean did in fact receive all these, he would have been able to provide weekly reports to Moscow of deliberations at the highest levels of the British and American governments, which, at this time, were in large part devoted to the conflict in Korea and planning in case of (the expected) wider war.

We have an unusually intimate view of Maclean as head of the American Department from Robert Cecil, who worked for him there, as he had in Paris and Washington, and would succeed him. "[T]he American Department ... had two Assistants and served two Under-Secretaries.

> The Assistant Under-Secretary supervising the Latin-American section, which was in my charge, was the late Sir Andrew Noble." Sir Roger Makins supervised the US section himself. (Sir) John Curle, Cecil's opposite number for the US section, observed "I never noticed [Maclean] the worse for drink. I thought him a good head of Department; he was never fussed or flustered." A comparatively junior official from the Latin American section one afternoon found Maclean "with his heels on this desk, and reading a paper-bound French novel. For once he was less impersonal than usual. Had I read it? Did I like it? It was Camus' *La Peste* ... and I told him that I like neither it nor *L'Etranger* ..."[15]

In other words, at this highly pressured point in his dual career, Maclean appeared to his subordinates, as well as, no doubt, to his colleagues and supervisors, as he had always been seen: the very model of a Foreign Office official (although an occasional reader of contemporary French literature), still destined, as many thought, for at least an ambassadorship and a "k."

Aside from his daily reading of official papers and French novels, "As Head, Maclean was responsible for the efficiency of the department, and he made sure it supported the embassies abroad, and Whitehall at home.

For example, Maclean saw that the Washington Embassy needed more current information to counteract anti-British propaganda, and arranged for more information to be sent out. Maclean was once again at the centre of Anglo-American relations. Ministers would ask his department for advice on American matters, and Maclean or a member of his staff would draft position papers, speeches and replies to parliamentary questions. Maclean had contact with Ministers … his minutes were read by Strang, the Head of the Foreign Office and the Foreign Secretary, Bevin, and later Morrison [who, Lord Astor-like, denied meeting Maclean]. Maclean supervised key position papers, for example a paper on neo-isolationism for Bevin to use at the Commonwealth conference. Maclean often commented on the weekly political summary from Washington, this was still a key document which helped to form opinion in Whitehall.[16]

After Donald Maclean moved to Moscow there was a considerable amount of disinformation promulgated by the Foreign Office about the scope of his duties and access to materials while head of the American Department. Then-Foreign Secretary Harold Macmillan, in his 1955 House of Commons speech about Maclean and Burgess, mischaracterized the responsibilities of the American Department, minimizing those and also the importance of the documents Maclean was able to see. However, Verne Newton found that "When purging the files, government document weeders neglected to purge those preceding Maclean's tenure.

So it is possible to track what was flowing to the American Department prior to his appointment. At the time Maclean assumed his new duties this included highly secret operational military information originating from the British mission in Peking, the British Cabinet, the American Joint Chiefs of Staff, and from General Douglas MacArthur himself ... The government would later claim that it withheld vital documents from Maclean once he was a suspect in the 'Homer' case. But, no one has suggested this occurred before March of 1951. For example, an advance copy was found of a cable to Maclean (head of the American Department) from Ambassador Franks bearing the highest classification, 'FO Immediate/Top Secret OTP' (one-time pad–a code never to be repeated) dated April 5, 1951.[17]

Therefore not March, but April 5th, at the earliest.

In some ways in the winter of 1950/51 Anglo-American relations were not good. Britain had implemented the Labour Party's socialist agenda while Washington was implementing the Republican Party's anti-New Deal and anti-Communist agenda. During the period that Donald Maclean was head of the American Department, the Minister of War was John Strachey, perhaps the most prominent Communist publicist of the 1930s, and long-time Socialists Emanuel Shinwell and Herbert Morrison were Minister of Defence and Foreign Secretary, respectively. This occasionally made American authorities uneasy; reciprocally, admiration for "the American way of life" was not widespread in the British Cabinet, nor in much of the rest of the British administration, ruling and working classes, with the signal exception of the very pro-American Foreign Secretary. Toward the end of 1950 Bevin thought that the Government might not win a vote of confidence on the issue of his policy of an ever closer Anglo-American alliance. Indeed, Ritchie Ovendale has found that "early in 1951 ... several members of the Cabinet and sections of the establishment tried to break with the American alliance."[18]

The British Cabinet and Chiefs of Staff were close to panic, considering withdrawing the somewhat more than token British forces from Korea, as they did not at that moment think the war winnable and believed that it was more important to concentrate on Western Europe. Perhaps knowing this, on November 28, 1950,

Secretary of State Acheson sent a secret telegram to the British Embassy in Washington for Foreign Secretary Bevin, summarizing the Korean situation. It stated, inter alia, "our purposes in Korea remain the same, namely, to resist aggression, to localize the hostilities, and to wind up the Korean problem … in such a way as not to commit US forces in large numbers indefinitely in that operation."[19] Then, on the morning of November 30, President Truman held a news conference during which the following exchange took place:

"The President: We will take whatever steps are necessary to meet the military situation, just as we always have.

Q. Will that include the atomic bomb?

The President: That includes every weapon that we have.

Q. Mr. President, you said 'every weapon that we have.' Does that mean there is active consideration of the use of the atomic bomb?

The President: There has always been active consideration of its use.[20]

Later that day, Attlee announced in Parliament that he was traveling to Washington and would meet with Truman on December 4.

Peter Boyle observed that "The deterioration in Anglo-American relations reached a crisis in early December [1950], with Truman's careless remarks in a press conference regarding the possible use of the atomic bomb in Korea. The American Embassy in London cabled Acheson on December 1$^{st}$ that "British opinion from top to bottom … is strongly opposed to any action that would contribute to UN forces becoming entangled in war with [the People's Republic of] China."[21] However, by December 2 the American cabinet and Chiefs of Staff saw the alternatives as war with China or an immediate evacuation of American forces from Korea. They were doubtful of the possibilities of success of the latter. "General Marshall said that even a Dunkirk type of evacuation might be prejudiced if the Chinese brought in their air."[22] The next day MacArthur sent a cable to the Joint Chiefs of Staff predicting the total destruction of his army unless it were drastically and immediately reinforced.

Discussions in Washington became focused on the choice between asking for a ceasefire and evacuation or destruction of all UN forces. There was no more talk of bringing the boys home by Christmas or the inferiority of "oriental" soldiers.

Attlee was accompanied in the Washington meetings by Ambassador Franks; Field Marshall Slim, CIGS; Marshall of the Royal Air Force Tedder; Sir Roger Makins, Robert Scott, and Edwin Plowden. Ambassador "Franks attended the sessions of talks between Truman and Attlee and reported that the British and American positions on most matters relating to China and a Korean settlement were at serious variance."[23] (Guy Burgess and Kim Philby apparently remained at the British Embassy, where Philby controlled secure communications.) According to Dean Acheson, "The first purpose of the British group was to find out what was going on and why in North Korea ...

> As the Prime Minister became reassured that alarm over the safety of our troops would not drive us to some ill-considered use of atomic weapons, his purposes in coming emerged more clearly. He wished us to end our conflict with the Chinese in order to resume active participation in security for Europe; to resume also ... a joint control with Britain of the allocation and pricing of raw materials [commodity prices then being driven up by American stock-piling] ... and, finally, he wished Britain to be admitted to some participation with [the U.S.] in any future decision to use nuclear weapons.[24]

Kerr found that: "Maclean not only read the brief for Attlee's meeting, but he also contributed to its drafting."[25] Specifically, "The briefing paper for the summit meeting revealed a detailed picture of British perceptions of the impact of the Korean war on international affairs, their objectives in Korea, their fears about escalation and their doubts about General MacArthur.

> Britain had two central aims in the Korean War, to maintain Anglo-American solidarity and to localise and settle the war. Their two main fears were that the war would escalate because of communist behaviour or General MacArthur and that allied

325

forces would not be able to hold on to Korea. The brief revealed that Britain was under considerable strain to supply forces in Korea, and could not redeploy forces from Hong Kong, Malaysia, Western Europe, or the Middle East. Britain would have to call up reservists which would take months.[26]

Once the Attlee group arrived in Washington, Maclean "also had access to the daily reports of the meetings, and Attlee's appraisal of the talks.

From these materials he could provide Stalin with complete, accurate and timely intelligence on British and American objectives and tactics in Korea, the issues upon which they agreed and disagreed and the degree of unity within the Anglo-American alliance. This intelligence from within the British Government could be compared to the communiqué Truman and Attlee released. Stalin would be able to distinguish between the image of the alliance Truman and Attlee sought to project and the real state of Anglo-American relations. He would be able to distinguish between the signals Truman and Attlee wished to communicate and their real intentions ...

And to close the circuit, Maclean (and therefore Stalin) also received a copy of Attlee's report to the Cabinet on the talks once they were concluded.[27] Perhaps one through official channels and another from Philby or Burgess.

Attlee's report, of December 12, 1950, laid out the agreements and disagreements between the British and American governments in the field of foreign affairs. "The United States Government fully recognised the importance of building up military strength in the West, and the dangers of becoming too deeply involved in the Far East. At the same time they tended to believe that Chinese policy was dictated by Russia, and they had been considering the idea of a limited war against China." Attlee "had stressed the need to avoid major war with China and had indicated that the broad choice was between a settlement of the Korean problem or a general drift to world war ... Before the end of the talks the President's advisors had developed doubts about the value of a limited war against China ..."

On the other hand, "it had not proved possible to reach agreement about the recognition of the Chinese People's Government and Chinese representation in the United Nations." However, most importantly, "President Truman had entirely satisfied him about the use of the atomic bomb ... He had assured the Prime Minister that he regarded the atomic bomb as in a sense a joint possession of the United States, United Kingdom and Canada, and that he would not authorise its use without prior consultation with the other two Governments save in an extreme emergency ..." Finally, the President and Prime Minister had agreed on a plan for "Western Germany to contribute military forces for the defense of Western Europe."[28] This last was not something that would be greeted with joy in Moscow.

Reading the reports of the Washington meetings, according to Yuri Modin, "Stalin was sure that a Third World War was imminent ... [Maclean's later] information strengthened Stalin's certainty. In March, 1951, Maclean sent us [Soviet foreign intelligence] the minutes of a meeting that had taken place in the Foreign Office, along with an account of his own alarmist view of the situation. The British Government's experts were apparently convinced that American aggressiveness was "pushing the world into a pointless war."[29] This appraisal of British governmental (and public) opinion was confirmed by the American ambassador in London in a cable to the Secretary of State on March 14, 1951.[30] The Chinese army had taken Seoul on January 4th, 1951 and Inchon the next day. An American counter-attack recaptured both by mid-March and the advantage passed from one side to the other, with the front stalled near the 38th parallel for more than two years until an armistice agreement was signed on July 27, 1953. Ernest Bevin, whose health had been declining since 1939, resigned on March 9, 1951, and died soon afterwards. Attlee appointed Herbert Morrison, the architect of the London County Council, in his stead. MacArthur, having unsuccessfully challenged the authority of the President, was fired on April 10th, 1951, returning to the United States for a hero's welcome, in spite of which he faded away.

327

On April 16, 1951, Maclean wrote a memorandum on political developments flowing from Truman's confrontation with MacArthur: "Truman's position would probably be strengthened in the end and the administration will find itself free to pursue its own Far East policy—they were handicapped by not having a policy, at least not one easily apprehended by the citizens.

Americans have for some time had a steady diet of "fighting communism" etc. and Truman's present accent on "avoiding a third world war" will have an unfamiliar ring. MacArthur's return will evoke temporarily at least violent and unreasoning expression of deep unease over the Far East and Britain will in the process get a quite irrational share of the blame. Dust will no doubt settle, but the President and the administration are unstable and unless they can lead strongly in favour of some comprehensive policy on China and Korea, and Truman has little domestic credit to keep him afloat.[31]

He may well have produced this appraisal in duplicate.

Commenting on a report from the Washington Embassy, on May 15, Maclean wrote: "I believe our prestige on Far East matters in the US was a good deal higher when we clearly stood for a policy of our own, for example at the time of Mr Attlee's visit. We now suffer the disadvantage of appearing to tag voluntary behind the US ..." The political report from Washington dated May 19 (a few days before Maclean left England), covering the previous week, "reported that while MacArthur's influence was waning, the administration had moved some way towards the policy he advocated. This meant the administration was having difficulty in holding a moderate line because of pressures from the Republican party."[32] Maclean minuted: "I do not find any comfort in this report.

It seems to me that American opinion, and the administration with it is drifting into a more and more dangerous attitude towards the Far East from our point of view. As was the case last December I should guess that only some arresting statement of policy by ourselves (preferably by the Commonwealth as a whole) would stand a chance of turning the tide.'"[33]

A reading of the British Cabinet papers and similar American materials gives an overwhelming impression of governments convinced that war could begin at any moment. In this case Truman, Attlee, Stalin and their advisors were in agreement. The tone of Maclean's commentary on the May 19$^{th}$ report is not notably different from his usual bureaucratic calm, which is rather surprising in the circumstances.

Philip Toynbee had turned up in London with his new wife early in 1951 and Donald Maclean began missing the last train home, drinking with Toynbee and their friends at the Gargoyle Club and other places that sold drinks. Maclean liked Sally Toynbee (he seems to have liked American women) and introduced her to people he knew, but he was losing patience with Toynbee and his new-found anti-Communism. Toward the end of January when Alger Hiss was convicted of perjury Toynbee had written an article taking the side of the prosecution. "Next time Toynbee encountered Maclean in the Gargoyle, he was already very drunk and showed him his most menacing face. Maclean advanced on his friend, muttering, 'I am the English Hiss.' As Toynbee wrote later, 'Donald threw me backwards into the band, pint-glass in hand.'"[34] Perhaps. The story is not found in Toynbee's available contemporaneous diaries.

In May Guy Burgess returned to London from Washington, sent home after a series of events not unlike those of Maclean in Cairo (and involving, as it happened, Maclean's younger brother, Alan, in New York). Modin claims that Burgess had arranged for his own departure, in disgrace, from Washington in order to carry Philby's warning about Maclean's identification as "Homer" to Maclean and arrange for the latter's defection.[35] It is not clear why it would have been necessary to use this dramatic means to contact Maclean. Perhaps the Soviet foreign intelligence service was insecure about the secrecy of its communications. In any case, Burgess contacted Blunt; Blunt contacted Modin; Modin and his superior Nicolai Rodin ("Korovin") contacted Moscow Center. Moscow Center agreed to exfiltrate Maclean.[36] At about the same time Melinda Maclean's sister and brother-in-law, Harriet and James Sheers, arrived from

Paris for a weekend (James Sheers was a writer and producer of documentary films).[37] "Harriet immediately noticed a great change in Donald; he was tense, strained, and, she thought, really desperately worried ...

> One day Donald took Jay Sheers to have a drink in the local pub. There he railed bitterly at his life and his job; he mocked at himself as a sheep among hordes of other sheep, going off to London every day with his black hat and neat black suit and little black briefcase; and he said that he was sick of it all and longed desperately to "cut adrift."[38]

Maclean having told that story, towards the end of May, 1951, Burgess went to the Foreign Office to talk with him about an analysis of current affairs that he had written while in Washington.[*] That was his story. Maclean, Burgess said, suggested lunch; the Reform Club dining room was full; they walked down Pall Mall to the Royal Automobile Club, where Maclean at once said that he was being followed "by the dicks," that he suspected that his telephone was tapped and that he had been removed from the routing of secret documents (which must have happened only a week or two earlier). They lunched twice more in the following days. Burgess later told Tom Driberg that it was at the third lunch that Maclean said that he wanted to go to Moscow and asked Burgess to help him.[39] According to Anthony Blunt, Burgess then discussed the matter with "his Soviet contact," perhaps Yuri Modin. It was soon decided that Burgess should go with Maclean, as Maclean was not in a fit state to carry out on his own the complicated arrangements which had been made.[40] Modin says he suggested to Burgess that Maclean talk over his projected defection with Melinda Maclean, who was nearing the end of her pregnancy. He did. "'They're quite right, she said briskly. 'Go as soon as you can, don't waste a single moment.'" Here we have Melinda Maclean acting as a counterintelligence advisor. She, too, thought he was too far gone to be able to resist interrogation.

---

[*] Burgess's essay may have influenced Maclean's thinking about Anglo-American policy in the Far East, cited above.

The M.I.5 officer in charge of the Homer investigation, Geoffrey Patterson, had told Philby in Washington that his final report would reach London on 22 or 23 May. At Blunt's suggestion, as border officials would no doubt be alerted to watch for Maclean, Modin and his colleagues decided to use a local excursion ship, the *Falaise,* for Maclean's and Burgess's travel to France. Ships of this kind, according to Blunt, oddly expert in these matters, were often used by senior civil servants and business men for short trips to France with women who were not their wives and therefore were purposefully not watched. Much has been made of the incompetence of the British secret police's watchers, who followed Donald Maclean from his arrival at the station in London to the time that he returned there to travel home. Modin comes to their defense: "I knew by experience how hard it was to arrange a tail outside town.

> In the urban milieu, it's a simple matter for a watcher to keep out of sight, but in the country, in a village for example, it's another story ... On the train ... Donald [Maclean] would know the other passengers by sight, all of them being people who had taken the same trains for years, to and from their offices. A follower would stick out like a sore thumb at the little station at Tatsfield, especially since Donald always went home from the station by car, never by foot.

Four years later, on November 7, 1955, after a Soviet defector had stated that Maclean and Burgess were in Moscow, Harold Macmillan, then the Secretary of State for Foreign Affairs, spoke in the House of Commons on the subject of "Former Foreign Office Officials (Disappearance)." He began, as we have begun, by placing Maclean's and Burgess's actions in the context of the times: "To understand—though not, of course, to excuse—this story, it is necessary to cast our minds back to the 1930s and to recall the kind of background against which the two principal characters grew up." He briefly did so, then went on to lay out the official version of the story of Maclean's "disappearance."

> As soon as he fell under suspicion, in the middle of April, 1951, one of those informed was Sir Roger Makins, now our

distinguished and highly successful Ambassador in Washington. Sir Roger was then his immediate chief, being the Superintending Under-Secretary of the group into which [the American] Department fell. It is, however, quite untrue, as has been suggested, that Sir Roger Makins was in any way responsible for the conduct of an inquiry, or that he checked or cleared Maclean. It is not the case at all and such a suggestion is false and grossly unfair to Sir Roger Makins ...

Except that Makins was one of those deciding that his long-time colleague Donald Maclean should be interrogated.

But, even when suspicion narrowed down to Maclean, the evidence was both inconclusive and circumstantial. The best, perhaps the only, chance of obtaining evidence which could be used to support a prosecution lay in obtaining admissions from him ... A watch was, therefore, put upon him for the primary purpose—indeed, the sole purpose—of securing such information. As was said in the White Paper, everything depended upon the interview, and its success depended also on the use of an element of surprise. If he were alerted to the fact that he was under investigation or suspected it, all hope of obtaining the essential confirmatory evidence would probably have gone for good. For that reason, the decision not to watch him at Tatsfield was deliberately taken after a careful survey had been made of the technical problems involved in keeping him under observation in the neighbourhood of his home. The conclusion was that the risk that he would be put on his guard would be too great. Obviously, it is far more difficult in the country to conceal from a man the fact that he is being watched than it is to watch his movements or his contacts in London ...

In this the Soviet and British intelligence services were in agreement.

Burgess set up a false trail, as advised by Modin's superior, Rodin, telling his latest lover that he was going to take him on a short holiday and making a show at the Reform of planning a trip to Scotland. The morning of Friday, May 25th, the Foreign Secretary, Herbert Morrison, decided, on the basis of VENONA, to have

Maclean interrogated.[41] Given that certain preparations would be necessary, the decision was taken to begin the interrogation when Maclean arrived at the Foreign Office Monday morning. Too late, of course. "In the early evening [of the 25th, Burgess] ... drove down to Tatsfield in his rented car.

> It happened to be Donald's thirty-eighth birthday. Melinda was busy preparing a special dinner in the kitchen when Burgess appeared at the door and introduced himself as "Roger Styles", a fellow employee of Donald's at the Foreign Office. Melinda, who knew Burgess perfectly well, called her husband; the two men spoke in private for a few minutes, then everybody settled down to dinner. At around 9 p.m. Maclean went upstairs to kiss his sons good night, while Burgess waited in the hall. Donald then took his leave of Melinda, and the two men vanished into the night.[42]

Something like that.

*    *    *

Melinda Maclean continued to play her role in this Soviet secret intelligence service operation. She waited until the Monday to place two calls to the Foreign Office, one to the American desk, asking if Donald Maclean was there or had left a message for her, the other to the chief of security, reporting that Donald Maclean had gone out the Friday night and that she had heard nothing from him after. "It wasn't until 30 May, five days after Donald's disappearance," Modin gloated, "that Melinda was finally interviewed by MI5." They did

---

* Many years later Donald Maclean told his brother Alan that the name came from a couple of Agatha Christie novels Burgess happened to have with him: *The Mysterious Affair at Styles* and *The Murder of Roger Ackroyd.* (Maclean, Alan. No I Tell a Lie, It was the Tuesday: A Trudge Round the Life and Times of Alan Maclean. London: Kyle Cahtie Limited, 1999, p. 108. The remark that Melinda Maclean knew Burgess "perfectly well," is of interest.

these things more expeditiously in Moscow.

> She was at the Kensington home of her mother-in-law, Lady Maclean, when a couple of inspectors rang the doorbell. She stated that her husband had gone away on the previous Friday evening with a Foreign Office colleague named Styles. She described Style's appearance and made a show of deep anxiety. The officers asked both women to say nothing to anyone about the matter till further notice, and went back to their headquarters.[43]

Alan Maclean, who had just been appointed press attaché to Gladwyn Jebb at the United Nations, was immediately recalled to London, interrogated and forced to resign from the Foreign Office, as was Donald Maclean's brother-in-law.

Melinda Maclean gave birth to a baby girl in June, 1951 and in July went with her mother to France, to her sister's villa in Beauvallon, Cote d'Azur. Before leaving England she was interviewed by William Skardon, the man who had "broken" Klaus Fuchs. He seems to have believed that Melinda Maclean was, as many thought her, a simple woman, a mother and housewife, who knew nothing about her husband's work for the Soviet Union. Move along; nothing to see here. Upon her return to England she was taken under the wing of Violet Bonham Carter, which kindness led to a newspaper tempest and the coining of the term "the Establishment."[44]

Bonham Carter had maintained the acquaintance with the Macleans that dated back to Sir Donald's alliance with her father, H. H. Asquith. Donald Maclean had been part of the group to which her daughters, Laura and Cressida (and Philip Toynbee) belonged and during the war he had seen Lady Violet from time to time. After Maclean's "disappearance," Bonham Carter had tea with Lady Maclean on Sunday, June 8th, when they would presumably have discussed the Maclean family's troubles. A journalist from the *Daily Express* published a story on July 16th, 1952, asserting that Melinda Maclean had decided to move to Switzerland. The story was presented as an interview with Melinda Maclean. Violet Bonham

Carter, who wrote a note in red ink in her diary under the 15th, "Daily Express Interview with Mrs Maclean," (perhaps having received an advance copy) drafted a letter to *The Times* on the 18th, launching an extensive correspondence with that newspaper, with David Astor, publisher of *The Observer,* Randolph Churchill and others. Bonham Carter defended Melinda Maclean's assertion that no interview had taken place, that there had been a telephone call from the journalist, during which he had requested an interview, which she refused. Other letters from Lady Maclean and Lady Maclean's mother, who said that they were in the room with Melinda Maclean at the time the call came through, supported Melinda Maclean's position. Actions of various kinds, formal and informal, were threatened, reputations were put on the line and impugned, columns of newspapers and weeklies were filled. But, as a matter of fact, the sense of the story, if not its circumstances, was true.

Modin again: "Part of our plan for the defection of Maclean was that Melinda Maclean ... should stay in England with her children till the scandal blew over, and would then take her family to rejoin him in Moscow." Which means, of course, that Melinda Maclean had been "witting" of the exfiltration plan and much else. Modin's vivid account of his implementation of this decision gives a somewhat different image of Melinda Maclean than the usual one of a housewife meek and mild: "Eighteen months after Donald's departure, the moment seemed to have come to make good our promise, and I was given the job of re-establishing contact with Melinda ...

> We finally decided to intercept her on her way home from the school, just after she dropped the boys. The road was a narrow lane through wooded country, with hedges either side ... All we needed to do was drive ahead of her, pull up in a suitable spot— and show Melinda half of a postcard. The other half had been handed to Melinda by her husband a year and at half before ... our driver gently pulled up on the verge, signaling the young woman behind to do likewise. This she did, but not quite in the way we had expected. She burst out of her car like a deer

335

breaking cover, yelling abuse at us for our bad driving. I was stunned by the speed of her reaction and by her sure reflexes— this woman ... was certainly not one to be pushed around ... She was very attractive, a handsome woman in a simple skirt and white blouse. I recovered my wits and drew the half postcard from my pocket. She calmed down instantly, reached across for a bag on the passenger seat of her car and produced the other half ...

Modin says that the Soviets tried to arrange with Melinda Maclean (who arrived at the meeting arranged at the roadside in "an extremely elegant light beige suit") for a procedure to bring her and her family out of England to Moscow. She, however, preferred to do it herself, moving to one of her mother's houses, this in Montreux-Terrilet, Switzerland, having refused Soviet help and funds. In September, 1953, "the Center decided to contact Melinda once again and, if she were still willing, to mount a simple operation to bring her out of Switzerland." She was willing. In Natasha Walter's telling, "She prepared for her great flight in the way you might expect of a bourgeois American, rather than a closet Red.

The day before, she spent hours at a salon having her hair and nails done. That morning she had gone shopping, then returned to tell her mother that she had bumped into an old friend who had invited her to spend the weekend with the children at his villa at Territet. After lunch, at which she seemed no more than preoccupied, she got the children and herself ready, throwing an electric blue Schiaparelli coat over a black skirt and white blouse.[45]

Melinda Maclean left an unmailed letter in her flat in Geneva. It had been written on June 14, 1951, three weeks after Donald Maclean's departure, as she was about to have the Caesarean that would result in the birth of her third child. "A previously used white envelope was sealed with a wide band of blue paper on which was written in pencil, "To Donald Duart Maclean from  Melinda Maclean."

My dearest Donald.

336

If you ever receive this letter it will mean that I shan't be here to tell you how much I love you and how really proud of you I am. My only regret is that perhaps you don't know how I feel about you.

I feel I leave behind and have had a wonderful gift in your love and the existence of Fergie and Donald. I am so looking forward to the new baby. It seems strangely like the first time and I think I shall really enjoy this baby completely. I never forget darling that you love me and am living for the moment when we shall all be together again.

All my deepest love and wishes for a happy life for you and the children.

Melinda[46]

On September 11, 1953, Melinda Maclean drove to Lausanne with her children and took a train to Vienna. From there Modin's colleagues took care of the rest.[47]

## Chapter Nine: Notes

---

[1] Cambray, Joseph. Synchronicity: Nature and Psyche in an Interconnected Universe. Texas A&M University Press, 2009, p. 9.

[2] Cecil, p. 109-10.

[3] Cecil, p. 112.

[4] Steel, Ronald. Walter Lippmann and the American Century. Boston: Little, Brown and Company. An Atlantic Monthly Press Book, 1980, pp. 476-7.

[5] TNA CAB/131/9.

[6] Hoare, p. 97.

[7] Makins's personal papers (FO 800/432) in The National Archives have been weeded to such an extent that there is a gap in his otherwise extensive correspondence with Strang, the gap extending from 1944 to 1953.

[8] Advertisement by White & Sons: www.whiteandsons.co.uk

[9] Hoare, Geoffrey. The Missing Macleans. New York: The Viking Press, 1955, pp. 182-3.

[10] Weathersby, Kathryn, "'Should We Fear This?' Stalin and the Danger of War with America." Cold War International History Project Working Papers Series, #39. Washington, D.C.: Woodrow Wilson International Center for Scholars, July 2002.

[11] Kerr, pp. 326-7.

[12] Modin, pp. 183-4.

[13] Kerr, p. 335.

[14] Kerr, p. 333.

[15] Cecil, pp. 118-9.

[16] Kerr, p. 331.

[17] Newton, Verne W. The Cambridge Spies: The Untold Story of Maclean, Philby, and Burgess in America. Lanham, New York: Madison Books, 1991, p. 284.

[18] Ovendale, Ritchie. "William Strang and the Permanent Under-Secretary's Committee" in Zametica, John (ed.). British Officials and British Foreign Policy: 1945-50. Leicester: Leicester University Press, 1990, p. 225 citing Ovendale, Ritchie. The English Speaking

Alliance, Britain, The United States, The Dominions And The Cold War, 1945-51, 1985, pp. 224-9.

[19] FRUS, 1950, Vol. VII, p. 1251.

[20] FRUS, 1950, Vol. VII, pp. 1261-2.

[21] FRUS, 1950, Vol. VII, p. 1296.

[22] FRUS, 1950, Vol. VII, p. 1313.

[23] Boyle, Peter G. "Oliver Franks and the Washington Embassy, 1948-52," in Zametica, John (ed.). British Officials and British Foreign Policy: 1945-50. Leicester: Leicester University Press, 1990, p. 203.

[24] Acheson, pp. 480-1.

[25] TNA PO 371 81637/AU 1053/29 General Brief for the Prime Minister's Visit to Washington, 2 December 1950

[26] Kerr, pp. 345.

[27] Newton, p. 300.

[28] TNA CAB/128/18.

[29] Modin, pp. 183-4.

[30] FRUS, 1951, Volume IV, pp. 906ff.

[31] TNA FO 371 90907/AU1015/6.

[32] Kerr, p. 366.

[33] TNA FO 371/90904/AU 1013/23, Weekly Political Summary, 12-18 May 1951, and AU/1013/21, Weekly Political Summary, 17 May 1951.

[34] Cecil, p. 121.

[35] Modin, p. 200ff.

[36] Modin, p. 197-99.

[37] "SHEERS--Harriet Marling, 89, of New York City and Dennis, Massachusetts, died in her sleep on October 23, 2009 at her home on West 92nd Street in Manhattan. After graduating from Smith College in 1941, she served in the United States Navy during the Second World War as a Lieutenant in the Waves. Living in Paris after the war, she met and married J.C. Sheers, a writer and producer of documentary films. Harriet raised her family in North Stamford,

Connecticut and, for three years, in Rome and London, before moving to Waltham, Massachusetts following her husband's death in 1970, and then to New York City, where she worked for many years as Director of Intake and Referrals at the Ackerman Institute of Family Therapy. A constant student of literature and passionate lover of music and the arts, Harriet was a longtime supporter of many cultural organizations in New York City, including the Metropolitan Museum of Art, the 92nd Street Y and the New York Society Library. She is survived by her sons, James Campbell Sheers III, Nicholas Minor Sheers and Alexander Marling Sheers, her sister Melinda Maclean, nine grandchildren and an extended, much loved family." Death Notice of Harriet Marling Sheers. New York Times, November 1, 2009.

[38] Hoare, p. 102.

[39] Driberg, pp. 92-4.

[40] Blunt Memoir, British Library, ADD Ms. 88902/1, p. 76.

[41] Cecil, p. 135. This is an interesting, and interested, assertion, not to be accepted without corroborating evidence, but, in this case, the date is widely accepted.

[42] Modin, pp. 205-9. In 1959 Burgess told Michael Redgrave: "I did all that was required of me by bringing Maclean safe to Russia." The implication was that he had not himself intended to stay there. TNA KV 2/3822.

[43] Modin, p. 210. Later in the year, if not immediately, the British secret police put a tap on Lady Maclean's telephone. See TNA KV 2/3436.

[44] MS. Bonham Carter 186, Special Collections, Bodleian Library, Oxford University.

[45] Walter, Natasha, Spies and Lovers. The Guardian, May 10, 2003.

[46] Hoare, p. 25.

[47] Modin, 225-227.

# Chapter Ten

## *Moscow and Another Career*

The "disappearance" of Maclean and Burgess ignited a media frenzy that continued for years, dying down from time to time for lack of news, then, with each new tid-bit of information (or misinformation), reigniting. Cyril Connolly, serialized in *The Sunday Times,* then published as a book in 1952 his *The Missing Diplomats.* In March, 1956, Goronwy Rees committed professional suicide with his sensationalizing, self-implicating, articles about Burgess and Maclean in *The People.* Philip Toynbee waited until 1967 to publish "Maclean and I: A Personal Memoir" in *The Observer.* These provided the basic Cold War storyline for narratives about Donald Maclean.

Maclean and Burgess seem to have been under the protection of secret police chief Lavrentiy Beria in those dangerous final months of Stalin's life. There was a celebratory NKVD party in a hotel near the Kremlin, then they were taken to Kuibyshev, an industrial city on the southern Volga, perhaps coincidentally beyond the range of the B-29 bases in England and the Canal Zone. After some unpleasant weeks, including the no-nonsense Russian system of detoxification for their alcoholism, Maclean began to study Russian (and Burgess to study Georgian wine). Stalin died in March, 1953. Maclean and Burgess were brought to Moscow, Burgess to drink himself to death, Maclean to make himself over into the Soviet academic, "Mark Frazer." Maclean worked for a time on a newspaper specializing in world economic matters, published by the Ministry of Foreign Affairs[1] and, with Burgess, as an advisor to the Foreign Literature Publishing House.

Modin saw Maclean for the first, and last, time in September, 1953, when Melinda Maclean and their three children arrived in Moscow. "He was just as I had imagined: cold, distant, supercilious and thoroughly aristocratic. The weight of his presence was overwhelming ...

The Maclean family were temporarily housed in a small apartment, before being moved in 1955 to a splendid six-room home on Bolshaya Dorogomilovskaya Street in the centre of Moscow. The building was in the purest Stalin-era style, brand-new, with windows facing the Ukraine Hotel [now the Radisson Royal] and the Moskva [River]. There was a market just below. Fergus and Donald Junior, who were aged ten and eight, went to school in the normal way and quickly learned to speak Russian perfectly; later the older boy, Fergus, spent several holidays in a camp and the younger became a Pioneer. They had no difficulty blending into Soviet life."[2]

The apartment was filled with books from Bowes and Bowes in Cambridge, replacing those left behind in Surrey.[3]

Mrs. Dunbar had left France for New York in May, 1953, establishing contacts with both the FBI and the CIA. She stayed with her youngest daughter, Catherine Terrell, in Great Neck, Long Island, for six months, returned to Europe, and then in May, 1954 went back to New York where she moved into the San Carlos Hotel in Manhattan and resumed connections with the FBI. She spent the summer of 1955 on Cape Cod with her daughters Harriet and Catherine and their families. Maclean and Burgess emerged from what the latter called their "purdah" at a press conference February 11, 1956, just before the Twentieth Party Congress. They read an official statement, attributing their presence in the Soviet Union to a desire to further the cause of peace. By then Maclean's Russian was fluent and he was a member of the Soviet Communist Party (later serving in the Party organization of his Institute). Unlike Burgess, who met with anyone from Britain who happened by, and drank with those who were in the least bit willing, Maclean avoided foreign visitors.

After the Maclean/Burgess news conference Mrs. Dunbar formally requested assistance from the CIA in locating Melinda and the children. A few days later she received a letter (sender redacted but probably Alan Maclean), containing a cablegram from Donald Maclean requesting various family addresses and commenting that he and Melinda and the children were "flourishing" in Moscow. At the beginning of April there was a cable from Melinda Maclean:

"All happy and well. Longing for news of you," and then on the 20th a letter expressing regret at having left her to face "the fury of the press" . . . "Believe me I did the right thing and don't regret it" except for the suffering it caused her family in America. "Donald is well and happy to be with his family again. This is absolutely the best place for us to be. The life here is good in every way." Mrs. Dunbar telephoned Walter Roetting, her FBI contact and read the letter aloud to him. "'Donald is well and very happy to be with his family again. The children are also well and happy and have adapted themselves thoroughly to life here.'" Roetting then recorded that

> Following this is a rather long discussion of the Russian school system, which Mrs. Maclean praised highly, and the activities of Mrs. Maclean's children at school and in sports. Mrs. Maclean has a television and a nice modern flat with all the conveniences. She has a part-time maid and may have to get a full-time one. She is kept very busy at home and is about to take lessons in the Russian language. She also attends a course in sewing. She mentioned that she has been given some translation work to do. She discussed the activities of her little daughter, and mentioned that the child's favorate books are the Beatrix Potter series, such as Peter Rabbit, etc.

Mrs. Dunbar asked the FBI to make this information available to CIA.

In January, 1958, the FBI was informed that Melinda Maclean was said to be editor of the English language "Moscow News" and Donald Maclean was chief of a section in a foreign language printing house. They were also told by the American embassy in Moscow that Melinda Maclean wished to return to the United States with her children and began to plan to interview her if she did in fact arrive in the United States.[4] However, Melinda Maclean was to remain in the Soviet Union for another twenty years.

Kim Philby had arrived in Moscow just before Burgess's death in 1963, but was not allowed to—or did not wish to—see him. In due course Philby was joined by his American wife, the former Eleanor Brewer, who claimed to have thought she had married a journalist,

343

not a spy. We have her detailed description of the personal lives of the Macleans in Moscow. It largely tallies with that of observed by Modin ten years earlier. The "Macleans' apartment was high up in one of the massive, heavily-ornamented piles, characteristic of Stalin's reign.

> They had a fine view over the Moscow River from their drawing room which, with its good furniture and western bric-a-brac, had an unmistakable flavour of London, S.W.1. The older boy attended Moscow University, and his brother a technical institute. None of the children looked Russian, perhaps because they dressed themselves from parcels of clothes which Melinda's mother and sister were constantly sending from America and England ... I sometimes wondered why Melinda, who had clearly been close to divorcing Donald a number of times, had chosen to join him in Moscow. *She may have shared his convictions and been an accomplice of his espionage,* but she seemed to yearn for the luxuries of Western capitalism—from which she was not wholly cut off thanks to her mother's packages of food and clothes ... Melinda had an old car, perhaps six or seven years old, in which she used to get about the city.[5]
> (Emphasis added.)

If Melinda Maclean's car was six or seven years old in 1963, she might have purchased it (or been given it) new soon after her arrival in Moscow.

The Macleans lived in Moscow at a level relatively similar to that at which they would have lived in London (given the absolute difference in standards of living); that is, at the standard of the higher governing class. Again from Eleanor Philby: "Ordinary Russian citizens queued for hours for tickets to the Bolshoi and the Tchaikowski Conservatoire, but we could see whatever opera, ballet or concert we chose.

> [In October 1963] we decided to take a short trip to Leningrad before the long cold winter began. The Macleans agreed to accompany us and so the four of us boarded the night express— the Red Arrow—the poshest of Russian trains and a source of

344

great pride to them. There were small pink lampshades in each compartment. It was most luxurious, each of us having our own compartment. Buxom women attendants rushed up and down the corridor selling champagne, caviar and chocolates. In Leningrad we stayed at an enormous hotel with miles of corridors. Relay posts, in the form of little buffets on each floor, served vodka, caviar and tea, to cheer you on your journey to your room. The Macleans knew the city well and were enthusiastic guides. Donald occasionally throwing in a scholarly explanation of some historical feature of the Peter and Paul Fortress or of Peterhof, the beautifully restored summer palace a few miles out of the city.[6]

Two or three times a year the Macleans would send an order to a Danish importer for "luxury foods unobtainable at GUM" the famous Soviet department store. Donald and Melinda Maclean each had a sterling account in London[7] (his had received his inheritance from a maternal grandparent—spoils from colonialism). Melinda Maclean had made herself an expert on the city, knowing the best shops in Gorky Street, old palaces re-cycled as office or youth clubs, out-of the way churches and the museums.[8] They had a dacha in a birch forest outside the city in the resort area of the higher officials of the Ministry of Foreign Affairs. Molotov's dacha was nearby. Eleanor Philby thought it "unspoiled country of great beauty."[9] Maclean "lived there from spring till late fall, cultivating his orchard, flower beds and garden like a true Englishman. Often his daughter came to stay with him. He particularly loved his little granddaughter, who [later] would stay with him for weeks at a time."[10] Less idyllically, Donald Maclean's alcoholism had returned and he continued to have periodic violent drinking episodes, "Gordon" replacing Sir (or Comrade) Maclean. During one of these episodes he wrecked a bar near his dacha. The rather gigantic Donald Maclean, run amuck, must have been a terrifying sight.

In the winter 1964, while Eleanor Philby was in America, Kim Philby went skiing with the Macleans and began an affair with Melinda Maclean. "In February, Melinda's sister arrived suddenly from England to look after her (with a new fur coat and boots to cheer her up) ..."[11] Eleanor Philby, who had returned to Moscow for Christmas, discovered the affair, and in May, 1965, when Eleanor Philby again left Moscow, Melinda Maclean moved in with Kim Philby. Roy Medvedev attributed the Macleans's unhappy family life in the Soviet Union to Donald Maclean's persistent alcoholism. There is a story about Melinda Maclean and the children huddled on the staircase landing outside the apartment while Donald Maclean raged within, smashing things. Melinda Maclean returned to Donald Maclean in 1966. It may have been around this time that Donald Maclean finally overcame his alcohol addiction.

The 1956 Twentieth Party Congress, highlighted by Khrushchev's denunciation of Stalin and Stalinism, had facilitated Donald Maclean's second career, as an academic researcher, writer and teacher. After Khrushchev's speech, "Millions were engaged by the literary-cultural thaw ...

> hundreds of intellectuals—historians, writers, economists, scientists, and policy analysts of all stripes—benefited from burgeoning ties abroad and new or rejuvenated research centers at home that now permitted remarkably frank examination of most domestic and foreign issues. In these "elite congregations," encouraged by the broader climate of reform, began the systematic study of international affairs, something that had simply not existed for nearly 30 years.[12]

Intellectual life in Moscow became less isolated. Books and academic journals from the West began to be allowed into the Soviet Union. Roy Medvedev said that in the 1950s Maclean had become part of the group "that formed around the journal International Life [*Mezhdunarodnaya Zhizn*], and he enjoyed the complete trust of its members." There was also the journal Foreign Literature *(Inostrannaia Literatura)*, begun in 1955, with which both Maclean and Burgess had some role. Cultural exchange programs with Western European countries and the United States were signed in 1957 and 1958; there were trade fairs and exhibitions. Soon there were hundreds of thousands of foreign visitors, international radio, television. The grey tones of the usual journalistic depictions of the lives of the Macleans in Moscow corresponded less and less to reality as they entered their second decade of Soviet life.

Maclean joined the Institute of World Economy and International Relations (IMEMO), in 1961.[13] IMEMO, re-opened after the Twentieth Congress, was the Soviet, is now the Russian, equivalent of the London School of Economics: "the country's largest and most respected research centre in the field."[14] It "soon became the 'incubator' for a new generation of international economists ... and foreign-policy experts."[15] Donald Maclean wrote a dissertation there, received a doctorate, gave courses and conducted research, notably on the foreign policy of the first Labour Government in Britain. In 1962 he published "Colonial Tactics of the English Monopolies," in the IMEMO journal MEMO. In it he discussed "monopoly capital as one of the major supports of imperialism and colonialism; maneuvers used in preparation of the colonies for independence—meaning above all the use of class, ethnic, tribal and religious differences to ensure the transfer of political power to the hands of those friendly with London and English ultracolonialism ..."[16] Maclean published an article, similar in tone, in MEMO as early as 1963 ("Contradictions between Centers of European Imperialism"). He wrote a 4,000 word appraisal of the foreign policy of the Wilson government for the MEMO, in which he damned the Wilson government for failing to support national liberation movements, but approved of it for "a partial departure from the rules of the cold war."[17] IMEMO flourished during Khrushchev's "Thaw," and, with some other similar organizations, continued to prosper with ever-widening contacts with the West during the difficult years that followed.

At first the Prague Spring appeared to promise an acceleration, or renewal, of the liberalizing trends of the Thaw. Researchers at IMEMO and other institutes, as well as younger staff in governmental agencies, such as the Foreign Ministry and various planning groups, began to look to the theorists of Eurocommunism for ideas about a way forward from Stalinism. Roy Medvedev met

Maclean in the late 1960's, when he gave Maclean the manuscript of *Let History Judge,* Medvedev's book on Stalin. It is an indication of Maclean's reputation in 1968 that Medvedev entrusted him with his explosive manuscript. "Maclean and I subsequently met on several other occasions. He ... offered to help in translating certain English texts. 'Samizdat' was at its peak and he wanted to read many other manuscripts circulating in Moscow." In May, 1968, Andrei Sakharov circulated his samizdat *Reflections on Progress, Peaceful Coexistence, and Intellectual Freedom,* focused on the dangers of nuclear warfare and overpopulation and the importance of protecting the environment and human rights. Sakharov states in his *Memoirs* that he gave a draft of the *Reflections* to Roy Medvedev in April and that Medvedev had shown it to "friends" and passed along their comments.[18] It would be interesting to know if Maclean saw it at this point. In any case, within weeks Sakharov's manuscript was all over Moscow and early in July it was published in Holland. A few months later the tanks were sent into Prague. Soon enough Medvedev had been expelled from the Party and the KGB took responsibility for his welfare. "Certainly for many, the end of the Prague Spring was also the end of hopes for liberalizing change, a deep disillusion that led to conformism and cynical careerism. But others drew the opposite conclusion: that the Prague Spring had shown that reforms *were* possible, but only under an enlightened leader ..."[19]

Two years later Maclean published *British Foreign Policy Since Suez (1956-68),* in Britain, with the assistance of his brother, Alan, and then published in the in Russian in the Soviet Union.[20] It has a flavor not of Samizdat, but of Cambridge University or the LSE: a fairly typical work of British diplomatic history, similar, in a way, to Victor Rothwell's *Britain and the Cold War.* It would not have been out of place on the publications list of a professor at, say, the School of Postgraduate European Studies at Reading University, where Maclean's former deputy, Robert Cecil was Chairman at the time. In the foreword, Maclean wrote: "When, after having spent the first sixteen years of my working life in the Diplomatic Service, I found myself faced with the necessity of finding a new profession, I decided, after some casting about, that what I was best qualified to do was to contribute ... by making a continuous study, as objectively as possible, of the process of development of contemporary British foreign policy."[21] *British Foreign Policy Since Suez* was an early result of that study.[*] It is academic in tone, leftist, to be sure, but not so much so as would have been out of place in a publication from the LSE itself. The historical narrative is underpinned by scholarly references, overwhelmingly British, varying from statistical analyses to speeches from Hansard's.

*British Foreign Policy Since Suez* is divided into three parts: "Policy towards the other Western powers," "Policy towards the Third World," and "Policy towards the Communist powers." It is a detailed indictment of all three of those areas of British foreign policy from 1956 to 1968. A typical judgment is to be found in the second part: "[N]ot only in the Middle East, but also in Africa the general picture has been not of a wise and far-sighted government conducting a liberal experiment in freeing the subject peoples, but of men compelled reluctantly to retreat farther and farther along a road upon which they did not want to travel."[22] Maclean concludes the book with a diagnosis of the causes of the ineffectiveness of British foreign policy: "There is one common factor in these and a large number of other blunders, namely an over-estimation of the real strength of Britain's position in the world.

> Bearing in mind that most of the present generation of policy-makers formed their conceptions of British power before and during the war, this strongly suggests that the particularly high rate of error is a function of the particularly rapid change in the post-war balance of forces to the disadvantage of all the imperialist systems, particularly the British. It also seems likely that the present generation of top people, by age, training and bent, has more difficulty in grasping the foreign political consequences of the scientific and technological revolution than will the succeeding generation.[23]

---

[*] According to George Blake, it was Maclean's dissertation.

349

The problem with the foreign policy of Britain in decline was a failure of leadership. Given the choices facing it: Europe, the Commonwealth or the Atlantic Alliance, it hesitated and delayed as its assets dwindled and its potential partners lost interest. (Maclean published a related article, "Looking Toward Europe? London Diplomacy on the Threshold of the Seventies" in MEMO, No. 6, 1970.) The underlying issue was the chronic financial deficit, which itself was a product of a similar period of indecision and self-delusion in the mid-nineteen forties. The connection, as Maclean pointed out in the quotation just cited, was that many of the policy-makers were the same.

The year of the publication of *British Foreign Policy Since Suez* saw widespread dismay at the Soviet police tactic of committing dissidents to insane asylums. Zhores Medvedev (brother of the historian Roy Medvedev) was confined in the Kaluga psychiatric hospital toward the end of May, 1970. After protests by Sakharov and others he was released on June 17.[24] It was reported on August 21, 1970 that a Moscow University student, Olga Ioffe, had been charged with anti-Soviet agitation and sent to a psychiatric institute. In his obituary of Donald Maclean, Roy Medvedev wrote that "In Moscow, Maclean did not seek meetings with the dissidents, although he observed their activities and struggle with interest.

He never refused to make small contributions when collections were made in support of the families of the arrested. On one occasion he learned that the daughter of a family he knew had been arrested for distributing leaflets ...That year elections were being conducted ... Maclean went to the voting place and inside the booth, wrote on the form: "While girls like Olga Ioffe are kept in mental institutions, I cannot participate in the elections."

Maclean also protested to Yuri Andropov, then Chairman of the KGB, against the March, 1971, arrest of Vladimir Bukovsky, a dissident and member of the Human Rights Committee, was arrested at the end of March.[25] When Maclean's sons were at Moscow University, in the 1970s, they "not infrequently brought home young friends who were opposed to the government. Maclean listened to their conversations with interest, but this was already a different generation with its own ideas about political and moral values."[26]

In 1973 Maclean published an article, "The Plans for Military Integration of Western Europe: the British Variant," in *International Affairs* under the name S. Madzoevsky. He wrote other articles, some on the British Conservative Party, which appeared in IMEMO's publication, MEMO, also under the name S. Madzoevsky. IMEMO continued to sponsor increased scholarly exchanges with the West. In 1978 it began coordinating the U.S.-Soviet Joint Committee on International Issues on behalf of the U.S. and Soviet academies of science. "Over the mid-to-late 1970s, IMEMO produced many studies viewing European political and economic union in an increasingly favorable, even glowing light."[27] MEMO published "Great Britain in Today's World" by Maclean with E. Khesin in 1980 and "Growing International Tensions and Western Europe," which Maclean wrote with D. Tomashevskii, published in its 1982 issue.

Professor Sergei Peregudov, recalls: "I knew Donald Maclean for most of his time at IMEMO.

Mainly we collaborated in co-authoring articles on British politics, which we published in the Institute's journal ... These articles and other publications by Maclean were very professional and offered a deep analysis based on a scrupulous study of sources and literature. The level of scientific research he did was very high, and they were highly apprized in the Institute and in wider circles, including in the so-called Soviet periphery. I can judge from contacts with scholars from Perm how important and interesting his works were considered.

Maclean's research was an organic part of the research activities of those scholars in the Institute who held nondogmatic views of the situation in the USSR and in the world. As the same "revisionist" positions were shared by a greater part of the Institute's directorate, including the then IMEMO director Nikolai Inozemtsev, Donald Maclean's authority as a first-class specialist and researcher at IMEMO was extremely high.

351

I can definitely say that the colleagues who collaborated with him in research activities at IMEMO and I myself were very much impressed by the remarkable dimension of his personality. We felt that research was only one of the spheres, and not the main one, where his potential could be successfully implemented. This was my personal opinion from my interaction with him.

His personality manifested itself in his quick learning of the Russian language, and in the way he rigorously kept a self-imposed taboo on alcohol.

Evaluating Maclean's personality and his life, I can say that my impression of him (and, I am sure, not only mine) was that of a person of a tragic fate. The illusion so common in the 1930s for many Western intellectuals broke his life. He found the strength to start life anew and to find his place in this new life with the dignity of a real Englishman, and this confirms the high appraisal of his personality and the high esteem for him we had.[28]

"Some Reflections of a Communist on the Soviet Union," was published in the November 1990 issue of MEMO from notes made by Maclean in the spring of 1981, "two years before his untimely death and four years before the beginning of perestroika," as the editors remarked.[29] In "Some Reflections of a Communist on the Soviet Union" Maclean begins with a claim that his "Reflections" have "a general application, since it bears on the Marxist conception of the transition of human society from capitalism to socialism ... I doubt if it is possible to understand [the history of any] socialist state without the aid of one of the key conceptions of historical materialism—the contradiction between superstructure and base common to all social formations including socialism." This may seem today as a pro forma declaration of faith, but the last phrase would have been read as a "deviation" when Maclean arrived in Moscow, perhaps a fatal deviation, as contradictions between base and superstructure were then held to be characteristic only of capitalist society, not the society that Stalin had built. As the "Reflections" are little known, here follows some extensive extracts:

The Soviet Union ... is a society in which calculations of return on privately owned capital have been replaced by calculations of the common good as the main determinant of the way in which all necessities of life, material and spiritual, are produced and distributed ... On this central question, my thoughts about the Soviet Union are basically the same as they were nearly fifty years ago. The differences relate to the nature of the "calculations of the common good" as they have in fact been, and still are being, made by the people who have run and now run the country ...

[S]ince the mass destruction of the Soviet intelligentsia in the second half of the 30s, the political and cultural level of the ruling elite ... has on the whole been, and still is, entirely inadequate for the tasks it is supposed to perform ... Since 1964 ... the record of the present leadership and its penumbra shows, it seems to me, a persistent, regressive tendency to substitute the aim of preserving its own power for the aim of finding ways of realizing the energy of the society which they rule ...

I believe that the Soviet Union itself is bound sooner or later to develop on Eurocommunist lines ... [There is] a feeling of unease, a critical mood, among the hundred thousand, say, men and women who have direct responsibility for day-to-day decision-making ... who have become aware that the highly complex problems of running the Soviet Union are now beyond the range of the present leaders at the top, that a new quality of top leaderships is required ... [This] presages an eventual mass demand ... for the democratization of the political life of the country ... In this country, the immediate initiative for creative change is still likely to come ... from inside the upper reaches of the Party-state hierarchy ... it seems more probable than not that the next five years, owing to favorable changes at the top, will see an improvement in the political, cultural and moral climate in

353

the Soviet Union and the introduction of a complex of reforms affecting most major aspects of the life of the Soviet people ... Gorbachev became General Secretary of the Communist Party in 1985.

Maclean argues that the changing nature of the Soviet economy, from centralized heavy industry to more complex technologically based modes, requires a parallel change in governmental structure. He writes that many of his friends are less optimistic, believing that the "hundred thousand" will not easily give up their privileges. He agrees that those whose work was within the Party apparatus were an obstacle, but believes that the technocrats will move toward decentralization, not least because the ideals of Socialism were still strong.

After predicting, and calling for, what would be Gorbachev's "new thinking," Maclean's "Reflections" turn to foreign policy. "In terms of getting things wrong, there is little to choose between Chamberlain's "It's peace in our time" (1938) and Molotov's "the danger of war between Germany and the Soviet Union has been eliminated" (1939) ...

The era of the 20th Congress brought a major turn towards a more rational view of the outside world and the needs of Soviet society, the adoption of a course centered on the aim of peaceful co-existence ...

Underlying long-term social and political tendencies within the capitalist and former-colonial worlds are predominantly favorable to the interest of the Soviet people and state and to socialism generally, but those responsible here for top-level foreign policy decisions have in recent years ... to an increasing extend misjudged the global dynamics of international relations, failed to foresee the consequences of their own actions and, in certain cases, lost ground which appeared already to have been gained ... the feature of contemporary Soviet foreign policy which ... does most damage to the interests of the Soviet Union is an undialectical, one-sided conception of the role in world politics of the country's armed forces ... the views of the military authorities [prevail]... the Soviet Union, as if it were hypnotized by the size and variety of American nuclear forces, is continually adding to its own overkill capacity, not only with no advantage to itself, but with seriously harmful consequences ...

The Soviet leadership evidently believed that the introduction of the SS 20 rockets would not compel the FRG [Federal Republic of Germany], Britain and some other Western European states to accept upon their territories a new generation of American weapons of roughly comparable capacity, but in fact it has ... it costs Washington far less than it costs Moscow to maintain a high military share of GNP ... the American ruling class has a long-term political interest in forcing the Soviet Union ... into a spiral of irrational military expenditure ... I ... regard the substitution by military force of a [Vasil] Bilyak for a Dubchek as part of a long chain of events highly damaging to the interests of the Soviet Union ...

[T]he central imperative of international relations today [is] the absolute necessity for everyone's sake ... of lowering the level of military confrontation in the Euro-Atlantic region, of turning the upward spiral into a downward spiral ... the fate of socialism in the long run depends ... on the outcome of ... [the} competition between ... the capitalist and socialist ... formations and on the avoidance of a mutually annihilating war between them. But it also depends on the outcome of the conflict between creative and what the Russians call "dark" tendencies within the Communist system ...[30]

*       *       *

The MEMO editors prefaced the "Reflections" with the comment that "Working for more than 20 years on the IMEMO staff, right up until his death, [Maclean] gained wide renown as a major expert and talented scholar of British and world politics, a subtle analyst of events and patterns in contemporary international

355

relations, a solicitous mentor of young scholars, and a person of immense charm ...

> [He] combined a scholar's powerful intelligence with irreproachable decency, devotion to principle, and courage in defending his convictions—and not just his convictions in the scholarly realm. A concern for the true interests of our country and party and for human rights suffused his numerous appeals to the Central Committee of the Communist Party of the Soviet Union and the KGB, including his appeals on behalf of Zhores Medvedev and Vladimir Bukovskiy, who had suffered abuses in psychiatric institutions.[31]

Geoffrey Hoare thought that "There was always one guiding principle ... to which Donald remained steadfast, even if it was sometimes obscured: he believed in peace and he believed in human liberties. Deep down in his heart, Donald was a reformer—he wished to remake the world ... It was this reformatory zeal more than anything else, I feel, that made Donald a Communist in the early thirties ..."[32]

We also have an appraisal of Donald Maclean from Yevgeny Primakov, briefly Prime Minister of Russia under Yeltsin, deputy director then director of IMEMO. "Donald Maclean ... [actively campaigned] for political dissidents ...

> One cannot say that Maclean did not like Britain, and especially Scotland ... But he was a patriot of the Soviet Union. I would not want to simplify things, however. Together with us he lived through the drama of the exposure of Stalin and the crimes that did not fit into the framework of ideologically pure socialism, in which he believed so reverently. We spoke a lot on this subject, but there wasn't even a trace of complaint about his fate in anything he said ... A fatal disease with which Maclean struggled courageously finally took the life of this outstanding man. The entire institute and all of Maclean's colleagues in the intelligence community attended the funeral.[33]

\*   \*   \*

Melinda Maclean stayed with her husband until 1979, living, for the last ten years or so before that, something of the life of a faculty wife.    She then went back to New York, where she lived in Sunnyside Gardens, Queens (once a famous socialist colony), until her death in 2010. In the mid-1970s, their sons, who had married Russians, had emigrated with *their* children to London, Fergus Maclean, then 30 years old, with his wife Olga and son Dmitri, to take a three-year course in modern history at University College, London.[34] The Macleans's daughter, "Melinda," of course, married a dissident painter named Aleksandr Driuchin and taking with her Donald Maclean's favorite granddaughter Melinda, joined her grandmother, mother and aunts in New York.[35]

During the last few years of his life Donald Maclean lived alone in his dacha and Moscow apartment, at each of which he had a caretaker. He died on March 9, 1983. His ashes were taken by his son Fergus to England, where they were placed in the family vault at Penn, Buckinghamshire.[36]

## Chapter Ten: Notes

[1] "The Committee of Information was . . . [detached from the secret intelligence services, became] a subsidiary department of the Ministry of Foreign Affairs, and it was there that Burgess and Maclean started to work in 1952, after their defection from the West." Sudoplatov, Pavel and Anatoli Sudoplatov. Special Tasks: The Memoirs of an Unwanted Witness—A Soviet Spymaster. Boston: Little, Brown and Company, 1994, p. 237.

[2] Modin, p. 246.

[3] Cecil, p. 170.

[4] FBI FOIA documents, in the possession of the author.

[5] Philby, Eleanor. Kim Philby: The Spy I Loved. London: Hamish Hamilton, 1968, pp. 81-83.

[6] Philby, Eleanor, p. 85.

[7] Philby, Eleanor, p. 134.

[8] Philby, Eleanor, p. 104.

[9] Philby, Eleanor, p. 116.

[10] Medvedev, Roy. A Spy's Lonely Loyalty to Old, Betrayed Ideals. Washington Post, Sunday, June 19, 1983, p. B1; B4.

[11] Philby, Eleanor, p. 166.

[12] English, Robert D. Russia and the Idea of the West: Gorbachev, Intellectuals, and the End of the Cold War. New York: Columbia University Press, 2000, p. 51.

[13] It is interesting that the career of Robert Cecil, Maclean's deputy in Washington and then again at the American Department, followed a similar trajectory. Cecil left the Foreign Service in 1968 to become an academic, teaching and writing at Reading University. A later career for a possible Donald Maclean at, say, LSE, is not difficult to imagine, always with the proviso that he had not met Arnold Deutsch.

[14] Walker, Martin. The Cold War: A History. New York: Holt Paperbacks, 1995, p. 284.

[15] English, p. 76.

[16] The Middle East, Abstracts and Index, Volume 23, Part 4. Northumberland Press, p. 93.

[17] See also, Peregudov, Sergei, S. Efimov and S. Madzoevsky. "Angliiskie conservatory u vlasti," MEMO, 11 (1979), pp. 114-21, Madzoevsky, Sergei Peregudov and Efim Khesin, "Pravye konservatory u vlasti," MEMO, 6 (1981), pp. 73-85 and G. Kolosov and S. Madzoevsky. "The Plans for Military Integration of Western Europe: the British Variant," International Affairs, Moscow, 1973, pp. 52-58.

[18] Sakharov, Andrei. Memoirs. Trans. Richard Lourie. New York: Alfred A. Knopf, 1990, p. 284

[19] English, p. 114.

[20] Modin, pp. 248-9.

[21] Maclean, Donald. British Foreign Policy Since Suez. London: Hodder and Stoughton, 1970, p. 9.

[22] Maclean, Donald. British Foreign Policy Since Suez, p. 220.

[23] Maclean, Donald. British Foreign Policy Since Suez, p. 330.

[24] Sakharov, pp. 310ff.

[25] Sakharov, p. 334.

[26] Medvedev, Roy. A Spy's Lonely Loyalty to Old, Betrayed Ideals. Washington Post, Sunday, June 19, 1983, p. B1; B4.

[27] English, pp. 152-3.

[28] Personal communication.

[29] Hirsch, Steve (ed). MEMO 3: In Search of Answers in the Post-Soviet Era. Washington, D.C.: The Bureau of National Affairs, 1992, p. 195. The provenance of these "reflections" is unclear. George Blake, who also worked at IMEMO, quotes from them and claims that they had been given to him for safe-keeping. Blake, George. No Other Choice. London: Jonathan Cape, 1990, p. 268.

[30] Hirsch, p. 195ff.

[31] Hirsch, p. 196.

[32] Hoare, p. 195.

[33] Primakov, E. M. Russian Crossroads: Toward the New Millennium. New Haven: Yale University Press, 2004, pp. 111-2.

[34] Niesewand, Peter. "Defector's Son Returns For Study." Manchester Guardian, January 27, 1974.

[35] Modin, pp. 260-61. Blake, who emphasizes Donald Maclean's importance within the KGB, writes that their emigration was facilitated by his connections.

[36] Modin, pp. 260-61.

# Some Reflections on the Macleans

The lives of Donald and Melinda Maclean are technically challenging for the biographer. Aside from the scattered letters published by Geoffrey Hoare, which are almost exclusively to do with personal, emotional, matters, there is virtually nothing available about Melinda Marling Maclean's intellectual and political life. This has been taken, implicitly, to mean that she was first to last simply a denizen of Manhattan's Upper East Side, who happened to drift into forty-year marriage with a man she knew was a Communist and a spy. It is not a very plausible story. She told Donald Maclean that she was a Communist sympathizer virtually as soon as they met. After some years in Moscow she continued to present herself in that way. She remained in Moscow for a quarter of a century, when at any moment she could have walked into the American Embassy with her children and asked to be repatriated.

The material concerning Donald Maclean is difficult in other ways. The official files have been severely edited, "weeded"; diaries, memoirs and correspondence of those who knew him have been treated similarly. Slander has been given a free rein and accepted as fact. Thanks to the work of Sheila Kerr and, more recently, the release of files from the British National Archives, we know approximately what Donald Maclean did as a diplomat and what he knew. From this we can infer what he sent to Moscow, although there is little in the way of confirmation of those inferences beyond summary statements in the published history of the Foreign Intelligence Service of the Russian Federation and similarly reliable publications by people like Yuri Modin. Nonetheless, we can be fairly confident that Maclean comprehensively deprived the British Government of secrecy for its plans and decision-making, at least between 1944 and 1951, and only slightly less deprived the American government of its ability to make policy in secret during that period. There are few, if any, parallels to this record.

It is likely that the standard histories of the period of Maclean's activity as a Soviet agent will eventually include his influence on

Soviet decision-making in regard to the run-up to the Second World War and during the early Cold War. Munich, the Molotov-Ribbentrop Pact, the end of the Russo-Finnish War, the Marshall Plan negotiations and, most dramatically, the part played by American nuclear power in the early Cold War, will all be re-evaluated in the light of the question: What did Stalin know and when did he know it?

Some historians, and more journalists, have been puzzled by why Donald Maclean became and remained an agent of the Soviet secret intelligence service. It is probably best to accept his own explanation in his "Reflections." He became a Communist out of conviction that the order of British society was unjust and he became a spy to change that. Later, while in Washington, he became convinced that various groups in the American government were intent on creating what he thought of as a fascist society at home and something very like the informal British Empire everywhere else, even at the cost of a Third World War. These, rather than admiration for Stalin, were his motives.

Once in the Soviet Union there was no going back for Maclean. He would have faced a life in prison or, as likely as not, assassination. There was nothing for him to do other than what he did: study, teach, write; garden in the summer, go to the opera in the winter; with Melinda Maclean bring up their children. There was the additional factor of his political activities in the space between the dissidents and the KGB, about which only hints are known, and the dynamics of the marriage of Melinda and Donald Maclean, about which nothing is known, as is the case with most of the marriages of others. Given the cards dealt him it was not a bad end game, not very different from the later years of his associate Robert Cecil or from those of his brother Alan Maclean, the publisher; much better than the later years of Philip Toynbee. Of course Maclean could have gotten to those quiet academic last years by another route: ambassadorships, a knighthood, perhaps other honors. It was a choice he made long before, while sitting on a bench in Regent's Park, talking with a man from Vienna.

# Bibliography

A Note on Sources

"However disappointing these spy histories might be for those who are looking for documented facts and objective analyses, they should not be rejected out of hand, because they are all we have ... Unless there is a drastic change in the way Russia's security and intelligence services operate, the FIS will continue to dole out its archival secrets for profit, selling only those documents that uphold its version of history. But this should not stop us from reading what they have to say now. Probably the best approach is to treat these books with the same kind of skepticism we applied to Soviet publications - from which the discerning reader could glean a great deal. In other words, read between the lines, and always consider the source." Amy Knight, The Wilson Quarterly, Winter, 2000, writing about *The Sword and the Shield; KGB: The Inside Story; Deadly Illusions; Special Tasks; The Haunted Wood* and similar books purported to be based on Soviet secret police archives.

Robert Cecil, Donald Maclean's some-time deputy in London and Washington, published *A Divided Life: A Biography of Donald Maclean* in 1988. An excellent book, it contains extracts from many documents, a compilation of stories and interviews, and an insider's view of Maclean's career. Cecil is sympathetic to Donald Maclean as a friend and mentor, and sympathetic, if condescending to Melinda Maclean. He is not sympathetic to the politics that shaped the lives of the Macleans and he allows his hostility to that commitment to influence his account of their actions. There is also a question of how much of the narrative is affected by Cecil's own implication in Donald Maclean's career. Did his certainly understandable wish to maintain a certain distance influence not only his interpretations, but also decisions about what to include in the biography?

Geoffrey Hoare's *The Missing Macleans* was written by a journalist who benefitted from conversations with Melinda Maclean, her mother and sister, as well as access to some of their papers. It is a primary, often the only source, for Melinda Maclean's part of the story. Finally, Sheila Kerr, a graduate student advisee of Robert Cecil at the London School of Economics wrote a thesis entitled "An Assessment of a Soviet Agent: Donald Maclean, 1940-1951." Kerr systematically explored the resources of The National Archives (Kew) for Donald Maclean's professional papers. As the thesis is now digitized and accessible on the Internet, those Foreign Office files can be read in it, where they are extensively quoted. Kerr's "assessment" is useful, especially as read with Cecil's interpretations. The Kerr material should be supplemented, as they have been here, by further work in the National Archives and in other archives, such as those in Oxford (Bodleian Special Collections) and Trinity College, Cambridge.

The Foreign Relations of the United States (FRUS) and Documents on British Policy Overseas contain official material not found in Cecil or Kerr. The archives (some of which are now on-line) of the United States Federal Bureau of Investigation contain thousands of pages of interviews and newspaper clippings concerning the Macleans (with those concerning Burgess and Philby), primarily for their time in the United States. I have obtained additional FBI material by means of a Freedom of Information Act request. These, too, are, as is usually the case, more or less heavily censored (redacted). Finally, the in-house history of the Foreign Intelligence Service of the Russian Federation has some interesting pages giving their view of the Macleans and their associates.

## Works Cited

Acheson, Dean. Present at the Creation: My Years in the State Department. New York: W.W. Norton & Company, Inc., 1969.

Aldrich, Richard J. British Intelligence Strategy and the Cold War, 1945-51. London: Routledge, 1992.

Aldrich, Richard J. "Secret intelligence for a post-war world: reshaping the British intelligence community, 1944-51," in Aldrich, Richard J. British Intelligence Strategy and the Cold War, 1945-51. London: Routledge, 1992.

Aldrich, Richard J. and Zametica, John. "The rise and decline of a strategic concept: the Middle East, 1945-1951" in Aldrich, Richard J. British Intelligence Strategy and the Cold War, 1945-51. London: Routledge, 1992.

Aldrich, Richard. The Hidden Hand: Britain, America, and Cold War Secret Intelligence. London: John Murray, 2001.

Andrew, Christopher and Gordievsky, Oleg. KGB: The Inside Story. London: Hodder & Stoughton, 1990.

Andrews, Geoff. James Klugmann, a complex communist 27 February 2012 accessed on May 12, 2013 at http://www.opendemocracy.net/geoff-andrews/james-klugmann-complex-communist

Auden, W. H. "Honour," in Greene, Graham. The Old School. London: Jonathan Cape, 1934.

Barnes, John and David Nicholson (eds.). The Empire at Bay: The Leo Amery Diaries, 1929-1945. London: Hutchinson, 1988.

Blake, George. No Other Choice. London: Jonathan Cape, 1990.

Blunt, Anthony. Memoir, British Library, ADD Ms. 88902/1, p. 76.

Blythe, Ronald. The Age of Illusion: England in the Twenties and Thirties, 1919-1940. London: Phoenix Press, 2001.

Bohlen, Charles and Robinson, Gerold T. "The capabilities and intentions of the Soviet Union as affected by American policy," Diplomatic History, I (Fall, 1977), 389-99. December 10, 1945.

Borowski, Harry R. "A Narrow Victory: the Berlin blockade and the American military response." Air University Review, July-August 1981.

Botman, Selma. Egypt from Independence to Revolution, 1919-1952. Syracuse, New York: Syracuse University Press, 1991.

Boyle, Peter G. "Oliver Franks and the Washington Embassy, 1948-52," in Zametica, John (ed.). British Officials and British Foreign Policy: 1945-50. Leicester: Leicester University Press, 1990.

Brooks, Philip C. Oral History Interview with Sir Edmund Hall-Patch, Chairman of the Executive Committee, Organization for European Economic Cooperation, 1948. Harry S. Truman Library & Museum, http://www.trumanlibrary.org/oralhist/hallpatc.htm          accessed December 5, 2013.

Brooks, Philip C. Oral History Interview with Sir Roger Makins. Harry S. Truman Library & Museum, http://www.trumanlibrary.org/oralhist/makins1.htm, accessed December 5, 2013.

Brown, Andrew. J. D. Bernal: The Sage of Science. Oxford University Press, 2005.

Bullen, Roger and Pelly, M.E. Documents on British Policy Overseas, Series I, Volume IV. London: Her Majesty's Stationery Office, 1987.

Bullen, Roger and Pelly, M.E. Documents on British Policy Overseas, Series I, Volume III. London: Her Majesty's Stationery Office, 1986.

Bullen, Roger and Pelly, M.E. Documents on British Policy Overseas, Third Series, vol. I, no. 250. London: Her Majesty's Stationery Office, 1949.

Bullock, Alan. Ernest Bevin: Foreign Secretary, 1945-1951. New York & London: W. W. Norton & Company, 1983.

Bullock, Alan. The Life and Times of Ernest Bevin. Volume One: Trade Union Leader, 1881-1940. London: Heinemann, 1960.

Burke, David.   The Lawn Road Flats: Spies, Writers and Artists. Woodbridge, Suffolk: The Boydell Press, 2014.

Cairncross, John. The Enigma Spy: The Story of the Man Who Changed the Course of World War Two. London: Century, Random House, 1997

Cambray, Joseph. Synchronicity: Nature and Psyche in an Interconnected Universe. Texas A&M University Press, 2009.

Caute, David. The Great Fear: The Anti-Communist Purge Under Truman and Eisenhower. New York: Simon and Schuster, 1978.

Cecil, Robert. A Divided Life: A Biography of Donald Maclean. London: The Bodley Head, 1988.

Channon, Sir Henry. 'Chips': The Diaries of Sir Henry Channon. Ed. Robert Rhodes James. London: Orion, 1996.

Clarke, Peter. The Cripps Version: The Life of Sir Stafford Cripps, 1889-1952. London: Allen Lane, The Penguin Press, 2002.

Cole, Margaret. Growing Up Into Revolution. London: Longmans, Green and Co., 1949.

Connolly, Cyril. The Missing Diplomats. London, Queen Anne Press, 1952.

Costello, John. Mask of Treachery. New York, William Morrow and Company, 1988.

Costigliola, Frank. Roosevelt's Lost Alliances: How Personal Politics Helped Start the Cold War. Princeton: Princeton University Press, 2012.

Dale, Robert. Re-Adjusting to Life After War: The Demobilization of Red Army Veterans in Leningrad and The Leningrad Region 1944-1950, dissertation, Queen Mary, University of London.

Damaskin, Igor with Geoffrey Elliott. Kitty Harris: The Spy with Seventeen Names. London: St Ermin's Press, 2001.

DeConde, Alexander. A History of American Foreign Policy, 1963.

Deighton, Anne. Britain and the Cold War, 1945-1955, in Westad, Odd Adne. The Cambridge History of the Cold War, Volume I: Origins. Cambridge: Cambridge University Press, 2010, pp. 115-6.

Devereux, David R. Britain and the Failure of Collective Defence in the Middle East, 1948-53. in Deighton, Anne (ed.) Britain and the First Cold War. New York, St. Martin's Press, 1990.

Dilks, David. (ed.) The Diaries of Sir Alexander Cadogan, O.M.: 1938-1945. New York: G. P. Putnam's Sons, 1972.

Dorril, Stephen. MI6: Inside the Covert World of Her Majesty's Secret Intelligence Service. New York: Free Press, 2002.

Douglas, Roy. Biography of Sir Donald Maclean. http://www.liberalhistory.org.uk/item_single.php?item_id=51&item= biography, accessed May 1, 2013.

Edwards, Jill. "Roger Makins: 'Mr Atom'" in Zametica, John (ed.). British Officials and British Foreign Policy: 1945-50. Leicester: Leicester University Press, 1990.

Edwards, Jill. Anglo-American Relations and the Franco Question, 1945-1955. Oxford: Clarendon Press, 1999.

English, Robert D. Russia and the Idea of the West: Gorbachev, Intellectuals, and the End of the Cold War. New York: Columbia University Press, 2000.

Fahmy, Isis. Around the World With Isis. London: Papadakis, 2006.

Falin, V., ed. Soviet Peace Efforts on the Eve of World War II (September 1938-August 1939). 2 vols. (Moscow: Novosti, 1973, 2: 144-7 (No. 379).

Flanner, Janet. Paris was Yesterday: 1925-1939. San Diego: Harcourt Brace Jovanovich, Publishers, 1988.

Forbes, Duncan. "Politics, Photography and Exile in the Life of Edith Tudor-Hart," in Behr, Shulamith and Marian Malet. Arts in Exile in

Britain 1933-1945: Politics and Cultural Identity. Amsterdam and London: The Yearbook of the Research Centre for German and Austrian Exile Studies, 6, Institute of Germanic Studies and Romance Studies, University of London.

Gerolymatos, Andre. Red Acropolis, Black Terror: The Greek Civil War and the Origins of the Soviet-American Rivalry, 1943-1949. New York: Basic Books, 2004.

Gormley, James. From Potsdam to the Cold War. London: Rowman & Littlefield, Publishers, 1990.

Gorodetsky, Gabriel. "The Dramatis Personae behind the Ribbentrop-Molotov Pact." February 26, 2013.
http://www.youtube.com/watch?v=ZVOh1yS-Qag

Graham, Katherine. Personal History. New York: Vintage, 1998.

Hahn, Peter L. The United States, Great Britain, and Egypt, 1945-1956. Chapel Hill and London: The University of North Carolina Press, 1991.

Hennessy, Peter. The Secret State: Whitehall and the Cold War (London: Penguin, 2002).

Hirsch, Steve (ed). MEMO 3: In Search of Answers in the Post-Soviet Era. Washington, D.C.: The Bureau of National Affairs, 1992.

Hitchcock, William I. The Marshall Plan and the creation of the West. In Leffler, Melvyn P. and Westad, Odd Arne (eds.). The Cambridge History of the Cold War, Volume I: Origins. Cambridge University Press, 2010.

Hoare, Geoffrey. The Missing Macleans. New York: The Viking Press, 1955.

Hobsbawm, Eric. Interesting Times: A Twentieth-Century Life. London: Penguin, 2002.

Holzman, Michael. James Jesus Angleton, the C.I.A., & the Craft of Counterintelligence. Amherst: University of Massachusetts Press, 2008.

Honigmann, Barbara. A Chapter from My Life. An extract translated by John S. Barrett from Ein Kapitel aus meinem Leben. Munich: Carl Hanser Verlag, 2004. http://www.litrix.de/mmo/priv/15847-WEB.pdf

http://blogs.spectator.co.uk/books/2013/08/amartya-sen-interview-india-must-fulfil-tagores-vision-not-gandhis/ accessed November 13, 2013.

http://www.cafedeflore.fr/accueil-english/history/1939-45/ accessed May 16, 2013.

Ignatieff, Michael. Isaiah Berlin: A Life. London: Chatto & Windus, 1998.

Jeffery, Keith. The Secret History of MI6. New York: The Penguin Press, 2010.

Kennan, George F. The Kennan Diaries. Costigliola, Frank (ed.). New York: W. W. Norton, 2014.

Kerr, Sheila. "Investigating Soviet Espionage and Subversion: The Case of Donald Maclean," in Hoare, Oliver (ed.) British Intelligence in the Twentieth Century, London: Routledge, 2003.

Kerr, Sheila. An Assessment of a Soviet Agent: Donald Maclean, 1940-1951. Unpublished thesis, Department of International History, London School of Economics and Political Science, January 1996.

Kerr, Sheila. Secret Hotline to Moscow in Deighton, Anne (ed.) Britain and the First Cold War. New York, St. Martin's Press, 1990.

Kimball, Warren F. Churchill and Roosevelt, The Complete Correspondence, Volume III, Princeton: Princeton University Press, 1984.

Klugmann, James. History of the Communist Party of Great Britain. Volume One: Formation and Early Years, 1919-1924. London: Lawrence & Wishart Ltd., 1968.

Klugmann, James. History of the Communist Party of Great Britain. Volume 2: The General Strike: 1925-1926. London: Lawrence & Wishart Ltd., 1969.

Kolosov, G. and S. Madzoevsky. "The Plans for Military Integration of Western Europe: the British Variant," International Affairs, Moscow, 1973, pp. 52-58.

Lewis, Julian. Changing Direction: British Military Planning for Post-war Strategic Defence, 1942-1947, Second edition. London: Frank Cass, 2003.

Louis, Wm. Roger. The British Empire in the Middle East 1945-1951: Arab Nationalism, The United States and Postwar Imperialism. Oxford: Clarendon Press, 1984.

Luke, Michael. David Tennant and the Gargoyle Years. Weidenfeld and Nicolson. London, 1991.

Maclean, Alan. No, I Tell a Lie, It was the Tuesday: A Trudge Round the Life and Times of Alan Maclean. London: Kyle Cathie Limited, 1997.

Maclean, Donald. British Foreign Policy Since Suez. London: Hodder and Stoughton, 1970.

Macmillan, Harold. Winds of Change: 1914-1966. London: Macmillan, 1966.

Madzoevsky, Sergei Peregudov and Efim Khesin, "Pravye konservatory u vlasti," MEMO, 6 (1981), pp. 73-85.

Maisky, Ivan. Memoirs of A Soviet Ambassador: The War: 1939-43. Trans. Andrew Rothstein. New York: Charles Scribner's Sons, 1967.

Mastny, Vojtech. NATO in the Beholder's Eye: Soviet Perceptions and Policies, 1949-56. Washington, D.C.: Woodrow Wilson

International Center for Scholars, Cold War International History Project, Working Paper No. 35, March, 2002.

May, Ernest R. Strange Victory: Hitler's Conquest of France. New York: Hill and Wang, 2000.

Medvedev, Roy. A Spy's Lonely Loyalty to Old, Betrayed Ideals. Washington Post, Sunday, June 19, 1983, p. B1; B4.

Miliband, Ralph. Parliamentary Socialism: A Study in the Politics of Labour. London: Merlin Press, Second Edition, 1972.

Millis, Walter. Ed. The Forrestal Diaries. New York: The Viking Press, 1951.

Modin, Yuri. My Five Cambridge Friends: Burgess, Maclean, Philby, Blunt and Cairncross. New York: Farrar Strauss Giroux, 1994.

Morris, Benny. 1948: The First Arab-Israeli War. New Haven: Yale University Press, 2008.

Mosley, Charles. editor, Burke's Peerage, Baronetage & Knightage, 107th edition, 3 volumes (Wilmington, Delaware, U.S.A.: Burke's Peerage (Genealogical Books) Ltd, 2003), volume 1.

Mosley, Charlotte, ed. Love from Nancy. The Letters of Nancy Mitford. Boston and New York: Houghton Mifflin Company, 1993

Muggeridge, Malcolm, Like It Was: The Diaries of Malcolm Muggeridge. London: HarperCollins Publishers Ltd, 1981.

Newsletter, Foreign Intelligence Service, Russian Federation, April 3, 2008, "Returning to the Cambridge Five: Triumph or Failure?" http://svr.gov.ru/smi/2004/bratishka20040125.htm

Newsletter, Foreign Intelligence Service, Russian Federation, January 25, 2004, http://svr.gov.ru/smi/2004/bratishka20040125.htm.

Newton, Verne W. The Cambridge Spies: The Untold Story of Maclean, Philby, and Burgess in America. Lanham, New York: Madison Books, 1991 .

Niesewand, Peter. "Defector's Son Returns For Study." Manchester Guardian, January 27, 1974.

Ovendale, Ritchie. "William Strang and the Permanent Under-Secretary's Committee" in Zametica, John (ed.). British Officials and British Foreign Policy: 1945-50. Leicester: Leicester University Press, 1990.

Page, Bruce, Leitch, David and Phillip Knightly. Philby: The Spy Who Betrayed a Generation. London: Andre Deutsch, 1968.

Pappe, Ilan. "Sir Alec Kirkbride and the Anglo-Transjordanian alliance, 1945-50," in Zametica, John (ed.). British Officials and British Foreign Policy: 1945-50. Leicester: Leicester University Press, 1990.

Pechatnov, Vladimir O. The Big Three After World War II: New Documents On Soviet Thinking About Post War Relations With The United States And Great Britain. Working Paper No. 13. Woodrow Wilson International Center For Scholars, Cold War International History Project.

Pechatnov, Vladimir O. The Soviet Union and the World, 1944-1953, in Leffler, Melvyn P. and Westad, Odd Adne. The Cambridge History of the Cold War, Volume I: Origins. Cambridge: Cambridge University Press, 2010.

Peregudov, Sergei, S. Efimov and S. Madzoevsky. "Angliiskie conservatory u vlasti," MEMO, 11 (1979), pp. 114-21.

Perrault, Gilles. Henri Curiel, Citizen of the Third World. Le Monde Diplomatique, English Edition, April, 1998, http://mondediplo.com/1998/04/13curiel.

Philby, Eleanor. Kim Philby: The Spy I Loved. London: Hamish Hamilton, 1968.

Pottle, Mark (ed.). Champion Redoubtable: The Diaries and Letters of Violet Bonham Carter: 1914-1945. London: Weidenfeld & Nicholson, 1998.

Primakov, E. M. Russian Crossroads: Toward the New Millennium. New Haven: Yale University Press, 2004.

Ragsdale, Hugh. The Soviets, the Munich Crisis, and the Coming of World War II. Cambridge: The Cambridge University Press, 2004.

Rawls, John. A Theory of Justice. Cambridge, Massachusetts: The Belknap Press of Harvard University Press, 1971.

Reynolds, David. From World War to Cold War: Churchill, Roosevelt and the International History of the 1940s. Oxford: Oxford University Press, 2006.

Roberts, Andrew. "The Holy Fox" The Life of Lord Halifax. London: George Weidenfield and Nicolson, Ltd., 1991.

Robson, Dorothy. Memoirs. Unpublished. In the possession of the author.

Rothwell, Victor. Britain and the Cold War: 1941:1947. London: Jonathan Cape, 1982.

Rothwell, Victor. "Robin Hankey" in Zametica, John (ed.). British Officials and British Foreign Policy: 1945-50. Leicester: Leicester University Press, 1990.

Rucker, Laurent. "Moscow's Surprise: The Soviet-Israeli Alliance of 1947-1949. Woodrow Wilson International Center for Scholars, Cold War International History Project, Working Paper #46.
Sakharov, Andrei. Memoirs. Trans. Richard Lourie. New York: Alfred A. Knopf, 1990.

Sen, Amaryta. Interview: India Must Fulfill Tagore's Vision, Not Gandhi's." O'Malley, J. P. The Spectator, August 20, 2013,

Sfikas, Thanasis D. "Attlee, Bevin and 'A Very Lame Horse': The Dispute Over Greece and the Middle East, December 1946-January 1947." Journal of the Hellenic Diaspora, 18 (2) (1992), 69-96.

Simons, H.J. and R. E. Class and Colour in South Africa 1850-1950. London: Penguin, 1969.

Skelton, Barbara. Tears Before Bedtime. London: Hamish Hamilton, 1987, p. 27.

Sketches of History, the Russian Foreign Intelligence Service. Moscow: International Relations, 1997.

Smith, Bradley F. Sharing Secrets with Stalin: How the Allies Traded Intelligence, 1941-1945. Lawrence, Kansas: University of Kansas Press, 1996.

Smith, Raymond. Ernest Bevin, British Officials and British Soviet Policy, 1945-47 in Deighton, Ann (editor) Britain and the First Cold War. New York: St. Martin's Press, 1990.

Smoller, Sanford J. Adrift Among Geniuses: Robert McAlmon, Writer and Publisher of the Twenties. University Park and London: The Pennsylvania State University Press, 1975.

Spender, Stephen. Forward From Liberalism. London: Victor Gollancz Ltd, 1937.

Stansky, Peter. The First Day of the Blitz. New Haven: Yale University Press, 2007.

Steel, Ronald. Walter Lippmann and the American Century. Boston: Little, Brown and Company. An Atlantic Monthly Press Book, 1980.

Strachey, Julia and Partridge, Frances. Julia: A Portrait of Julia Strachey by Herself and Frances Partridge. Boston: Little Brown and Company, 1983.

Sudoplatov, Pavel and Anatoli Sudoplatov. Special Tasks: The Memoirs of an Unwanted Witness—A Soviet Spymaster. Boston: Little, Brown and Company, 1994.

Taylor, A. J. P. English History: 1914—1945. New York and Oxford: Oxford University Press, 1965.

Tharoor, Shashi. "The Ugly Briton," Time Magazine, November 29, 2010, citing Mukerjee, Madhusree, Churchill's Secret War.

Toynbee, Philip. A Tale of Terror. The Sunday Herald, Sydney, NSW, June 25, 1950, page 8, http://trove.nla.gov.au/ndp/del/article/18478215?searchTerm=%22Phi lip%20Toynbee%22&searchLimits=sortby=dateAsc, accessed November 11, 2013.

Toynbee, Philip. Arab States Have Legitimate Sense of Injury. The Mercury, Hobart, Tasmania, June 23, 1950, page 3, http://trove.nla.gov.au/ndp/del/article/18478215?searchTerm=%22Phi lip%20Toynbee%22&searchLimits=sortby=dateAsc, accessed November 11, 2013.

Toynbee, Philip. Communism Plays a Paradoxical Role in Israel. The Mercury, Hobart, Tasmania, September 5, 1950, page 3, http://trove.nla.gov.au/ndp/del/article/18478215?searchTerm=%22Phi lip%20Toynbee%22&searchLimits=sortby=dateAsc, accessed November 11, 2013.

Toynbee, Philip. Friends Apart: A Memoir of Esmond Romilly & Jasper Ridley in the Thirties. London: MacGibbon & Kee, 1954.

Vernon, Betty D. Ellen Wilkinson 1891 – 1947. London: Croom Helm, 1982.

Walker, Jonathan. Operation Unthinkable: The Third World War: British Plans to Attack the Soviet Empire 1945. Stroud: The History Press, 2013.

Walker, Martin. The Cold War: A History. New York: Holt Paperbacks, 1995, p. 284.

Waller, Maureen. London 1945: Life in the Debris of War. London: John Murray, 2004.

Walter, Natasha, Spies and Lovers. The Guardian, May 10, 2003.

Weathersby, Kathryn, "'Should We Fear This?' Stalin and the Danger of War with America." Cold War International History Project Working Papers Series, #39. Washington, D.C.: Woodrow Wilson International Center for Scholars, July 2002.

Weinberg, Gerhard L. A World at Arms: A Global History of World War II, Cambridge University Press, 1994.

West, W. J. Truth Betrayed. London: Duckworth, 1987.

Westad, Odd Adne. The Cambridge History of the Cold War, Volume I: Origins. Cambridge: Cambridge University Press, 2010.

Wiebes, Cees and Bert Zeeman. "The Pentagon negotiations March 1948: the launching of the North Atlantic Treaty," International Affairs (Royal Institute of International Affairs, Vol. 59, No. 3 (Summer, 1983).

Zametica, John (ed.). British Officials and British Foreign Policy: 1945-50. Leicester: Leicester University Press, 1990.

Zametica, John. "Three Letters to Bevin" in Zametica, John (ed.). British Officials and British Foreign Policy: 1945-50. Leicester: Leicester University Press, 1990.

Zubok, Vladislav and Pleshakov, Constantine. Inside the Kremlin's Cold War: From Stalin to Khrushchev. Cambridge, Massachusetts: Harvard University Press, 1966.

# Index

## A

# C

# M

# T

Printed in Great Britain
by Amazon